Great Parliamentary Scandals

Rumour is fleet of foot, and swift are her wings; she is a vast, fearful monster, with a watchful eye miraculously set under every feather which grows on her, and for every one of them a tongue in a mouth which is loud of speech, and an ear ever alert. By night she flies hissing through the dark in the space between earth and sky, and never droops her eyelids in contented sleep. In the daylight she keeps watch, sometimes perched on the rooftop of a house and sometimes on the tall towers of a palace. And she strikes dread throughout great cities, for she is as retentive of news which is false and wicked as she is ready to tell what is true.

Virgil's *Aenid*, book iv,
translated by
W. F. Jackson Knight

Great Parliamentary Scandals

Five Centuries of Calumny, Smear and Innuendo

Matthew Parris
and
Kevin Maguire

ROBSON BOOKS

First published in 1995 by Robson Books,
The Chrysalis Building, Bramley Road,
London W10 6SP
This revised edition first published in 2004

An imprint of Chrysalis Books Group

With thanks to the following for allowing Matthew
Parris to use relevant extracts and illustrations from
their publications: the *Daily Express*, the *Daily Mail*,
Edwina Currie, the *Mirror Group*, the *News of the World*,
Private Eye, the *Star*, the *Sun*, the *Sunday Times* and *The
Times*.

The authors have made every reasonable effort to
contact all copyright holders. Any errors that may have
occurred are inadvertent and anyone who for any
reason has not been contacted is invited to write to the
publishers so that a full acknowledgement may be made
in any subsequent editions of this work.

British Library Cataloguing in Publication Data
A catalogue record for this title is available from the
British Library

ISBN 1 86105 736 9

Indexed by Indexing Specialists (UK) Ltd
Typeset in Plantin by FiSH Books, London
Printed by Bell & Bain Ltd., Glasgow

CONTENTS

INTRODUCTION
to the Original Edition

'Feasting with panthers'

The death in February 1994 of a backbench MP in what the BBC called 'unusual sexual circumstances' was not a great parliamentary scandal. It was not really a scandal at all. But it was bizarre, it was shocking and it involved an MP – and that is enough for British newspapers. My own, *The Times,* asked me to write about the pressure MPs face and the temptations to which they are exposed. Why do they get into trouble so often when theirs, above most others, is a career to which scandal can be fatal?

Under the title 'Feasting with Panthers' my subject was not Stephen Milligan but scandal itself: the fascination scandal holds not for those who read about it, but for those who make it. I wrote:

I hardly knew Stephen Milligan. What is said of his death may not be true, or there may be special circumstances which explain it. It is dangerous to proceed from the particular to the general and so I would like to make it clear that in a case like this the particular may not be an example of the general. But it has aroused interest in the famous general question: 'Why do they do it? Why do MPs, and JPs, and DPPs and VIPs of every type . . . why do public figures of all people take such risks?'

When Oscar Wilde called it 'feasting with panthers' he meant seeking sex with working-class youths. But it's an apt expression for many sorts of adventure. It means hazard. It means foolish, reckless excitement. It means danger, secrecy and shame.

How we find it depends on us. Some will run up crazy gambling debts; some will philander, kerb-crawl, drink and drive; some turn to drugs; some will pursue boys, some girls. Some will pursue dodgy money in crazy schemes. Each to his own, but we all have this in common: that if we are found out, the world will say *'why?'* He had everything going for him. He must have known he risked ruin. And he seemed such a steady chap. *'Why?'*

But the world misunderstands. The secrecy and danger are not a regrettable side-effect of the folly: they are the reason for the folly. They are the spice, the drug. That the visible part of a man's life looks respectable and safe should be no cause for surprise that in the shadows between the real and the imagined he has sought for himself a perilous other-life. Crushed by decency, he embraces hazard as a means of escape. To regret that he could not find something safer is like suggesting to those who crave furtive love-making behind the shelves of busy supermarkets that they buy a container-load of cornflakes and recreate the Tesco backdrop in their own bedrooms. It misses the point.

So what is the point? I shall talk about men, because the problem is mostly with men. I am clear from the start that I include myself in these observations.

The public has the impression that MPs take more personal risks than other citizens and I suspect the public is right. Of course, disproportionate publicity follows an MP's exposure and inflates the impression of the Commons as an exotic hot-house of sin, but I doubt whether this is the whole explanation. If the proportion of my ex-colleagues who philandered is true to the national average, then this is a philandering nation. If, proportionately, as many citizens are gay as MPs are, then homosexuality in Britain outruns even the wildest calculations of Outrage. I suspect MPs do take unusual risks in unusual numbers and the suspicion is reinforced whenever another is found out. He is almost never one of those I knew about.

And another misconception needs to be corrected. Miscreant MPs do not 'always get found out in the end'. I never was, and nor were any of my gay Tory friends. The calculation is not between safety and certain ruin, but between safety and risk.

But why does a career in public life in the Commons and in the constituency dispose an MP towards such risk? First, we must ask whether the risk-takers are self-selected. Are men with a weakness for surprising private behaviour especially drawn towards a political career? Secondly, we must ask whether the job itself, once secured, turns previously cautious men into secret risk-takers. The answer to both questions is Yes.

Nobody without a gambling streak, a taste for uncertainty and a belief in his own luck would embark upon a Commons career. Statistically, most must 'fail' within their own terms, which are (usually these days) the achievement of high ministerial office. The hours and conditions are arduous and the salary no more than what most MPs could have hoped to attract in a career outside. For many it is less. You may sacrifice a career in the hope of securing a seat which you may at any time subsequently lose, without compensation. However a candidate may present himself to his electors, no unadventurous family man in search of security is likely to want a career in politics.

And there is something, too, which I believe attracts men with a streak of exhibitionism, buccaneering or bravado. MPs are a miscellaneous bunch, but united by this: a craving for applause. They are attention-seekers. The job rarely offers real power or influence. But regularly it offers publicity. You may do little, but you *are* somebody. It is remarkable how few MPs' biographies reveal boys who were the 'rounded' type at school: popular enough, clever enough, good enough at sport. The balanced all-rounder beloved of school reports does not, typically, seek election to Parliament. You will find that many MPs were unhappy, lonely or unpopular.

Men often go into politics to prove something which they feared might be in doubt. 'One day I'll be popular. I'll be Prime Minister, and be driven around in a big car, and everybody will cheer.'

In short, the parliamentary selection process attracts adventurers with more bravado than self-confidence, more *chutzpah* than emotional security. Then it lands them in what is, for long stretches, a spectacularly boring job. What follows, follows.

But, if the trait is not already there, the job itself creates deep dissatisfactions. Let me try tactfully to explain why, and I hope I shall not lose any of my MP friends in doing so. Being an MP feeds your vanity and starves your self-respect.

You are a little prince in your own constituency. In the House you may be a smaller fish, but still feel you belong to a most important – *the* most important – club. Your head swells.

But your heart troubles you because you know it's not true. You know you are only there because your party association chose you. Few ever voted for you as an individual, or ever will. You know, too, that your power at Westminster is almost zero – the whips humiliate you privately – and your influence in the constituency consists mainly in using your headed notepaper to help a pushy handful jump the queues in which more patient constituents quietly wait. You know you are a fraud and your position is a fraud.

It breeds an awful internal cynicism and an imperceptibly opening gap between your public life and your private, internal life. The latter becomes a world of its own in which you increasingly choose to dwell, all the while developing the skills you need to keep up appearances in the external world. The gap between these two worlds becomes, for some, almost unbridgeable. It generates terrible fears and anxieties.

I offer two examples. While I was an MP I found myself, once, in a gay pub called *The Two Brewers* in Clapham. A man came up to me and asked if I was Matthew Parris MP. I recognised him as a lobby correspondent at the House of Commons. I was immediately struck by complete terror and the absolute conviction that he had come there to find and expose me. Of course, he was gay himself and that is why he was there. But I shall never forget my immediate and irrational reaction.

The second example took place not long before I resigned. A mill was moving out of my constituency and I had invited a delegation of workers (all women) to come down and see the minister with me to try to stop it. The (Labour) leader of the county council had, like me, muscled in on this, and decided to accompany the women. He and I walked along with them from the little mini-bus that had brought them, towards the minister's office. Each of us was resentful of the presence of the other. Each of us was trying to impress the women with our own mastery of the situation. Both of us knew that nothing we could do would make the least difference.

One of the women turned to me and asked how I thought she should address the minister if he spoke to her. I looked at her and realised how completely genuine and how very nervous and how timidly hopeful she was. She believed in me. I suddenly felt a complete heel. Tears filled my eyes but as it was dark in the street nobody saw this.

It is not surprising that MPs learn to despise if not themselves then the thing they are pretending to be. It is not surprising that they sometimes try to escape this, sometimes in a manner which to the rest of us looks desperate.

Re-reading that, it is not surprising that writing this book proved less of a giggle than perhaps I hoped.

Not that much within these pages isn't richly comic. Toe-sucking and Chelsea strips (both stories, incidentally, disputed) amused rather than horrified 1990s Britain. The corpulent figure of Horatio Bottomley, sewing mail bags in gaol after swindling the poor of millions as an MP in the 1920s ('Sewing, Horatio?' asked a visitor. 'No, reaping,' he replied) is a fit subject for amusement now, though Robert Maxwell isn't yet.

The thought of William Ewart Gladstone bringing prostitutes back to 10 Downing Street in the 1880s, to read them the Bible, raises a smile. The duel with pistols on Putney Heath in 1809 between two members of the same Cabinet now looks more hilarious than shocking. One can chuckle at the eighteenth-century John Wilkes's remark that, ugly as he was, lechery was easy and it only took 'half an hour to explain away his face', or his reply when a French visitor asked how far liberty of the press extended in England: 'that is what I am trying to find out'.

The seventeenth-century Commons Speaker Sir John Trevor, so cross-eyed that confusion reigned as two members caught his eye at the same time and so corrupt that on being found out by the Commons he simply stayed at home and sent in a series of sicknotes until they sacked him, seems with the benefit of 300 years' distance more ludicrous than wicked. And the Elizabethan and Jacobean Sir Francis Bacon was so great an essayist that his literary legacy has outlived his reputation for enjoying bribes, and boys, as Lord Chancellor.

Yes, there is enough to smile about. But after a year's work on this book, and re-reading what I have written, I cannot brush aside a pervading sadness. Most of the stories related here were a complete catastrophe for somebody. Almost every tale over which we now smile or tut-tut was for somebody a drawing back of the curtains one morning to realize, with hollow stomach, that everything was lost. As often as not it was not just a career which was wrecked, but a life.

Some deserved it. Sometimes there were other victims too – the women scorned or husbands cuckolded, the citizens robbed by a corrupt politician's wickedness – but more often than not the principal victim was the politician himself. On occasions he had nobody but himself to blame, but still I read these chapters with a growing feeling that the British press (and arguably the British readers whose appetites we serve) emerges too often as more than bystander, more than reporter; more, even than investigator: we emerge as aggressor. The problem is not diminishing.

Some who people these pages were badly wronged by reports, others destroyed by untruth or mere rumour. Many were hounded into ignominy by a press or public which had got its teeth into *something* which was culpable, got it all out of proportion, and simply would not let go. Some of the cruellest injustices you will find here arose not from media lies but from media half-truths: not from invention, but from too narrow a view of the facts. Readers will make their own judgement.

This vague but insistent unease has been renewed as I discussed my draft manuscript with many of those, still living, whom it fingers. I tried to send to most of those surviving parliamentarians and ex-parliamentarians who appear here (many of whom I know) my proposed words about them. It seemed a common courtesy and a good way of ironing out the many errors that creep in as journalists base stories on cuttings written by other journalists; but I committed my drafts to the post or fax with gritted teeth and bated breath, waiting for the explosion, the bellow of 'How dare you venture here!'

It almost never came. A few did not reply (and a few I never tracked down) and the reader must certainly not suppose that every modern politician here has vouchsafed the accuracy of my report; but I was overwhelmed by the helpful, matter-of-fact way most responded to what must have seemed an unwanted raking over of coals by which they were once badly burned.

As a result I have spent days discussing my text with some of the principal actors in these stories, and received reams of sensible corrections. Interestingly, very few have asked me to alter opinions, judgements or even gibes: wrong facts vex them more. Time and again the person concerned would ask me not to withdraw what had been alleged, but to add what was never printed at the time. Surrounding circumstances can greatly alter the light in which we see an otherwise isolated incident, complicating the moral perspective and fudging simplicity. That is why popular journalists so often ignore them.

Of these exchanges and conversations I would mention just this: that to interview a man who has been felled or crippled by scandal is like talking, long after the event, to the survivor of a road accident or natural disaster. He becomes gripped by a kind of post-traumatic horror, very intense, sometimes staring at the desk as though he were alone in the room, or talking to a psychiatrist.

Many of my interviewees said this had forced them to think again about a chapter they had buried from recollection. Some, amazingly, said this was the first time they had revisited those memories. Most found that painful, but a number also said that it had been interesting: they were surprised to realize that they had never mentally reviewed the episode before now, or written about it, or asked anyone else to do so.

I have tried to. There is therefore much in the later chapters of this book which, though not a 'revelation' (in the *News of the World* sense), has hardly been mentioned before. Do not read this book for revelations: there is only one, and its subject is a rather minor character.

What to include and what to leave out? Not every political scandal is a personal scandal, and this book concentrates on allegations which imply (sometimes unfairly) private disgrace as well as political error. Some readers may be disappointed not to find every peccadillo of the last decade, but many are notorious only for being recent. In terms of enduring disgrace, the late twentieth-century harvest looks rather disappointing.

A number of ex-colleagues and still (I hope) friends have asked me rather sadly why I chose to add to the number of words already squandered in a distasteful realm of modern journalism. Let me avoid the pious excuse-making of modern newspaper editors and reply that I write for money, and for fun. People want to read about parliamentary scandal; I know something about it; and so I will write for them. I hardly expect to improve the world. But this does not relieve me of a duty (and the wish) to be fair. Perhaps by retailing stories honestly, so far as we can, and in proper context, we can add something to readers' own grasp of history and sense of proportion.

Readers might like to glance at my remarks concluding the chapter on Disraeli. Disgrace is too easily assumed to be disabling to a man's political career and personal development alike. But a certain knocked-about quality in a statesman can add proportion, compassion and a redeeming cynicism to his judgement. I include, at the close of this book, a poem by D. H. Lawrence. Readers may care, too, to review what the *New Statesman* of 3 June 1922 wrote of that unequalled rogue, Horatio Bottomley MP:

He had elevated roguery to an art. He possessed the sort of genius that repeatedly drew our eyes from his victims, and even the moralist could on occasion suspend his moral sense in order to admire a brilliant display of effrontery.

Seventy years later, a press which succeeds in being both dirty and pious, has lost the generosity which once could admit an impish delight in the wickedness of the wicked. There is a sort of drabness in late twentieth-century disapproval, a meanness.

I expect this book will be read for amusement – and I hope so. But I hope also that it might be read with understanding, and sometimes sympathy. And that, most of all, it might be read for *perspective* too.

Matthew Parris
September 1995

INTRODUCTION
to this Edition

Trust in Tony?

Tony Blair offered an unusually large hostage to fortune on the doorstep of 10 Downing Street. 'It will be a government that seeks to restore trust in politics,' he promised, on his first day as Prime Minister. Where Margaret Thatcher preached harmony and recited the prayer of St Francis of Assisi and John Major offered a nation at ease with itself, the first Labour tenant for eighteen years of the UK's most famous address proffered honesty and integrity that sunny day.

Well, Thatcher struck a distinctly discordant note, Major united the country in exhaustion and Blair spectacularly failed to deliver his new dawn. The heavy tramp of the hostage's boots could be heard, heading in the direction of the newspapers' front pages, as soon as Downing Street's much-filmed black door closed behind him. It's been pretty much business as usual in Parliament since May 1997 as con men, philanderers, cheats, liars, brawlers, dodgy dealers, sycophants and 'a moment of madness' joined the prostitutes, gropers, rent boys, swindlers, hypocrites, Soviet spies and Reggie Perrin characters who have been such a colourful feature of five centuries of calumny, smear and innuendo. And, I must confess, I've loved every incident. Scandal may not be good for politics or the politicians involved, indeed it may be dangerously corrosive, but a scandal makes a good story and puncturing the pomposity of those who seek to govern us is immensely satisfying. Ministers, lulled into a false sense of importance by salaries, titles, private offices, red boxes and comfortable back seats of chauffeur-driven cars, believe they are masters of the universe – until that inquiry, that question, that confrontation results in an uncomfortable reality check. I suspect most, if not all, ministers looking back with invaluable 20–20 hindsight, would avoid the mistakes that brought them down to earth with a bump.

From Blair back to Francis Bacon, surveying events since the sixteenth century, this book records the low side of high office over 500 years. This edition of *Great Parliamentary Scandals*, updated with Matthew Parris to encompass the New Labour era and the continuing tribulations of the Tory Party, includes characters whose foibles and failings not only scandalised but also brightened up politics, as we marvelled at their audacity, shaking our heads in disbelief at their antics and subsequent explanations.

Inevitably, with two authors there were occasional differences, yet they were rare and, when they occurred, were of emphasis rather than fact. Writing this edition was therefore a joy.

So who to include and who to leave out? Not every political scandal is a personal scandal, and this book concentrates on allegations that had some form of public dimension. Readers may be disappointed not to find every peccadillo and sensation of the Blair era on these pages. If they were to be included, there would be little room left for episodes from earlier eras. It is also the case that many are notorious, or at least newsworthy, only for being recent. Those people who make it into this updated edition will, I am sure, hope they will be left out of any future version – and they may well be. Others, issuing a sigh of relief at escaping inclusion, may yet merit a chapter if, or when, further and better particulars emerge. Writing about parliamentary scandals is akin to painting the Forth Bridge: a task never completed.

A lack of trust between politicians and the public is not new but it is also true that cynicism about politicians is plunging new depths: turnout at the 2001 June General Election plunged to the lowest level recorded since universal suffrage and the principle of one person-one vote was won. This book is not designed to restore trust or raise the turnout, however desirable both might be. That is another task. The firm intention here is to inform and above all to entertain, rather than to preach. A number of 'victims' are worthy of our sympathy; others deserve our contempt. You, the reader, can judge from the sentences that follow.

Kevin Maguire
May 2004

ACKNOWLEDGEMENTS

Time marches relentlessly on and Four Centuries of Calumny, Smear and Innuendo is now Five Centuries of Calumny, Smear and Innuendo. This revised, updated edition of *Great Parliamentary Scandals* includes the trials and tribulations of political figures in the Blair era as well as revisiting some of the more serious offenders from earlier periods.

Inevitably one or two 'victims' included in previous editions had to be dropped to make way for newcomers, but we endeavoured to retain as many as possible, morphing some into other chapters, in order to preserve the crucial historic perspective of the book. Axing the foreword, epilogue and even a poem seemed to us less brutal than cutting the characters who are the essence of this work.

Thanks go to Julian Glover who cast his well-informed eyes over the new chapters and offered sound advice, seeking to ensure this volume is fair as well as accurate. Gratitude is also owed to those who helped research and draft earlier editions: David prosser, Andrew Pierce, Edward Pearce, Mark Mason, Simon Christmas, Christopher Hope, Nick Fitzpatrick. Jeremy Robson has, again, proved to be an understanding publisher while there would be no new century of scandals without the understanding and expert editing of Joanne Brooks.

As the cover reveals and introductions confirm, Kevin Maguire took the lead in bringing this book up to date with the New Labour years, but he asks friends in the party who may take exception to any particular passage to rest assured that any such passage will almost certainly have been been written by Matthew Parris. For his part, Parris reminds his Tory friends that the more disobliging of the book's remarks about troubled Tories can probably be attributed to Maguire.

Finally, a big 'thank you' to all those politicians included in the pages that follow. Without their troubles, there would be no *Great Parliamentary Scandals*.

Matthew Parris
Kevin Maguire
2004

FRANCIS BACON – 1621
'I am guilty of corruption and do renounce all defence'

Four centuries of sleaze catches in its web both the noble and the ignoble. Whatever his sins, Francis Bacon was among the noble. His vast abilities have rescued his name from clouds which would have cast lesser reputations into shadow. This brilliant lawyer, judge, philosopher, homosexual philanderer, adviser to Queen Elizabeth I and Lord Chancellor to James I – a man who in his spare time wrote some of the most thoughtful essays of his age – deserves (and usually receives) a broader assessment than the simple assertion that his was one of the most corrupt Lord Chancellorships in English history.

But it was so. Part of the problem was carelessness. The King's most senior minister was accused of taking bribes, and the evidence was overwhelming, but how many of these bribes he actively sought, and how many he was too disorganized to return, is less clear.

Modern politicians would do well to learn from Bacon's mistakes. With his head in the philosophical clouds and his lackadaisical approach to office administration, the Lord Chancellor became an easy target for his opponents. He did receive gifts, probably far more than were alleged at his trial, probably far more than he knew about. Most were arranged and then pocketed by his beloved servants. Bacon cared little for worldly possessions, even less for professional niceties, and trusted too much. But neither carelessness nor gullibility is any defence for a minister of the crown, alas.

Yet Bacon's background should not suggest naivety. He was born in 1561 amid the grandeur of York House, off the Strand. His father was Lord Keeper to Queen Elizabeth I, in effect deputy Lord Chancellor. By safeguarding the Great Seal of England, the Lord Keeper held huge executive sway.

Together with his elder brother Anthony, three years his senior, Francis went up to Trinity College, Cambridge. They were devoted companions, although over-influenced by their mother, whom the historian A. L. Rowse describes as 'very religious in the most tedious Protestant fashion'. Brilliant but both physically frail, they shared one other characteristic: homosexuality.

After Cambridge, Francis was sent to Paris with the English ambassador, Sir Amyas Paulet, but was recalled abruptly when his father died in 1579. Within three years he became a barrister and moved into Gray's Inn. Although he was one of the best jurists of his day, the law did not satisfy his political and philosophical ambitions, and in 1584 he was elected MP for Melcombe Regis on Weymouth Bay. He then sought a job in the government of Elizabeth I.

Anthony, on the other hand, left Cambridge to travel on the continent and fell in with the Protestant King, Henri of Navarre – the future Henri IV of France. Anthony lived happily in Montauban, near Toulouse, with a succession of obliging page-boys. He sent the English Queen regular intelligence reports.

That was until Anthony's own brush with scandal. His alliance with Henri made him an attractive match, but the 34-year-old bachelor showed little interest in women. When he refused to marry a young noblewoman, he encountered her mother's wrath. The affronted mama had him charged with sodomy. The accusation was serious: a priest at nearby Cahors had recently been burned alive for the same offence. It was not difficult for the authorities to frighten a number of boys into testifying. Anthony was found guilty, but was saved when his royal friend stepped in to champion his appeal.

Nevertheless Anthony, by now suffering from gout in both hands and legs, returned to England in 1592. He moved into Francis's chambers in Gray's Inn. Much to their religious mother's horror, the two brilliant brothers also shared lovers and attendants.

Francis Bacon, Viscount St Alban, by an unknown artist
(courtesy of the National Portrait Gallery)

The following year, Francis temporarily wrecked his hopes of political advancement when he took a principled stand in Parliament against the Government. The Queen was demanding more subsidies to meet the huge cost of the war with Spain. Elizabeth was furious at Bacon's disloyalty. He refused to apologize. She left him to wander in the political wilderness.

In 1597, with one eye on regaining the Queen's favour, Francis dedicated his *Essays* to his invalid brother. In a Europe only recently emerged from a dark age, the work was one of the more significant contributions to human thought since the Greeks. He dedicated it to

> our love, in the depth whereof I sometimes wish your infirmities translated upon myself, that Her Majesty might have the service of so active and able a mind, and I might be with excuse confined to these contemplations and studies for which I am fittest.

The Queen did not take the hint. Francis had one other motivation for trying to gain office: he was chronically in debt. His father had left less money than he had hoped for. In 1598 Bacon, the future Lord Chancellor, was arrested for debt, but kept himself afloat by borrowing.

Anthony died in 1601 and was bitterly mourned by his brother. Two years later the Virgin Queen followed suit and James of Scotland was crowned English King. Now widely regarded as the best mind in England, Bacon could gain the official recognition he so richly deserved. For a time, though, his cousin and deadly rival, the Earl of Salisbury, kept him in lowly jobs. His star was not set to rise until Salisbury's death in 1612 when Bacon was already 51.

Meanwhile, partly to ease financial worries, in 1606 Bacon married Alice Barnham, an heiress and a London alderman's daughter. They had no children. Historians express surprise that there is almost no evidence of their spending time together and it is likely that Bacon saw very little of Alice.

In 1607 Bacon became Solicitor-General, and after Salisbury's death Attorney-General, in 1613. It was a job the greatest lawyer in the land should have held twenty years earlier. His rise was now steep. James I fully recognized his skills. In 1617 Bacon followed his father's footsteps, becoming Lord Keeper; and the following year he finally achieved his ambition when he was appointed Lord Chancellor. He moved back to the royal residence of York House where he had been born and in 1620 took the title Viscount St Alban.

Bacon was the 'justest judge' England had seen but he was too detached, too relaxed and too philosophical to take notice of the bribes flowing in to his servants. His head in the clouds, he was absorbed in grander matters. Part of Bacon's problem was that he could never decide between the active and contemplative life. He had 'musique in the next room where he meditated', sweet herbs or flowers were always before him as he dined, and he was notoriously easygoing with his servants. In the words of one parliamentary diarist of the time, he had a habit of 'making his servants his bedfellows . . . [he keeps] still one Goderick, a very effeminate youth, to be his catamite and bedfellow'. The Lord Chancellor saw to it that all his servants wore boots made from Spanish leather – less a kink than an affectation: the smell of common English oxhide offended him.

His young charges did much as they pleased. It was partly thanks to Bacon that the Churchills are a wealthy family today. The first of their clan to drag themselves from the Dorset mire was John Churchill, who ran a very lucrative little bribe-collecting business as Bacon's Registrar in Chancery. There was no National Lottery fund to assist the Churchills at this time. Presents to Bacon himself were accepted graciously but (studying the Lord Chancellor's court judgements) probably without favour.

Bacon had an international reputation. In January 1621 he was at the height of his philosophical career with the publication of his great work on logic, *Novum Organum*. But he had enemies. Chief among these was the Catholic-baiter Sir Edward Coke, the Lord Chief Justice, who had made his name prosecuting Sir Walter Raleigh; and the Gunpowder Plotters. The Civil War was little more than twenty years away and already the battle-lines were being drawn. On the one side were ranged the parliamentarians: dry and puritanical, personified by Coke. On the other, those like Bacon defended the inconsistencies of the Royal Prerogative against the follies of Parliament.

Parliament had been looking for some time for an excuse to attack the excesses of the court. There were plenty to choose from.

The King was homosexual. Once he had produced an heir from his wife, Anne of Denmark, a suitable match from a Protestant kingdom, he could barely abide seeing her. He outraged Puritan sentiment with his choice of favourites and lavished gifts of land and titles on a beautiful 22-year-old boy, George Villiers.

Aware of the King's proclivities, the youth's mother had presented her son to the court in 1614. Villiers, described as 'the best male specimen in the land' and the last of the King's favourites, rose from being a threadbare hanger-on at court to become the second richest nobleman in England. We know him today as the Earl, later Duke, of Buckingham, but to the King he was 'Steenie' because of his resemblance to a stained glass depiction of St Stephen in the royal chapel. The fact that Steenie's tastes were at least partly heterosexual only seemed to inflame the King's desire. James once told his Council of Ministers: 'I love the Earl of Buckingham more than anyone else... Christ had his John, and I have my Steenie'.

When Buckingham's brother, Sir John Villiers, wanted to marry the daughter of Bacon's hated rival, Sir Edward Coke, Bacon unwisely tried to block the match. But the King could refuse his favourite nothing and the ceremony went ahead in 1617 with the King, rather than the father, giving the girl away. Coke was readmitted to the Council. Bacon was forced to grovel but he soon made it up to the King's favourite, for whom he had a genuine affection. Steenie's younger brother Christopher was made a Gentleman of the Bedchamber, then Master of the Robes, each job attracting a considerable pension. And there were other jobs for the favourite's half-brothers, and for other relatives too.

It seems that the court had few problems with homosexuality, but this is not to suggest the Puritans in Parliament and the country approved. When Steenie finally married, the King wrote to the newlyweds: 'The Lord of Heaven send you a sweet and blithe awakening, all kind of comfort in your sanctified bed, and bless the fruits thereof, that I may have sweet Bedchamber boys to play with me (and this is my daily prayer)'.

The former Bedchamber boy should have kept out of politics. Buckingham's political dalliances spelt danger for the King, but more immediately for the Lord Chancellor.

Bacon was essentially a moderate man, whose idea was to bring King and Parliament together. He served both tirelessly, but by the likes of Coke was seen as too closely allied to Buckingham and the excesses of the court. Coke, who had the ear of the Commons, attacked the monopolies the courtiers enjoyed. His real target was Buckingham and his brothers. Coke's complaints were justified and received widespread support. The court needed a scapegoat. Bacon was expendable. He was accused of accepting bribes to affect cases in the Court of Chancery. One concerned a man named Aubrey. He had heard that he would win his case if he gave 100 guineas to the Lord Chancellor. When he lost, his anger was turned upon Bacon. Another man, Egerton, told a similar story, although the price in his case was 400 guineas.

Facing the charges, Bacon felt he could rely on the King's support. He wrote of being in

> purgatory . . . but my mind is calm . . . I know I have clean hands and a clean heart, and I hope a clean house for friends or servants. But Job himself, or whoever was the justest judge, by such hunting for matters against him as hath been used against me, may for a time seem foul.

He tried to make a pre-emptive speech in his defence during a parliamentary debate, but was rebuked and forced to apologize.

By mid-March 1621, Bacon was becoming anxious about the increasing level of public disapproval. New charges seemed to be laid daily. The Lord Chancellor hurried home from the Lords, pretended to be ill, and waited for the King to step in. 'If this is to be a Chancellor,' he wailed, 'I think, if the Great Seal lay upon Hounslow Heath, nobody would take it up.'

James did try to help. He suggested a special tribunal – a delaying tactic fashionable right through to our own time – but Parliament refused. Asserting its new sense of authority, it insisted on pronouncing the items of impeachment. Bacon pleaded for time, writing from his 'sick bed' that he would not 'trick up an innocency by cavillations, but plainly and ingenuously (as your Lordships know my manner is) declare what I know or remember.'

The King did his best. He adjourned Parliament early to let the dust settle, an old trick. This proved counter-productive. Away from London, MPs measured the atmosphere in the country. Resentment against the King's courtiers was strong. When

Parliament returned on 17 April, MPs were determined to bring the Lord Chancellor to justice. There were by now no fewer than 23 charges.

Hoping to throw enough meat to the wolves, Bacon wrote to the Lords giving a qualified admission of guilt: but in such general terms that he could not be said to have admitted any particular allegation. The House was having none of it, resolving that

> the Lord Chancellor's submission gave not satisfaction to their lordships; that he should be charged particularly with the briberies and corruptions alleged against him, and that he should make a particular answer thereunto with all convenient expedition.

At this point Bacon suddenly caved in. 'I do plainly and ingenuously confess that I am guilty of corruption, and do renounce all defence.'

The country was stunned. An incredulous House of Lords sent a delegation to inquire whether Bacon's confession was genuine. 'My Lords, it is my act, my hand, my heart.' He begged them: 'Be merciful to a broken reed.'

Bacon's sudden capitulation has never been satisfactorily explained. It is possible he hoped to be saved by procedure. While he retained the Great Seal of Office as Lord Chancellor, he would be required to pass sentence *on himself*. The historian A. L. Rowse suggests there was another reason: he was being blackmailed. A charge of sodomy was about to be brought against the sixty-year-old Lord Chancellor. Such was the atmosphere of the time, the King could not possibly allow that can of worms to be opened. Bacon had to surrender, and surrender completely.

With the King's support gone, four senior Lords were sent to retrieve the Great Seal. Bacon, in bed, handed it over with one hand while covering his face with the other. Bacon wrote to the King, rather pathetically offering to write a 'good History of England, and a better Digest of your laws' if he intervened. But it was too late. On 3 May, Bacon received his sentence: a massive £40,000 fine, imprisonment in the Tower at His Majesty's pleasure, and banishment from court, Parliament or any public office.

Only now could James be of service. The King saw to it that the prisoner was taken to the Tower by Thames barge to avoid the shame of having to proceed through the streets. Once there, he was given a comfortable apartment. James then released him after only two days, and annulled his fine. Although Bacon never regained any real degree of honour at court, he was given an annual pension of £1,200, and went on to write several more distinguished academic works.

By the end of his first year of disgrace he had finished his *History of Henry VII*. It was a model for future historians: compact and interpretative, unlike the heavy chronicles of the past. Then came the Latin translation of his *Advancement of Learning*. However, he was not for two years admitted to kiss the King's hand, and the full pardon that would have cleared his name never came.

The end of Bacon's life was absurd yet strangely typical. He was a keen amateur natural scientist. Travelling in Highgate one winter's day, he saw a dead chicken by the roadside. Wondering whether freezing would delay the onset of putrefaction, he jumped from his cab and stuffed the chicken with snow. It was one of the world's earliest experiments in refrigeration. But in the process he caught a chill, the chill led to pneumonia, and shortly afterwards, on 9 April 1626, he died aged 65.

It was a great loss. Bacon pre-empted the Enlightenment. He believed in the progress of man. He strove all his life to resolve the political and religious disputes that dogged the age. Within a generation after his death, but only after the idiocy of the Civil War, the Royal Society was founded to advance his programme of scientific exploration and discovery.

In his essays, Francis Bacon wrote that 'all rising to a great place is by a winding stair . . .'

The rising into place is laborious, and by pains men come to greater pains; and it is sometimes base, and by indignities men come to dignities. The standing is slippery, and the regress is either downfall, or at least an eclipse.

Bacon had a difficult life. He might well have found in his own death confirmation of the epigraph in one of his essays: 'The sweetest canticle is *nunc dimittis*'. His epitaph, sad and perhaps a little bitter, read: 'For my name and memory, I leave it to men's charitable speeches and to foreign nations and the next ages.' The next ages have judged him well.

SIR JOHN TREVOR – 1694

An Unusual Sicknote

Possibly the ugliest Commons Speaker ever to occupy the chair, Sir John Trevor was probably also the most corrupt. 'He created a most unfavourable impression on all who saw him,' say Philip Smith and Arnold Wright in *Parliament Past and Present* as 'an ungainly figure, and with a lowering countenance which was made more repellent by a villainous squint'. Trevor's speakership was famous for the confusion caused whenever he chose a member to speak. He would appear to be looking at a different MP from the one he intended to call, and two or more would rise, each under the impression that Sir John was looking at him.

Trevor found it difficult in more ways than one to look Honourable Members in the eye. After a few years in the chair, his reputation for taking bribes to secure desired outcomes in Parliament began to grow. The East India Company was rumoured to have bribed him, successfully, for his influence over legislation touching its interests. He was also said to have accepted a large payment from the City of London Corporation to secure the passage of a measure compensating them for debts its members incurred through their responsibility for orphans.

The House appointed a committee (in the way that, as you turn these pages, you may note the House always does) to investigate, chaired by a Mr Foley MP. The committee uncovered a written record of the City's instructions: '. . . that Mr Chamberlain do pay to the Hon. Sir John Trevor, Knight, the sum of 1,000 guineas so soon as a bill be passed into an Act of Parliament for satisfying the debts of the orphans . . .' There was even a written endorsement of these instructions, confirming that the Act had passed and the money had been paid.

MPs drew up a resolution, effectively convicting their own Speaker of a 'high crime and misdemeanour'. It fell to Sir John himself, as Speaker, to put the motion to the House. 'Shame would have overwhelmed a less sensitive man,' say Smith and Wright, 'but Trevor was not constituted that way, though it was with blanched cheek and quivering lip that he put the fatal question'. The ayes had it, by overwhelming acclamation. Sir John slunk out. He never returned. To put the motion for his own expulsion was more than he could bear. The next day an expectant House was delivered a note:

> GENTLEMEN – I did intend to have waited on you this morning; but, after I was up, I was taken suddenly ill with a violent cholic. I hope to be in a condition of attending you to-morrow morning. In the meantime, I desire you will be pleased to excuse my attendance. I am, with all duty, Your most obedient humble servant,
>
> J. Trevor. SPEAKER

The House adjourned. The following day another sicknote was brought.

The House expelled its Speaker and elected another one, William III raising no objection. No more was heard of Sir John.

JOHN WILKES – 1763

The Cross-eyed Ladies' Man

Having something wrong with you is a necessary, if not sufficient, condition for becoming a Member of Parliament. Boys who were bullied in the playground, teased by teachers or mocked on the playing fields, have, since the earliest times, resolved to have the last laugh on a persecuting world by raising themselves above it through political office.

John Wilkes, a member of the Hellfire Club whose members devoted themselves to depravity as a creed, was a scoundrel, a gambler, a vulgarian, a womanizer, and one of the ugliest men in England. He was convicted and imprisoned for libel and expelled from Parliament repeatedly – though for his politics rather than his morals. He was also one of the wittiest men to grace the Commons. When Lord Sandwich told him he would 'die either on the gallows, or of the pox', Wilkes replied, 'That must depend on whether I embrace your lordship's principles or your mistress.'

He was an idealist whose fight against privilege earned him the epitaph he penned: John Wilkes, 'a friend of liberty'. He has many modern admirers, not least the Labour MP Tony Banks.

The son of a wealthy distiller, Wilkes studied at Leyden, and then gained further financial security in 1747 by marrying an heiress. He was 21. Such was the vigour with which he pursued his debauchery and gambling that he was soon in debt. He joined a secret society, set up by the MP Sir Francis Dashwood, whose members became known as the 'Mad Monks of Medmenham' because of their obscene cavortings in the ruins of Medmenham Abbey in Buckinghamshire. Even without the mad monks' help, Wilkes overcame his chronic ugliness and severe squint to indulge in serial womanizing. It was Wilkes's boast that he only needed 'half an hour to talk away my face'.

He was famous for his barbed put-downs. When an elector told him, 'I'd rather vote for the devil,' Wilkes replied, 'Naturally, but if your friend is not standing, may I hope for your support?'

Wilkes made his first attempt to enter Parliament in 1754, standing in Berwick-on-Tweed. Part of his election strategy had been to bribe the captain of a ship bringing opposition voters from London. A generous inducement persuaded the captain to encounter navigational problems during the journey and the ship docked in Norway rather than Berwick. By the time it reached Berwick it was too late for the passengers to cast their votes. But Wilkes still lost the election.

His wife left him in 1757, fed up with his lechery. Wilkes redoubled efforts to deal with his mounting debts: his plan was to get elected to Parliament, where as an MP he would be free from arrest for debt. At a cost of £7,000, largely spent on bribes to the voters of Aylesbury, he was returned as an MP later that year.

He became a deadly enemy of the hated Tory, Lord Bute, the champion in Parliament of the Prince of Wales (later George III). Bute, 49, ousted the popular William Pitt from his administration when he became Prime Minister in May 1762. The same year Wilkes started his own newspaper, the *North*

John Wilkes, by William Hogarth

Briton, to launch his attacks on Bute's government and, the following year, the government of George Grenville. In edition number 45 in April 1763, he finally went too far. He alleged that the speech from the throne was the result of ministers putting lies into the King's mouth. A general warrant was issued for the arrest of everyone connected with the *North Briton*, and Wilkes was thrown into the Tower of London.

Within a week, however, he was released. Lord Chief Justice Pratt decreed that Wilkes was immune from arrest for libel on the grounds of parliamentary privilege. The irrepressible Wilkes not only carried on precisely as before, but sought and won damages against the Government for arresting him in the first place. Asked by a French acquaintance how far liberty of the press extended in Britain, Wilkes replied: 'That is what I am trying to find out.' His actions in fact secured a significant advance in civil liberties by establishing the illegality of general warrants: those which did not name a specific person.

To rid itself of the troublesome Wilkes, the Government tried to remove his immunity from arrest by getting him thrown out of the Commons. The errant MP gave them every assistance. As well as reprinting the offending *North Briton* article (he had to do it on his own press as no other printer would touch it), he published a poem: Thomas Potter's *Essay on Women* which parodied Alexander Pope's *Essay on Man*. Both are reprinted below.

> O blindness to the future! kindly given,
> That each may fill the circle marked by Heaven:
> Who sees with equal eye, as God of all,
> A hero perish, or a sparrow fall;
> Atoms or systems into ruin hurled,
> And now a bubble burst, and now a world . . .
> Alexander Pope, *Essay on Man*

> O blindness to the future! kindly given,
> That each may enjoy what fucks are marked in Heaven:
> Who sees with equal eye, as God of all,
> The man just mounting, and the virgin's fall;
> Prick, cunt, and ballocks [*sic*] in convulsions hurled,
> And now a hymen burst, and now a world.
> Thomas Potter, *Essay on Women*

Potter was the son of the Archbishop of Canterbury.

At the start of the November session of 1763, both Wilkes's reprinting of the allegations about the King's lies and the pornographic poem were voted breaches of privilege. In the Christmas recess Wilkes decided to go and stay in Paris. He knew what was coming. In January 1764 the motion for his expulsion from the Commons was carried, and in February he was found guilty in his absence of publishing a seditious libel (about the King) and an obscene and impious libel (the poem). Sentence was deferred until his return.

This was not to be for some time. Wilkes was now living in Paris in the manner to which he had become accustomed in England. His friends included Madame de Pompadour. His wit never failed him. Declining the offer of a game of cards, he told a fellow gambler he was these days unable to 'tell a king from a knave'. Wilkes was no respecter of monarchs. Dining once in company which included the Prince of Wales he unexpectedly raised his glass and proposed a toast to the King's health – something he had never been known to do. The Prince asked him how long he had felt such concern for his father's health. 'Since I had the pleasure of your Royal Highness's acquaintance,' replied Wilkes.

He waited in France for a more sympathetic government in Britain but after four years there was still no sign of it. By then Wilkes had run up so many debts in Paris that to stay there any longer might have seriously damaged his health, so in early 1768 he returned to England. By March he had succeeded in becoming MP for Middlesex. Parliament continued to expel him. Anti-government feeling was running high. Wilkes, encouraged by the public support he was getting, tried a high-risk strategy. He voluntarily submitted himself to arrest. He was sentenced to 22 months in prison and a £1,000 fine for the outstanding charges against him.

His gamble paid off. There were riots outside the prison in St George's Fields where he was held. Troops were called and one man was killed. This profligate, womanizing, bankrupt, rich man's son had become a national hero for the poor and dispossessed and at the same time the moral leader of the middle-class campaign to assert popular control over Parliament. So when the Commons expelled him again in February 1769, the voters of Middlesex immediately re-elected their imprisoned candidate. A constitutional tug of war followed, in which Wilkes was again and again returned to the Commons, where he was denied his seat. At the fourth election, the Commons insisted on declaring Colonel Luttrell, the runner-up to Wilkes, as the winner, leading to widespread public anger.

A Society for the Defence of the Bill of Rights was formed in February 1769, primarily to fight his case, and even raised and donated £16,000 to pay off his debts. But his off-hand treatment of the Society alienated supporters.

In 1771 the Commons, wearying of the fight, decided not to prosecute three newspapers which had defied the ban on reporting parliamentary proceedings – one of Wilkes's chief demands. For the first time the right of the press to scrutinize and report Britain's elected representatives was accepted. The same year Wilkes, released from prison, was elected sheriff of Middlesex. Three years later he became Lord Mayor of London.

In 1774 the Commons allowed Wilkes to be elected without fuss for Middlesex. He had won all his major battles and remained the county's MP until 1790. He died on Boxing Day 1797 at the age of 72.

With much scandal, a politician starts as a good chap, until unmasked as a sex beast. Wilkes reversed the process. He began as a man famous for his sexual activities but was finally discovered, constitutionally and politically, to be a splendid chap.

SPEAKERS NORTON and CORNWALL – 1770–89

Contrasting Pitfalls for a Commons Speaker

The late 1700s was a time when the parliamentary spotlight often moved from the benches and turned – to his embarrassment – on the Speaker himself.

Charles Wolfran Cornwall had difficulty keeping his own house in order – as well as his House to order. When his immediate predecessor, Sir Fletcher Norton, once cheerfully announced that he would treat the resolutions of the House 'as those of so many drunken porters' (a reference to *Macbeth*), he cannot have anticipated a successor who came to be seen in just this role. Cornwall sat – or slouched – in the Speaker's chair from 1780 until his death in 1789. He slurred his words and relieved his boredom with regular swigs of porter. A porter on porter.

> There Cornwall sits, and ah! compelled by fate,
> Must sit forever, through the long debate.
>
> Like sad Prometheus fastened to the rock,
> In vain he looks for pity to the clock,
> In vain th' effects of strengthening porter tries,
> And nods to Bellamy for fresh supplies.

Thus did the author Sir Nathaniel Wraxall commemorate Mr Speaker Cornwall. His overall summing-up was less poetic: 'Never was any man in public situation less regretted or sooner forgotten.'

Philip Ziegler, author of *Addington*, describes Cornwall as a 'lazy non-entity who diverted the House by keeping a supply of porter underneath his chair and noisily sipping at it during debates'.

He was also a Tory political defector, who changed sides to the Whigs for a short time, following a fall-out with his brother-in-law, Charles Jenkinson, Secretary-at-War. Staggering from party to party, he lurched from constituency to constituency, too, representing Grampound in the Parliament of 1768, Winchelsea in those of 1774 and 1780, and Rye in the 1784 session, before dying in office in 1789.

He could not have presented a more ludicrous contrast with his predecessor in the chair, Sir Fletcher Norton. Cornwall cared little. Norton cared far too much, and ended up being burned in effigy outside the Tower of London.

A far more interesting and vital character, Norton did not mix, or slur, his words. Vehemently anti-government, he was drawn towards controversy, drawing back before things became impossibly uncomfortable. But his intensity and courage earned him friends.

Sir Fletcher Norton, already a controversial lawyer, was elected Speaker on 22 January 1770, with a huge majority over the Whig candidate, Thomas Townsend the younger. He created a sensation while presenting a bill voting funds for the King's expenses on 7 May 1777. He memorably barked that the Commons 'have not only granted to your majesty a large present supply, but also a very great additional revenue – great beyond example, great beyond your wants'. MPs and courtiers cringed. Norton was accused of having substituted the word 'wants' for 'expense'. Friends swiftly organized a damage-limitation exercise, and a resolution was carried that the Speaker had expressed 'with a just and proper energy the zeal of this House for the support of the honour and dignity of the Crown in circumstances of great public charge'. And for having declared 'in manly terms the real state of the nation to his majesty on the throne'.

Norton's candour brought him popularity with many, and he was awarded the freedom of the City. Undaunted by the fuss he had caused, he turned the Civil List into something of a hobby-horse.

This incident had occurred when Norton's popularity was already secure. He had been unanimously re-elected Speaker in 1774, even after a colossal furore in 1771, when Norton signed the warrant imprisoning Brass Crosby, the much-loved Lord Mayor of London and MP, in the Tower. Norton was a clever survivor and his battles helped advance privilege: the right of newspapers to report parliamentary proceedings with no fear of libel proceedings.

With neither the porter beneath his chair to console him, nor the perils of being burned in effigy to unnerve him, Speaker Martin in the 21st century has a more arduous, if less colourful, role than his predecessors more than 200 years ago.

CASTLEREAGH and CANNING – 1809

Pistols at Putney: a Duel Between Two Cabinet Ministers

These days, neither honour nor ambition would induce a politician to risk his life. Not so two centuries ago, when a summer of bitter feuding between two Tory Cabinet ministers led to pistols at dawn. Two days after Viscount Castlereagh resigned as War Secretary he challenged to a duel his scheming arch rival George Canning, who had just stood down as Foreign Secretary.

On a misty autumn morning in September 1809 the two men met at Putney Heath to take pot shots at each other. Canning missed. Castlereagh was more successful. His 39-year-old opponent was carried from the field with blood pouring from his left thigh. The press called it a 'disgusting exhibition'. George III, suffering increasingly frequent bouts of insanity soon to incapacitate him, privately hoped his entire Tory Cabinet would be carried off the field in wooden boxes. But both men lived to fight another day.

Historians describe the duel as epitomizing the struggle of interests in Britain during the Napoleonic Wars. The great landed aristocracies, which were represented by the 40-year-old Castlereagh, had been losing power to the new bourgeoisie: the thrusting mercantile class represented by Canning. The military threat from Napoleon had given the old reactionary élite a breathing space and, under the cloak of national security, they resisted demands for greater political participation from the new breed.

The cool, Cambridge-educated aristocrat Castlereagh was looking for a chance to thwart the ambitions of George Canning. Canning, considered the sharpest mind in Parliament, never hid his desire to become Prime Minister. His biting wit made him popular in the country, but hated in Parliament where, despite being an Etonian, he lacked 'tone'. Was he entirely a gentleman? His background was a disadvantage. Canning's father had died in 1771, leaving his wife and year-old-son, George, destitute. Mrs Canning took up with an unemployed actor, to whom she bore five children. Her marriage in 1783 to another actor, by whom she had another five children, did nothing to rescue her from poverty and shame.

The young George was plucked from all this by a wealthy uncle, Stratford Canning, who sent him to Eton and Oxford. He proved a clever student, but eighteenth-century snobbery meant Canning was considered rather an *arriviste*. After graduation he decided on a political career and came under the protective wing of the Prime Minister, William Pitt, who, impressed by Canning's wit and intelligence, found him a safe seat. His ascent up the political ladder was rapid. By the spring of 1809, when Britain seemed to be losing against Napoleon, he was Foreign Secretary.

Canning took the credit for planning the brilliant seizure of the Danish fleet, allied to Napoleon: the cause of the biggest outpouring of patriotic joy since the Battle of Trafalgar in 1805. But the Foreign Secretary was quick to dissociate himself from military setbacks. In the disaster at Corunna – the Napoleonic equivalent of the retreat at Dunkirk – he made sure the blame was laid at the door of Castlereagh, the War Secretary. On 2 April he wrote to the Prime Minister, the Duke of Portland, threatening to resign as Foreign Secretary unless Castlereagh was sacked.

The ailing 71-year-old Prime Minister was not the master of his own destiny. At a dangerous time in the country's history, the King had charged Portland with the delicate task of keeping Britain's two most able politicians in the Government. Neither the King nor the Prime Minister held Castlereagh responsible for Napoleon's string of stunning victories, and Portland, who delegated most decisions to his ministers, could not afford to lose either man. He tried to placate Canning. But the Foreign Secretary would not compromise. The Prime Minister delayed. It was to prove a disastrous and near-fatal delay for both rivals.

Portland discussed Canning's ultimatum with three other members of the Government including Castlereagh's uncle, Lord Camden, the Lord President of the Council. Castlereagh himself was kept in the dark over Canning's demand. Besides, with Napoleon an imminent threat, he was busy planning an ambitious invasion force to capture the French naval base at Antwerp. While the King tried, and failed, to arrange a compromise solution under which War Office duties would be divided between Castlereagh and Canning, a huge British invasion force of 39,000 men – the Walcheren expedition – was dispatched to do battle with Napoleon. It proved to be England's most spectacular disaster in the Napoleonic era.

In Castlereagh's association with this disaster, Canning saw his chance. He repeated his demand that Castlereagh be sacked. For the Prime Minister it was too much, and Portland tendered his resignation to the King on 6 September.

The following day Canning offered himself as Prime Minister on condition that Castlereagh was made the public scapegoat for the Walcheren humiliation. The demand was refused. Believing that no creditable government could be formed without his involvement, Canning resigned as Foreign Secretary. Britain, in the middle of a long and debilitating war with the French, had gone from a weak and divided government to no government at all. An extraordinary twelve days elapsed before a new Prime Minister was chosen.

Puzzled about the sudden resignation of Canning, Castlereagh quizzed his uncle, Lord Camden. Camden came clean and told his nephew the full story of that summer's plotting. Remarkably, Castlereagh seemed to be the only member of the Government who had not known. 'It is impossible for me to disguise,' he said, 'the extent to which my confidence in my colleagues has been shaken by what has passed.' He resigned too.

DUEL
BETWEEN LORD CASTLEREAGH AND MR. CANNING

We regret to state, that a Duel took place early yesterday morning, between Lord CASTLEREAGH and Mr. CANNING, in which the latter received a wound in the left thigh, but happily it is not dangerous, being merely a flesh wound. The meeting took place at Putney Heath. Lord YARMOUTH seconded Lord CASTLEREAGH, and Mr. R. ELLIS accompanied Mr. CANNING. We understand they fired by signal, at the distance of ten yards. The first missed, and no explanation taking place, they fired a second time, when Mr. CANNING was wounded in the left thigh on the outer side of the bone; and thus the affair terminated. The wound, as we have already stated, is not dangerous. He was put into a coach, and conveyed to Gloucester Lodge, his newly purchased seat at Brompton; and Lord CASTLEREAGH returned to his house in St. James's-square, where he was shortly afterwards visited by Lord LIVERPOOL.—This very unpleasant affair was yesterday reported to have originated in the failure of the ulterior objects of the Expedition to the Scheldt, respecting which Mr. CANNING had expressed himself very pointedly; but this we are assured is not the fact. Lord CASTLEREAGH resigned the Seals of his office as Secretary of State last week; and Mr. CANNING having also tendered his resignation, remains in office only till a successor is appointed. Some misunderstanding has since arisen between them, the nature of which has not yet been publicly stated, but we understand it bore more of a private and personal, than of an official or public character. Indeed, as we have already stated, Lord CASTLEREAGH had ceased to be in office upwards of a week before the dispute took place. The challenge was given by his Lordship. Beyond this, we deem it prudent, at present, not to venture any statement. It is a delicate subject, and we are desirous of avoiding any statement, of the accuracy of which we are not perfectly assured.—In contemplating the event, we derive considerable consolation from the consideration that the cause of combat was more of a private than of a public nature, and Lord CASTLEREAGH being no longer a Minister, that it was not between Members of the Administration. Were the case otherwise, it would, indeed, be most lamentable; for if our Statesmen were to vindicate their public measures by the sword or the pistol, what would become of the dignity, the controul, and the authority of Parliament?

The Morning Post, 22 September 1809

Canning waited for his summons from the Palace. It never came. On 18 September George III called upon Spencer Perceval, the Chancellor of the Exchequer, to form an administration. (Perceval was later shot by John Bellingham, forebear to the present MP for Norfolk North-West, Henry Bellingham.)

The following day, with Britain's two most able ministers out of government, Castlereagh challenged Canning to a private duel to restore honour. Canning had never fired a gun in his life, but to refuse would have meant public shame. The same evening he made his will, signing off with a message to his wife: 'I hope I have made you a happy mother and a proud widow. I am content. Adieu. Adieu.'

The duellists met at six o'clock the next morning on Putney Heath after their aides failed to broker a last-minute compromise. Castlereagh, rumoured to have successfully duelled in Ireland, was calm and hummed songs by his favourite opera singer, Catalini, in the cab on the way to the showdown. Canning's aide, Ellis, was a bag of nerves. He gave his master the pistol, saying: 'I must cock it for him. I cannot trust him to do it himself.'

A distance of twelve paces was set between the duellists. They both fired and missed. Castlereagh's aide vainly pleaded with him to leave the field. He refused. They took aim a second time. Shots rang out. Canning missed. A piercing cry rent the air. Castlereagh's bullet had passed through Canning's left thigh. The wounded man exclaimed: 'But perhaps I ought to remain. Are you sure we are done?' before he was dragged from the field. The wound was not serious. Within a few hours Canning was propped up on a sofa at home writing letters to family and friends declaring all was well.

The affair was considered a monstrous scandal. There was an incredulous public reaction to the fact that two distinguished former ministers of the Crown had resorted to a duel: an ancient custom introduced by William the Conqueror, common in nineteenth-century French politics but, by 1809, astonishing between senior British politicians. The *Morning Chronicle* wrote: 'To suppose it possible, after the disgusting exhibition they have made, to form out of their dispersed and disordered ranks a government that could stand, is the height of absurdity.'

Publicly the King let his displeasure be known, but privately he was fascinated. After an audience at the Palace, Canning wrote

that he had to 'show the situation of the wound which he made
me point out to him on his own royal thigh'.

Castlereagh was blamed for demanding the duel and insisting
on a second shot, but his career quickly recovered. He was back
in his old job within two and a half years. Historians credit him
with much success, but he never enjoyed public affection.

> Why is a pump like Viscount Castlereagh?
> Because it is a slender thing of wood,
> That up and down its awkward arm doth sway,
> And coolly spout and spout and spout away,
> In one weak, washy, everlasting flood.

wrote Thomas Moore.

In 1821 the great Tory aristocrat began to show signs of
paranoia. After a supposedly happy 28 years of childless marriage,
he was, or thought he was, being blackmailed for homosexual acts.

It was said that he had picked up a soldier whom he afterwards
claimed had appeared to be a woman. He committed suicide in
1822. When his corpse was carried into Westminster Abbey, the
solemn proceedings were disrupted by boos.

After the duel, Canning remained out of office until 1816. He
did not return to the Foreign Office until after Castlereagh's
suicide. Then, in 1827, after 33 years in Parliament, Canning
finally achieved his dream and became Prime Minister. Half the
Cabinet refused to serve under him. His tenure at Downing Street
was short-lived. He died four months later, his health broken by
the strain and his own sanity questioned. Duelling was outlawed
in 1819.

BENJAMIN DISRAELI – 1826

'Youth is a blunder'

It was Disraeli who called politics a greasy pole, and the remark is usually applied to the snakes-and-ladders quality of high office. But for the young Disraeli, a low-born immigrant's grandson facing the nineteenth-century triple-whammy of debt, sexual scandal and Jewish ancestry, the pole was nowhere greasier than at its base. Disraeli got off to the most awful start. Just how awful is suggested in a book by the historian Jane Ridley: *The Young Disraeli, 1804–1846*. Ridley goes further than previous studies in indicating the mess Disraeli got himself into as a young man, and from which he struggled to free himself as a politician. His career was a triumph over adversity. It points the lesson that when scandal looms, all is not necessarily lost.

Unable to afford a proper public school or university, Benjamin Disraeli's father, Isaac, had him trained as a solicitor. Benjamin had little love for his law textbooks. He plundered the literary classics and took a growing interest in Tory politics. A dandy at the age of eighteen, he followed the Byronesque craze of dressing almost entirely in black. Ridley describes him shocking the wives of solicitors by appearing at their dinners in a black velvet suit with ruffles and black stockings with red clocks (ornamental designs) on their sides. This was a youth with ideas and dreams way above his means or station.

At the age of twenty, with less than fifty guineas to his name, he saw an opportunity to make money. Canning had just recognized the newly independent republics of South America. London was awash with rumours of the untold riches that would accompany those who invested in the joint-stock companies springing up to exploit the gold and silver mines of that continent.

Disraeli borrowed heavily to finance his speculation: a thousand pounds from an uncle, around £1,500 from a money-lender called Robert Messer, more from his publisher friend John Murray. He agreed with Murray to set up a Tory newspaper, to be called *The Representative*, as *The Times* in the early 1820s was seen by Tories as politically unreliable. How different from today.

In December 1825, the City suffered a disastrous crash. Disraeli, just turned 21, was ruined, his mining shares worthless. He owed many thousands of pounds – a considerable sum in those days, though the exact amount is not known. Because he had been under 21 when he had purchased the shares he could not be held legally liable for his debts, but this did not stop his creditors pursuing him. He spent much of the next two decades avoiding them and running up further debts.

Adding, now, to his political ambitions was the knowledge that a Member of Parliament cannot be imprisoned. Disraeli was unable to pay his promised share of the start-up costs of *The Representative*, and fell out with his friend Murray, who went ahead without him. The paper failed after six months.

Partly as therapy, partly as a means to pay off his debts, Disraeli resorted to writing a novel loosely based on his financial misadventures. But *Vivian Grey*, which appeared anonymously soon after, parodied too closely Disraeli's former friends and business associates, and the secret identity of its author was soon revealed. Society was appalled and fascinated in equal measure at his apparent peddling of confidences. Duels were threatened, but never fought. Disraeli had made his name and bought a valuable breathing space from his creditors. A sequel was hastily brought out the following year, 1827.

Soon after its publication, the stress of the past two years took its toll. Disraeli was sitting in his room one evening, when he heard a loud ticking noise. Checking his watch, he realized the sound seemed to come from within his head. He slept badly, and the following morning was unable to write. The noise returned in the evening. 'I could compare it to nothing but the continuous roar of a cataract,' he later wrote. With his debts still unsettled, his nervous condition worsened. He languished in Bloomsbury doing nothing. Doctor after doctor was called. 'I was bled, blistered, boiled, starved, poisoned, electrified, galvanized; and at the end of a year found myself with exactly the same oppression on my brain.'

Ten years later, a doctor diagnosed his condition as 'chronic inflammation of membranes of the brain.' Disraeli later admitted he had suffered 'exhaustion of the nervous system'. Today we might call it a nervous breakdown.

Slowly, and with rest, he recovered. In 1831, with his creditors increasingly vocal, he felt fit enough to embark on a sixteen-month grand tour around Europe and the Middle East. He travelled as far as Constantinople and enjoyed several audiences with the Sultan. As for what Disraeli did on these travels, we have few details other than the highly fictionalized material in his novels. But we do have some clues. Back home in 1833 he was attending dinner parties dressed in 'green velvet trousers and ruffles' and shocking guests with his passion for the East, which, according to the painter Benjamin Haydon, 'seemed tinged with a disposition to palliate its infamous vices . . . I meant to ask him if he preferred Aegypt, where Sodomy was preferment, to England, where it very properly was Death.'

Jane Ridley suggests Haydon was hinting at a little-discussed aspect of Disraeli's nature. He was a dandy, and dandies were notoriously effeminate, but Disraeli, she believes, went further. 'Like his political Radicalism, it was an attitude Disraeli found no difficulty in reconciling with the more conventional frameworks of Toryism or heterosexuality; bisexuality came as naturally to Disraeli as did Tory Radicalism,' she says.

An image of Disraeli at this time was provided by the Countess of Montalembert who thought him 'an egregious coxcomb . . . outraging the privilege a young man has of being absurd'.

This is all very speculative. Being a dandy in those days meant aping the dress and manner of a set, some of whose members would have been bisexual or gay, but that does not mean that all who followed these fashions were themselves bisexual or gay.

It was certainly heterosexual affairs which landed him in trouble over romance. Disraeli sounds as though he was in love at least with the idea of love. After dalliances with a series of women, most of them older than him and some of them married, he became involved with Henrietta Sykes, the daughter of a wealthy sporting Norfolk brewer. Their affair became a public scandal. Henrietta had been married for eleven years to the sickly Sir Francis Sykes, by whom she had four children. Bored, tempestuous, voluptuous, and significantly older than Disraeli, she would sign her letters to him 'your mother'.

They would be seen at parties and the opera together, but although gossip was rife, it suited Sir Francis to turn a blind eye for the time being. He was busy in adultery with the married Clara Bolton, who happened to be one of Disraeli's former lovers. But Clara was less willing to ignore Disraeli's affair. Resentful that she had been discarded by Disraeli, she encouraged Sir Francis to break the pair up. By 1836, when they parted, this suited Disraeli well enough. His prospects of a political career were brightening.

A year later, Henrietta's husband found her in bed with a new man. Late one night he shut Henrietta out of the house, refused to allow her to see her children, and then placed an advertisement broadcasting her adultery.

It could so easily have been Disraeli. Even now, he did not emerge unscathed. At the time Disraeli was making his fifth attempt to enter Parliament, standing for the winnable seat of Maidstone, and rumours dogged his campaign.

Although he finally won the election, his appearance, at the age of 33, on the hustings in dandified dress astonished the people of the town. They howled abuse, and there were cries of 'Shylock' and 'Old Clothes' as the mob offered him stinking lumps of ham and bacon.

His Commons career began badly. He was nervous, he was, at first, an unsuccessfully pretentious orator, there were rumours about his dalliances with married women, and he was still seriously in debt. A Maidstone lawyer, Charles Austin, accused the newly elected MP of promising bribes to the voters of Maidstone during the election, bribes which he had failed to honour. (Bribing electors was a common practice, but a gentleman paid the bribes he promised.)

Austin's claim is probably true, but Disraeli's handling of the affair shows his genius – and shows why, in these pages, he joins the ranks of those who got away.

Instead of ducking, Disraeli went on to the offensive. Taking Austin's onslaught as an attack on his honour, he wrote a letter to the *Morning Post*, alleging worse by Austin. Rather than challenging Disraeli to a duel, as Disraeli had expected, Austin instead sued for libel. Disraeli was allowed to apologize flamboyantly in court. Though he had incurred costs, he had succeeded in switching the issue from that of his unpaid election bribes to his libel. Fortunately his legal bill was paid by the latest older woman in his life: Mary Anne Wyndham Lewis, the widow of his deceased running-mate in the Maidstone election.

Disraeli had written in a private letter dated December 1837, soon after his election: 'I am not married, but any old, ugly and ill-tempered woman may have me tomorrow.' Mrs Wyndham Lewis was a good deal more attractive than that, and though she was twelve years older than Disraeli, she was also rich. Disraeli's haste to conclude the match appeared almost crude, but their affection for each other seemed genuine. She was to act as a stabilizing influence over him for the rest of her life.

He despaired of Maidstone shortly after his election, and began searching for a cheaper seat with fewer voters requiring fewer bribes. He chose Shrewsbury for the 1841 election. His need to remain in Parliament became evident the moment the dissolution was called. A handbill was plastered over the town, listing the judgement debts against him during the past three years. They totalled over £21,000. In the list were included

> the names of unhappy Tailors, Hosiers, Upholsterers, Jew Money Lenders (for this Child of Israel was not satisfied with merely spoiling the Egyptians), Spunging House-keepers, and, in short, persons of every denomination who were foolish enough to Trust him . . . He seeks a place in Parliament merely for the purpose of avoiding the necessity of a Prison, or the benefit of the Insolvent Debtors Act.

In the end most of the debts were, if not settled, made subject to agreements. The others he brushed off, with some success, as collateral raised for other people. The voters of Shrewsbury accepted his excuses and his money, and elected him.

Disraeli's political career began to prosper. As middle age approached, the MP made headway against his debts with his wife's assistance. He could concentrate on the pursuit of power. By the time his wife died of cancer, in 1872, he had already been Prime Minister once.

When the widower returned to power in 1874, his curious relationship with the widowed Queen Victoria began. Disraeli had learnt how to flatter lonely middle-aged women without appearing over-familiar. He addressed the delighted Queen, who had just produced a slim volume of her own, with the phrase 'we authors, ma'am'. Early lessons were paying off.

Early lessons in risky speculation did not, however, seem to have been learned. Disraeli was still a gambler. But this time his gamble succeeded. Disraeli bought almost half the Suez Canal without Parliament's authority. A patriotic journalist in the area informed the Foreign Office that the extravagant and spendthrift ruler of Egypt, the Khedive Ismail Pasha, was keen to sell. The Foreign Office, identifying no tangible gain for Britain, could not justify the purchase. Disraeli however saw a bargain and at the end of December 1875, with Parliament in recess, he borrowed the money from his friends the Rothschilds and boldly bought shares for the Government. Fortunately Parliament, sunning itself in the enhanced national prestige, approved the purchase in the New Year.

Disraeli was an uncensorious man. Once, when Palmerston was in power, the 79-year-old Prime Minister was cited as co-respondent in a divorce case involving a Mrs O'Kane (prompting the inevitable popular joke: 'she was Kane but was he Able?'). Disraeli remarked that it was a pity this had got out, as Palmerston would now sweep the country at the next election. He did.

The story Jane Ridley tells runs rather counter to the course of much political scandal. The more common tale is of the idealism of youth giving way in a politician to cynicism and corruption – and ending in scandal. But Disraeli started in scandal. As a young man he was reckless and amoral, and very nearly ruined himself. He remained an artful pragmatist for the rest of his career, but it may be argued that, burned by his early experience of debt and disgrace, the mature Disraeli had learned something. His personal difficulties had lent him a certain alienation from the herd. His 'One Nation' Toryism steered the Conservative party away from class politics and away from unthinking opposition to reform. Cynicism is not always a degrading force. Disraeli became cynical about the rich, about privilege, and about the Christian Establishment in nineteenth-century Britain. He learned both to use and to despise 'the system'. His alienation may have saved him – and his party – from too deep an attachment to faction, class and privilege. A brush with scandal can be a redeeming experience.

'Youth is a blunder, manhood a struggle, old age a regret,' Disraeli wrote in *Coningsby*. But the blunders of youth arm us for the struggle, and need be no cause for regret.

GEORGE HUDSON – 1849

The Railway King

'In society but not of it,' said Lady Dorothy Neville of George Hudson, in her celebrated memoirs. Those making a quick buck out of railway privatisation would do well to read Hudson's tale. The massive expansion of the railway network in Britain during the middle of the last century gave many men the chance to make their fortunes, but the greatest fortune of all was rapidly won – and spectacularly lost – by George Hudson MP, the 'Railway King'.

Born in 1800 near York, Hudson became a draper in the town. In 1828 he inherited £30,000, invested heavily in the North Midland railway and threw himself into politics. He bought three estates, served as Deputy Lieutenant for Durham and was thrice Lord Mayor of York. At 45 he was elected Conservative MP for Sunderland.

In the years 1847–8 Britain was experiencing 'railway mania'. Hudson acquired railway companies until he came to exercise more power in the industry than anyone before or since. And he used his seat in Parliament ruthlessly in the expansion of his business empire. This was not unusual: at the time, 155 MPs were directors of railway companies and it cannot have been a coincidence that their services had been so sought after. But Hudson went too far. He bribed other MPs to support the private bills authorizing his railway purchases.

Once, he advised the Duke of Wellington's two sisters to sell their large holdings in a railway company he knew to be rotten, and they did so, shortly before they would have lost a fortune in its downfall. The grateful Wellington asked whether there was any way he could repay the MP. Hudson replied that his daughter, whom he had sent to an expensive private school, was being victimized for her humble origins. Could Wellington help? The great man responded by a personal call, with flowers, and an outing to tea, so that her reputation among schoolfriends and staff was swiftly secured.

Hudson's dream was to build up a unified system, based on his home-town, that covered the whole of the country. An early slogan he used was 'Mak all t' railways cum t' York'. And certainly, as the 1840s neared their end, he found himself well on his way to achieving that aim. He controlled 1,450 of the 5,000 miles of track in England, and was in charge of the Midland, the York and North Midland, the York, Newcastle and Berwick, and the Eastern Counties companies. His empire stretched from Bristol to Berwick.

To achieve this level of control, he had sought to gain influence wherever it might be of use to him – legitimately or otherwise. As well as being elected to the Commons in 1845, he was Lord Mayor of York and served on the magistracies of York, the North Riding, and Durham. He was part proprietor of the *Yorkshire Gazette*, the *Sunderland Times* and the *Railway Chronicle*.

In the financial field, Hudson used the York Union Bank (he was chairman) to borrow heavily in the City, to fund his operations. Moreover, he influenced prices on the London and York Stock Exchanges by buying and selling shares whose prices he wanted to move. He falsified accounts and fraudulently paid dividends out of borrowed capital instead of profits, in order to give an impression of greater success than was actually being achieved. Of great assistance to him in these deceptions was the fact that he kept all the accounts in his head.

But like Maxwell's a century and a half later, Hudson's deceit caught up with him. He was not alone in using creative accounting to drum up cash for his investments, and his core businesses were mostly bona fide. In Hudson's day (as in ours) the perpetrators of many potential financial 'scandals' were rescued by the ultimate profitability of their ventures and Hudson may have been the visible tip of a parliamentary iceberg. But what did for him was geometry. Hudson was conveying passengers from Newcastle and York to London via Derby and Birmingham, piggy-backing on George Stephenson's line. Edmund Denison took the straight line down the East coast. A railway between Cambridge and Lincoln to shorten Hudson's route failed, and his prospects faded.

'Off the Rail', *Punch*'s cartoon of the fall of Hudson, 1849

By the beginning of 1849 Hudson's empire was crumbling. He had overstretched himself. Keen-eyed shareholders, who had become suspicious and started to study the accounts, found discrepancies. In February the York, Newcastle and Berwick Company set up a committee of investigation. Its report two months later signalled the end of the reign of the Railway King. In October 1846, Hudson had recommended to the company that they buy shares in another company, the Great North of England. They agreed, and put Hudson himself in sole charge of the purchases. What Hudson hadn't told them was that earlier in the month he had bought some GNE shares himself, in a personal capacity. So he sold his own shares to his own company. He sold them at £23 10s per share, while their true market value was only £21. In the age of the directors' share option, we can only marvel at his restraint.

Hudson was forced to buy back the shares, and repay the £9,000 which he had defrauded from the company. *The Yorkshireman* newspaper, in the lapel-clutching prose of the day, took up the case: 'Mr Hudson shall not escape us. The thousands he has duped, and the breaking hearts from whence spring curses both loud and deep, shall have ample satisfaction for the injuries they have suffered and the torments they have endured.'

Another of Hudson's companies, the Eastern Counties, set up their own committee. Until now Hudson had been the hero of the company, having 'rescued' it from near bankruptcy in 1845. But now it was discovered that of the £545,714 he had paid out in dividends between 1845 and 1848, £320,572 had come not from profits but from capital. The committee found that as well as stealing the company's money to pay his own hotel bills, Hudson and David Waddington (another MP on the company's board) had stolen £9,000 with which to bribe other MPs into supporting Hudson's purchases of other companies. The committee petitioned Parliament.

Hudson was lost. He was forced to resign all his chairmanships. His brother-in-law, Richard Nicholson (a co-accused) killed himself in shame. Nine days later, Hudson was forced to make a Commons reply to the allegations of bribery. He was in such a state that for several moments he could not even speak. Even when he did start, building up to a defiant performance, his fellow MPs heard little to impress them. From now on he was to be an outcast (but, as an MP, an unarrestable one) in the Commons and outside it. In the months that followed, he was forced to pay back the sums he had stolen from his various companies. In York he was particularly unpopular – he didn't even dare show himself there. His name was removed from the Aldermanic roll, and the new approach to York train station, which had been named Hudson Street, was given the rather plainer title of Railway Street.

The following year his co-swindler, James Richardson, sued *The Yorkshireman* for libel over an article condemning him and Hudson. He lost, so damning Hudson even further. But Hudson was determined to stay in the Commons, a determination based less on stubborn pride than on the legal protection his status as an MP gave him.

In the 1852 election he managed to avoid defeat, largely because two years earlier he had secured the opening of a new dock in his Sunderland constituency. But even while he sat as an MP, he would always flee to Paris when Parliament was in recess, in order to escape his creditors. He lost his Sunderland seat in 1859 and spent the remaining years of his life in litigation, in Boulogne, making efforts to operate financially outside England. He died in 1871, virtually penniless.

We must not be too hard on George Hudson. He wasn't a Maxwell, more an improviser who moved money on casters. The statue planned for him outside York was replaced by one of George Leeman, his chief tormentor, the sort of high-toned creep who inspires in us a sneaking affection for men like Hudson.

ROBERT LOWE – 1873

An Albino Chancellor with an 'Unhappy Knack'

Robert Lowe, Chancellor of the Exchequer in Gladstone's first government, cut a curious figure. An albino, with one eye malformed and the other so sensitive to light that he had to keep his eyelids almost shut, he was described by *Punch* as having an 'unhappy knack of offending his subordinates and quarrelling with all with whom he comes into contact'. His desire to 'get things done', without due regard to the niceties of the rule book, led to two financial scandals in quick succession. His cantankerous refusal to apologize spoiled his rehabilitation.

Lowe was born in Nottinghamshire in 1811. From Winchester he went on to University College, Oxford, where he taught for a time. Called to the Bar in 1842, he emigrated the same year to Sydney, Australia. He built up a lucrative practice there and played a major role in the state legislative council from 1843 until 1850.

Home again in 1850, Lowe began writing editorials for *The Times* and in 1852 he entered the House of Commons, holding office under both Aberdeen and Palmerston. He led the renegade wing of the Liberal Party which opposed their own Prime Minister, Lord Russell, over his moderate attempts to widen the franchise. Lowe's grouping became known as the Adullamites. John Bright, who supported household suffrage, had called them the 'Cave of Adullam' because everyone who was discontented or in distress resorted there. Despite this disloyalty, Gladstone later chose Lowe as his Chancellor in 1868. His abilities were so conspicuous as to outweigh his disobliging manner and bizarre appearance. He was still at Number 11 when his first scandal came to light in March 1873.

In recent years the newly nationalized telegraph service had been expanding rapidly with a trebling in the number of stations. Rates had been reduced and standardized. The man Lowe had placed in charge of this task, the ultra-efficient and hard-working civil servant Frank Scudamore, was widely credited for this success. Unfortunately, Scudamore's success had been partly financed by illegal borrowing. In order to pay the often unpredictable bills for expanding the network of telegraph lines, he had been dipping into the savings of working men in the Post Office Savings Bank. In 1871 he borrowed £171,775; the following year it was £400,000.

The man who should have spotted this, the Financial Secretary William Baxter, was kept out of the picture by Lowe. Like Scudamore, Lowe was a doer, and considered Baxter too pedantic. The request for Treasury funds to pay back the savings accounts went straight to Lowe, who agreed to them straight away, without inquiring too closely why Scudamore needed these funds.

When Opposition MPs revealed in the Commons what had been going on, the ambushed Lowe had little choice but to promise an investigation. Although it found that the payments had been due to over-enthusiasm rather than fraud, the press were hard on him. He was not popular.

Hot on the heels of this affair came the exotic-sounding Zanzibar scandal. The Sultan of Zanzibar, a keen patron of the slave trade, had been the subject of growing public protest. To dissuade him from permitting slavery, the British government promised him a mail service from Zanzibar to Aden and the Cape Colony.

But who would provide it? It was not a commercial proposition. The Union Steamship company offered to take the franchise for a mere £5,000, as long as their subsidized government contract for the Britain to Cape Town service was renewed. In fact there was no need for a subsidy on this latter route: a Mr Donald Currie had started a service unsubsidized.

Lowe knew that the nit-picking Baxter would insist on a tendering process, so he didn't tell him, but signed the contract and told the Union Steamship Company to commence the service immediately – ignoring the requirement for prior parliamentary approval. Parliament, Lowe promised, would ratify the contract later.

When Mr Currie learned that the Union Steamship Company's contract had been renewed without a tender, he protested, forcing the Government to look into the matter. The contract with Union for the England–Cape run was thrown out.

Lowe was now fighting for his political life. Without the subsidy of the England–Cape service, he settled with Union on £26,000 for the Zanzibar to Cape run. But so mistrusted was the Chancellor by now that it became clear he was unlikely to get parliamentary support for this either. He used a procedural device to postpone a vote, thus gaining a ten-day delay.

When he returned for the second debate, Lowe refused to apologize and plead human error. Backbenchers would have accepted nothing less. He made unconvincing excuses for his procedural short-cuts. The Commons demanded a commission of inquiry, which finally shaved £6,000 off Union's contract.

Both scandals simmered on into the summer. It became obvious that the cantankerous Lowe would have to depart. Gladstone wanted this to happen quietly after the heat had died down. Baxter wrote to Gladstone in fury about the Zanzibar affair, offering his resignation. Gladstone was forced to bring forward his reshuffle. Lowe was demoted to Home Secretary, a post he held until the election the following year. He never held office again.

Lowe was created Viscount Sherbrooke in 1880 and died twelve years later.

GLADSTONE – 1880

'When you're out saving fallen women, save one for me'

. . . So Disraeli is reputed – almost certainly inaccurately – to have remarked to his rival. William Ewart Gladstone was a great statesman – strong, grave, deeply religious, the personification of Victorian respectability. But frequently, the Grand Old Man of Victorian politics would leave the Dispatch Box and turn his remarkable rhetorical skills on a different audience. Four times Prime Minister, he would stalk the seedier pavements of London in search of prostitutes, driven by a craving he had battled against since university days.

Precisely what that craving was we shall never be quite sure. How far he satisfied it we do not know. There are many views, and from the story which follows the reader may form his own. Ours is that – despite evidence which any modern tabloid newspaper would interpret in the obvious, crude way – it is entirely possible and on the whole likely that Gladstone, an immensely complicated man of almost unfathomable depth, never slept with the prostitutes whose company he sought. Professor H. C. G. Matthew quotes W. E. Gladstone (on Leopardi) thus in *Gladstone: 1875–1898*:

> There is scarcely a single moral action of a single man of which other men can have such a knowledge, in its ultimate grounds, its surrounding incidents, and the real determining cause of its merits, as to warrant their pronouncing conclusive judgement upon it.

Gladstone was tortured by questions of morality and fascinated by sin. He was undoubtedly capable of resisting temptation. He exerted cruel self-discipline. He seemed to enjoy tormenting himself. We believe that Gladstone was in the curious, twisted business of arranging temptation, enjoying it, and resisting it.

39

He had plenty to choose from. Late-nineteenth-century London was said to boast one prostitute for every eight 'gentlemen' and, over a forty-year period, Gladstone got to know a fair few of the former. He made no secret of this. He was so unashamed he even brought some of the gaudily dressed women back to 10 Downing Street. Sympathetic biographers say that, once there, he recited passages from the Bible to them. No one knows whether the fierce moralist and respected lay preacher actually had sex with those he called his 'erring sisters', whether he paid them anything, or if so how much.

The risks were enormous. Cabinet colleagues begged him to stop. At first many of his contemporaries were content to believe his protestations that his aims were purely charitable and he did find a sizeable number of his harem honest employment. Yet it emerged seventy years after his death, with the publication of Gladstone's fourteen volumes of diaries, that he was not himself convinced of his charitable aims. In one passage he explains how his motives were partly 'carnal or the withdrawal of them would not leave such a void'. He never much interested himself in the political movement for the reform of the laws on prostitution, or prostitutes' rehabilitation.

His wife Catherine, whom he married in 1839, knew about his interest in prostitutes. How much she knew, or cared to know, about his feelings and motivations is unclear. H. C. G. Matthew, whose study of Gladstone and his diaries has been as meticulous and thoughtful as any we are likely to have, writes: 'What she knew of her husband's sexual temptations, we do not know. Had she seen the scars on his back when in the 1840s and 1850s he used the scourge after meeting prostitutes?' Racked by guilt he would flog himself with a vicious scourge. Even then he could not prevail. As a student he had written (probably of masturbation) about 'this besetting sin' which returned 'again and again like a flood'.

In his diaries the whipping sessions were recorded thus: ß. His diaries suggest this self-administered justice was retributive rather than deterrent, although even retribution seems questionable as an explanation. Might it have been recreational? He seemed to enjoy it. In 1843 when he had just entered Robert Peel's government, he wrote:

Has it been sufficiently considered, how far pain may become the ground of enjoyment? In which case be it observed not only are the pleasure and the pain simultaneous and the first superior, but the latter is actually the occasion, the material, the substratum of the former.

Prostitutes had bewitched Gladstone since his Oxford days in the late 1820s. The anguish returned in the 1840s when he joined Peel's government. The pressures of ministerial life and the financial problems of his wife's family, from whom he had inherited Hawarden Castle in Flintshire, created a 'severe psychological crisis whose expression took a sexual form', according to one biographer.

In 1843 Gladstone, a High Church Tory, and at this time President of the Board of Trade, wrote in his diary: 'Fearful is the guilt of sin returning again and again in forms ever new but alike hideous.' He saw all sexual temptation as evil and a cause for guilt. At first he had sated his desires by reading what he regarded as pornography: Restoration poems, French verse fables, and classical authors such as Petronius!

In his diaries Gladstone gives a partial but revealing account of his encounters with more than French literature. On 13 July 1851, he wrote: 'Went with a note to EC's [Elizabeth Collins was a prostitute he saw regularly] – received (unexpectedly) and remained two hours: a strange and humbling scene – returned and ß.' It is clear by this time that Gladstone was forsaking the comforts of home very often.

15 July 1851: 'Fell in with EC and another mixed scene somewhat like that of forty-eight hours before – afterwards ß.'
23 July 1851: 'I then in a singular way hit upon EC: two more hours, strange, questionable, or more: followed by ß.'
7 May 1852 [about to become Chancellor of the Exchequer]- 'Saw E. Collins: bad: and there must be a change.'
1 April 1856 [back in Opposition]: 'Saw a Spaniard: and had a warning.'

Who was the mysterious Spaniard? What was the warning?

Gladstone clearly never heeded it. During this time he was subjected to at least one serious blackmail attempt in 1853 while still Chancellor. A man named William Wilson was astonished to see him in furtive conversation with a prostitute near Leicester Square. He saw a chance to make a few farthings. Gladstone's response to the blackmail attempt was swift: he immediately turned Wilson over to the police. Wilson received twelve months hard labour.

The press reported the incident briefly and factually. There was not even a hint of scandal. But thirty years later, when Victorian morality was more rigid, the Grand Old Man, now the Liberal Prime Minister, was forced to accept that he faced a political, if not a moral, problem.

In 1880 the Prime Minister, now turned seventy, was visiting brothels in pursuit of his 'rescue work'. In a sort of 'back to basics' moral climate – his own leadership had helped foster it – his ministers intervened and implored him to stop. They feared a scandal. The Government was in peril.

Rumours that Gladstone was a philanderer had persisted throughout his career. Earlier he had enjoyed what was, at the very least, an emotional, intense and sexually charged relationship with a courtesan called Laura Thistlethwayte. In his early letters to her, he began 'Dear Spirit'. She had showered him with gifts, and as her general extravagance was ruining Captain Thistlethwayte, her husband, Gladstone came to fear that their friendship might eventually be probed in the courts. 'What,' asks H. C. G. Matthew, 'was [Catherine Gladstone's] view of the regular letters to and from Laura Thistlethwayte and the visits [to her London town house] and later to Laura's cottage in Hampstead?'

Gradually, his relationship with the woman he called 'Mrs T' cooled. His friendship with the actress Lillie Langtry was probably sexually innocent, but it raised eyebrows. It may have been acceptable for the Prince of Wales but not for the Prime Minister of the world's greatest imperial power. There had also been rumours in the 1870s that a close political friend, Madame Olga Novikov, upon whom Gladstone relied for advice and information about Russia, was a mistress. Modern biographers regard these rumours as absurd. What is more likely is that Gladstone's powerful sex drive allowed shrewd women like Novikov to tease his susceptibilities and gain political influence with him.

In 1882 Lord Rosebery, a junior Home Office minister, who was to succeed Gladstone as premier, demanded an urgent audience. Agitation over Irish home rule had led to threats on Gladstone's life. He now received round-the-clock police protection. Rosebery saw the potential danger and spelt out the risk of a badly paid bobby passing on the secrets of the bordellos to a press far more hostile than it had been thirty years earlier.

Despite the grave risks, the Prime Minister still could not break the spell. Three months after the warning, and with gossip running through the Palace of Westminster, Rosebery's worst fears were realized. A Tory MP spotted Gladstone talking to a prostitute.

Colonel Tottenham MP seized on an opportunity to discredit the Prime Minister. The news spread like wildfire through Westminster and respectable society. It became the talk of the Victorian chattering classes. But, lacking hard evidence, the press never ran the story. Gladstone denied impropriety: 'It may be true that the gentleman saw me in such conversation but the object was not what he assumed or, as I am afraid, hoped.' Gladstone survived. But to the amazement of his colleagues and his long-suffering wife he had not learned his lesson.

Two years later there was a temporary halt after another desperate plea, this time from his private secretary Edward Hamilton, but Gladstone only took the hint after a final showdown in July 1886 when Hamilton presented the newly re-elected Prime Minister with compelling evidence that a strong blackmail case was imminent. Gladstone, who was by now 77, made a solemn promise to Hamilton. According to his diaries he kept it.

'15 and 17 June '92 are the penultimate examples of encounters with prostitutes,' writes Professor Matthew. 'Significantly, Gladstone refers to being "accosted", i.e. the initiative was the prostitute's, not, as in the past, his.'

Still with years of public life ahead, Mr and Mrs Gladstone celebrated their golden wedding anniversary in 1889. Of their four sons and four daughters, two became MPs, one became a baron, one became a clergyman, and another married the Dean of Lincoln. Two years before he died, still troubled by guilt, he tried to set the record straight when he gave his son, Stephen, who had taken holy orders, the carefully worded statement that he had 'not been guilty of the act which is known as that of infidelity to the marriage bed'. This may be partly borne out by the nicknames bandied around the brothels during the 1880s: 'Old Glad-eyes' and 'Daddy-do-nothing'. But his diaries are littered with contradictions. When writing in his diary of one prostitute's second visit to his home, he felt he had been 'certainly wrong in some things and trod the path of danger'.

The man Queen Victoria called 'old, wild and incomprehensible' died at the age of 84 in 1898, having left office four years previously for political reasons unconnected with scandal. The country mourned, as the great Victorian Prime Minister was buried with full honours in Westminster Abbey. *The Times* wrote:

> Gladstone's extraordinary career owed much to his happy domestic surroundings and the sympathy and watchful care of his wife . . . Mr Gladstone has known the truest blessing and joys of family relationships. He could truly have repeated the saying of Edmund Burke that once he crossed the threshold of his home all the troubles he had encountered outside would vanish.

Others thought differently. 'Gladstone . . . founded the great tradition . . . in public to speak the language of the highest and strictest principle, and in private to pursue and possess every sort of woman,' wrote one commentator, Peter Wright – his remarks occasioning a libel action from Gladstone's sons, after the old man's death.

In general, it may be said that attempts to discredit Gladstone failed. It is a testament to his enormous personal moral authority – an authority which perhaps no British Prime Minister had achieved before or could ever hope for now – that Gladstone was enabled to prevail against so powerful a tide of national rumour. The rumour continues to this day; he still prevails against it. It is quite an epitaph.

CHARLES STEWART PARNELL – 1880–90

'This man is wonderful – and different'

'In leaning forward in the cab to say a good-bye a rose I was wearing in my bodice fell out into my skirt. He picked it up and, touching it lightly with his lips, placed it in his button-hole' – thus wrote Mrs Kitty O'Shea of her first encounter with Charles Stewart Parnell.

Parnell was a remarkable Irish phenomenon. He had a political party at Westminster named after him. He united his divided homeland behind his dream of Home Rule, made and unmade ministries and mercilessly obstructed the British Parliament. He won over one of the century's great statesmen, Gladstone, to his dream. By 1890 it was in sight. It had taken Parnell fifteen years to get this far. And for the last ten of them he had been living with another man's wife.

The lady was born Katherine Page Wood in Essex in 1846, but would gain notoriety 44 years later as the adulteress, Kitty O'Shea. Kitty's father had once been chaplain to Queen Caroline, and her upbringing was comfortable but modest. An uncle, Lord Hatherley, was Lord Chancellor in Gladstone's 1868 government (a connection which later proved useful).

In January 1867, on the eve of her 21st birthday, Kitty married the dashing 26-year-old British army captain William O'Shea. Dublin-born and a Roman Catholic, he had joined the 18th Hussars at the age of eighteen but retired from the army before his marriage. A vain man, with little income from his estate, he soon squandered the money his solicitor father had left him.

The O'Sheas had three children, but their marriage sank quickly into one of convenience. It was in the husband's interest to continue the pretence: he took generous hand-outs from his wife's rich aunt, Mrs Benjamin Wood. Fluent in French and

Spanish, O'Shea had relatives in both countries and spent long periods abroad, including one in which he bought and managed a sulphur mine in Spain which, like most of his business ventures, failed. In 1874, when he had been gone for eighteen months, 82-year-old Aunt Ben, concerned for the children, bought her niece Wonersh Lodge, near her own home in Eltham, Kent.

Thereafter Kitty O'Shea lived in Eltham. Her husband, when not abroad, stayed at their London flat in Victoria. Partly to keep up appearances she would make the trip to London, hosting suppers for her husband's business associates at Thomas's Hotel, Berkeley Square. As the decade wore on, when O'Shea turned to politics, his guests would include the leading Irish politicians of the day. One of his targets was the rising political star among the new crop of Irish MPs elected in 1875: the member for County Meath, Charles Stewart Parnell.

Born in Wicklow, the son of a Protestant landowner, Parnell enjoyed an impeccable anti-British pedigree. His mother was the daughter of Commodore Charles Stewart of the United States Navy, a hero of the US war against the British in 1812 whose own parents had emigrated from Belfast before the American Revolution. The prevailing anti-British sentiment in the Parnell household did not stop his parents sending their son to school in England, where he hated everything except the cricket. Passionate in this un-Irish activity, he sustained his own XI.

He gained a place at Magdalen College, Cambridge, but never finished his degree. In 1869 Parnell got into a drunken street fight, the first of many quarrels. The fiery Irishman thought his victim was a pompous 'swell student'. In fact he turned out to be a respectable Cambridge merchant, who sold manure. About to be arrested, Parnell followed standard procedure and offered the policeman a bribe 'to settle the affair'. In his drunkenness he handed over a shilling, thinking it was a sovereign. Underbribed, the policeman persisted with an arrest for assault. Suspended by his college, Parnell turned his back on Cambridge.

And England. He returned to Ireland – a land now seething under Britain's coercive attempts to keep control. The revolutionary Fenians stood for armed resistance to British rule. Parnell was a striking, handsome and forceful presence, and a powerful recruit to the cause. He favoured a hard-nosed assault through securing the election of anti-British MPs to Westminster. In 1870 the Irish Home Rule League was established. Mostly Catholic, it succeeded in getting 56 MPs elected to Westminster in the 1874 election. The following year Parnell joined them.

Within two years he distinguished himself through his radical oratory. He cared little for Commons tradition but had a careful eye for Irish nationalist sensitivities. With other Home Rulers he used the obstruction of debates in the Chamber to draw attention to Irish concerns. In 1877 the Home Rule Confederation of Great Britain elected Parnell their president. He was now 31 and already the most conspicuous figure in Irish politics. William O'Shea recognized Parnell's growing strength and sought his friendship and support. At first he seemed to meet rebuffs.

In 1878 Ireland faced another famine. There were cases of families, unable to pay rents to absentee landlords, being mercilessly evicted from the countryside. Parnell saw his chance. He identified himself with their plight and the violent methods of the Irish Land League, which was resisting evictions and making rent-collection a life-threatening occupation.

Parnell thus became the centre of the 'new departure' in Irish nationalism: agitation at home and obstruction in the Commons. At the General Election in the spring of 1880, he was comfortably returned along with 85 other Home Rulers. One of these was Captain O'Shea, whose dinner parties in his Victoria flat had paid off. Elected MP for County Clare, O'Shea supported Parnell when he was voted leader of his party in Parliament. O'Shea was anxious to cement a close relationship with the powerful Parnell. He sent his wife to Westminster with a dinner invitation for his leader.

In her memoirs, Kitty gives her own account of that fateful first meeting when both were 34:

> He came out, a tall, gaunt figure, thin and deathly pale. He looked straight at me smiling and his curiously burning eyes looked into mine with a wondering intentness that threw into my brain the sudden thought: 'this man is wonderful – and different'.

After taking the rose that had fallen from her bodice, and placing

it in his buttonhole, he then sealed it in an envelope on which he wrote her name.

He accepted the dinner invitation. The following year he moved in with her at Wonersh Lodge. Her husband later denied any knowledge (at this stage) of their affair. But he challenged Parnell to a duel in 1881, after arriving at Eltham to find the Irish leader's portmanteau in the house. Parnell accepted the challenge, whereupon the captain backed down. 'From the date of this bitter quarrel,' wrote Mrs O'Shea, 'Parnell and I were one, without further scruple, without fear and without remorse.' O'Shea threatened divorce, but when his wife listed O'Shea's own infidelities, the threat subsided. He was still dependent on Aunt Ben's money.

Parnell's politics were as stormy, opportunistic and intuitive as his capture of Kitty. His success at obstructing Parliament had led to the suspension of 36 Irish MPs, wringing from Gladstone the 1881 Land Act, giving Irish tenants 'the three Fs' – fixity of tenure, fair rents and free sale.

The Land Act presented Parnell with a problem. He was not the only Irish politician to note his compatriots' preference for martyrdom over results, where these involved compromise with the English. He had done business with the English and, though the 1881 Land Act, dragged from Parliament, was a significant concession, it did not challenge British rule. This could have compromised him.

With rural Ireland in near-anarchy after four years of agrarian protest, Parnell cleverly set about testing the new law by putting cases to the Land Commission the Act had created, and he travelled through the countryside talking up sedition. As a result he was sent to Dublin's Kilmainham gaol on 13 October 1881. Biographers have suggested that imprisonment was his aim all along.

Now Parnell's ascendancy was assured. He was a nationalist hero, imprisoned for his cause. Inside Kilmainham he could not be held responsible for subsequent events: the suppression of the Land League and a winter of widespread terror against British rule. But he was also separated from his beloved Mrs O'Shea, who was now expecting their first child. Claimed by O'Shea as his own, the baby lived only two months, dying in April 1882, before Parnell's release.

Gladstone's government realized that Parnell was the only man who could restore order in the countryside. With Captain O'Shea as the intermediary, the government began negotiating with Parnell. The resulting Kilmainham Treaty guaranteed further concessions to Irish tenants in return for Parnell's promise to quell the agitation.

On 2 May 1882, Parnell was released. Four days later the Chief Secretary, Lord Frederick Cavendish and his (Catholic) senior civil servant, Thomas Burke, were gunned down by Fenians as they walked through Dublin's Phoenix Park. The murders affronted the nationalist movement, as the IRA bombing in Warrington was said to have done a century later. Parnell, dissociating himself from the killings, used them to bring the nationalist movement under his control at Westminster.

He was put under 24-hour police surveillance, something which caused news of his unconventional domestic arrangements to filter back to the Cabinet. Gladstone already knew, as throughout the 1880s it had been Mrs O'Shea who had drafted Parnell's letters to Gladstone and she had met the Liberal leader on three occasions. On 17 May, Lord Harcourt, the Home Secretary, warned his colleagues that the Kilmainham Treaty would not be popular 'when the public discovered that it had been negotiated by Captain O'Shea, the husband of Parnell's mistress'. The Home Secretary revealed how O'Shea's earlier divorce threat had only been silenced by the potential exposure of his own affairs.

Kitty and Parnell settled down to something not far from domesticity, given their adultery. Two daughters, Clare and Katharine, born in 1883 and 1884, were undoubtedly Parnell's. Christmas 1883 saw the couple in Brighton at a rented house. To their surprise the husband turned up. With only moments to spare, Parnell clambered down the fire escape. Composing himself outside, he then presented himself at the front door ten minutes later. The ignominy (when the story was related years later by Mrs O'Shea's cook during the divorce case) diminished Parnell's standing. Cartoonists sketched Parnell clinging to an outside stairway. An enterprising toy maker created a miniature Parnell clattering down a fire escape.

Parnell had never acknowledged O'Shea's efforts in negotiating his release from gaol and O'Shea grew increasingly resentful and distrustful towards his party leader and cuckolder. Though O'Shea pretended he did not know of the affair, a pretence in which his wife and Parnell colluded, tongues wagged. Aunt Ben, however, continued signing cheques. In the election campaign of 1885, Parnell was pointedly questioned about matrimonial fidelity in front of a noisy crowd. He refused to answer.

That election saw O'Shea re-elected, with the support of the radical Joseph Chamberlain. Chamberlain was hostile to Parnell's Home Rule, but talked alternatives with O'Shea – perhaps aiming to split the Irish party. O'Shea, re-elected as a Home Ruler, refused to sign a pledge supporting Parnell, but Parnell was still riding high, in Ireland as well as England. Gladstone's Reform Bill in 1884, giving agrarian workers the vote, increased his support. In 1886 Gladstone formed his third government, reliant on Parnell's backing, with the specific pledge to 'pacify Ireland'.

Parnell was now pivotal in British as well as Irish politics. Gladstone needed the votes he could deliver. Home Rule for Ireland depended upon him too. Only illness, or scandal, could threaten Parnell. It was now that his health began to deteriorate, and the likelihood that his adultery would be exposed started to grow.

In 1886 the *Pall Mall Gazette* ran a report headlined 'Mr Parnell's suburban retreat'. The MP had been involved in a slight accident with a market gardener's cart on his way 'home'. The

---

MR. PARNELL'S SUBURBAN RETREAT.

Shortly after midnight on Friday evening, Mr. Parnell, while driving home came into collision with a market gardener's cart. During the sitting of Parliament the hon. member for Cork usually takes up his residence at Eltham, a suburban village in the south-east of London. From here he can often be seen taking riding exercise round by Chiselhurst and Sidcup. On Friday night as usual his carriage met him at the railway station by the train which leaves Charing-cross at 11.45. As he was driving homeward a heavy van was returning from Covent-garden market, and this came into collision with Mr. Parnell's conveyance, damaging it, but fortunately causing no serious injury to its owner, who after a short pause continued his journey.

Pall Mall Gazette, 24 May 1886

paper added that Parnell often slept at Eltham when Parliament was sitting. Disingenuously, O'Shea demanded an explanation from his wife. She claimed the report was an invention of Parnell's enemies. Letters between the O'Sheas were becoming more bitter.

Gladstone, pledged to 'pacify Ireland', tried to introduce a limited version of Home Rule. But times were changing. The ageing statesman had not heard the new voice of Protestant Ulster, nor grasped Britain's sense of imperial ascendancy, as Chamberlain had. As Britain prepared for Victoria's silver jubilee, all classes united behind Empire. The mood was not for relinquishing territory.

Parnell backed Gladstone's Home Rule Bill. A miscellany of Whigs and Radicals led by Chamberlain quit the party rather than support it, joining the Tories in the No lobby. The bill fell. The Liberal party split. A Conservative and Unionist government took over. The argument over Home Rule was becoming a cruel tug-o'-war, and the looming scandal over Parnell was to give perhaps the decisive tug. The last century of Irish history may have been shaped by its brush with Captain O'Shea's bruised ego.

We know from correspondence that from 1886 until he filed for divorce in December 1889, O'Shea was well aware of the living arrangements in Eltham. We also know he was close to Chamberlain. O'Shea was embarrassed by his wife's antics. Newspapers dropped hints. In October 1886 the Sussex *Daily News* reported that Parnell had been staying with Mrs O'Shea in Eastbourne. Parnell was now adopting aliases (such as 'Mr Fox') as a shield against snooping.

In April 1887 a further bombshell hit. *The Times* published a letter, ostensibly signed by Parnell, expressing support for the Phoenix Park murders of 1882. Parnell's position as the unchallenged leader of nationalist opinion in Ireland was in jeopardy. He denounced the letter as a forgery but it took nearly two years for his name to be cleared: a needy Irish journalist called Richard Piggott, accused of composing the forgery, collapsed under cross-examination, and soon afterwards committed suicide. Not many years later, G. B. Shaw remarked: 'Put an Irishman on a spit and you can always get another Irishman to turn him.'

That summer, 1889, with Parnell wronged, judged harshly, then fully vindicated, the prospects for Home Rule and peace in

Ireland looked brighter than for many years. Furious negotiations continued through August.

A few days before Christmas Parnell went to Hawarden for talks with Gladstone, now Leader of the Opposition, returning triumphant with the promise of a Home Rule bill. The next election, due in 1892, might have delivered a majority for Gladstone, and thus for his hugely controversial Home Rule. The historian G. M. Trevelyan comments:

> No one can ever tell what chance there was of a solution of the Irish question by that generation of men, nor whether Civil War or Settlement would have resulted from a decisive majority for Home Rule at the polls. The question was never put to the test, owing to the downfall of the Irish Chief.

Captain O'Shea filed for divorce on 24 December 1889, citing Charles Stewart Parnell as co-respondent.

Had the Captain's patience finally snapped? Or had the financial inducement shifted? Aunt Ben had died in 1889, leaving her huge fortune to Kitty, his wife; O'Shea, always skint, was now interested in the estate. Other relatives contested the will and O'Shea saw the opportunity to join them, bidding for a share for himself rather than continued dependence upon his wife. This too may have precipitated the divorce. Or was his motive political? O'Shea may well have been acting for Chamberlain, hostile to Gladstone's and Parnell's Home Rule. This was a chance to sink their alliance.

The divorce would not be heard for nearly a year. Parnell, his health deteriorating, remained optimistic throughout 1890, but Gladstone wrote: 'I fear a thundercloud is about to burst over Parnell's head and I suppose it will end the career of a man in many respects valuable.' Parnell's supporters dismissed the rumours as just the latest slur.

Mrs O'Shea had no defence but her husband's own infidelities (she had listed seventeen). The evidence against her and Parnell looked stronger. The 1886 cutting from the *Pall Mall Gazette* was produced in court. The cook told of the fire escape episode. As the ignominy grew, the lovers chose to stay away from court. Unchallenged, Captain O'Shea emerged cruelly wronged by a deceitful wife. The divorce was granted, and he gained custody of the children, including Parnell's. Parnell gained his Kitty and lost his reputation.

> 'Do you believe in Mr Parnell?' is the question which will be asked on every hustings. And if there is not one solitary Englishman left among us, from Mr Gladstone downwards, who could answer that question in the affirmative, how dare we ask the nation to trust him in an affair involving the integrity and future prosperity of the realm?

wrote W. T. Stead, editor of the *Pall Mall Gazette*, at the time. (As will be seen later, such indignation was his trademark.) The *Methodist Times* summed up Nonconformist opinion:

> This man has been guilty of deadly sin, and no healthy and honest Christian could accept him as a leader. Mr Parnell admits that he has been guilty of immorality of the grossest type . . . If the Irish people deliberately accept such a man as their representative, they are morally unfit to enjoy the privilege of self-government. We do not for a moment believe that the Irish people will really degrade themselves at this momentous crisis. But if they took the unscrupulous and obscene advice which has been given them they would sacrifice the support of the most powerful section of the Liberal Party, and the moral sympathy of the civilised world.

Back in Ireland he lost the Catholic Church, too. The Archbishop of Ardagh thundered: 'I cannot but look forward with dismay to our interests, religious as well as civil, being placed under the guidance of a convicted adulterer.'

Mrs O'Shea was portrayed as an evil behind-the-scenes manipulator. *Vanity Fair* wrote: 'The political princess O'Shea who must be obeyed' (a pun on Rider Haggard's best-selling novel). The last straw was when the Irish *Freeman's Journal*, which had always supported Parnell in the past, turned against him.

Gladstone, collusively allied to Parnell, tried to remain aloof. 'It is no part of my duty as the leader of a party in Parliament to form a personal judgement on the moral conduct of any other leader or fellow member.' The following Sunday in sermons up and down the country Nonconformist churches – the backbone of Liberal

opinion – came out against Parnell. By now Gladstone had only
one choice: Parnell or Home Rule? he asked the Irish MPs. Cecil
Rhodes cabled Parnell from S. Africa: 'Resign. Marry. Return.'

But Parnell would not resign. Facing Gladstone's ultimatum,
the Irish parliamentary party met for six days in committee room
15 at the Commons. Exhausted by their differences, 45 MPs left
the room on 6 December 1890, to found their own party under a
new leader. Inside the room, Parnell looked about him: only 25
had stayed.

Ireland now had two bitterly opposed parties committed to
Home Rule, one for Parnell and one against him. He commuted
between Eltham and Ireland to fight hopeless by-elections for his
own faction. His message became increasingly revolutionary, and
although rejected by the majority of voters, it left a deep
impression on the young.

In the summer of 1891 he and Kitty married in a simple register
office ceremony in Sussex. Lovers for more than a decade, their
marriage was not to last long. Parnell's health was fading.

Shortly after their honeymoon, he was forced to return to
Ireland to support a candidate in a by-election in Cregas. Ignoring
doctors' orders, he addressed the crowd. Refusing an umbrella, he
stood bare-headed in the wind and rain, railing against the anti-
Parnellites: 'We shall continue this fight. We fight not for faction
but for freedom . . . the fight my friends throughout Ireland are
now waging and waging so bravely. I honour them for their
courage and I will not leave them until they get a better leader.'
Parnell had lost the suitcase his new wife had packed for him, and
sat up in his wet clothes all night, chatting to a journalist. Ill, he
left Ireland the next day, 30 September 1891, telling his ragged
army in Dublin they would soon see him again. They did, a
fortnight later, but not as he expected.

In England, at Brighton, Kitty nursed her 45-year-old husband
for a week. Parnell had contracted rheumatic fever. Her account
of his death on 6 October is moving:

Late in the evening, he suddenly opened his eyes and said:
'Kiss me, sweet wifie, and I will try to sleep a little.' I lay down
by his side, and kissed the burning lips he pressed to mine.
The fire of them, fierce beyond any I had ever felt, startled me,
and as I slipped my hand from under his head he gave a little

sigh and became unconscious. The doctor came at once but no remedies prevailed against this sudden failure of the heart's action, and my husband died without regaining consciousness, before his last kiss was cold upon my lips.

As the lid was closed on Parnell's coffin, his wife dropped inside the withered rose he had kept since their first meeting eleven years earlier. Kitty Parnell, whom Ireland considered the ruin of her lover, was advised not to accompany his corpse to Dublin. Public disapproval, the bane of their lives together, pursued her even now.

Dublin, loyal to the end, gave him a magnificent funeral.

It was a decade before Irish politics recovered from the split. Kitty, financially ruined by the divorce, published her memoirs in 1914, moved often and never remarried. Norah (her daughter by O'Shea) wrote: 'She has never stopped mourning Parnell.' Before her mother's death in 1921 at the age of 76, Norah observed: 'She has the happy delusion that Parnell comes back to her at night, when things are worse, and draws her out of the black waves as she lays dying.'

CHARLES DILKE – 1885–6

'He taught me every French vice'

'In the case of a public man a charge is always believed by many, even though disproved,' wrote Charles Dilke, one of the most prominent Liberal politicians of his day – before his fall. He was to star in a bedroom farce of such fiendish complexity that the story might be offered to trainee tabloid journalists as an Advanced Level examination question, to see if they can render what follows in more easily grasped outline than we can.

Sir Charles Wentworth Dilke was elected MP for Chelsea in 1868. By 1883 he was in the Cabinet, as President of the Local Government Board, a position he retained until Gladstone's election defeat of 1885. Many saw him as a potential Prime Minister.

But the promising career of this doctrinaire radical with Republican sympathies collapsed on Saturday 18 July 1885. Returning home at midnight he innocently opened a letter from his friend Mrs Christina Rogerson. She had 'grave information' to impart.

Early the following morning the lady ushered him into her drawing room and dropped a bombshell. Her lawyer brother was acting in the divorce case of a Mr Donald Crawford. Crawford's 22-year-old wife, she explained contemptuously, was intent on destroying Dilke. Virginia Crawford was related to Dilke by marriage: his deceased brother's widow was one of her sisters. Virginia was an extraordinary and colourful woman, in many ways more interesting than Dilke. She had a history. The daughter of a Tyneside shipowner, she had been forced to marry a man (Crawford) twice her age, and with a sister, Helen, had for years secretly enlivened her married life in the arms of medical students from a nearby hospital. She and Helen also frequented a Knightsbridge brothel, where both women had been conducting an affair with a certain Captain Henry Forster.

Virginia was now claiming that the 42-year-old Dilke had been her lover from February 1882 to the late summer of 1884. Their secret trysts, she alleged, had been conducted at his Sloane Street flat and her home in Kensington. For good measure she threw in more: claims that Dilke had a string of other lovers, including one of his maids, Sarah, and her own mother, Mrs Eustace Smith. Unfortunately for Dilke, this last allegation was true.

Mrs Rogerson then relayed the name of the next lady on Crawford's list: it was her own. Dilke gasped: 'Are there any more?' There were. Mrs Rogerson had left the worst till last. Crawford was claiming she had been coerced into three-in-a-bed romps with Dilke and Fanny Stock, a buxom serving girl at his Sloane Street address (also referred to by some contemporaries as Fanny Grey). Crawford was later to allege that, tucked up in bed with Fanny and herself, the MP 'taught me every French vice . . . He used to say that I knew more than most women of thirty.'

It was clear to Dilke that Mrs Crawford had created the web of deceit to throw her own husband, Donald, off the scent. She was portraying him as what would now be called a 'sex beast'. If Virginia had a serious lover at all, though, it was not Dilke, but Captain Forster and, consumed by jealousy, her middle-aged husband had hired private detectives to report on his wife's infidelities. When he had confronted her she said that her only lover had been Dilke. He had filed for divorce.

It has never been established whether Dilke, undoubtedly a ladies' man, had enjoyed the kind of affair alleged, or any affair, with Virginia Crawford. Something about his self-defeating attempts to prove his innocence suggests that these allegations, at least, really were not true. But because he was known as single and susceptible, her choice of him to name would have been shrewd, whether true or not. It has been suggested that Crawford was anxious for a divorce anyway, but anxious also to protect Captain Forster; and that she had resented Dilke's affair with her mother. There was gossip that she had also been encouraged by Mrs Rogerson to frame Dilke – because Rogerson was bitter, believing herself to have been jilted by the politician.

Others have suggested that Dilke was framed for political reasons: he was a rising Liberal star; he was controversial; he was a republican. Queen Victoria, it was said, was amused.

Framed or not, Dilke saw at once how serious these accusations were. To have one affair might be manageable: but to bed so many, and to stoop below the stairs, and then get caught, was a bed too far.

As it happened, Dilke was himself engaged to be married. He wrote a painful letter to his fiancée, the upright widow Emilia Pattison. 'In my belief the conspiracy comes from a woman who wanted me to marry her – but this is guesswork. I only know that there is a conspiracy, from one of two women, perhaps from both.' Then, boiling with rage, he went to Mrs Crawford's house, insisting she withdraw the farrago of lies. She refused.

Dilke was in despair. His diary entry two days later says:

'Left for the last time the House of Commons . . . A sudden fall indeed! Such a charge – even if disproved – which is not

Sir Charles Dilke and his second wife (courtesy of Roy Jenkins's *Sir Charles Dilke*, HarperCollins and of Hulton Deutsch)

easy against perjured evidence picked up with care, is fatal to supreme usefulness in politics. In the case of a public man a charge is always believed by many, even though disproved, and I should be weighted by it throughout life. I prefer therefore to at once contemplate leaving public life for ever.'

Even from a Liberal, to split an infinitive in 1885 indicated immense personal strain.

His wedding went ahead in Chelsea on 3 October under the shadow of the Crawfords' impending divorce case. Gladstone was re-elected Prime Minister four months later but, famous for his virtue, could not risk giving Dilke Cabinet office with the divorce hearing only ten days away.

At the hearing on 12 February 1886, Dilke was represented by the newly appointed Attorney-General Sir Charles Russell. (It was acceptable in those days for government law officers to take private briefs.) Joseph Chamberlain sat by his friend's side. The only substantial evidence offered by Crawford was his wife's confession. It had no legal force so Dilke had no case to answer.

The Attorney-General refused to put Dilke in the witness-box. Then he blundered badly. Without Dilke's permission, he told the court: 'In the life of any man there may be found to have been possible indiscretions.' He was, of course, referring to Dilke's affair with Crawford's embittered mother. The Crawford team had employed four people to muck-rake. The newspapers had a field day omitting the crucial word 'possible' and instead speculating entirely on Dilke's 'indiscretions'. Mr Justice Butt compounded the MP's misery when he granted Crawford his divorce. If Crawford's wife had not slept with Dilke, why was the divorce granted?

It was at this point that the *Pall Mall Gazette* swung into action. The editor, W. T. Stead, who was later mercifully to drown in the *Titanic*, shrewdly combined the sensationalism needed to sell papers with a self-appointed role as guardian of public morals. The previous year, in order to expose child prostitution, he had bought a thirteen-year-old girl for £5 from her parents: a criminal offence (though his behaviour toward her was unimpeachable) for which he received three months' imprisonment. He served his sentence ostentatiously, and every year thereafter wore his prison uniform in public on the anniversary of his conviction. His protest did succeed in getting the age of consent raised from twelve to sixteen in 1885. Now, after Dilke's court appearance, Stead called on the MP to clear his name. Dilke responded. He asked the Queen's Proctor to use his powers to annul Crawford's decree nisi before it was made absolute.

The Proctor granted his embattled friend's request and ordered a second hearing that July. Dilke was confident of success. By now he had tracked down the infamous Fanny Stock, who was happy to deny the three-in-a-bed claim. He also had proof of Mrs Crawford's adultery with Captain Forster, which she was still denying.

Even before the trial started, things began to go wrong. Dilke had been cleared at the first hearing; he was a witness, not a defendant, at the second. His lawyers could not therefore demand to cross-examine the treacherous Mrs Crawford.

Dilke's problem was therefore an almost intractable one in law: without the key witness, he had to pin all his hopes on counsel to prove a negative: that he had never slept with a named individual, whom he could not call as a witness.

Just eleven days before the trial Dilke suffered a further humiliation when he was rejected

Virginia Crawford (courtesy of Roy Jenkins's *Sir Charles Dilke*, HarperCollins)

by the electors of Chelsea in a massive swing against the Gladstone government.

The trial started on 16 July 1886. The courtroom was packed. Rarely had a simple divorce case attracted such massive public interest. Dilke was at an immediate disadvantage by being called first to the witness-box. Mrs Crawford had the benefit of hearing Dilke's evidence before responding. Although she was forced to admit her adultery with Captain Forster, she stuck resolutely to her claim that Dilke had been her main lover.

The case lasted a week. The jury took only fifteen minutes to reach their verdict – the decree nisi was *not* contrary to justice. Such an outcome did not absolutely imply that Dilke was Mrs Crawford's lover, but it was enough for chattering tongues. Dilke's political career was finished and he immediately wrote an address to the electors of Chelsea:

> As far as public life goes, I have no option but to accept the verdict, while protesting once more against its justice. I can only, gentlemen, assure you, as I have already often assured you, and with equal solemnity sworn in court, that I am innocent of the charges brought against me, and respectfully and gratefully bid you farewell.

Dilke's plea of innocence received substantial but belated backing from a committee established by his supporters. They uncovered convincing evidence (which they published in a pamphlet in 1891) that Mrs Crawford's affair with Captain Forster was much more involved than she admitted at the second trial. There was also evidence of other lovers, and they established strong alibis for Dilke on three of the nights she had claimed to have spent with him. But all this was too complicated, and it was too late.

In 1892, Gladstone was elected Prime Minister for the fourth time. Reeling from Parnell's adultery, the new Premier wanted no further suspicion of infidelity in his administration. Although Dilke had been re-elected by the burghers of the Forest of Dean, this gifted politician was never again rewarded with public office. He held his seat until his death in 1911.

Historians generally doubt that any adulterous relationship between Dilke and Crawford ever took place. Virginia herself was by no means finished. She survived until 1948, becoming a public figure in her own right: as a writer and thinker, a Labour councillor, and so ferocious a campaigner against fascism that Mussolini blacklisted her.

JABEZ SPENCER BALFOUR – 1892

'Liar, adulterer and cheat'

Compared with Jabez Spencer Balfour, a Victorian Liberal MP, the likes of Jonathan Aitken and Jeffrey Archer appear almost saintly. This astonishing rogue, who perpetrated the most destructive fraud of the nineteenth century, escaped inclusion in the last edition of *Great Parliamentary Scandals*. That wrong is righted only because of the perseverance and investigative skills of *Guardian* journalist and author David McKie. Stumbling across a record of the incarceration in Portland Prison of an MP with whom he was unfamiliar, McKie proceeded to uncover an astonishing tale of a deception that resulted in the destitution of thousands of ordinary people. What follows draws from McKie's writings and his riveting book, *Jabez: The Rise and Fall of a Victorian Scoundrel*.

Jabez, as he was universally known, was, on outward appearances, an entrepreneur, politician, philanthropist, temperance campaigner and all-round charming individual. But his mantle of respectability concealed a liar, adulterer and cheat with a reckless disregard for the law. He was Liberal MP for Tamworth from 1880 to 1885 and for Burnley from 1889 until he came badly unstuck. The institution that built and broke him was the Liberator Building Society he set up – a name intended to appeal to nonconformist

England and Wales as it echoed that of the Liberation Society, which was the principal voice of nonconformity directed against the established church. Nonconformist ministers, keen to augment their meagre earnings, were employed as agents to enhance the odour of sanctity that was so vital to the enterprise. The Liberator soon became the biggest building society in the land, ringed with satellite companies and even its own bank. Hard-working people, desperate to escape the clutches of avaricious landlords, saw the Liberator as the route to liberation and a home of their own. The building society opened its doors for business in June 1868, having adopted the slogan '*Libera sedes, liberum facit*' ('a free home makes a free man'). Its growth was phenomenal. After three years, assets had increased to £70,000; after seven to £500,000. By 1879, it had overtaken the Leeds Permanent to become Britain's biggest building society.

Increasingly, Jabez turned his hand to big prestige projects in central London, including the building of the Hotel Cecil. This, with its 100 feet long by 66 feet wide ballroom and towering 46 feet high ceiling, he intended to be the grandest hotel in Europe. His reputation in the City soared and companies eager to better themselves queued up to print the name of the trusted businessman MP with the Midas touch on the top of their headed notepaper.

In Croydon, his home town, Jabez's reputation as its leading citizen was confirmed in 1883 when the place achieved borough status. Though not a Croydon councillor, Jabez accepted a nomination as mayor and repaid his supporters with lavish banquets in his handsome mansion. While insisting he had no such ambition, his real aim was to become MP for Croydon because the borough was much handier for his Westminster and City interests than Tamworth, a seat due to be abolished by the boundary commissioners. In a humiliating blow, however, Jabez failed to win the constituency in the 1885 General Election. To rub it in, the local Tories arranged for the death march to be played outside his house. Jabez promptly gave up on Croydon and installed himself at grand addresses in London. He also bought most of the village of Burcot near Abingdon, where he continued to entertain on a lavish scale and lorded it as squire.

The apparent success of Jabez's empire was built on an illusion in the style of that great swindler of the late twentieth century,

Daily Mirror publisher and former Labour MP Robert Maxwell. Profits of Jabez's companies declared at the close of each year, complete with handsome dividends and bonuses for Jabez and his fellow directors, were massively inflated and almost entirely fictitious. Very few of Jabez's schemes made any serious money: his real gift, as with Maxwell, was for cooking the books. As the 1890s progressed, suspicion grew. The *Financial Times* and *Economist* warned investors against him. But as McKie discovered, it was too late. In September 1892, the portrait of Jabez that hung in an honoured place on the wall of the Croydon Liberal Club inexplicably crashed to the floor. Within days, his bank, the Liberator Building Society and all the companies with which he was linked, also hit the floor.

Resigning his seat at Burnley, Jabez promised to revive the failed businesses largely to avert the catastrophe feared by shareholders and investors. It soon became clear, however, that the scale of the commercial disaster made rescue impossible. His victims, convinced by the names of solid God-fearing men on the companies' letterheads, had been outrageously conned. Thousands were ruined. Suicides were regularly reported and people who had saved for old age in the hope of avoiding the workhouse found themselves now condemned to it. Thomas Henry Pexton of Scarborough, a father of four, killed himself out of remorse at having persuaded his mother to lodge her money with Jabez. Emily Ekins, a seventy-year-old Huntingdonshire spinster, was found by an inquest to have committed suicide after losing most of her savings. The human toll was heavy.

When the police arrested two of his main subordinates, Jabez fled. Alleged sightings were reported around the world. Jabez had, in fact, scarpered some 7,000 miles away to Argentina after he had established that the South American country had no extradition arrangement with Britain.

By March 1893 with the case followed as closely in Australia and the Americas as in Britain, much of the world knew the fugitive was living in a suburb of Buenos Aires. Jabez, uncomfortable at the press interest, fled again, this time to Salta, a town not far from the border with Chile. Here he set up home with a daughter of former business colleague Henry Freeman. After Freeman's death, his daughters had been regarded as Jabez's wards yet now he had taken one of them to be his mistress. She was half his age. The two daughters, Ethel Sophia and Lucy Mary, had travelled to Argentina under the pseudonyms Miss Baker and Miss Ferguson. One now claimed to be Mrs Butler, the other Mrs Butler's sister-in-law. McKie warns that the records are inconclusive as to which of the sisters was his mistress, though the author believes it was Ethel Sophia. What is certain is that both the public and authorities were fascinated with the attractive young woman and her portly, waddling, fifty-year-old companion and absconder. The great champion of temperance was also buying a brewery.

Although the Argentinian Government was sympathetic to British attempts to get their man, nothing could be done except through an extradition treaty. Here Jabez had read things wrongly. An extradition treaty *had* been agreed, and was now awaiting ratification. Jabez and his supporters now hit on an ingenious tactic to avoid justice. Argentinian law stipulated that no one could leave the country if litigation was pending against him; so Jabez's friends organised a rota to take turns to sue him. Furthermore, judgments made in Buenos Aires in favour of Jabez's return were consistently blocked by local officials in Salta, not least because local people believed that having this famous English financier was set to bring them prosperity. The British embassy in Buenos Aires despaired of ever getting Jabez back until an extradition expert at Scotland Yard, Inspector Frank Froest, was swung into action. Dispatched by the police commissioner with instructions not to come back until he had Jabez in handcuffs and warned that he could be in Argentina for five years, he came up with his own ingenious, if questionable, plan. The solution Froest devised, as he boasted to his family later, was to kidnap his target. He commissioned a train, hid it in sidings just outside Salta, waited until the federal courts gave their latest ruling in favour of extradition and then had Jabez aboard the train before Salta officials knew what was happening.

The officer and his reluctant guest were barely out of the town before a posse on horseback set off in pursuit, armed with a warrant for the return of Jabez and the arrest of Inspector Froest. As the train thundered southwards, the inspector, who had stationed himself on the footplate to prevent any delay, saw the horsemen approaching. One rode his horse on to the line ahead, waving the warrant and commanding the driver to stop. Froest intervened, obstructing the controls by throwing himself across them. The train sped on and ran over and killed both the hapless rider and the horse. Later, the British government offered $50 as compensation, to cover both man and beast.

Back in Buenos Aires, there were further foiled attempts at a rescue before a handcuffed Jabez was brought home on the steamboat *Tartar Prince*. In November 1895, he was sentenced to fourteen years' imprisonment with hard labour, rather than the three years many expected him to receive. 'You will never be able,' the trial judge told prisoner V460, 'to shut from your ears the cries of the widows and orphans you have ruined.' *The Times* declared: 'The great imposture has collapsed with satisfying completeness.'

McKie asks rhetorically:

> So what should we make of him, this Jabez, this J Spencer Balfour, with his huge business talent and his phenomenal losses, his piety and his pretty young mistress, his temperance and his splendid hoard of champagne, his philanthropy and the money-grabbing? His mother had said of her eager, garrulous five-year-old: 'He will be either good or evil – there is nothing negative about him.' Contemplating the ruin not just of his companies but of thousands of decent, deserving people who trusted him and paid such a heavy price for that trust, the world as a whole must have judged him if not evil, then, certainly, wicked.

Freed from jail in 1906, Jabez began a new career as a journalist, writing a series of prison memoirs that led page one of Lord Northcliffe's *Weekly Dispatch* for 26 consecutive weeks. Later, he set up as a mining engineer. Later still, at the age of 71, Jabez took a post in Burma until he was ordered back to London on the grounds that he might not survive such heat. He returned to a bitter British winter that probably killed him. Jabez died in February 1916 on a train which was taking him, at 72, to South Wales to begin a new job at Morriston Colliery. Twenty years earlier, Jabez had been the most notorious man in the land, burned in effigy on bonfire night after his companies crashed. Now, until they examined his papers, no one knew who he was.

He was interred in the grave of his parents. The headstone in London's Paddington Old Cemetery carries no inscription to indicate that Jabez's remains are there.

LORD ROSEBERY – 1894

An Abominable Rumour – or a Snob Queer?

One of the most intriguing, yet unproven, scandals of the Victorian age involves the Liberal Prime Minister, Lord Rosebery. It is alleged that when he was Foreign Secretary in Gladstone's last government, he had a homosexual affair with his 27-year-old private secretary, Viscount Drumlanrig. Fear of exposure led, it was said, directly to the young man's suicide in 1894. Drumlanrig's father was the odious 8th Marquess of Queensberry. This half-mad Scottish peer, famous for introducing new rules for boxing, certainly believed the Foreign Secretary had seduced his son.

Queensberry had plenty to worry about. His younger son, Lord Alfred Douglas, was, as they say, romantically linked to Oscar Wilde. After the playwright's public exposure it was rumoured that the Foreign Secretary had known about and condoned the liaison between Douglas (his private secretary's brother) and Wilde. There were strong suggestions that the Government's determined and surprising persecution of Wilde, through two trials, was intended to scotch this rumour.

Lord Rosebery had succeeded his grandfather as 5th Earl in 1868 at the age of 21. Though an impressive speaker, this learned and bookish man has been remembered less for his political than for his literary skills. He published works on Pitt, Peel, Napoleon and Chatham and became Lord Rector of Aberdeen, Edinburgh and Glasgow universities. In 1878 he married the heiress, Hannah Rothschild, who died after twelve years of marriage, aged 39.

Rosebery entered Gladstone's government in 1881 as a junior Home Office minister. He was probably better known as the owner of a Derby winner. When the party split two years later over Irish Home Rule, Rosebery followed Gladstone, who later rewarded his loyalty by making him Foreign Secretary in 1892.

It was around this time that young Viscount Drumlanrig, a good-looking, hard-working but fairly dim 25-year-old, was introduced to Rosebery, then a 45-year-old widower. A fellow Scot and heir to the Queensberry title, Drumlanrig had just left the Coldstream Guards, where he was a lieutenant. He was unmarried. Though lacking qualifications for the post, he was soon found a position as Rosebery's private secretary. The Foreign Secretary, impressed with Drumlanrig's hard work, sought advancement for his young charge as a Lord-in-Waiting to the Queen. As such he needed to be made an English peer in his own right, for Drumlanrig's father, the Marquess of Queensberry, had not been re-elected as a representative peer since 1881, and could not sit in the House of Lords.

The Marquess was a wealthy and hot-headed atheist, well-known in cycling circles, and had enjoyed his fair share of scandal. His first wife won a divorce from him in 1887 on grounds of his adultery with a lady called Mabel in Camden Town. He remarried very soon after, but this union lasted only a few months before it too was dissolved. When he heard of Rosebery's plans to elevate his eldest son to the peerage his reaction was startling, and strange. Queensberry sent angry letters to Rosebery and Gladstone. He even wrote to the Queen, complaining of the Foreign Secretary's 'bad influence' on his son: he seems to have meant in the direction of homosexuality.

To no avail: Drumlanrig became Baron Kelhead on 22 June 1893, and Lord-in-Waiting to the Queen. From this moment on he almost never spoke to his father, who was outraged. In August the Marquess pursued Rosebery to the Hessen resort of Bad Homburg in Germany where the Foreign Secretary was holidaying with the Prince of Wales. Queensberry took with him a dog whip. He was found, whip-in-hand, near Rosebery's hotel. The Prince of Wales persuaded the Chief Commissioner of Police to intervene, thus saving the 46-year-old politician from a painful thrashing. The Commissioner was able to report to Rosebery the next day: 'The Marquess of Queensberry, in consequence of the entertainment I had with him, found it advisable to depart this morning with the 7 o'clock train for Paris.' Rosebery told the Queen he found one of the more taxing parts of his job was 'to be pursued by a pugilist of unsound mind'.

Queensberry's attempted assault started society gossip about the nature of the relationship between Rosebery and Drumlanrig.

Many suspected that the Foreign Secretary was indeed homosexual. He opened all his letters himself. Lewis Harcourt, the son of Rosebery's political rival Sir William Harcourt and no stranger himself to scandal (see pp.88–90), later wrote that this was not surprising 'considering some of the things which, to my knowledge, some of them must contain'.

The following March, 1894, the 84-year-old Gladstone finally gave way to a younger man. Rosebery, at 46, began his undistinguished sixteen months as Prime Minister. He was more successful on the turf than he was in Parliament: both that year and the following his horses won the Derby, which only served to make him unpopular with the nonconformist wing of his party. Virtually every piece of legislation the Rosebery government introduced was blocked by the Conservative-dominated House of Lords.

During the summer Drumlanrig was engaged to a young woman by the name of Alix Ellis. On the weekend of 18 October he accepted an invitation for a weekend's shooting at Quantock Lodge near Bridgwater, the home of his new fiancée's uncle, the MP Edward Stanley. At one point he left the other shooters and went into the next field. After a few minutes his companions heard a shot. They ran and found the 27-year-old Viscount lying dead with gunshot wounds. Suicide was widely believed, although the newspapers the next day reported a 'shooting accident' and the coroner recorded a verdict of 'accidental death'. Later the dead man's nephew, the 11th Marquess, told the writer H. Montgomery Hyde that he was 'positive' that his young uncle had 'taken his own life in the shadow of a suppressed scandal'. Another possibility is that he could not face the prospect of marriage.

Oscar Wilde's biographer, Richard Ellmann, believes the young man was being blackmailed. Nine years earlier the Labouchère amendment – 'the blackmailer's charter' – had been slipped through during a late-night sitting of the House of Commons. The Criminal Law Amendment Act of 1885 made, for the first time, all forms of male homosexual activity illegal, on pain of imprisonment for up to two years with hard labour.

Despite their estrangement, Drumlanrig had been the only one of Queensberry's sons whom he seemed to love. He wrote in grief and rage to his ex-wife's father – the young man's grandfather, who had arranged the first meeting between his grandson and Rosebery – Alfred Montgomery, on 1 November 1894.

Queensberry Estate Office

> Comloncon Castle
> Ruthwell, N.B.

Sir

Now that the first flush of this catastrophe and grief is passed, I write to tell you that it is a *judgement* on the whole *lot of you*. Montgomerys, the Snob Queers like Rosebery and certainly Christian hypocrite Gladstone the whole lot *of you* set my son up against me indeed and made bad blood between us, may it devil on your own heads that he has gone to his *rest* and the quarrel not made up between him and myself. It's a gruesome message: if you and his mother did not set up this business with that cur and Jew friend (?) *Liar* Rosebery as I always thought –

At any rate she [Lady Queensberry] acquiesced in it, which is just *as bad.* What fools you all look, trying to ride me out of the course and trim *the sails* and the poor Boy comes to this untimely end. I smell a tragedy behind all this and have already *got Wind* of a more *startling one.* If it was what I am led *to believe,* I of all people could and would have helped him, had he come to me with a confidence, but that was all stopped by you people – we had not met or spoken frankly for more than a year and a half, I am on the right track to find out what happened, *Cherchez la femme,* when these things happen. I have already heard something that accounts *for it all.*

> QUEENSBERRY

Having lost one son in a homosexual scandal, Queensberry was now determined not to lose a second. It is perhaps helpful to remind ourselves that homosexuality was not then seen so much as an inescapable orientation to which some were prone, but more as a dangerous habit into which someone might be led by another more wicked than himself. The parallel is more with an addictive drug than with a personality trait. The whole thing could be seen as Rosebery's fault.

At the moment of Drumlanrig's death, some believe, Wilde had been intending to leave the spoilt and indiscreet Douglas for good, and announce it to Queensberry. But after reading the papers that morning in Brighton where the couple were staying, he felt such 'infinite pity' for his 'Bosie' that he did not catch his intended train back to London.

Queensberry now plotted his final revenge against the author. By bringing down Wilde's reputation as a playwright, which was riding high, Queensberry hoped to revive his own, which had been battered by his divorce and the suicide of his favourite son. On the opening night of *The Importance of Being Earnest* (14 February 1895) the Marquess planned to barge into the theatre and make a speech denouncing Wilde, but the author got wind of this and had guards block his entry. Queensberry contented himself with leaving a bouquet of vegetables for the author at the stage door.

Queensberry then left his calling card at Wilde's club, something which was to lead to the author's imprisonment and exile. On the card Queensberry had written, with aristocratic misspelling, 'To Oscar Wilde posing as a Somdomite'. Queensberry had finally committed himself to paper. Wilde, who understood Queensberry to have meant 'ponce and sodomite', was persuaded to sue, not wisely as it turned out, for criminal libel.

Though his family were embarrassed by their father, Lord Alfred Douglas's surviving brother agreed to pay half the costs, while his mother, Lady Queensberry, would provide the other half.

Wilde lost the Old Bailey case, but what made his subsequent prosecution for gross indecency so certain? Some have suggested that this was because Rosebery's and Gladstone's names came up during the six-day hearing. In fact at the start of the trial, Wilde's counsel, Sir Edward Clarke, seemed preoccupied with this. He accidentally called Queensberry 'Lord Rosebery'. The case was going badly for Wilde. Young men had been found who would confess to having had homosexual relations with the author. In a last desperate effort, Clarke attempted to demonstrate the fragile state of the Marquess's mental health by releasing recent letters he had written. One of these he sent to his ex-wife's father, Alfred Montgomery, on 6 July 1894, complaining of Lady Queensberry's support for the continuing friendship of 'Bosie' and Wilde. The angry Marquess wrote: 'Your daughter must be mad by the way she is behaving . . . I am now fully convinced that the Rosebery–Gladstone–Royal insult that came to me through my son, that she worked that.' [*sic*]

British newspapers chose to ignore the existence of the names of senior politicians. The Continental press, however, were less inhibited. They repeated what Queensberry had been suggesting all along: the Prime Minister, taking a benign view of Lord Alfred Douglas's relationship with Wilde, had created a top-level conspiracy to silence the father.

After Wilde lost his libel case against Queensberry, it was a matter of hours before he was arrested and charged with indecency. The evidence Queensberry had unearthed, including damning statements from a number of young men, had condemned the playwright. With Rosebery himself the target of homosexual slurs, accused of having supported Wilde against Lord Alfred Douglas's father, the authorities could not now be seen to go lightly on Wilde. Yet the Prime Minister did consider trying to do something to help Wilde. His Home Secretary, Herbert Asquith, warned him: 'If you do, you will lose the election.'

Wilde's first trial began on 26 April 1895. The large crowd which gathered outside Bow Street Magistrates Court was hostile to the middle-aged champion of aesthetics. They jeered Wilde as he arrived. But inside the court the jury could not agree a verdict. In the febrile atmosphere of the day, this increased suspicions that they had been influenced in order to protect Rosebery and his cohorts.

Tim Healy, the Irish nationalists' leader at Westminster, who had successfully challenged Parnell after the O'Shea divorce case (see p.52), begged the Solicitor-General, Lockwood, not to try his countryman a second time. The law officer replied: 'I would not but for the abominable rumours against Rosebery'.

Fearing accusations of a cover-up, Lockwood had a further reason for ordering a second trial. The name of his own wife's nephew, Maurice Schwabe, had come up. One of the chief prosecution witnesses, the self-confessed male prostitute, Fred Atkins, claimed at the first trial he had seen the Solicitor-General's nephew-in-law in bed with Wilde.

At this point, with the second trial looming, the *New York Herald* chanced its arm. On 20 May it reported that 'there is still a continued prevalence of gossip concerning well-known people whom it is attempted by current rumour to connect with the case'.

Sir Edward Hamilton, Gladstone's former private secretary, wrote in his diary the next day:

> The Oscar Wilde and Taylor cases have been brought forward again; and unless there is some cantankerous jury-man a verdict is confidently expected this time. A verdict of guilty would remove what appears to be a wide-felt impression that the Judge and Jury were on the last occasion got at, in order to shield others of a higher status in life.

This time Wilde was found guilty. On 25 May 1895, he was sentenced to two years with hard labour. There was no mercy shown. All of the author's possessions, including his children's toys, were auctioned to pay his debts.

In the General Election the following month, Rosebery's Liberal Party was heavily defeated. He resigned the Liberal leadership the following year but remained active in the House of Lords for a further decade, and lived on until 1929, publishing historical works and arguing for imperial federation. One of his horses brought him further triumph at the 1905 Derby. The former Liberal Prime Minister grew increasingly out of step with his party and by 1909 was considered an Independent or Conservative. In 1911 he was created Earl of Midlothian. His elder son, a keen cricketer and huntsman, succeeded him as 6th Earl. His younger son was killed in Palestine in 1917. In his later years Rosebery spent ever more time in his Italian villa at Posillipo near Capri – a resort, it has been pointed out, which was popular with homosexuals at the time.

After his release from Reading Gaol, short of cash in 1897, Wilde spent the remaining three years of his life in France and Italy. The guest of a M. Dupoirier, he said of the hated wallpaper in his room 'one of us will have to go'. He died in Paris on 30 November 1900, at the age of 44, a broken man.

In 1896 his one-time lover, Lord Alfred Douglas, had written to a French magazine to complain of Wilde's treatment:

> I am confident that the Government did not wish to let the prosecution of Oscar Wilde take its regular course . . . Why did the Crown take the very irregular course of having a second trial – why was the prosecution conducted with this

extraordinary animosity; briefly why did the Crown manifest so eager a desire to obtain a verdict of guilty? The reason is very simple. The Government was intimidated; the second trial was the result of political intrigue. I would wish to ask Mr Asquith, the then Home Secretary, that if a second trial was not instituted and a verdict of guilty obtained against Mr Wilde, the Liberal party would be removed from power. The fact is that the Liberal party then contained a large number of men whom I have referred to as the salt of the earth [homosexuals]. The maniacs of virtue threatened a series of legal actions which would have created an unprecedented scandal in political circles. If Oscar Wilde was found guilty the matter would be hushed up. This was the cause of the second trial, and the verdict of guilty. It was a degrading *coup d'état* – the sacrifice of a great poet to save a degraded band of politicians.

There can be no doubt that such a view was held by many at the time, and that – even though it was endorsed by the unreliable Alfred Douglas – it was a reasonable suspicion. What is hard to establish is whether or how far the political establishment actually did act to secure Wilde's conviction; there is no question that the conviction suited them. It was at the point of decision whether to order a second trial that figures in the Government could have exercised a decisive influence.

Rosebery once described politics as 'this evil smelling bog'. For many, a faint whiff is discernible here.

TREBITSCH LINCOLN – 1910

Revelations of an International Spy

Fraudster, spy, Anglican curate, German revolutionary, journalist, secret agent, international outlaw, Chinese cult leader and – in 1910 – the Liberal MP for Darlington, Trebitsch Lincoln was born into a prosperous Jewish family in Hungary in 1879 and died, perhaps poisoned by Nazi agents, in a Shanghai hospital in 1943. He lived a life so extraordinary we fear readers of this book may accuse us of invention. 'The election of Trebitsch Lincoln to the House of Commons in January 1910 stands out as one of the oddest aberrations of British political history,' writes his biographer, Bernard Wasserstein.

Short, dark-skinned, heavily-accented and a flagrant exhibitionist, Lincoln was given to bouts of childish rage, sentimentality, fantasy and self-destruction. Friendless and untrustworthy, he destroyed the lives of his family (one son was executed aged 23, another, abandoned in Java before the Japanese invaded, killed himself). And yet, as a politician and religious messiah, he eased his way to the top of three closed and xenophobic elites: Edwardian Liberalism, German militarism and Chinese Buddhism. It was a unique achievement. He owed it to his astounding self-confidence, his charm and his fluency. He was one of the best linguists ever to sit in Parliament, and one of the most unsuccessful MPs.

Evidence of Lincoln's enthralling personality emerged when, aged sixteen, and under the first of his many names, Ignácz Trebitsch, he defied his family and enrolled in the Royal Hungarian Academy of Dramatic Art. His time there was short – nothing ever lasted for Lincoln. Charged with petty theft, he fled Hungary and began a lifetime of voyaging. For Lincoln, writes Wasserstein 'travel was not a pleasure but a disease'.

In 1899, pausing in England, Lincoln trained as a Christian missionary. Sent to Canada to proselytize among Jews, he married. A wife-to-be, briefly encountered in Hamburg, was summoned from Germany by telegram. As the Reverend Trebitsch he enjoyed short-lived success, then returned in disgrace to England. Here he enlisted the Archbishop of Canterbury's help, in the hope of becoming a real vicar. Awarded a curacy in Appledore, Kent, he failed his exams and soon quit, much to the Archbishop's relief.

Next he was appointed private secretary to the chocolate millionaire philanthropist, Benjamin Rowntree (they met on a train). Lincoln crisscrossed Europe, living in style, ostensibly researching Belgian land-management for Rowntree. He later claimed to have been working as a German double agent. If so, he was a poor one: by demanding in Paris that the French Government pay for his book purchases he provoked an international crisis which involved three French Government ministries, assorted British Embassies and the Foreign Secretary, Sir Edward Grey. The incident earned him the lifelong hostility of the British Foreign Office.

Rowntree was a Liberal, and it was thanks to his patronage that Lincoln was unanimously chosen as a parliamentary candidate by the Darlington Liberal and Progressive Association in April 1909. This was a peculiar achievement; Lincoln, not yet thirty, was still a Hungarian citizen. The General Election came early. Even the most earnest Liberals in Darlington thought their unusual candidate had little chance. Though the Rowntree-owned *Northern Echo* had announced that 'his most intimate friends have the strongest faith in his future as a statesman,' Liberalism was on the wane from its 1906 triumph, beset by a constitutional crisis, and Lincoln faced a sitting Unionist candidate.

Despite repeated (and unexplained) trips to the Balkans, Lincoln had nursed the seat expertly since selection and he fought a vigorous if eccentric campaign, backed by letters of support from Winston Churchill and Lloyd George. Though denounced in the street by Darlington Unionists as a 'damned foreigner' Lincoln picked an issue which went down well with the Darlington middle classes: animal rights. Germany's tariff laws, he argued, drove working men into such poverty that they had to eat dogs to survive. If the Unionists, with their tariff plans, won, the people of Darlington, too, he explained, would have to feed off their pets. This combined appeal to sentimentality towards animals and resentment of foreigners proved the sure-fire hit with English voters which it has done so many times since. It is ironic that it took an outsider to notice the possibilities, and that the message was delivered in a heavy Hungarian accent.

The result was a majority of 29 for Lincoln. Telegrams of congratulation flooded in. But not everyone was impressed. Esmé

Howard, a British diplomat in Budapest and a past victim of Lincoln's continental travels, declared: 'I do not congratulate the people of Darlington on their choice of an MP but if Mr T Lincoln comes back here I shall always treat him with the respect due to an Elect of the people - and the reserve necessary in dealing with a liar.'

To Howard's dismay, Lincoln did visit Budapest in the weeks after his election. 'I am in the fortunate position of being able to travel in these countries and speak to the people in their own tongue' he told the Commons on his return. But his maiden speech was a letdown; hack rhetoric delivered to an almost empty chamber. This did not deter the MP – six years later, in his biography *Revelations of an International Spy*, he wrote 'My maiden speech dealt with my favourite theme: I was a great success.'

As ever, Lincoln's finances were in disarray. Though given huge sums by Rowntree, he resorted to defrauding him of more. He earned nothing as an MP and spent wildly. His venture into east European oil, the Austrian Petroleum Syndicate, collapsed. Meanwhile, the Austrian Government, angered by Lincoln's parliamentary questions on the Balkans, informed Sir Edward Grey of his backbench colleague's juvenile career as a petty thief.

And unluckily for Lincoln, the budget crisis caused a second 1910 election. Deeply in debt, and under pressure from the Foreign Secretary, Lincoln resigned the Liberal nomination a week before polling day. His successor, who lost badly, blamed the 'contumely and scandal' which had engulfed his predecessor.

In January 1911, no longer an MP, Lincoln faced his creditors, including Rowntree, at the Station Hotel in York. He paid them five shillings in the pound. It was the end of Mr I T T Lincoln, MP (as *Hansard* recorded him). Strictly speaking, his subsequent career is beyond the scope of this book. But here is a taste.

After losing his seat, Lincoln founded a string of oil companies. None made a penny. But when war broke out in August 1914, he scented opportunity. He was briefly employed at the Mount Pleasant sorting office in London, censoring mail to Hungary, but was fired for writing comments on the letters. Desperate for money, he turned to fraud, stealing letters from the National Liberal Club (where he had lived as an MP) and altering them to authorize payments to his account. Scotland Yard was soon on his tail.

At this, he launched a new career as an international spy. He offered his services to the War Office in London, but was summarily

Paks Vobiscum; or, The Lincoln Handicap.
'We weel not zend ze Büdg-ett to ze Haus of Lörrdz to be zrown out on-ly a-gen!!'
(Mr J.T.T. Lincoln – born at Paks in Hungary.)
Punch, 1910

turned away by 'Blinker' Hall, the director of Naval Intelligence. This led Lincoln to turn traitor: he caught the next ferry to neutral Holland, and presented himself at the German consulate. The German intelligence service, which could hardly ignore a former MP on its doorstep, engaged him and sent him back to London. But Lincoln suddenly departed for New York.

America, not yet at war, offered scope for the ex-MP's flair for publicity. He wrote two articles for the *World* newspaper, under the headline: 'Revelations of Mr Lincoln, former Member of Parliament who became a German spy'. He moved in with his brother who, in dismay, volunteered for the US Army: a disastrous move because as Lincoln's brother he was under immediate suspicion, watched, discovered in bed with a fellow-soldier and jailed at Alcatraz for sodomy. That was the end of him.

Meanwhile, Lincoln's New York journalism infuriated the British into asking for his extradition. He was arrested. He escaped before he could be deported ('most annoying' noted a British civil servant) and gave a press conference while on the run. But he was recaptured in February 1916 in an operation that tied up hundreds of New York policemen. Back in Britain he was sentenced to three years imprisonment for fraud. He was jailed in the cell next to Sir Roger Casement.

1919 was not a good time to release a character like Lincoln. The Foreign Office feared 'he might easily become a sort of Lenin of central Europe.' Their fears were justified. Freed from prison, Lincoln turned up in Berlin. He began to write articles advocating the restoration of the German monarchy, and though his attempt to meet the ex-Kaiser failed he did sail to the remote Dutch island on which the allies had imprisoned the Crown Prince. This activity led Lincoln to play a prominent part in the failed German Freikorps putsch of 1920: for five days he was part of the German government. Adolph Hitler was a fellow (though more junior) conspirator. The two men met, briefly, in Berlin.

The early 1920s saw Lincoln involved in various east European nationalist movements, all unsavoury. In fear for his life he fled to China in 1922. No one is quite sure why: though he had a long-standing interest in eastern mysticism. Within weeks, despite speaking no Chinese, Lincoln was giving counsel to warlords in Szechwan.

Lincoln spent most of the rest of his life in China, interrupted only by wanderings in India, California and Europe. The British authorities banned him from entering British territory, an inconvenience he overcame by forging new passports. By the early

1930s he had become a Buddhist. Known as the 'Venerable Chao King' he was never seen in western clothes again. Lincoln gathered a group of slave-like followers around him, some of whom were wont to defect, like Soviet ballet dancers, during his tours of Europe. It would be easy to dismiss this conversion to Buddhism as fraudulent: it was almost certainly not. It appears to be the most genuine feature of Lincoln's life, certainly more firmly based than his forays into politics.

But Lincoln never quite lost his political instincts. In the late 1930s, as Japanese troops swept China, he became a noted supporter of Japan. And in early 1941, by this time living in Shanghai, he was entwined in the Nazi security apparatus in the Far East. He convinced the Gestapo that, if allowed to meet Hitler alone, three Tibetan wise men would appear from the wall and save Germany. Absurd, of course, but the Germans hungered for reassurance, and Trebitsch sensed it. When Rudolph Hess landed in Scotland in 1941 his plane contained two phials of 'sacred liquid', supposedly provided by a Grand Lama in Tibet. Both Ribbentrop and Heydrich considered bringing Lincoln to Germany.

Instead the Gestapo turned against him, as the Japanese occupied Shanghai, and accused him of arms dealing. For two years, he survived: an elderly Hungarian Jew, former MP and self-proclaimed Buddhist Abbot. But Lincoln's self-destructiveness overcame him. He wrote a public letter to Hitler denouncing the extermination of the Jews; Lincoln's family in Hungary were among those killed in the Holocaust. Arrested by the Japanese he died two days later in a Shanghai hospital. Many people assumed he had been murdered by his former Nazi associates.

What to make of this bizarre career? Wasserstein, in his biography of Lincoln, is clear. 'Trebitsch should be seen as the performing flea of politics and diplomacy in the early twentieth century.' He had more than the con man's art, though. Wasserstein concludes that the former MP for Darlington was merely one of the most able of a string of false messiahs which occur throughout history. The tale can be told as fantastic but of no ultimate consequence. But what separates Trebitsch Lincoln from an Adolf Hitler, a Mahatma Gandhi, Joan of Arc, Mother Theresa, Robert Maxwell or James Goldsmith? For good or evil, the border between vision and fantasy is an uncertain one. Couple either with a powerful intellect, total self-confidence and a silver tongue, and we may be led to glory and immortality – or, like Trebitsch Lincoln, disgrace and obscurity.

THE MARCONI SCANDAL – 1912

From Whitewash to Won't Wash: the Marconi Octopus

Though the mere mention of a minister in a divorce case was enough to warrant immediate resignation before the First World War, ministerial misbehaviour in the world of financial wheeling and dealing was regarded as a lesser offence. That is, until the Marconi 'octopus' wrapped itself around Asquith's Liberal government in 1912. Three senior ministers, including the Chancellor of the Exchequer, secretly cashed in (or tried to) on the boom in radio telegraphy.

The wireless was much in focus at the time, a symbol of progress. In 1910, radio captured the public imagination when the captain of a transatlantic liner off the coast of Quebec signalled Scotland Yard that a certain Dr Crippen was on board, the first time the recent invention had been used in police work. In 1912, impressed, the Government awarded the English Marconi Company a huge contract to build six radio stations linking Britain to the Empire.

Rufus Isaacs, the Solicitor-General in the Liberal government, was impressed too. Before the award of the contract, he surreptitiously bought 10,000 shares in the sister company, American Marconi, from his brother, who was its managing director. These shares were not due to go on the market for several days. Although expected to do well anyway, they were given a huge boost when the stricken *Titanic* sent out SOS signals on the new wireless at 2.20 a.m. on 15 April. Seven hundred people were saved from certain death. Two days later, the Solicitor-General sold 1,000 shares to two of his friends, David Lloyd George, the Chancellor (see pp.90–101 to find out how else Lloyd George raised money), and Alexander Murray, the Chief Whip.

On 19 April the American Marconi stock opened at 65 shillings and closed the day at 80 shillings. But the three ministers tried to ride the boom for too long and lost their profits.

Although the Government contract with English Marconi was widely known, there was a series of conflicts of interests though a less clear link with any hoped-for financial gain. In terms of 'standards in public life' the position was actually rather confused. However, Isaacs, as Solicitor-General, was responsible for the legal side of the deal and Lloyd George as Chancellor controlled the purse strings. Rumours spread that ministers of the Crown had exploited their position in the run-up to the flotation.

On 8 August, *Eye-Witness* broke the story. It got it only half right. In an anti-Semitic outburst the magazine named (wrongly) Herbert Samuel, the Postmaster General, and (correctly) Rufus Isaacs, as beneficiaries of inside information. The Prime Minister, H. H. Asquith, rashly dismissed the allegations claiming that 'scurrilous rubbish was best ignored'.

But *Eye-Witness* had no intention of dropping its investigations. Meanwhile, *Outlook*, another magazine, dragged the Chancellor of the Exchequer into the controversy for the first time. The national press was forced to follow. Lord Northcliffe, the owner of the *Daily Mail*, launched a strident attack on the 'Welsh solicitor and the Jew barrister' (Lloyd George and Isaacs).

When Parliament reassembled after its summer break on 11 October, the growing scandal dominated the first day's proceedings. In a highly charged debate Rufus Isaacs, the Solicitor-General, denied that any ministers had bought shares in 'that company': English Marconi, the beneficiary of the Government contract. He failed conspicuously to add that they had tried to get rich by an early raid on associated shares: those of the American sister company. MPs were unimpressed. Asquith, ruing his offhand dismissal of the reports, was forced to concede a Select Committee to examine the affair.

It proved a meagre concession. The committee was given an inbuilt government majority of three, and one star witness had disappeared. Alexander Murray, the Chief Whip, had clearly tired of the pressures. He had left politics and was on business in Colombia, beyond the reach of even the new wireless. He was fourteen days' mule ride from the nearest telegraph office.

In February 1913, Leo Maxse, editor of the *National Review*, appeared before the committee and seemed well informed about the case. Isaacs decided that he and Lloyd George should come

PUNCH, OR THE LONDON CHARIVARI.—June 18, 1913.

THE MARCONI OCTOPUS.

Liberal Party. "ANOTHER TENTACLE OR TWO AND I'M DONE!"

Punch, 18 June 1913

clean about their purchases of the American shares. When the committee accused them of having misled the Commons five months earlier, Isaacs and Lloyd George feebly protested that to explain the distinction between the two Marconi companies would have been too complicated. Both men had offered their resignations to Asquith when the scandal first broke, but he had refused to accept them. Now he was privately enraged. On 4 April he told George V that their actions were 'lamentable' and 'difficult to defend'.

Then further news broke about Murray, the former Chief Whip. MPs – their intelligence and trust already insulted – were mortified to learn that Murray had launched a solo investment exercise, gambling £9,000 of Liberal Party funds on the shares.

The findings of the Select Committee with its government majority became known as the Whitewash Report. A minority report issued by Lord Robert Cecil concluded:

> The acceptance by a public servant of a favour of any kind from a government contractor involves so grave and obvious a danger of corruption that if the . . . action is to be condoned by parliament we feel that a wide door will be opened to corruption in the future.

The official report, far milder in its conclusions, was now dubbed by *Punch* as the 'Won't Wash' report. However it was this, not Cecil's version, which was discussed for two days by the Commons. It was finally rubber-stamped on 19 June. No one resigned. Shortly afterwards, Rufus Isaacs was rewarded with the post of Lord Chief Justice of England. Lloyd George went on to become Prime Minister.

> 'More whitewash!' said the Falconer,
> Doing the Party trick,
> 'Throw it about in bucketfuls;
> Some of it's bound to stick.'
> 'Very poor art!' the public cried;
> 'You've laid it on too thick!'

Punch

HORATIO BOTTOMLEY –
1922

'The greatest swindler of the century'

Horatio Bottomley could have been anything he wanted, said his *Daily Mail* obituary in 1932: a brilliant journalist, a first-rate lawyer, a powerful industrialist. Instead, the former Liberal parliamentarian came to be remembered as undoubtedly the greatest confidence trickster ever to boast the initials 'MP' after his name, and arguably the greatest confidence trickster, in or outside politics, of his age. He is reckoned to have amassed at least £50m in today's terms, from scheme after scheme of shameless, ceaseless and compulsive deceit.

Some seventy years later, and long after abandoning a political career, Robert Maxwell crashed to the tune of larger sums, but his losses arose from real business ventures, albeit failed ones. Maxwell left significant companies and publications behind and it can be argued that his deceits only multiplied, born of desperation, as his honest ambitions grew too grandiose to sustain. But Bottomley was a cheat from the start. Bottomley's enterprises were always and by design hollow, he never seriously tried to build anything genuine, and he left nothing useful behind. Knowingly, he took £150,000 from the poor alone, plus tens of thousands more from any board of directors that happened to be passing. His gifted oratory lubricated him through a diverse career – from professional gambler to jingoistic war recruiter.

We may argue the toss as to which man – Bottomley or Maxwell – was fatter, which more colourful, or which the more brazen public performer; but for sheer moral contumely, Horatio Bottomley leaves Robert Maxwell standing. A useful review of his career by the late Gerald Rawling published in *History Today* (vol. 43) provides a timely reminder that twentieth-century political sleaze was off to a flying start by 1922: in a style and on a scale that later politicians have emulated but never matched.

It is apt that Horatio Bottomley's verbal skill was first celebrated when he defended himself so cleverly against fraud charges (before a jury and the notoriously severe Mr Justice Hawkins) that, to public amazement, he walked coolly away. Hawkins took Bottomley aside and urged him to read law. If he had, he might never have found – and lost – a seat in Parliament, risen into – and fallen spectacularly from – public grace, and ended up in Wormwood Scrubs.

Bottomley's story is a classic snakes and ladders tale. Born in 1860, he was orphaned at the age of four (though authorities suppose his real father to have been not William Bottomley, but a neighbour and Freethinker, Charles Bradlaugh). After five harsh years at an exceptionally cruel Birmingham orphanage, young Horatio escaped to a nearby aunt, Mrs Praill, who accepted him on condition he buckle down to hard work. This he did, and then at fourteen he went to London where an uncle found him employment as an errand boy.

It was when he moved to a Coleman Street solicitors' practice and began working as an office boy that Bottomley had his first recorded introduction to the swindler's art: the managing clerk was coining a living from those city firms he induced to pay non-existent county rates. Bottomley learned well and by fifteen knew thoroughly the intricacies of the Lord Mayor's court at the Guildhall and was *au fait* with the swearing of affidavits and serving of writs: knowledge which would later prove useful.

At 24 Bottomley was making progress. He had for some time been working on *Secularist* and *Freethinker:* newspapers published jointly by Bradlaugh – whom Bottomley came to see as his 'political and spiritual mentor' – and his guardian and uncle, George Holyoake. He had excelled at shorthand while working as a court reporter with a company in which he became a partner. Now married (and unfaithful) to Eliza Norton, he began to produce transcripts of local political and municipal speeches in his *Hackney Hansard* and *Battersea Hansard*.

Next was born his *Financial Times* (no relation!) which came on stream and began to pay just as his *Hansards* went into liquidation. The official receivers took action leading to his first run-in with the courts. Bottomley was to say later: 'I hold the unique distinction of having gone through every court in the country – except the divorce court.' This last was a tribute only to

Eliza's forbearance. The legal tangle, centring around kickbacks from overpriced property transactions, was but the first from which he walked sweetly away, saying: '... though not of an advanced age, I see that I have committed 21 pages of crimes.' With £600,000 unaccounted for from £1m capital, his guilt has never been seriously disputed.

Bottomley careered off into newly discovered Australian gold, made a mint floating companies only to liquidate and wind them up, leaving the shareholders deftly diminished. To his increasingly crooked holdings he added what he called his 'stable'. This did not house his horses (for which indeed he had an expensive passion) but solicitors, accountants and retired boxers acting as 'heavies'.

In 1906 he ran successfully for Parliament under the Liberal banner in South Hackney. After a previous unsuccessful attempt in Hornsey, he unleashed a box of dirty tricks directed by Tommy Cox – friend, campaign director and general claque-leader for any Bottomley project – who defaced rival posters. One vote-puller was Bottomley's line of horses trotting down the High Street with saddlecloths reading: 'Vote for my owner.'

But *John Bull* was Bottomley's business *par excellence*: an early draft of the *Sun*. This vulgar, cheeky, populist newspaper carried the slogan: 'Politics without Party – Criticism without Cant'. With or without cant he was soon in court again, over the collapse of his goldmining activities and the location of moneys from the sale of almost ten million elegant five-shilling shares, with forged certificates. Again he defended himself; again he walked away. It is difficult, at a century's distance, to credit the survival and growing success of such an obvious and complete fraud.

Louder and stouter by the month, Bottomley successfully recontested his seat in 1910. At a key constituency meeting organized by the Tory challenger, Cox recruited fifty men to march out in steel-toe-capped boots, drowning out the speaker. But then Liberals have long been known for the inventiveness of their campaigning methods.

His political career was soon to be thwarted, however. In 1912 he went bankrupt with liabilities of £233,000. Obliged to give up his seat in the House and lose his Pall Mall flat, Bottomley's career in scandal was only just hitting its stride. He now flung himself into lotteries, which had to be routed through Switzerland to remain within the law.

With the outbreak of the Great War, *John Bull* became ever more jingoistic, and Bottomley a prize recruiter of fighting men. For £200 and a percentage of the gate, he would take to the stage and rant for England. He returned to the post-war Commons as an independent, with a majority of 8,315 and a temporarily clean financial slate.

Through *John Bull* Bottomley had sold government Victory Bonds at £1 each, against Whitehall's price of £5. The enticement to buy from Bottomley was the opportunity of a £20,000 prize in a sweepstake. But instead of buying Victory Bonds with the money customers gave him, he spent nearly £42,000 on two other newspaper projects, both of which ran at a loss.

Truth magazine began to expose Bottomley. Characteristically, the MP's instinct was not to take cover, but to renew battle. He began an action against a former colleague, Reuben Bigland, who had circulated pamphlets denouncing the Victory Bonds obtainable through *John Bull*. Bottomley was advised by friends not to sue – and indeed it proved a lawsuit too far. Its indirect result was that the Director of Public Prosecutions now brought action against him for fraudulent conversion in Victory Bonds.

For once, oratory could not save him, though in court he did manage to persuade the prosecution to adjourn each day at 11.30 a.m. so that he, now an alcoholic, could drink a bottle of champagne. The prosecution may well have reckoned it helpful to their chances. Another favour he sought was that the name of Peggy Primrose, his favourite mistress, who worked as an actress, be kept out of the proceedings though she had received £1,000 in bonds. Nevertheless, the prosecution dissected Bottomley, revealing that he had received up to £4,000 a week from receipts at his recruiting meetings.

He served five of seven years after good behaviour. Peggy Primrose remained devoted to him after his wife Eliza's death, and backed his unsuccessful second attempt at a comeback. Still regarded as a phenomenon, the would-be Lazarus toured the Empire, lecturing. But when he reached the Windmill Theatre in London in 1932, he collapsed. A second heart attack killed him several months later.

Horatio Bottomley is remembered for his reply to a prison visitor who, finding him sewing mail bags, inquired 'Sewing, Bottomley?' 'No,' was the grim reply, 'reaping.'

LEWIS HARCOURT – 1922

'Loulou'

Lewis (later 1st Viscount) Harcourt, known to his friends as 'Loulou', was the only surviving son of the great radical Liberal statesman Sir William Harcourt (1827–1904) who was Home Secretary, later Chancellor of the Exchequer. Sir William is best remembered as the man who introduced Death Duties in 1894 with the words 'we are all socialists now'. A celebrated orator, Sir William would probably have succeeded Gladstone as Prime Minister, if the Queen had not tipped the balance in favour of the erratic Rosebery.

Loulou was a sickly child: his mother died soon after his birth and he was passionately attached to his father. Until the age of forty his career consisted in being his father's private secretary. When Sir William died, Loulou entered Parliament, where he was to sit in Cabinet from 1905 to 1916, initially as First Commissioner of Works (he was responsible for giving London's parks much of their present aspect) and, from 1910, as Colonial Secretary. He left the Government in sympathy with Asquith in 1916, ascending to the peerage the following year. After the war, his house remained a notable political salon.

In 1899, Loulou had married the fabulously rich American heiress Mary Burns, niece of the banker Pierpoint Morgan. Her parents' wedding present was a magnificent double house in Brook Street, which Mrs Harcourt decorated in the eclectic, ornate style then fashionable in New York. The decor, dubbed *Loulou Quinze'* by visitors of the day, has been retained by the Savile Club which has occupied the building since 1927 – only a few years after Harcourt's death and the family's departure.

If the outward trappings of Loulou's life and career were conventional, the private side was less so. The Harcourts were an apparently contented couple with a son and two daughters, but Loulou's true romantic and sexual interests lay elsewhere. He was an enthusiastic practising paedophile, absorbed by children of both sexes. A great friend was Reginald (Reggie) Brett, 2nd

Viscount Esher, Edwardian *éminence grise* and professional *confidant* – not least – of the King, as well as many prominent politicians. They saw much of each other: Reggie was Secretary to the Board of Works while Loulou was Commissioner. Reggie shared his friend's infatuation with youth but was homosexual, and a romantic and sentimental fantasist rather than (like Loulou) a pouncer. He was obsessively attached to his own second son, Maurice, who introduced a number of Eton schoolfriends. Loulou tried to interfere with Maurice, as well as indecently assaulting Reggie's young daughter Dorothy (the 'Brett' of D. H. Lawrence), putting her off men for life. (Loulou was not a physically attractive man; many found him repulsive.)

Reggie, who kept his affairs within bounds, became concerned about his friend, believing his indiscretion and high public profile might lead to eventual exposure. Both men were Fellows of Eton, and, according to James Lees Milne's excellent biography of Esher, *The Enigmatic Edwardian* (1986), boys there were warned to avoid taking walks alone with either Lord Harcourt or Lord Esher.

Some time during the autumn of 1921, Loulou pounced on an Eton boy who, with his mother, was visiting Nuneham Court, the Harcourts' country house in Oxfordshire. The boy was Edward James (the future millionaire homosexual aesthete, patron of Betjeman and the surrealists, and owner of Monkton Hall). James recalls in his memoirs that he fought off Loulou's advances ('a hideous and horrible old man') and told his mother what had happened. She gossiped indignantly about the assault among friends in London society, and the story slowly made the social descent until it reached the police.

On the morning of 24 February, Loulou, who had been looking preoccupied for days, was found dead by his valet in his dressing room at 69 Brook Street – where he had been sleeping since ceasing relations with his wife some years earlier. (The room was Bedroom no. 1 at the Savile, but in late 1995 became the library room of the Flyfishers' Club.) He had swallowed a whole bottle of the sleeping draught known as Bromidia.

Every effort was made to achieve a British standard of graceful untruth. At the inquest held a week later, Loulou's doctor claimed he had been in precarious health and the overdose might not have killed a man with a strong heart. Lady Harcourt also gave evidence and insisted that her husband had been 'most cheerful' the day before his death. The coroner concluded that 'there was not the slightest motive for suicide' and (according to *The Times* of 1 March 1922) brought in a verdict of death by misadventure. Loulou's *Dictionary of National Biography* entry, by his friend Lord Onslow, claims he died suddenly at his country house after being unwell for some time, adding nothing more about the circumstances.

Political society evidently knew the truth about what was unquestionably the great politico-sexual scandal of the 1920s. Meanwhile, Esher quickly went through Loulou's archives to extract his child pornography collection, said to be the best in the world, which he carried off to his own house. Its ultimate fate is unknown.

The family, including the new Viscount, aged thirteen, left London soon afterwards and proceeded to live quietly on their estate in Oxfordshire.

This scandal, famous at the time but only ever among 'people who know', was kept out of the newspapers and has rarely appeared in print. The story was stumbled on by Matthew Parris quite by accident, while dining with the retired Labour MP and psycho-political writer, Leo Abse, at his club, the Savile. Leo mentioned the club's link with Harcourt, and provided the outline. Historian Michael Bloch supplied from his own research the details set out above.

DAVID LLOYD GEORGE

Lloyd George Knew My Mother – 1897

The Victorian era and its long after-breath in the early twentieth century set enormous store upon the eleventh commandment. In the world of politics the peccadilloes of Ministers were well enough known. The drunkenness of Asquith, 'Squiffy' to his friends, the liaison of Hartington, Gladstone's lieutenant, with that Queen of Tarts, Catherine Walters, which won him the admiring soubriquet 'Harty-Tarty' and the trail of debt and adultery behind the comet Disraeli, were chuckled at – but privately. The political world also knew about Charles Parnell and Katherine O'Shea. Women had an undoubtedly worse deal, but so had politicians. Having somewhere to fall from, they fell.

Nobody much doubted that Lloyd George did have an affair with Mrs Catherine Edwards, the wife of a Montgomeryshire doctor. Given his lifetime record, failure to have a whirl with her could only have been an administrative oversight. But in this particular case, where the doctor brought a divorce petition against his wife, citing one Wilson as co-respondent, a confession made by Catherine Edwards said that she had also had sexual intercourse with Lloyd George. She was very specific. She said she had slept with him on the night of 4 February 1896. Lloyd George, MP for Caernarvon Boroughs since 1892, was an overnight guest in his friends' house; the doctor was called out on a case and 'criminal conversation', as it was sweetly termed, took place.

David Lloyd George, Prime Minister for six years, is among the greatest British statesmen of the twentieth century. He lacked Churchill's sense of the historic, but he had a better grasp of domestic policy, over which he was our single most effective individual radical. He was by a short head an even finer orator, one with a genius for annihilation by short phrase, dismissing the House of Lords as 'five hundred men chosen at random from the ranks of the unemployed'.

'Lloyd George won the war' is a large simplification, but his organizing talent, energy, nerve in adversity and ability to gather in and use the talents of the country, did more to win it than those of anyone else, certainly the hapless High Command. He introduced the old age pension and national insurance, used tax for income redistribution and forced upon uncertain colleagues a reform of the legislature: the Parliament Act which effectively removed the aristocratic veto from political life. Significantly, having removed it, he finally achieved a negotiated settlement with Irish nationalism, the 1922 treaty settlement.

But if the case involving Mrs Edwards in the Divorce Court in 1897 had, as they say, gone the other way, Lloyd George would

"I COULD NOT LOVE THEE, DEAR, SO MUCH,
LOVED I NOT HONOURS MORE."

Punch, 26 July 1922

have at very best sat on the backbenches as an unemployable man of genius, another Charles Dilke. More likely, he would have lost his Caernarvon Boroughs seat and lived a life cut off from metropolitan life and its creative friendships with Beaverbrook, Churchill and F. E. Smith, his natural peers. He would have kicked out a life of frustration in a provincial law practice.

For what was alleged was not just adultery, the black shuddering word which if publicly proved, meant social death, but betrayal of a trust and a friend.

The luck for Lloyd George lay in the specifics. Mrs Edwards had also said that he was the father of her child. But that child had been born, to term, in August, six months after the alleged love-making. And Lloyd George had conclusive proof of a London engagement on 4 February. The railways had done much for mobility, but they hadn't reconciled voting in the House of Commons and a sexual romp in North Wales on the same evening. It was therefore possible for Lloyd George to argue fantasy, a crazy imagined notion on poor Catherine Edwards's part – to insinuate everything which today is gathered under the word 'groupy'. This central inaccuracy caused this part of the evidence to be withdrawn, but as Lloyd George's vengeful son, Richard, remarked in his disagreeable personal life *Lloyd George* (1960) the lady had also referred to 'previous occasions' and these were never investigated. There was enough evidence of adulteries with other men for Dr Edwards to get his decree and Lloyd George, like the man acquitted by a Limerick jury, was dismissed with no other stain on his character.

Lloyd George was luckier than Parnell to whom, after the latter's disgrace, he had once said in the Commons: 'Come and let me introduce you to a Welsh friend who wants to meet you,' Parnell smiled, 'I did not know I had a friend left in Wales.' Parnell suffered all the malignancy of the Irish Roman Catholic hierarchy of the day. A Lloyd George brought down by Catherine Edwards would have been exposed to the comparable charity of militant Welsh Nonconformity, Lloyd George himself having been brought up in the Church of the Disciples of Christ. It cannot be said that Lloyd George took his deliverance to heart and mended his ways. In 1908–9, after he had become Chancellor of the Exchequer, *The Bystander*, a hard-hitting publication of the day, published a short squib, 'Mr Chancellor's Troubles':

All is not going well with Mr Lloyd George in his new and
exalted sphere. Not only is he having a most uncomfortable time of it politically . . . but rumour is
now busy as to the existence of embarrassment of another
kind which is even less likely to prove of assistance to
his career. Mr George has of course been overloaded
with flattery of late, especially from the fair sex, which
is always difficult for a man of 'Temperament' to resist.
The matter may of course be kept quiet. Also it may not.
Nous verrons.

But, in fear of libel proceedings, *The Bystander* then lost its
nerve and sent £300 to Caernarvon cottage hospital. This
victory was, however, followed up by a piece in the *People* giving
chapter and verse. The Chancellor was allegedly about to be
named as co-respondent in another divorce suit. He sued. As
counsel he engaged F. E. Smith, a Tory politician, a supposed
violent opponent of Lloyd George's ministerial proposals and a
close personal friend.

F. E. Smith – and Rufus Isaacs, later Attorney-General and
Asquith's clever son Raymond – were thrown at the court. So
was Mrs Lloyd George. Morality schmorality, the right thing
was done.

Doing the right thing involved Margaret accompanying her
husband to court on 12 March 1909, sitting beside him and
hearing him, before a packed society audience, make a single
answer to his own counsel. 'The paragraphs are an absolute
invention, every line of them.' There was no cross-examination
and the defence silk, Edward Carson, the man whose questions
had destroyed Oscar Wilde, offered a sincere and frank apology
saying that the allegations were without foundation or
justification. A thousand pounds, a subtly small sum in the
official circumstances, went to another Welsh charity. Welsh
Charity was doing rather well out of Lloyd George.

He was a persistent philanderer. His son Richard is a bluff
settler of family scores, alternately resentful and admiring, but
there is no reason to disbelieve him. And his biography speaks
of a regular and renewable stream of ladies, Mrs J, Lady H,
secretaries, society types and general female admirers. Lloyd
George had a nickname, 'the goat'.

The name was apt. Lloyd George wasn't a romantic lover, nor an idealistic Romeo. He had a high sex drive and a passion for efficiency. There was an element of hygiene about his brisk dispatch (according to one legend, sometimes on the Cabinet table) of a steady stream of sexual partners. He bears comparison with Edward VII, for whose mistresses a separate pew was reserved at his coronation and given the name 'the Loose box'.

But the Welshman was no dull Hanoverian hedonist stewing in lethargic concupiscence. He was attributed with the view that sex was a harmless invigorating pleasure which did not interfere with work, for which he also had a strong appetite.

He was in no sense a slack man, and was intolerant of slackness in others. Though Lloyd George confined humbugging to the witness box or the affidavit and never moralized about sex, he had a deep Nonconformist contempt for drunkenness. In his view it was the destroyer of intelligence and coherent thought, something which slowed a man down and turned him into a fool. Just how far this coloured his attitude to the torpid Asquith with one besotting mistress and many bottles, is worth reflection. Nothing slowed Lloyd George, with no bottles and many mistresses. He had vast energy, a thirst for creative ideas, and if sex cleared his head for important work, sex was in the national interest.

But though the generality of his sex was of the therapeutic sort without emotional attachments, a kind of work-out such as press-ups might be for others, there was an exception. In just one case he was held and involved for the rest of his life.

This was the woman his son can only bring himself to call by her full name, Frances Stevenson. Sex had played its part, of course. The tutor taken in 1912 for his daughter, Megan, was a handsome woman. She was still handsome when, after Margaret's death, they finally married thirty years later. But Frances had an excellent mind, she was a political animal, she shared his political and intellectual tastes and could talk to him as Maggie could not. All sorts of unhappiness flow from an official union linked with a discreet real one. But as long as divorce was a disgrace, with clergymen to maunder over it, lies had to be sustained, and they were lifelong.

Lloyd George, never malicious or wilfully cruel in his selfishness, had in his life one great attachment, a multitude of quick tumbles and a wife and family to whom he gave affection, but with whom he most emphatically did not want to spend more time. There was a price, and Margaret for one, paid it. But Lloyd George's calibre was never going to come cheap, and the price paid for similar pre-occupation by the children of chaste Winston Churchill and cold, cuckolded Harold Macmillan ran to death by suicide or other forms of self-destruction. Lloyd George was more rational, his wife more resigned. As his son Richard's biography tells it he had squared her before perjuring himself in his libel action against the *People*.

'You must help me, Maggie. If I get out of this I give my oath you shall never have to suffer this ordeal again.'

'And you will give your oath that this story is untrue?' she asked.

'I have to.'

Maggie then, asked: 'And you give *me* your oath that I shall not have to suffer this sort of thing again. How can I rely on your "oath"?'

'One day,' said the adulterer and perjurer-to-be, 'I shall be Prime Minister. I shall be a force for the public good. If you help me you shall never forget your decision.'

He was, and she never did. Lloyd George was the man he was, did the things, great and silly he had to do, and, thankfully, got away with it.

The Honours Scandal:
Lloyd George Knew My Father –
1922

Many of today's peers have David Lloyd George to thank for their position. Lloyd George knew their fathers, or grandfathers, and they gained something from the acquaintance. They took advantage of the Prime Minister's great post-war liquidation sale when honours were available for retail.

'Lloyd George spent his whole life in plastering together the true and the false and therefrom extracting the plausible,' commented Stanley Baldwin of the great man's career. Lloyd

George had survived the Marconi scandal of 1913, and the war had disposed of Asquith, making him Prime Minister in 1916. At the head of a coalition government after the war, he enjoyed – in the fullest sense – the Prime Minister's gifts of patronage.

The sale of honours was nothing new in the early part of this century. As today, a generous party benefactor could find himself rewarded with an honour he might not have received on the basis of his good works alone. What made Lloyd George's abuse a full-blooded scandal was its brazenness: the sheer scale of the operation, with its permanent office hawking titles.

Money always had charm, but before Lloyd George cash alone had not usually been enough. The recipient of an honour had to have the right background and social trappings. There was an element of subtlety, coupled with a care that the practice didn't go too far. Things carried on pretty nicely for all concerned. Unfortunately, no one told Lloyd George, who came to rely on the widespread sale of honours as income. Liberal funds were under the control of the Asquithian wing of the party, while those of the Conservative Party (led by Bonar Law) were reserved for their own use. Hence Lloyd George found himself in need of what would effectively be a personal campaign fund to fight a general election.

To raise this money, he simply increased the sale of honours to audacious levels. The need for those purchasing honours to have the tedious 'cover' of a plausible claim was dispensed with. Anyone with the cash could purchase the desired honour in what became an effective, if seedy, marketing operation.

In charge of proceedings were the Liberal Chief Whip Freddy Guest (replaced in March 1921 by Charles McCurdy) and Lloyd George's crass, cigar-smoking press agent, Sir William Sutherland. But the real driving force, enlarging the scandal to its ultimately calamitous proportions, was the man they in turn appointed as 'broker' – a colourful character: one Maundy Gregory.

Gregory, the son of a Southampton clergyman, had failed as a teacher, actor, playwright and theatre impresario, and had served ingloriously in the war. But in this new guise a natural talent for fraudulent impersonation and deception flowered. Established in offices in Parliament Square, and claiming to be powerful and well-connected, he began selling honours to anyone who was interested, and who had the requisite (and very large) amounts of cash. For he *was* powerful and well connected.

A price list for honours offered knighthoods at £10,000. A baronetcy would set you back £30,000 (dearer because it was hereditary). A peerage cost upwards of £50,000.

Like any good businessman, Gregory proved adept both at creating products and developing his market. He would seek out possible customers himself, not wait for an approach from them. The OBE was invented specially at this time: in four years over 25,000 were awarded. Gregory would also scrutinize the list of those in the running for honours for legitimate reasons – and persuade some to pay up, unaware that they would have received the award anyway!

An example of this skilful marketing was cited in the debate in the House of Lords, after the scandal had broken. The Duke of Northumberland quoted from a letter sent by a government tout (probably Gregory):

> There are only 5 knighthoods left for the June list – if you decide on a baronetcy you may have to wait for the Retiring List. It is not likely that the next Government will give so many honours, and this really is an exceptional opportunity, but there is no time to be lost if you wish to take it. It is unfortunate that Governments must have money, but the party now in power will have to fight Labour and Socialism, which will be an expensive matter.

Trade grew brisk. Peerages were awarded at the previously unheard of rate of fifteen a year, while the same annual number of baronetcies meant that the average of the previous twenty years was doubled. Between December 1916 and July 1922 over 1,500 knighthoods were awarded. By 1922 Lloyd George had amassed more than £2 million.

Not surprisingly, quality of recipient was in inverse proportion to burgeoning quantity. Gregory was tolerant about the background of his clientèle. Money alone talked. Richard Williamson, who received his CBE for 'untiring work in connection with various charities', turned out to be a Glasgow bookmaker with a criminal record. The 1921 New Year list saw Rowland Hodge become a baronet 'for public services, particularly in connection with shipbuilding'. No mention was made of his 1918 conviction for hoarding flour, sugar, bacon and other foodstuffs. In June 1920 John Stewart, a Dundee whisky distiller, received a baronetcy for 'public services'. It cost him £50,000. In 1924 he committed suicide with a shotgun, leaving debts of £500,000. The money he had paid for his honour was returned to his creditors.

Besides selling honours, Lloyd George gave some away – to newspaper barons. Between 1918 and 1922 Fleet Street received 49 Privy Councillorships, peerages, baronetcies and knighthoods. For a while it worked. But by 1922 Viscount Northcliffe (owner of *The Times* and the *Daily Mail*), Viscount Rothermere (*Daily Mirror* and *Sunday Pictorial*), Lord Beaverbrook (*Daily Express*) and Sir George Riddell (*News of The World*) were to turn against Lloyd George, and the days of his premiership would be numbered. The gods who had cherished him, and been rewarded, abandoned him.

Such widespread and shameless corruption could hardly escape public notice. London became known as the 'City of the Dreadful Knights', while music-hall comedians christened the OBE the 'Order of the Bad Egg'. In some Pall Mall clubs, when a newly honoured member entered the room, others would sing under their breath (to the tune of *Onward Christian Soldiers*) 'Lloyd George knows my father, Father knows Lloyd George.' In P. G. Wodehouse's *The Inimitable Jeeves*, Bingo Little refers to a peerage costing 'the deuce of a sum. Even baronetcies have gone up frightfully nowadays, I'm told.'

By February 1919, even the unfastidious Freddy Guest warned Lloyd George that the belated New Year's list was a 'grave risk' because 'the bulk of the recommendations' were for '(a) the press, (b) the trade, and (c) the capitalists'. Lloyd George took little heed, and the business flourished.

Patience was now running thin at the Palace. King George V objected strongly to the abuse of the honours system. He had begun holding up some awards for a year or so, agreeing to others with the utmost reluctance. As the abuse grew, so did the monarch's anger. Sooner or later, patience must snap. And it did – at the July 1922 Honours List. Published on 3 June, it contained awards brazen by even Lloyd George's standards. Sir John Drughorn, a shipowner recommended for a baronetcy, had in 1915 been convicted of trading with the enemy. Sir William Vestey, recommended for the same honour, was a wartime tax dodger.

But the most notorious name on the list was Sir Joseph Robinson. The 82-year-old South African businessman had been fined £500,000 for defrauding the shareholders of his mining companies. His appeal had been turned down by the Judicial Committee of the Privy Council as recently as the previous November. No one in either the South African or British governments would accept responsibility for nominating him.

Not surprisingly, there were massive public protests. Members of both Houses of Parliament complained, while King George V's verdict was that 'the Robinson case must be regarded as little less than an insult to the Crown and to the House of Lords'. Despite his efforts to avoid it, Lloyd George was forced to concede a debate in the Commons.

It took place on 17 July 1922. His long and rambling speech brought derision from MPs. Claiming that the war had been the reason for the award of so many honours, he said that the sale of honours to the highest bidder was a 'discreditable system. It ought never to have existed. If it does exist, it ought to be terminated, and if there is any doubt on that point every step should be taken to deal with it.'

It is interesting to compare these public words to those Lloyd George uttered in private to J. C. C. Davidson (a respected adviser to the government and later a Conservative MP): 'You and I know that the sale of honours is the cleanest way of raising money for a political party. The worst of it is you cannot defend it in public.' He further commented (also in private) that 'a man gives £40,000 to the party and gets a baronetcy. If he comes to the leader of the party and says, I subscribe largely to the party funds, you must do this or that, we can tell him to go to the devil.'

Whatever defences of the practice he offered in private, Lloyd George was determined that public scrutiny of matters should be limited to the minimum possible. Two hundred and seventy-nine MPs had signed a motion calling for a Select Committee, but he prevailed with the tenuous argument that, as the Royal Prerogative was involved, a Royal Commission (with, as it happened, less extensive powers) would be more appropriate for conducting the investigation. His will prevailed. Further, the commission was instructed to examine general procedure for the future, not specific events of the past. (An interesting parallel with the similar limitation placed on the Nolan Committee's remit 72 years later.)

Somehow, Lloyd George managed on the whole to avoid direct blame for the affair. Revisited today, it stands out as far worse than many other parliamentary scandals at which society has blanched and enjoyed itself. It is hard at this distance to understand why the scandal never quite blew itself into the storm which the facts – perfectly well known – justified.

It seems the abuse had become so well known that a certain cynical tolerance had set in. Shock thresholds had been levered gently upwards, and too many people had become involved for Lloyd George alone to be identified as the moving force. Then again, many members of the establishment had come either to owe their position to the sale of honours or to have close friends or associates who did. They were hard-faced men who had done well out of the racket.

The scandal did, however, help destroy an already discredited administration. Lloyd George resigned in October (the commission reported a month later). His successor, Bonar Law, accepted the need for change. A Political Honours Scrutiny Committee (comprising three Privy Councillors), and the 1925 Honours (Prevention of Abuses) Act which made it a criminal offence to traffic in titles, were consequences. Stable doors were bolted. Horses within whinnied; horses without grazed in tranquillity.

And Sir Joseph Robinson had to be persuaded to decline his peerage. When the messenger arrived in his Savoy hotel room to deliver the bad news, the almost totally deaf businessman thought at first that more money was being requested, and grudgingly reached for his cheque-book.

Further down in the undergrowth, the seedy Maundy Gregory had maintained his network of connections within the honours system and actually managed to continue for a while trading in honours. But in 1933, he offered a knighthood for £10,000 to Cdr Edward Billyard-Leake, who went straight to Scotland Yard. In his resultant prosecution under the 1925 Act, Gregory was persuaded to plead guilty and remain silent in exchange for a quarterly pension. There were no doubt many prominent people, from those with humble OBEs up to men in strawberry and ermine, who found it in the national interest that Gregory was enabled to avoid a long and revealing trial. Some of their descendants sit in the Lords today.

RAMSAY MACDONALD – 1929

Prime Minister and Pornographic Love Poet

This is the slightest of stories yet curious indeed: a Prime Minister being blackmailed by a Viennese lady in Horseferry Road, over his pornographic love poems to her. The affair never reached the newspapers – never even reached the dinner tables of 1930s political society. It has been published only once, by the one surviving parliamentarian privy to the secret. Robert (now Lord) Skidelsky, in his book *Interests and Obsessions*, recounts the tale as Sir Oswald Mosley related it to him. Mosley is our only source and so before the story is accepted as history, the appropriate caveat should be entered.

Mosley (the future fascist leader) was a Labour minister at the time of the episode: Chancellor of the Duchy of Lancaster in Ramsay MacDonald's government. MacDonald went on to break with the Labour movement, head a coalition government in 1931, and end his career in personal political failure; but at this point, in 1929, he had just formed a government.

A Viennese woman of mature years, living near Victoria Station in Horseferry Road, was threatening to blackmail the Prime Minister over pornographic poems she said he had written to her. She was short of money and MacDonald had refused, she said, to provide for her.

Mosley was asked by the PM to act as secret mediator as Mosley and his wife Cynthia had introduced MacDonald to the woman while they and MacDonald were on holiday together in 1928. MacDonald had found her 'agreeable'. The Mosleys had been pleased to see MacDonald, a widower, with a companionable lady, and as pleased, some time later, to encounter the two of them together at a house party in Cornwall. Mosley told Skidelsky that it seemed MacDonald and the lady had interests in common: in particular he was told that MacDonald liked to read poetry to her. It was only after the election that Mosley discovered what kind.

In response to the blackmail threats, Mosley visited her flat in Horseferry Road. She had been threatening to sell MacDonald's letters to the French press. He did not see them, but persuaded her to delay action. Later she resumed her threat. When the issue was finally settled – she was paid £20,000 for the correspondence – the letters were in Paris, where it fell to the British Ambassador, Sir Charles Mendl, to retrieve them. Sir Charles read and destroyed the correspondence. He confirmed to Mosley its pornographic nature, but gave no further details.

The world may to this day read and enjoy MacDonald's *Socialism and Culture* and his *Labour and the Empire*, as well as the memoir he wrote of Margaret, his wife; but at the Prime Minister's talents in Lord Rochester's field, we can only guess.

HAROLD MACMILLAN – 1929

'No man has ever lost sleep over public worries'

Harold Macmillan was one of the most successful Prime Ministers of the post-war era, confidant of Churchill and Kennedy, and coiner of phrases like 'You've never had it so good'. Yet during all this time he nursed a private pain. His friend Robert Boothby (see pp.116–121) was continuing an open and frank affair with Macmillan's wife Dorothy and (it was said) had fathered a child. The effects were arguably profound. Many believe that ignoring the affair for so long resulted in the blind spot which allowed him to overlook the damage done by the Profumo affair (see pp.156–181).

The truth about Harold Macmillan, his wife Dorothy and his friend Robert Boothby only trickled out some years after the death of Dorothy Macmillan in 1966, such is the protection society affords its own. Indeed when Boothby died twenty years later in 1986 *The Times* obituary referred darkly to 'a grave personal wrong' he had done to Harold Macmillan. The 'wrong' continued through the most politically active years of Macmillan's life, beginning at the end of the 1920s.

Macmillan's biographer, Alistair Horne, puts it succinctly: '1929 was a year of disaster throughout the world: it was also one of the most wretched in Harold Macmillan's life.' For in the year of the Wall Street Crash, Macmillan lost his parliamentary seat in Stockton, and his wife to another man.

Robert Boothby was everything the younger Harold Macmillan, before he invented himself, was not. He was a handsome, dashing, assured fellow who drove a two-seater Bentley. His oratory was commanding, as was his sureness of touch, whether with dukes or dustmen, complete. He was as at home in grand country houses as in a fisherman's cottage in his Scottish constituency. His biographer Robert Rhodes-James wrote: 'He would sit back in his chair, and talk about his passion for jazz, for the music of Gershwin and his addiction for Hemingway.'

In short, he was the coming man: Prime Minister potential. Quoting a journalist who said he was 'always ahead of his time and always right,' Boothby replied: 'from this conclusion, I cannot dissent.'

If Boothby was telegenic, Macmillan was radiogenic. He provided a complete contrast to Boothby's glamour. He learned to affect the avuncular air of an English school master, with his horn-rimmed glasses, unstylish clothes, bushy moustache and uneven teeth.

His wife was Dorothy Cavendish, daughter of the Duke of Devonshire. By 1929, after nine years of marriage, Dorothy was growing bored with her husband. Dorothy was a highly sexed woman who craved excitement – she once took part in a mock burglary, using masks and toy pistols at the house of a royal equerry. There were further problems in the Macmillan domestic set-up. Macmillan's mother, Nellie, stayed in the family home, Birch Grove. Dorothy was forbidden from even replanting a border in the garden without permission from Macmillan's mother. 'It must have been like a strait-jacket,' said one of Dorothy's daughters-in-law.

Macmillan, the crofter's grandson, was mocked at Dorothy's majestic family home, Chatsworth House. At dinner the Cavendish girls used to vie for the honour of *not* sitting next to him. Robert Rhodes-James wrote: 'He was rated by them [the Cavendish girls] as the most stupendously boring man they had ever met, and they could not understand why the vivacious and attractive Dorothy had ever married him.'

Boothby met the Macmillans at Boothby's father's house in 1928 when they played a round of golf together. A year later, all three were invited to a house party at Bowood, the Marquess of Lansdowne's Wiltshire seat. During a parlour game Lady Henry Bentinck lost her glasses. Much amusement followed, at Lady Henry's expense. Some days later Dorothy received a parcel through the post – it was Lady Henry's glasses together with an invitation from Boothby to lunch. Boothby had apparently stood over her glasses, hiding them.

Some weeks later, Boothby, consoling Macmillan at losing his seat at the General Election, invited the couple to a shoot on his father's estate. Robert Rhodes-James takes up the story: 'It was on the second day on the moors, when Boothby was waiting his turn to shoot, that he was startled to find his hand being squeezed affectionately, and turned to see a beaming Dorothy beside him. That was when it all began.'

Each appears to have been equally implicated from the start. Boothby gave Dorothy excitement, an escape from a boring and tedious marriage and a sexual fulfilment it was whispered Macmillan was unable to provide. Dorothy gave Boothby form – and a ticket to the most elevated social circles.

There is no doubting that the relationship was genuine and intense. Between 1929 and 1935 Boothby and Dorothy lived together publicly. Boothby later described Dorothy as 'a very powerful woman'. He went on to describe the intensity of their relationship: 'She never suffered a pang of remorse, or she never showed it, anyway – absolutely none about me and Harold . . . Several times I got engaged, once in Venice, but Dorothy came all the way from Chatsworth to pursue me there . . . she was absolutely unafraid of anything . . . she broke off my engagements and stopped me twice from getting married . . . she was relentless, there was a streak of cruelty in her, I have to admit, and very selfish. But we were absolutely fixed upon each other.' The result, it was said, was Sarah, born in 1930 and widely thought to be Boothby's daughter. The pain of the affair was exposed in a letter from Boothby to his friend Cynthia Mosley in September 1932, when he was on holiday in Portugal with Dorothy: 'I love Dorothy. As much as I have ever loved her . . . She said to me tragically yesterday, "Why did you ever wake me? I never want to see any of my family again. And without you, life for me is going to be nothing but one big hurt."'

There was no secrecy in their love – it was not in Dorothy's nature to lie about anything. Letters from Boothby were left around the Macmillan house, telephone calls to Boothby were not disguised. The affair soon became known in Westminster and society circles, but it did not become generally known until after Dorothy's death in 1966. King George V was reported to have said at the time, 'Keep it quiet.' Macmillan only confided in his mother Nellie, who advised him not to divorce. In those days of stricter divorce laws, Macmillan said he had done nothing wrong and refused to accuse his wife of adultery. Politically, it would have been damaging. Macmillan had won back his Stockton seat in 1931 and any suggestion of his wife's adultery would have unsettled his constituents.

The strain took its toll on everyone apart from Dorothy. Macmillan, a proud and private man, was grievously wounded by the affair. His son Maurice later said: 'What he minded most was being dishonoured.' In 1931 he collapsed and was sent to a Munich sanatorium to recover. The official diagnosis was neurasthenia, a recurrence of war wounds. But this may have been a smokescreen brought on by a full-scale nervous breakdown caused by the strains of the Boothby–Dorothy affair. Before the breakdown, one witness described Macmillan banging his head against the wall of a railway carriage compartment in despair. An old family nanny hinted at a suicide attempt.

But Macmillan remained committed to his wife. In a rare moving, and rather astonishing interview he said: 'I have never loved anyone but her – never had a woman friend, or even knew anyone. On her side, there were transient things – unimportant . . . In middle age, things pass: I said jokingly, "Now you've had everything, husband, children, a home, a lover, what more?" In the way women do, she said it was my fault . . . but what's physical love compared to things you share, children? . . . But it took a lot of me, physically.' It is likely that the carefree cynicism of his widely quoted observation, 'No man has ever lost sleep over public worries,' was only affectation.

Boothby suffered too. In 1935, at his wits' end, he proposed over dinner to Diana Cavendish. By the morning, he regretted it. But it was too late. Her mother Lady Moyra had announced the engagement to the world and there was no turning back. Two days before the marriage, Boothby fell into a deep alcoholic depression. He sent an SOS cable to his former secretary, Marjorie Macrae, who was returning on a ship from China. She replied that he had got himself into this mess and that he would have to get himself out of it. Her sole insistence was that he did not take the wedding vows when drunk. Wedded bliss was short-lived, however, and soon he was seeing Dorothy again. Boothby and Diana divorced after two years, though the couple remained close for the rest of their lives.

Boothby said the dalliance with Diana was due to a desire to settle down. He wrote at the time: 'I married Diana because we were old friends, and she was a first cousin of Dorothy and we were both unhappy. It was a damned silly thing to do ... The reason I was unhappy was because deep down I was dissatisfied. And the reason I was dissatisfied was because I passionately wanted a home and children of my own.'

The affair put strains on the whole Macmillan family. All four of the Macmillan children suffered to a greater or lesser extent from alcoholism – the 'Cavendish' disease, as it was known. Sarah particularly was affected. She only found out in her teens at a college dance that Boothby was her father. She had earlier discovered she was pregnant and aborted the pregnancy after pressure from Dorothy who told her it would ruin Macmillan's career. When she later married, Sarah was unable to have children due to the abortion. Boothby later said: 'It is the one thing I could never quite forgive Dorothy: the one wicked thing she did ... I think it was part of her guilty conscience, but it killed Sarah.'

Dorothy appears to have remained unaffected by the unhappiness around her, constantly juggling the two men in her life. She kept in daily contact with Boothby, travelling at home and abroad with him as much as possible. Yet she was always at home to run Macmillan's household at Birch Grove and playing the dutiful wife to the Stockton MP.

The affair continued right up to Dorothy's death in 1966. In public, Boothby and Macmillan enjoyed civil relations. Both were in political agreement for most of their careers (both opposed Chamberlain's policy of appeasement in the late 1930s). This ability to separate public from private affairs continued into later life when, as Prime Minister, Macmillan rewarded the politically disgraced Boothby with a life peerage. This was remarkably generous.

During the years up to Dorothy's death, the two men saw contrasting fortunes. Boothby's star gradually sank. Financial scandal hit him hard, but he speculated morosely on whether it was his affair with Dorothy and the failure of his first marriage which spoiled his suitability for higher office.

The affair transformed Macmillan. Unhappiness at home turned his mind to politics. Many believe the affair proved to be the 'grit in the oyster' which was the making of Macmillan – it gave him a certain cynicism about life. R. A. Butler thought the affair 'enhanced his character'. Macmillan later admitted 'all this personal trouble did strengthen my character'.

Macmillan resigned the party whip in protest over unemployment in 1936. During the wartime administration, Churchill increasingly relied on him. Defeated in the Labour landslide of 1945, he was returned that year as MP for Bromley. He was Minister for Housing 1951–4, when he succeeded in getting 300,000 houses a year built. After spells as Defence Minister and Chancellor of the Exchequer, he became Prime Minister in 1957 when Anthony Eden resigned. His economic expansionism, resolution in foreign affairs, integrity and 'you've never had it so good' optimism inspired a mini consumer boom. During his time in office the Macmillans became close. After a successful Commonwealth tour in 1958, a new warmth entered their relationship. He increasingly relied on Dorothy's advice and judgement and leaned on her calmness, under the pressures of office.

His crowning achievement was winning a 100-strong majority in the 1959 election. His 'wind of change' speech in Cape Town in 1960 predicting the African continent's independence, enhanced this Edwardian actor's credentials as a modernizer. But after setbacks, including the Profumo scandal, Macmillan retired from office in 1963 during a bout of ill-health.

There was a curious postcript to the affair some years after Dorothy's death. Macmillan decided to burn Boothby's love letters to Dorothy at Birch Grove. There were too many to fit in the fireplace, so he took them to the garden incinerator. He had no one to help him, and was unsure how the incinerator worked. The wind picked up and blew the half-burnt letters around the garden. The picture of this partially-sighted elder statesman chasing half burnt *billets-doux* from his wife's lover around the garden caused amusement when he recounted the tale to Boothby afterwards.

'And so it ended,' said Macmillan. There was a long pause. 'And so it ended,' said Boothby.

T. I. MARDY JONES – 1930

MP Loses Seat on Train from Pontypridd

It is hard not to feel sorry for the obscure Labour backbencher T. I. Mardy Jones, who made a humiliating and unceremonious departure from Parliament weeks before the financial crisis which triggered the Great Depression. The House of Commons, poor Mr Mardy Jones discovered, can put on quite a show of retributive and socially selective justice, especially where a breach of its own privileges is concerned.

Thomas Isaac Mardy Jones had followed his father down the coal mines at the age of twelve. His father died in a pit disaster – frequent in those days. The son rose through the ranks of the Labour Party to become the MP for his home town, Pontypridd, in July 1922.

Once, MPs received no wages. Labour had successfully fought to secure small salaries – its working-class MPs had few other sources of income – and the socialist government of 1924 had secured a further privilege: MPs were eligible for vouchers which they could exchange for rail tickets between London and their constituencies. These were not transferable to friends or family. It was a clear rule. Mr Mardy Jones broke it.

He sent two rail tickets to his wife Margaret, and their twelve-year-old daughter, on 19 December 1930. Mrs Mardy Jones and the little girl, who made only rare excursions to the capital because of the cost, boarded the steam train at Pontypridd, excited at the prospect of seeing the bright lights of London.

A first class single in 1930 cost £1 12s 9d (19s 8d 3rd class). An MP's salary was £360. The price of such a ticket was thus about 20 per cent of his week's earnings. Mrs Mardy Jones and her daughter took their place in a first-class carriage when disaster struck. They were challenged by three ticket collectors.

Mr Mardy Jones had been careless. One of the tickets was six weeks out of date. There was an altercation during which a tearful Mrs Mardy Jones insisted that the tickets must be in order because her husband had said so, and he was an MP, so he must be right. The conductors from the Great Western Railway, a private company, were not impressed. They passed the distraught woman's name and address to the GWR police.

Christmas must have been a miserable affair in the Mardy Jones household as they anxiously awaited the knock on the front door of their small terraced home. The MP tried to get in touch with the general manager of the GWR but was refused a meeting. The GWR police waited until 6 January before calling. Mr Mardy Jones did not flinch from the truth. 'She had not got sufficient cash. I was short too. I am paid quarterly, and the cheque was not due until the end of December.'

The GWR showed no mercy. Charges were pressed. The day before he went to court on 6 February, Mr Mardy Jones, after consulting the Labour whips and his constituency officials, resigned from the House of Commons. He pleaded guilty to transferring two non-transferable tickets to his wife, and helping her to travel without paying a fare. His wife pleaded guilty to using non-transferable tickets and intending to travel without paying a fare.

In his defence, the former MP said he had needed important papers from his home in Wales and had been stranded in

Westminster because the Labour government had been defeated the night before. He was involved in protracted negotiations to reduce the working day in the coal mines, a subject close to his heart. 'I was at my wits' end,' he told Marylebone court. 'My wife was there so I decided to get her to bring me the papers. Knowing I could not get tickets in time for her to travel next day, I sent her the two tickets I had in my pocket.'

Mr Mardy Jones might have got away with it if he had sent only one ticket for his wife, but Mrs Mardy Jones refused to leave their twelve-year-old daughter in the house on her own.

Imposing fines of £2 on each defendant, the magistrate, Mr Hay Halkett, compounded the former MP's ignominy. 'It is rather disgraceful to find an MP involved in a case like this,' he said to the reporters packing the public gallery. 'However disgusting this case is, and I think it is very disgusting, we have to remember that Mr Mardy Jones has risen to his present position from a coal mine.' The magistrate then ordered the former coal miner to find costs of £31 10s or face the prospect of 42 days in jail.

Mr Mardy Jones found the money. He had lost his seat.

J. H. THOMAS – 1936

Cabinet Minister Turns Budget Tipster

Budget purdah was abolished in 1993 by the Chancellor of the Exchequer, Kenneth Clarke. Before then the rule had prevented ministers discussing any aspect of economic policy which might touch on the forthcoming Budget. The very existence of the Chancellor's famous battered briefcase could barely be mentioned. But even after Mr Clarke's relaxation, Jim Thomas would still have been out of order. A popular and racy speaker, Thomas was a big, ruddy-cheeked former railwayman as renowned for his witty asides as he became for his unfortunate loose tongue.

Born in Newport in 1874, James Henry Thomas started work at the age of nine as an errand boy. At twelve, he took up his first full-time job cleaning locomotives on the Great Western Railway, eventually earning seven shillings a week. He earned his spurs in the growing trade union movement when he led his first strike at the age of fifteen. Aged 36, he was elected MP for Derby – among forty Labour MPs returned in the 1910 election: the new party was taking wing.

As a young MP he was a victim of the vicious alcoholic wit, F.E. Smith. Thomas asked him the way to a toilet in the Commons. 'Downstairs,' said Smith, 'turn right and on the third door on your right you will see the sign "Gentlemen". But don't let that put you off.'

Thomas was by nature a moderate. He became general secretary of the National Union of Railwaymen at the end of the war, and his conciliatory stance helped settle the 1926 general strike peacefully. In the first Labour government in 1924 Thomas held Cabinet office as Colonial Secretary. He seemed to be on his way up.

Seven years later he was less popular among his old friends, having followed Ramsay MacDonald into coalition with the Conservatives. But by 1936, Colonial Secretary again, and quite at home with his new-found Conservative colleagues, J. H. Thomas was still regarded as potential Foreign Secretary material. That was until he breached what had become one of Parliament's more sacred traditions.

In the 1930s, the Chancellor of the Exchequer would normally announce details of the budget to the Cabinet 24 hours before he addressed the Commons, but with the Easter recess imminent, Chancellor Neville Chamberlain broke with convention and told surprised Cabinet colleagues on 19 April 1936 that he was planning the biggest tax rise since the war. Stanley Baldwin, the Prime Minister, felt ministers would require the full Easter break to recover from the shock: Chamberlain planned a threepenny rise in income tax and a hike in tea duties.

It was political dynamite. Coming a full thirteen days before the Budget statement there was an inevitable risk of a leak. Over Easter, Colonial Secretary Thomas shared his secret with his good friend Alfred Bates during a round of golf. When the Stock Exchange reopened a few days later the minister's golfing chum exploited his inside information and sold shares he thought were most sensitive to the tax increases. Days later he compounded Thomas's sin by taking out insurance policies against a threepenny rise in income tax. Betting on the Budget was a common practice during the 1930s but most punters insured themselves against a general tax rise. Bates got better odds by putting all his money on a startlingly precise figure.

On the morning of 21 April, Budget day, Sir Alfred Butt, the Conservative member for Balham and Tooting, went for tea and biscuits with his friend J. H. Thomas. It was a profitable meeting. As the Colonial Secretary lifted the teapot he told Butt to make the most of his cuppa as the price was set to soar. Before Chamberlain stood up to make his speech, Sir Alfred had obtained highly specific insurance cover.

Less than 48 hours later, with the country still reeling from the punitive tax rise and with housewives jostling each other in the stampede for pre-Budget-priced Brooke Bond, a keen-eyed MP, Sir Assheton Powell, asked the Speaker's permission to make a grave allegation to the House. MPs sat up. Powell told a hushed

PUNCH, OR THE LONDON CHARIVARI.—JUNE 10, 1936

THE FLYING SQUAD.

[Budget Inquiry Tribunal begins Sittings May 11th. Delivers Report June 2nd.]

Punch, 10 June 1936

Commons he had detected an unseemly interest by a certain member of the public in insurance immediately prior to the Chancellor's speech. The unthinkable had happened. The Budget had leaked.

Baldwin was mortified. An immediate tribunal was set up to find the culprit. All eyes were on the handful of civil servants and government printers, but after eight days of exhaustive interrogation, much to the embarrassment of the Government and the quiet contentment of the Opposition, the tribunal vindicated Whitehall's loyal public servants. Sensationally all the evidence pointed to a leak from within the Cabinet.

Butt and Bates were hauled before the tribunal. Neither could provide a convincing explanation for their windfalls. When recent social engagements were examined, the finger of accusation pointed at their mutual friend, the Secretary of State for Colonial Affairs. It was only surmise and would never have stood up in court; but shock rippled through Westminster. With his political reputation now annihilated, Thomas did the honourable thing and resigned before the tribunal damned him.

Meanwhile, some merry sideshows to the main event were uncovered. Thomas, it seemed, was a would-be author with a taste for insider-gambling. His golfing friend Bates had advanced him £15,000 for his autobiography which the Cabinet minister had not even started. And it emerged that using his Tory friend, Butt, as an intermediary Thomas had earlier gambled on the date of the election now behind them. Having placed a £1,000 bet on the country going to the polls some time in 1935, they netted a £600 profit from the venture. Sir Alfred Butt had no choice but to follow J. H. Thomas into the political wilderness.

On 11 June the former Colonial Secretary made a moving eight-minute resignation speech to the House and left Westminster for ever. He spoke of the 'humiliation and stain' of the tribunal's report. Thomas's forced departure from public life gave him time to write his by now much-trailed autobiography, *My Story*, which appeared in 1937. Not uncomfortable in his disgrace, he busied himself with his job as Chairman of British Amalgamated Transport Ltd and Vice-Chairman of Crystal Palace. He went to his grave in January 1949 protesting his innocence and insisting that he 'never consciously gave a Budget secret away'.

ROBERT BOOTHBY – 1940

'It never occurred to me'

Robert Boothby was one of those enhanced personalities who had seemed destined for high office. A supporter of Churchill's when few others would back him in the 1930s, his role at the forefront of British public life seemed assured. His *political* judgement in essentials was splendid. One of the earliest political disciples of Keynes and a day-one abominator of Nazism, he represented an enlightened and humane brand of Conservatism: a proto-Wet. But a scandal involving an undeclared conflict of interest in 1940 resulted in his resignation, and (until he took up the campaign for homosexual law reform twenty years later) estrangement from politics. He threw himself instead into television.

His biographer Robert Rhodes-James agrees with contemporaries that Boothby was an impulsive, rumbustious, easygoing and generous man. According to his cousin, Ludovic Kennedy, he had fathered at least three children by the wives of other men. His long love affair with Harold Macmillan's wife is dealt with on pp.103–9. Kennedy wrote in his autobiography: 'I once told him [Boothby] to his face that he was a shit of the highest order, at which he rubbed his hands, gave a deep chuckle and said: "Well, a *bit*. Not entirely".' Yet he was, said Kennedy, 'a companionable man of great charm'.

The cause of his downfall was his friendship with Richard Weininger, a businessman who had gained and lost a million dollars on the US stock market before the First World War. In 1923 Weininger became a Czech citizen, living in Munich and Berlin and with business interests in both Czechoslovakia and England. Horrified by the Nazis' persecution of the Jews in Kristallnacht, he had left Berlin for Prague. Boothby and Weininger both shared a concern for Czechoslovakia and in August and September 1938 Boothby – Conservative MP for East Aberdeenshire since 1924 and for four years the Parliamentary Private Secretary to Winston Churchill – visited the Republic and was greatly alarmed at its vulnerability.

Boothby's weakness was his gambling, made worse by not having enough money. It was his undoing. By 1939 previous investments had made his financial standing unstable and to ease his burden he got a temporary and unsecured loan from Sir Alfred Butt (see J. H. Thomas, pp.111–115) in August 1938. Here his problems began.

In January 1939 Weininger became concerned that his wife's personal assets, estimated at £200,000, were tied up in Czech banks. Weininger asked Boothby if there was anything he could do to negotiate their unfreezing. Boothby was currently working in the City as a banker and said he would try to help. This was to be a 'personal transaction' between client and banker, in which Boothby would take 10 per cent of any assets recovered. Rhodes-James says Weininger made the offer. The Zota Company was set up to secure the release of the funds and Boothby was given £1,000 expenses by Weininger to visit Czechoslovakia.

When Germany invaded Czechoslovakia on 15 March 1939, the trip was abandoned, and Czech bank balances in Britain were closed. The Bank of England swiftly set about trying to find the number of British holders of funds in Czechoslovakia and Weininger's wife put in a claim of £240,000 for herself and her daughters.

On 18 April a Committee for Claimants against Czech Assets was set up, representing most claimants in Britain. It was natural that Boothby would be proposed as Chairman, and he agreed. He omitted to mention his interest in one of the claims. It is here that he has been judged to have crossed the unstated and imprecise line in such matters. It was probably less clear at the time. Regulations governing members' interests were vague: they implied that an interest had only to be declared if a Commons vote was involved. The only payment Boothby received from the Committee was a small cigarette case presented in gratitude for his work on it. Nevertheless, rumours that Boothby was being paid for his work as Committee Chairman circulated in the City. Reputation counts there and such rumours were damaging. Blithely, Boothby dismissed them.

Interests became increasingly tangled. On 1 April 1939, for example, Boothby wrote to Weininger saying he would be staying the weekend with the Financial Secretary to the Treasury and that he would 'bring pressure to bear in that quarter'.

On 3 May Boothby received a letter from the Zota Company saying Zota would give Boothby 10 per cent of any assets recovered (about £24,000). The timing suited Boothby as creditors were pressing: he wrote to Alfred Butt stating that the 10 per cent of the Czech assets would pay off the debt. Meanwhile Boothby badgered the Treasury to get a speedy decision on compensation for the lost Czech assets. He was assured that Zota's application was proceeding duly.

He wrote to Sir John Simon, the Chancellor, enclosing a letter from Weininger and saying that British holders of assets in Prague should be compensated as soon as possible. Under pressure to settle his own debts, he wrote again on 31 May, pressing for an early settlement of the Czech claims. The clash of interests was now indisputable.

The efforts of the Committee were hampered by the fact that it did not speak for all the claimants. In fact the largest London claimants, the Petschek brothers, had not joined the Committee. This arguably weakened their case, and certainly undermined the Committee's standing. Boothby was understandably eager to get the Petscheks into the fold. He asked his lawyer, Colonel Harry Nathan, a Labour politician, to write to the Petscheks to encourage them to join the Committee. A letter was also enclosed from Weininger to the brothers. The brothers considered these letters threatening. They showed them to Sir Edward Reid, a prominent figure in the City. For Reid this confirmed suspicions about Boothby.

The matter was brought to the attention of the Chancellor, who interpreted the letters, writes Rhodes-James, as a 'form of improper pressure' being brought to bear upon the Petscheks. On the basis of the letters, Sir John Simon, who knew of Boothby's private interest, summoned the MP and accused him of using his position as Chairman to make money. Boothby, completely unprepared for such accusations, was dumbstruck, a silence later interpreted by Simon, according to Rhodes-James, as 'dejection'.

After leaving Simon, Boothby wound up the Committee and cancelled a cheque from Zota, but Sir Alfred Butt was threatening writs. Boothby gave him a £5,000 cheque. Shortly after this his father came to the rescue and paid off the rest of the debt; but the damage had been done.

Boothby carried on. He spoke twice in the House, on the Czechoslovakia (Financial Claims and Refugees) bill, about the special consideration which should be given to all claimants resident in Britain. He kept negotiating with the Treasury on Zota's behalf, still not mentioning that he expected his cut from any payment made to Weininger. By 9 August, Boothby was able to repay £3,000 of a £6,300 loan to Weininger, to whom he wrote 'I am hoping to receive a substantial amount when the second half of the Czech assets is paid.' On 17 August 1940, he wrote again on Ministry of Food notepaper complaining about the delay in the pay-out.

His fall came soon after. When the Emergency Powers (Defence) Act came into force, many innocent foreigners were put in gaol, Richard Weininger among them. Before his arrest he phoned Boothby and asked him to look after his papers. When the police arrived, Weininger's secretary phoned Boothby who said the secretary should hand over any papers – 'scarcely the act of a man with a guilt-laden conscience', writes Rhodes-James.

The seized papers were brought to the attention of Prime Minister Churchill and on 17 October 1940, he announced a Select Committee investigation into Boothby's activities. By then Boothby had been appointed a junior minister in the Ministry of Food. It was he who introduced the free milk ration for schoolchildren that would be removed some thirty years later by the Minister of Education, Mrs Margaret Thatcher.

The investigation was a disaster for Boothby. The Chairman was a pro-Munich Chamberlainite (Boothby was a Churchill ally), while Boothby's lawyer got hopelessly out of his depth. The Select Committee concluded that Boothby should have declared his special interest in Weininger's holdings. This was hardly disputable. What, however, can be maintained in Boothby's defence is that his omission was innocent, or no more than negligent, or at least only marginally culpable – something widely believed at the time. What was so damaging to Boothby was that the Committee went on to remark that 'Mr Boothby's conduct was contrary to the usage and derogatory to the dignity of the House and inconsistent with the standards which Parliament is entitled to expect from its members.' In the view of Rhodes-James, the report, and the subsequent destruction of Boothby's career, turned on the malice of a political enemy.

Boothby resigned from the Food Ministry. He had the sympathy of most MPs and Downing Street let it be known that it would oppose any effort to expel him.

On 28 January 1941, the report was debated in the Commons. Boothby made his resignation speech. Churchill wrote later that Boothby gave a 'remarkable Parliamentary performance that perceptibly affected the opinion of the House'. The speech was certainly remarkable in its candour: 'Looking back, the whole unfortunate business seems so unnecessary. A post-script in a letter, a sentence or two in a conversation or a speech – which could have altered neither the facts nor the course of events nor my conduct in relation to them are all, it seems, that were required. But it never occurred to me that they were necessary. It may be that I was thoughtless . . .' He echoed similar thoughts in his autobiography, years later: 'The single sentence "I have an interest to declare" would, it seems, have cleared me. I can only say that it never occurred to me to say it.'

He had been, after all, working for many people; and was paid by only one, a close personal friend. It is hard to see how non-disclosure affected his conduct.

Boothby remained in public life, although not in the way he might have anticipated. He had been knighted in 1953. In 1958 he became the 1st Baron Boothby of Buchan and Rattray Head. He had not lost the affection of the establishment.

He had a flair for the bold gesture and enjoyed publicity. Even as an MP he had raised smiles by a weekly dispatch of herrings to his friend Noël Coward, as part of his campaign to popularize the fish. 'Lord Boothby remembers the frisson,' writes Coward's biographer, 'that swept through his office in the City when a telegram arrived addressed to him: MEET ME TONIGHT IN DREAMLAND 10.00PM – NOEL COWARD.' Dreamland in Margate was one of Coward's beloved amusement parks. Boothby also turned himself into what we were learning to call a television personality. But scandal of a sort was again to seek him out. Boothby became a prominent homosexual law reform campaigner, championing the cause when it was taboo in the press. Michael Foot described him as a 'non-playing captain'. Others say different and it is not easy to square convinced attestations to his homosexuality with his scandalous heterosexual dalliance with Dorothy Macmillan. One must simply leave both reports lying on the table.

A speech in 1954 started off his personal campaign on homosexual reform, and he began putting down Parliamentary Questions. He went to see the charmless Home Secretary, Sir David Maxwell-Fyffe, who replied: 'I am not going down as the man who made sodomy legal.' But Maxwell-Fyffe referred the matter to a committee headed by Sir John Wolfenden. It is upon Wolfenden's work that twentieth-century homosexual law reform can be said to have been founded.

Years later, on 11 July 1964, scandal broke. The *Sunday Mirror* splashed: 'Peer and a Gangster: Yard Probe Public Men at Seaside Parties'. The front-page article alleged that Scotland Yard was investigating a homosexual relationship between a peer and a London thug. The following Sunday the same paper again splashed the story, claiming it had a photo: 'The Picture We Must Not Print'.

In fact a photo did exist: of Ronnie Kray, who was homosexual, and Boothby in the latter's flat. By not printing it, the paper inflated its importance. The article described it as 'of the highest significance and public concern', but in reality it was not. An outraged Boothby wrote to *The Times* on 31 May 1964, explaining all. Kray had been to his flat to discuss a business arrangement, but nothing came of it and no deal was struck. Before he left, Kray, who was in the habit of getting himself photographed with famous people, asked for a photo with Boothby, who obliged. Boothby maintained he did not know about Kray's gangster connections. Whether or not he did, the sexual innuendo may have been spurious.

A letter from Boothby was printed in full and without comment. The *Sunday Mirror* acknowledged there was no truth in the allegations and Boothby received a full apology. The paper's editor was sacked, and Boothby was paid £40,000 in compensation. The case never even went to court.

Reviewing Boothby's life in his sympathetic *Bob Boothby, A Portrait*, Robert Rhodes-James believes Boothby was unlucky. He is one of those unfortunate men whose reputations have become a smudge in public memory: 'some sort of scandal, wasn't there?' we murmur, remembering perhaps that there was something about his cut from a financial deal involving Czechoslovakia, something about homosexuality, and something about the Krays. Yet when each matter is viewed separately, as each ought to be, the vague impression of monolithic scandal, like some great rock, apparently glimpsed through a fog, scatters; and we see only shards of flotsam.

GARY ALLIGHAN – 1947

'Approaching the fringe of semi-sobriety'

Who, do you suppose, was the last MP to be expelled from the House? A rapist? A murderer? A war-traitor? An international crook? No. It was a man who admitted in print that MPs leak stories to journalists for reward, favours or drinks. He also suggested that MPs get drunk. The House was outraged. The full wrath of an affronted legislature came down upon his head.

Gary Allighan was both an MP and a journalist. The Labour MP for Gravesend had started his career working for Horatio Bottomley as an assistant editor, and worked on the *Luton News*. He had also been a news editor of the *Daily Mirror*. He had served two masters – press and Parliament – and when it came to the crunch, Allighan devoted his loyalty to the wrong one.

He was hauled up before the Commons Privileges Committee after writing an article in the *World Press News* 'exposing' the means lobby correspondents were using to obtain leaks and insider information. The technique, he said, was to ply MPs with drink until they collapsed into the proverbial 'well-placed source'. This was what enraged his colleagues, but what gave them the stick with which to beat him was the discovery that he was, himself, just such a source.

Under the headline 'Labour MP reveals his concept of how party news gets out. Public that pays is entitled to know', he wrote:

Every newspaper on Fleet Street has anything up to half a dozen MPs on its 'contacts' list . . . some of the contacts are on a retainer, some get paid for what they produce, some are content to accept 'payment in kind' – personal publicity. I, as news editor of the *Daily Mirror*, used to 'OK' payments to several regular MP contacts, both for stories, info' and tip-offs. At least two of them were prominent MPs – one is a Cabinet minister of such prominence as to be in the first four of potential premiers.

That is one way any enterprising newspaper gets what the Party calls 'leaks'. Another way more accurately justifies that description. MPs leak around the bar. Being no less human than subs, some MPs 'knock 'em back' at the bar and, being less absorptive than reporters, become lubricated into loquacity.

No worthwhile reporter could fail to get the stuff. If he knew no other way, and had no other contacts, all he would have to do would be to spend his time, and the paper's money, at the bar and if he did not pick up enough bits and pieces from MPs in search of refreshment to make a first-rate story, he ought to be fired. Herbert Morrison is not half the Party 'boss' he is accused of being – if he were he would put the bar out of bounds to Labour MPs, some of whom have succeeded in approaching the fringe of semi-sobriety.

Herbert Morrison was on the Privileges Committee. A motion was put to discharge Allighan for contempt.

The committee called in the editors of every daily title to give evidence. They were all sworn in, except Peter Zinkin of the *Daily Worker*, who affirmed. The *Evening Standard* editor admitted that he paid £330 a week to the *Trans-Atlantic News Agency* for political reports and that two detailed accounts of a private Labour Party meeting over the lowering of the length of National Service that had recently appeared in his newspaper were authored by Gary Allighan. Allighan, who admitted having a controlling interest in the news agency, though a nominee was registered as proprietor, told the gathering he had supplied reports of the meeting out of journalistic duty which he had seen ('wrongly' he said) as higher than his duty as a politician. (At the time, 22 MPs were members of the National Union of Journalists.) Allighan's article had appeared in the *World Press News* on 3 April 1947. The committee's inquiry began at a time when full details of the meeting were splashed across ten evening and daily newspapers.

The plot thickened when the editor of the *Evening News* admitted paying £35 weekly to an MP source, though he would not reveal whom. It was not Allighan.

The Privileges Committee Report, censuring the MP severely, said Allighan had aggravated his contempt by trying to cast suspicion on other MPs beside himself.

Allighan let off steam in the *Evening Standard*:

> Who could have taken the speeches down? I reply: anyone of the score or more MPs who can be seen at every Party meeting making voluminous notes. On one occasion – here I 'leak' – the chairman had to appeal to them to restrain their note-taking energy.

He admitted he had occasionally leaked a couple of reports, and called for the private meetings to be opened, saying 'secret diplomacy' was evil.

Next, the committee received a letter from Allighan's doctor, saying the MP was on the brink of a nervous breakdown and had made arrangements to travel to South Africa to rest.

On 4 August, Evelyn Walkden, Labour MP for West Riding, rose up nervously to make a 'personal statement' to the House. He admitted giving information to the *Evening News*, whose reporter had 'protected' him as a source. He described how he would receive the £35 payment more or less each week, sometimes over a cup of tea with the lobby correspondent. However, the former trade union official said that he had disclosed his £35 to the Inland Revenue. He survived.

On 30 October the same year, with the Privileges Committee Report on the table, the Commons voted to expel Gary Allighan, who thus became, in 1947, the most recent MP to be expelled from the House. He moved to South Africa, where he became Principal at the Premier School of Journalism in Johannesburg and wrote numerous books.

Allighan said that on the eve of his election in 1945, he, Hector McNeil and Michael Foot had made a solemn promise never to drink alcohol in the House. Perhaps if he had drunk a little more, and published a little less under his own name, he would have stayed the course. Dozens of other MPs quietly altered their arrangements with the press as a result of this episode, and some (though not all) of the practices Allighan alleged were swiftly and silently ended.

TOM DRIBERG – 1942–76

One That Got Away

'Sex is only enjoyable,' said the professionally outrageous left-wing Labour MP Tom Driberg, 'with someone you have never met before and will never meet again.' From the 'cottages' (public lavatories) of London, to the large underground urinal behind the Metropole Hotel in Moscow – the delights of which he revealed to the spy Guy Burgess – and his regular trips to Westminster privies with House of Commons kitchen staff, Driberg had, in his own words, 'a chronic, life-long, love-hate relationship with lavatories'. Tom Driberg was an early but enthusiastic apostle of the doctrine that there is no such thing as a heterosexual male, but some are a bit obstinate.

This was one great scandal which, ever hinted at, never functioned as a scandal. It is only thanks to Driberg's frank but unfinished autobiography, *Ruling Passions*, published after his death in 1976, that a wider public can share a secret which was common knowledge at Westminster. Indeed, even beyond. After Matthew Parris joined the Foreign Office in 1976 he was asked to compile a guest list of 'cultured' MPs to accompany the Foreign Secretary, Jim Callaghan, when he entertained his Scandinavian counterpart at the opera at Covent Garden. It struck him that Driberg was suitable and he included his name. His head of department struck it out. He asked him why. 'Can't say,' he said, 'but don't ever include Driberg. On anything.'

Everybody who needed to, knew. But somehow knowledge never went wider. Driberg had friends in Fleet Street and contacts in MI5 and MI6. His veiled threat to expose other gay parliamentary colleagues would, if carried out, have kept the headline writers occupied for years and taken us further 'back to basics' than we quite wish to go.

During his adult life it was rare for the MP for Maldon in Essex (and later for Barking) to go more than a few days without sex. Even two happily married Labour leaders were not safe from Driberg's voracious sexual appetite.

He had started early. At the age of ten, his first fumblings with another boy in the cubicles at school encouraged him to explore the local public lavatories. His first true sexual experience soon followed: 'the impatient sperm would not be contained and the coming was a good deal hotter and faster than that of the Magi', he recalled, with characteristic restraint, in his autobiography. At Oxford, seducing a don, he 'managed what I have experienced, otherwise, only once in my life – an exercise in soixante-neuf culminating in exactly simultaneous ejaculations'. He left Christ Church without taking a degree.

From 1933 to 1943 he wrote the William Hickey gossip column on the *Daily Express*, 'These Names Make News'. At the time he had his closest brush with scandal. He picked up two unemployed miners in the street and took them back to his flat. He later insisted that the reason they all ended up in his bed was that there was nowhere else for any of them to sleep. One of the men began to doubt Driberg's altruism when a straying hand stroked his groin. He went hotfoot to the nearest police station. Driberg's subsequent trial for indecent assault, at which he was found not guilty, was kept out of the press only after Lord Beaverbrook, proprietor of the *Daily Express*, brought his considerable influence to bear on the whole of Fleet Street.

It was 1942 when Driberg was first elected – as Independent MP for Maldon, at the age of 37. (He took the Labour whip in January 1945.) Early Essex man was kept in the dark from the very start about the bachelor MP's proclivities. 'In the often ridiculous document called an election address, which every candidate issues, such details as *Married, with two children* are usually included . . . I should have had to put *Homosexual, promiscuous*. I don't think there would have been many votes in that.'

At Westminster Driberg was less circumspect. How he avoided public scandal has long been the subject of debate among his contemporaries. Chapman Pincher suggests: 'Driberg's long relationship with MI5 solves the mystery of why such a notorious homosexual, who was repeatedly caught in the act publicly by the police, was never successfully prosecuted.' Driberg had a more down-to-earth explanation. He boasted to friends that no government would dare allow prosecution, because they could never be certain how many of Driberg's conquests would be revealed on their own benches. He also claimed that any British

Tom Driberg by Marc

police constable would take a bribe if it were large enough and in cash. The trick, he said, was to keep a substantial roll of banknotes on one's person at all times.

Driberg recalled only two close shaves during his time as an MP. The first was in Edinburgh during the Second World War, when he accompanied a Norwegian sailor to an empty air-raid shelter. He was just about to attend to the man's 'long, uncircumcized, and tapering, but rock-hard erection' when 'we were caught, almost wet-handed' by two policemen. The quick-thinking MP remembered that at his 1935 trial a policeman had told him that if he had known that Driberg was William Hickey of the *Express* he would never have arrested him. Driberg flourished his press card at the bobby. 'Good God, man, I've read ye all of my life! Every morning,' said the bobby. The danger having passed, Driberg got talking to the policeman; 'I liked him and thought him attractive, but judged that it would be going too far, in the circumstances, to make a pass.'

His second scrape was in one of his favourite public conveniences in Jockey's Fields, off Theobalds Road, London. His chosen mate turned out to be a policeman posing as an *agent provocateur*. Using the same approach as in Edinburgh, Driberg achieved the same result. He reinforced the message with 'an assurance that any charge would be hotly resisted, with benefit of learned counsel and the evidence of a genito-urinary specialist, if necessary in court after court'.

Columnist George Gale once pointed out that it was not only Driberg's own reputation which was at risk from his behaviour. His sexual appetite remained as strong as ever at party conferences, so that 'in a town crawling with delegates, reporters and photographers, he risked his own career, the success of his cause and the welfare of his party all for the sake of a snatched few seconds of mutual masturbation'.

Few attractive men were safe from Driberg's attentions. He was a regular at Ronnie Kray's flat, where as one biographer put it, 'rough, but compliant East End lads were served like so many canapés'. He once propositioned Mick Jagger with the line: 'Oh my, Mick, *what* a big basket you have!' The rock star did nothing more than blush. Francis Wheen, in his biography of Driberg, tells the story of the night when the MP met a uniformed policeman walking across Hungerford Bridge, and 'without a word, after the merest glance of consent, I knelt down and fellated him.'

One of his few dislikes – he shared it, as so little else, with Mrs Thatcher – was a horror of beards. The *Times Literary Supplement*, reviewing his autobiography, noted that 'men with beards were immune from his passions. This may explain the high incidence of beards on the Labour Left.' Driberg paid a high price for his one-man crusade to convert every clean-shaven male in the Palace of Westminster. He was denied the ministerial office his intelligence might have merited. He knew very well why, branding Attlee and Wilson 'deeply prejudiced puritans'. This seems a little harsh.

The announcement in 1951 of his intended marriage to Ena Binfield caused disbelief at Westminster. Churchill, shown a picture of the strikingly plain bride-to-be, remarked, 'Oh well, buggers can't be choosers.' A policeman at the Commons expressed sympathy for Binfield: 'Poor lady, she won't know which way to turn.' Evelyn Waugh, unable to attend the wedding, wrote to Driberg: 'I will think of you intently on the day and pray that the church is not struck by lightning.'

In his spare time, Driberg carved a reputation as a fairly serious figure on the Labour Left. He passed for a wit. Woodrow Wyatt says he could never take the Speaker seriously when he declared 'The Clerk will now proceed to read the Orders of the Day' after Driberg had dug the newly elected Wyatt in the ribs and, *sotto voce*, sung the lines to the tune of *John Brown's Body*.

He supplemented his MP's pay in the early 1970s by anonymously compiling the crosswords for *Private Eye*. One puzzle, fairly typical of his output, contained the clues 'seamen mop up anal infusions' (enemas) and 'sounds as though you must look behind for this personal lubricant' (sebum). The £2 prize on this occasion was won by a Mrs Rosalind Runcie of St Albans, Hertfordshire. It is not clear whether she had any help from her husband, the local bishop, later Archbishop of Canterbury.

One London cabbie, at least, had a lucky escape. On 12 August 1976, when Driberg was dashing to a lunch in the City, he keeled over in the back of a taxi and died from a heart attack. His autobiography had been started. Seventy thousand words had been written. Friends feared the worst. He had told colleagues that both the style and content would be forthright and explicit. When it finally appeared nearly a year after his death it provoked outrage from politicians, but they were lucky. The *Sunday Times* noted that he did not get beyond his entry into Parliament in 1942. 'Sadly, the author took the saucier secrets of the Palace of Westminster to the grave with him.'

Walter Terry, political editor of the *Sun*, labelled it a 'devastating, stomach-turning document. Probably the biggest outpouring of literary dung a public figure has ever flung into print.' Lord George Brown called it 'beastly' in the *London Evening News* and the usually restrained *Economist* titled its review: 'Pederast's Progress'. The *Sunday Telegraph* condemned Driberg's 'vicious life'. Immorality in high places was nothing new, the paper said, but 'Driberg's autobiography surely sets a new low which is unlikely to pass unnoticed in the rest of the world'.

The inconvenient timing of his death robs us of confirmation of two of Driberg's most daring alleged exploits. Francis Wheen, in *Tom Driberg: His Life and Indiscretions*, claims Driberg knelt to administer oral sex on his hero Nye Bevan in the Labour Leader's office at the Commons. The fiery Welshman is alleged to have shouted enthusiastically: 'Tell me a story, Tom, tell me a story!' – a request Driberg was in no position to grant. Driberg bragged that he could disprove the rumour that Bevan was a eunuch – his penis was, said Driberg, 'long, but a trifle thin'.

Woodrow Wyatt, in his 1985 memoirs, recalled a story told him, he said, by the former Labour Prime Minister, Jim Callaghan. Driberg and Callaghan were returning to London after a meeting, and stopped to urinate by the roadside. Driberg grabbed Callaghan's penis and commented, 'You've got a very pretty one there.' Callaghan retreated fast. Later he denied the story. Wyatt refused to comment and is now dead. Callaghan is in the House of Lords, while the late Mr Driberg is probably in the other Hades.

JOHN BELCHER – 1948

'A gift from some of John's acquaintances'

John Belcher was the only minister in Clement Attlee's astonishingly clean post-war government to resign after a scandal. We look back from an era of 'cash-for-questions' scandals to an era of post-war rationing, and a 'groceries-for-questions' affair. Sherry, burgundy, whisky, meals out, lunch and a suit featured among the gifts from an unscrupulous lobbyist, 'the Spider of Park Lane', who boasted that he had more than one government minister on his books. These boasts may have exaggerated both his influence and the complicity of politicians.

John Belcher was the first minister fingered. With Britain still in the grip of rationing, Mr Belcher's crime was allowing himself to be showered with gifts by one of Westminster's first political lobbyists. The junior Trade minister accepted a holiday for his family in Margate, another in Bournemouth, a £68 gold cigarette case, a three-piece suit, lavish entertaining at Harringay dog track and boxing matches at Bethnal Green. The gifts came from the Spider, Sydney Stanley, king of the fixers in the thriving black economy under post-war austerity. Belcher met him in April 1947, a year after becoming a minister. Within a month he was enjoying a holiday in Margate.

Polish-born Stanley, alias Kohsyzcky, Rechtand or Wulkan, was an undischarged bankrupt with a 1933 deportation order outstanding against him. Despite his physical appearance (one writer described him as 'five feet three . . . portly and ill-formed . . . a wide flat face and deep-set eyes') he persuaded the distrustful business community that it could work with the new socialist government, and that he could be a bridge. He spent more than £60,000 a year on entertaining to prove his point. Belcher, a former Great Western Railway clerk, had been elected MP for Sowerby in Yorkshire in 1945, and made a minister within a year. He was quickly ensnared in the web of the Spider.

Forty-three-year-old Belcher was genuinely keen to establish good relations with the business world. His 'door was always open'. Open, for instance, to Sir Maurice Bloch, head of the Glasgow distillers, Bloch Brothers Ltd. In a two-month period Bloch gave Belcher 56 bottles of sherry, burgundy and whisky – unimaginably precious commodities in post-war London – in return, it was said, for three import licences for 'essential' business supplies.

None could match the generosity of the Spider. For Belcher's birthday, Stanley threw a dinner party at the Garter Club. The bill for half a dozen people was £89, lavish at the prices of the day. At the same time, Stanley was promising businessmen that his friend the minister could open doors for them. Belcher's friends, and they were many, doubt that he did sell his influence in the way Stanley claimed, but he did accept gifts.

In August 1948 two business contacts became suspicious. Stanley had persuaded Harry Sherman, head of Sherman's Football Pools, that he could get Belcher to drop a prosecution against the company that had resulted from Sherman's breach of the paper-rationing regulations in the production of coupons.

Star, 3 February 1949

Another company, Stagg & Russell Ltd, had paid Stanley £10,000 for an import licence for amusement arcade machines. Harry Sherman complained to an official in Belcher's office; Stagg & Russell went to the police.

On 30 August Harold Wilson, then President of the Board of Trade and Belcher's boss, was told about Sherman's claims. He informed the police, the Prime Minister and the Lord Chancellor. A tribunal was set up under Mr Justice Lynskey and Belcher was asked to go on leave for the duration as the 26-day tribunal heard about the extent of the 'cash-for-favours' scandals.

The press (much of which were looking for sticks to beat the postwar Labour government) went to town. Other government ministers were named. Charles Key, the Minister of Works, had progressed from lunches and bottled beverages from Stanley, to a first fitting for a suit! George Gibson, a director of the Bank of England, was censured for abusing his position with Stanley to gain material advantage.

Lynskey's 50,000-word report was published in January 1949. It was withering in its denunciation of Stanley: 'a man who will make any statement, whether true or untrue, if he thinks that it is to his own advantage'.

Belcher was found guilty of using his influence as a minister in return for 'small gifts and hospitality'. His constituency party scheduled a meeting to consider his future as an MP for 26 February (he had already resigned as a minister during the tribunal's inquiry). He saved them the trouble and resigned on the day the report was debated in the Commons: 3 February 1949.

His wife, Louise, insisted she had never accepted any gifts. Tracked down in a West End restaurant, she held up her hands in reply to reporters' questions, and declared: 'Those are the hands of a working woman – not hands ready for gifts from anyone.' With quiet pride she claimed she had saved £20 out of her housekeeping to buy herself what in those days was called a 'costume'. 'But now how can I buy it? How can I escape the censure of women whose eyes tell me they believe it was a gift to me from some of John's acquaintances!'

There was sympathy for the couple. Calling the affair 'a terrible tragedy', Attlee said, 'He has spoken with dignity and with courage.' Herbert Morrison said MPs felt 'understanding'. Churchill heard the resignation speech 'with pain'. Many felt

Belcher had been more naive than corrupt in his choice of friends and acceptance of gifts.

Humiliated, Belcher had to return to his former job as a railway clerk. In 1960, Harold Wilson intervened personally to help his former minister, who faced prosecution for tax arrears. Belcher retired from the railways in 1963, and died the following year.

In a letter to one of the authors, John Belcher's daughter, Jill Mumford, said 'He trusted people who proved to be false and it cost him everything . . .

'My parents received hundreds of letters in the following months and they are notable for their support and sympathy. Many of these were from people of different political views who nevertheless felt that my father had acted honourably.

'In 1990 Radio 4 broadcast a series of programmes, *Public Affairs*, one of which examined the Lynskey Tribunal and concluded that my father had paid an incredibly high price for his unwise choice of friends. Although I was too young at the time to understand what was going on, I have since met many people who have expressed their sadness at my father's downfall. My sister and I recently visited his constituency and were fortunate to talk with Labour Party members who still remember those days. They all spoke warmly of our father and felt that he would have been re-elected if he had stood again for Parliament ...

'My mother, Louisa was cross-examined and forced to give details about her most private affairs. She was found to be transparently honest, but she collapsed after giving evidence and later suffered a series of nervous breakdowns, after which she never fully regained her mental health.'

It was after this case that Attlee set up a committee to look at the problem of middlemen and consultants. It reported in October 1949 that 'common sense and vigilance' were the only necessary safeguards against corruption, an observation of quite blinding futility.

CAPTAIN PETER BAKER – 1950

'I've been ill for a long time'

The Times of Wednesday, 1 December 1954, carried a photograph of the Queen in full regalia walking through the Royal Chamber at the Lords, to open the Parliament. But the new Commons session was to be without its member for South Norfolk. A headline above and just to the left of the Queen and her robe-carriers offers a brutal summary: 'MP Sent to Prison – Seven Years for Forgery'. Captain Peter Baker, at 33 the youngest MP in the House, was bound for Wormwood Scrubs, forged bills of exchange for thousands of pounds flying in the breeze behind him, his companies sinking, brandy and anti-depressants now his only comfort.

This would not be Captain Baker's first experience of being held captive. The son of an army major, his career had begun in the Royal Artillery and he had earned a Military Cross in the Second World War after working for the Dutch resistance movement, when he was twice captured and twice tried to escape. Elected in 1950, he was already running numerous businesses when he entered the House. Captain Baker had energy to spare. In his short parliamentary career he had had a dozen run-ins with the Tory whips, including the then Chief Whip, Edward Heath, over diverse issues. Each time he had been headed back into the fold. Party managers strained to control him: but neither his heart specialist, abdominal specialist, neurologist or three auxiliary doctors who 'drugged me, injected me, massaged me and cajoled me' could persuade him to rest. Sorrow in the whips' office at his jail sentence will have been mitigated.

When finally brought in to the Old Bailey, Baker blamed liquor, exhaustion, and his increasingly volatile mental state, for both his fraudulent actions and his inability to recall them: his failure, for instance, properly to remember the forging of signatures such as those on twelve bills of exchange worth a total of £13,200; or the letter which accompanied them, supposedly written by Sir John Mann, partner in the brewery, which Baker had simply dictated to his typist. The letter authorized him to use the bills as he chose, and helped secure an £8,500 loan from the Edgware Trust. Sir John was wholly unaware of it.

This is just a detail in a tangled picture, for which Baker was to apologize in an abject letter to the House; and on which he was to expand later in his autobiography, finished two days before he pleaded guilty at the Old Bailey. He called the book *My Testament*.

Testimony was certainly called for. Captain Baker had tried to combine his role as politician with the chairmanship of a raft of companies, including four publishing houses, a wine merchant, an aircraft company, a whisky company, and television, radio, investment and property companies based off Pall Mall and in their heyday employing over 500 people. Publishing was a fascination this MP shared with, for instance, Robert Maxwell and Horatio Bottomley. Indeed Baker dealt with Maxwell, selling him his British Book Center in New York, and considering the then unknown businessman 'a remarkable character.' The interest that publishing holds for MPs is curious. Michael Heseltine also began his business career in this way.

And it was publishing which most agitated Baker's finances and his health. In July 1950 his publishing houses were over-spending and under-selling. 'While publishing was the cause of many of my subsequent worries and certainly a contributory cause to my ill-health, it also brought me more happiness than any other activity except politics,' he wrote. At one stage his secretary was a Mrs M. Spark, who has included Baker in one of her novels.

Within three years, and facing a liquidity crisis, his business conduct turned seriously fraudulent. Four thousand pounds from the Edgware Trust loan went to his Falcon Press, and £2,500 to his father who, the court heard, was now a major creditor of many of his son's seventeen companies. Between December 1953 and May 1954, six of the Bills of Exchange matured and were paid. But on 9 June an attentive cashier noticed irregularities in the seventh signature. The bill was not honoured.

Baker then went to the Bank of America for £3,000. Asked for guarantors (the bank was not content with his father's word) Baker went back to his secretary's typewriter, producing a guarantee 'signed' by Bernard Docker, an industrialist, and another by one Owen David. He obtained a £2,500 overdraft. Next came a loan for £49,000 from Barclays, secured on three forged signatures – Docker, Mann and a Mr Reynolds. From this Barclays account Baker transferred £11,000 to his earlier creditor, the Bank of America, £4,500 to a firm of solicitors involved with his businesses, and £33,000 to the Peregrine Press account at the National Provincial Bank. Out of this £33,000 he drew £18,000 over ten days for his own Provincial account. Then he spent £12,000 on a controlling share in a whisky company. Barclays never saw its £49,000 again.

Baker's bizarre business activity was taking place against the backdrop of an ever more complicated political life. His mind was beginning to float off course. According to Baker, 'There were whole weeks in 1953 and 1954 that I cannot remember. Often I had to check up in *Hansard* to make sure I had attended the Commons and voted.' He may not have attended as assiduously as he should. Challenged in the Smoking Room by Sir Charles McAndrew, who as a Deputy Speaker ought to have known every MP but could not recall Baker, the MP replied: 'Please don't apologize, I have no idea who you are either.' This would have been funnier if it had been meant as a gibe.

In *My Testament*, Baker explained:

> Falcon proved a constant worry, and in Parliament, the Budget and the Finance Bill brought me the worst all-night sittings on record . . . for four days and nights in succession . . . with all-night sittings at the House and Board meetings during the day, I never went to bed. However, I needed a flask of brandy always by me to see me through it. Despite sedatives, sleeping pills and draughts, I had practically no sleep during these years, however tired I became.

It was a wonder he ever went into politics at all. 'I could not reconcile myself to the policies of either of the main parties,' he wrote, perhaps rather late in the day.

He corresponded with the whips several times, offering to resign, but was dissuaded. Persuaded to vote with his party for German rearmament, he said to the whips' office: 'I shall vote with you for three reasons. Firstly, because I believe that a rearmed Germany, with a European Defence Community, is just the least of four possible evils. Secondly, because I want my summer holidays. And thirdly because without a German Army, you [the Tory whips] would be the last survival of Prussianism in Europe.'

And still his businesses sank deeper into loss. In the end the banks lost a total of £102,000, of which £22,720 was traced directly to Baker. It was not, however, suggested that money was being diverted for his personal enrichment. Unlike Horatio Bottomley, Baker's crooked dealings were designed to shore up real but failing businesses: not as fronts to rob the public.

On 28 May Baker was summoned to an important meeting by the industrialist Bernard Docker and Sir John Mann. Docker waved a phantom guarantee at Baker. Baker paused, and said: 'I've been ill for a long time.' The breakdown had come at last.

He was arrested at the Holloway Sanatorium by a Chief Superintendent he already knew socially and he spent the night in a cell with drunken women and prostitutes. 'During the last twelve months before entering a Nursing Home I had at least thirty daytime blackouts and was twice taken to hospital after half-hearted attempts at suicide. My mind varied from unreliable pin-sharp brilliance to complete inability to record events and conversations. The rest that I had refused to take was bound to force itself upon me.'

Baker's first reaction was to plead not guilty at a Bow Street committal, but at the Old Bailey he admitted six charges of forgery. He received seven years. When Baker was ushered away, the prison escort whispered: 'Seems like a long time to me,' at which Baker hissed: 'Sounds a bloody sight longer to me.'

His term began at Wormwood Scrubs before he was transferred to Leyhill Prison Without Bars in Gloucestershire. In prison he wrote another book, *Time Out of Life*. Baker, who was married with two daughters, was released in 1959 and discharged from bankruptcy in 1962. In 1963 he petitioned unsuccessfully for a Queen's pardon and died in Eastbourne in November 1966.

IAN HARVEY – 1958

'The Eleventh Commandment: thou shalt not be caught'

Thus wrote Ian Harvey. 'Tory MP Caught in Bush with Guardsman', the headlines would proclaim today. '£5 fine on Ian Harvey. He will pay to end of life,' rumbled *The Times* on 11 December 1958. They were right. Ian Harvey was a minister. Fined for indecency with a young Coldstream Guard, he knew his parliamentary career was over. He was the first in a depressing roll-call of Macmillan's ministers brought down by scandal.

Harvey had started playing with fire and guardsmen five years before becoming MP for Harrow East in 1950. Now, living in fashionable Trevor Square, off Hyde Park, he was well placed to pick up troopers from the Knightsbridge barracks of the Household Cavalry. From a young age he had known he was homosexual, but ambition had dictated pragmatism and in 1949 he had married Clare Mayhew, sister of the Labour MP and broadcaster Christopher Mayhew, now a peer. The union satisfied his constituency supporters who, as he recalled in his autobiography, *To Fall Like Lucifer*, 'thought it was a mistake to have a candidate who was a bachelor and over thirty'. Glamorous Mrs Harvey was wheeled in. It worked and the following year her husband was elected MP for Harrow East.

Mr Harvey did not let marriage or political office interrupt his forays into Hyde Park. 'I discovered a very convenient place near the Peter Pan statue in Kensington Gardens. J. M. Barrie, unlike some of his predecessors, would hardly have approved. Peter Pan had his back to us so I could not be accused of polluting the young.'

Harvey, who had been singled out as a serious talent, was taking a great risk. In 1958 the maximum sentence for any form of homosexual conduct was five years in prison. 'In view of my undoubted political ambitions this conduct could well be adjudged as verging on insanity. Every time it was over I pretended to myself that this was definitely the last time. I knew

139

MP and Guardsman accused

JUNIOR MINISTER ON 'OFFENCE IN PARK' CHARGES

Daily Express, 21 November 1958

perfectly well . . . exactly what would happen if I were caught.' He would be back in his usual spot the very next night.

In 1953 he was given a stark reminder of what could lie in store. The Labour MP William Field, fined £15 for importuning in a public lavatory, was forced to resign. 'This should have shown me the red light,' said Harvey.

Born in Surrey in 1914 seven months before the outbreak of the First World War, Harvey enjoyed a comfortable middle-class upbringing. He attended Fettes College (Tony Blair's old school) in Scotland and Christ Church College, Oxford, where he was President of the Union. After a distinguished wartime career he went on to a successful job in advertising and wrote a noted book, *Techniques of Persuasion*.

He moved into politics, serving his apprenticeship in local government. His wartime service enabled him to make his mark in Parliament as a member of a Commons Select Committee whose advice reinforced draconian punishments for practising homosexuals in the armed forces. He rapidly became known as one of Macmillan's abler young supporters. In 1956 he was a popular choice as Parliamentary Secretary at the Ministry of Supply. When Macmillan became Prime Minister the following year, Harvey was promoted to the Foreign Office. Two years later, he fell like Lucifer.

After dinner at the Polish embassy on Wednesday 19 November 1958, temptation proved too strong. Just after 11 p.m. when the guardsmen would be returning from the pubs to the Wellington Barracks, Harvey followed his normal routine and walked along the Mall, another favourite pick-up point. A teenage guardsman in uniform caught the minister's eye. He caught up with him and they went into St James's Park. They had no intention of feeding the ducks. A few minutes after they disappeared into a bush the harsh glare of a torch beam interrupted them. A policeman and park-keeper had heard a rustling noise in the bushes. *The Times* reported: 'They saw two men standing under a tree misbehaving.'

Harvey panicked and on the way to Cannon Row police station attempted to make a run for it. But ministerial life had already taken its toll, he tired, and was swiftly recaptured. At first he gave the duty sergeant a false name and address. To no avail. They knew exactly who he was. Harvey owned up.

The following morning the 44-year-old minister and the nineteen-year-old guardsman, Anthony Walter Plant, were charged with gross indecency and breaching the park's regulations by behaving in a way likely to offend against public decency. The case was adjourned. A 100-strong crowd was waiting outside the court. The minister made his escape in a taxi in the direction of Whitehall, but his two-minute court appearance, standing next to the slim, fair-haired soldier in blue dress uniform, made the front pages of the evening newspapers.

Harvey's local party pledged to stand by him, but the day after his court appearance he told the Prime Minister he intended to resign from Parliament. Though Macmillan, who desperately wanted to avoid a by-election, begged him to reconsider over the weekend, Harvey's mind was already made up.

When the case came to court the second time on 10 December, the gross indecency charge had been dropped. Counsel for Plant said he was young and naïve, and 'as far as could be traced was not addicted in this way'. Returning from his fiancée's home in north London, he had only gone into the park with Harvey 'out of curiosity'. They were fined £5 each for breaching park regulations. Harvey paid Plant's fine. 'I felt it was the least I could do,' he said.

As he left the court he was mobbed by the press. Rather than run for cover he faced the music for ten minutes in the hope 'that if I got it all over there and then I was less likely to be plagued for interviews on the telephone . . . I felt no resentment because I knew that they were only doing their job and I wanted to make it as easy for them as I could.'

Harvey was resigned to being ostracized by former friends. 'The Conservative Party, quite understandably because of its outlook and make-up, did not want to know anything more about me.' Nor did any of his clubs. The Carlton Club accepted his resignation without comment. The Junior Carlton Club would allow him to keep his membership only if he did not set foot in it for two years. 'I thought this was rather an expensive indignity, so I declined to give the assurance and resigned.' The chairman of Pratt's showed mercy and urged him to stay. 'I knew, however, that there were a number of members who were less broad-minded.' He faced a further ordeal: dishonourable discharge from the Territorial Army despite his distinguished war record. It required the intervention of Hugh Fraser, a junior minister at the War Office, to spare him this fresh humiliation.

For more than two years he faced what he called 'purgatory. I went to several psychiatrists – the first treated me like a twit, as if I was simple-minded – and I drank a lot,' he told the *Daily Mirror* in 1972. After a period of total breakdown he became a Roman Catholic. He and his wife were divorced.

The disgraced Tory was persuaded to break his long silence by Lord Longford, the Roman Catholic Labour peer whose causes included Myra Hindley and who had consistently argued the evils of homosexuality. Harvey wrote his autobiography in 1971 and it was published by Longford's Sidgwick and Jackson publishing house. Lord Longford may have been disappointed that it shows more remorse for Harvey's folly than his homosexuality, and that he later became honorary president of the Conservative Group for Homosexual Equality. Ian wanted to help, but lacked confidence that his association would be helpful, drank too much, and would issue half-hearted invitations to members of the group to accompany him home. Everybody liked him for his self-mocking humility, but his self-denigration seemed sad. He was a broken man, and looked it. He never came to terms with his fall from power, remarking once, 'I am the best politician the Tories haven't got.'

What happened to guardsman Plant? A book of inquiries into the fates of the forgotten halves of such scandals would be absorbing, but cruel.

Ian Harvey died in 1987. His immediate successor at the Foreign Office was one John Profumo.

SIR IAN HOROBIN – 1962

A War Hero Disgraced

'I am afraid I have come to a decision which may put you to some trouble,' the war hero and former Tory minister Sir Ian Horobin wrote to Macmillan in April 1962. 'While I would not wish to be inactive, I have decided that I cannot undertake the amount of work which I now understand to be entailed by being an active member of the House of Lords.' The real reason was his impending trial for a series of sexual liaisons with East End boys.

Horobin had been a popular choice for elevation to the Upper House. After serving in the RNVR during the First World War, he was captured by the Japanese in the Second World War while serving as a squadron leader in the RAF. He was held in the notorious and overcrowded Soekaboemi prison camp in Java. He was tortured and forced to watch executions – an attempt to get him to reveal the escape route organized by his fellow inmate Sir Laurens van der Post, who called Horobin 'a person of great courage, wit and humour under appalling conditions'.

Born in 1899, Ian Horobin was the son of the Principal of

Homerton College Cambridge. Serving as an MP for Southwark (1931–5), he returned after the war as Conservative MP for Oldham East in 1951. Knighted in 1955, he served as a parliamentary secretary at the Ministry of Power in his final year, 1959.

Horobin's offer of a peerage reflected his life-long devotion to the East End. In 1923 he had practically re-founded the Mansfield House University Settlement, a young men's and boys' club, raising over half a million pounds for its upkeep. He was its warden, living in a small bedsit above the dining room.

After boxing bouts, the boys would occasionally find Horobin supervising proceedings in the communal bath area, perched on a shooting stick. They called him 'Spike'. One old boy, the actor Terence Stamp, recalls how 'there was all kinds of gossip about Sir Ian, the strongest being that he was a bit of a "ginger beer".' Despite the rumours, Stamp's autobiography describes how, aged fourteen, he was 'chuffed' to receive an invitation to Horobin's flat one Saturday afternoon to show off some paintings he had entered in a competition.

According to Stamp, Horobin, then still an MP, drew the curtains. 'He stood close to me, first looking over my shoulder, then leaning over me turning the paintings, resting his hand on my back.' But the MP's interest in the young man's artwork appears to have waned rapidly. 'He slipped his hand lightly on to my neck. It must have goose-pimpled. I was too scared to move. His other hand reached around me and rubbed the inside leg of my trousers. In spite of myself I was getting a hard-on.'

The young Terence Stamp made a run for it, but not before Horobin had pressed ten shillings into his hand and received a promise from the boy that he would not 'lag' on him. Down in the street Terence Stamp immediately told a friend, Teddy Debell, about his experience. 'He gave you half a nicker?' cried his wide-eyed mate. 'Cripes, d'you think he'll give me one?' 'Listen, Ted – he's you know, after yer ring!' 'Oh, don't worry about that. Listen, you hang about here and I'll see if I can get ten bob as well.' A few minutes later Ted was back. 'Haw, the old nanny said he was resting, still we got ten bob, where shall we go?' 'I had to laugh.' Stamp concludes, 'trust old Ted to put things in perspective.'

It is impossible to know how many such encounters, successful or otherwise, the MP attempted. When eventually confronted, he expressed surprise that it was a long-term boyfriend, seventeen-year-old Roy Girard, whom he had known for four years, who finally 'lagged'. 'I don't know how they it got out of Girard,' Horobin said, 'a boy to whom I have been virtually married (although apparently not monogamously) for some years.'

In 1961, Girard confessed after some heavy questioning from a concerned clergyman, who passed the information on to the Deputy Warden of the Settlement. When confronted, Horobin offered to resign saying he had had 'sweethearts for many years' and there was nothing wrong with his relationship with boys. 'It is natural for some men to love boys,' he told them. When offered treatment he replied: 'You must accept me as I am. I am too old to change now.'

In May 1962, both Horobin and his young friend were charged with indecency. The crown appointed Mervyn Griffith-Jones to lead the prosecution. He was later to lead the legal assault on Stephen Ward (see p.178).

The jury heard that one boy had been invited to see Horobin's stamp collection and had been 'assaulted'. Another was taken for a ride in his Rolls-Royce and offered an extra ten shillings pocket money. After declining a number of invitations to the bedsit, he finally agreed and yielded to Horobin behind locked doors. He went back a second time and received £2. When he refused a third time, Girard tried to persuade him to accompany him to the bedsit, arguing it would mean more money if he did. A third, a young groundsman who went to the bedsit 'for instructions', was said to have suffered a 'serious assault' and earned himself £1.

It was never suggested that any of the young men sustained any physical injuries from their encounters with Horobin. The liaisons were consensual, the term 'assault' being a peculiarity of legal language. The head groundsman at the Settlement told the jury that Horobin claimed to have helped the lives of far more boys than he had ever ruined. 'He told me I was lucky to be married and to love a woman,' the groundsman told the court. 'He had the misfortune to be otherwise. Referring to the law on homosexuality, he said it was a silly law and unfortunately homosexuality was against the law.'

Sentencing Horobin to four years in prison, Mr Justice Mocatta said: 'You have pleaded guilty to a number of grave and unnatural offences . . . You used your authority and position, as well as what can only be described as bribes, to persuade these young boys to submit to your indecent assaults . . . a man in your position owes a duty to others to set an example, and however unfortunate your own make-up may be, it cannot be allowed to be said that these Courts are prepared to allow this sort of conduct with boys to be carried on by people of education, position and responsibility.'

'You were led into this horrible state of affairs at a very early age and while still at school.' Girard was bound over and put on probation for three years.

Given the times, Horobin got off lightly – not just in his sentence, but also in the press. No longer an MP, his guilty plea at the trial caused even a newspaper like the *Mirror* to dwell as much on Horobin's war record as on the offences. The note struck in the article, 'Great Career of Sir Ian Ends in Jail', is regretful rather than scandalized.

Horobin served his sentence and moved to Tangier. He published a collection of poems, dedicated 'with gratitude and affection to my partners in crime', in 1972. Sir John Betjeman, whom he had met at a Soho club after his release, supplied an introduction. 'Say what you like about my odd career,' Horobin had asked the poet. 'Don't fluff anything or be apologetic. I broke the law with my eyes open all my life until I went to prison. I broke it while I was in prison. I broke it immediately I came out of prison, and have not the slightest intention of ever paying any attention to it . . . So war, warts, wit and all.'

Betjeman, describing Horobin as a 'slim, slight, cheerful man, with red cheeks, high collar, a tie-pin and a resounding voice . . . full of humour and without self-pity,' remarks: 'It seemed to me ironic that one who had been a prisoner of the Japs during the War, then served his country as a junior minister in the Macmillan administration, should have been a prisoner in the England which he loved and had served so well.'

Sir Ian Horobin died in 1976. He is still remembered with some respect by those who knew him.

> Happy lover, who can say
> 'Dear my love' by light of day;
> Nor need fear lest even night
> Should betray true love to sight.
> All my Hope can save from Dread
> Is time for Time to kill Instead.
>
> Sir Ian Horobin, *The Secret Lover*

THOMAS GALBRAITH – 1962

'Never catch a spy'

'We have arrested a spy who is a bugger and a minister is involved,' the Director of Public Prosecutions told the Attorney-General on the evening of 12 September 1962. 'Oh, that's bad news! Very bad news!' exclaimed Harold Macmillan, when told of the arrest at the Admiralty earlier that day. 'You know, you should never catch a spy. Discover him and then control him but never catch him. A spy causes far more trouble once he's caught.'

The Prime Minister was right. By the time the scandal had blown over, an obscure clerk, John Vassall, had been sent to prison; a junior minister had been forced out of office; a Cabinet minister had offered to resign; and – in a bombardment of press innuendo – Macmillan had retaliated and two journalists had been jailed. Macmillan admits in his memoirs that the outcome 'infuriated Fleet Street, at every level of activity, and made the newspapers anxious to seek and exploit any possibility of counter-attack'. Fleet Street was already prepared for its revenge. Barely twelve months later a new name would enter the popular vocabulary: Profumo.

On 22 October 1962, John Vassall, a 38-year-old clerk in the Admiralty, was sentenced to eighteen years at the Old Bailey. The Cold War was at its hottest (the Cuban Missile Crisis broke the following week). So soon after the discovery of George Blake and the Portland spy ring, the *Daily Mail* was not alone in castigating the Government for this 'latest woeful chapter in Britain's post-war catalogue of security failure'. The paper's hunt for Vassall's accomplices had already begun.

Vassall was a homosexual. When serving in the British Embassy in Moscow in the mid-1950s, he had starred in an orgy deftly stage-managed – and photographed – by the Soviet security services. Later, Vassall was helped in his decision to become a spy by a snapshot which showed him flourishing his underpants over his head in a Moscow hotel bedroom. The son of an Anglican clergyman, and a convert to Roman Catholicism, he commented in his *Autobiography of a Spy*: 'There I was, naked, grinning into the camera; naked, holding up a pair of men's briefs which must have been mine.'

The KGB's entrapment of Vassall paid off for them. Back in London he worked from 1957 until the autumn of 1959 as Assistant Private Secretary to Thomas Galbraith, Civil Lord of the Admiralty, and Conservative member for Glasgow Hillhead. Wellington and Oxford-educated and the son of the Tory peer, Lord Strathclyde, Galbraith had seemed a natural choice for the Admiralty after wartime service in the Mediterranean fleet.

Vassall's dutifulness towards the Civil Lord and his lady brought rewards. Galbraith would invite his underling to lunch and drinks in the family home in London. Vassall would make the long journey carrying secret documents to Barskimming, Galbraith's mansion in Ayrshire. Unknown to the minister, copies of the same documents were destined for the Kremlin.

After Vassall's arrest, there were rumours of a sexual liaison between the KGB spy and the 45-year-old minister. Unknown to the Government, the tabloid *Sunday Pictorial* had paid £5,000 for Vassall's story. The treacherous clerk handed over to the newspaper handwritten letters and postcards from Galbraith and his wife. These surfaced two weeks after the key was turned on Vassall at Brixton Prison. While some of the letters merely dealt with mundane office matters, the most damaging were the ones written after Galbraith moved from the Admiralty to the Scottish Office in October 1959. Vassall was then working in the military branch and did not like it. He was determined to keep in touch with his former boss, and sent him fawning postcards from his expensive holidays abroad paid for by the proceeds of his spying.

The Annual Register for 1962 later remarked that the letters revealed 'nothing more damaging than the former Civil Lord's interest in his office carpets, crockery and paper clips. The most that could be said against Mr Galbraith was that he had suffered a socially pressing and plausible junior colleague a trifle too gladly.'

The press, meanwhile, was demanding to know why a spy, working at the heart of the Government, had remained undetected for so long. Vassall was reviled by the press who, after his conviction, branded him 'a fawning mediocrity' and 'mother's boy'. The newspapers did not pull their punches: they reported that Vassall was known as 'Aunty' to junior clerks and typists, went shopping for women's underwear, and 'liked to spend the evening in the West End haunts of perverts'. They even unearthed friends from his old school, Monmouth, who were willing to turn the knife. One, Norman Stone (not the Oxford academic), described as a respectable country club owner, said: 'He was a sissy and a snob. No one who knew him then would be surprised to hear he is a homosexual.'

Newspapers asked a series of telling questions: how had Vassall charmed his way into the minister's inner circle? When it emerged that Vassall lived in an 'extravagantly furnished' Dolphin Square flat costing £10 a week on a salary of £15, they asked which minister or official had written the landlord a reference. The pressure grew on Galbraith when it emerged he had been a visitor at Vassall's luxury flat, a gaudy residence full of 'perfume bottles to an extent one would expect to find in a lady's accommodation', according to the *Pictorial*. Only after Galbraith's resignation did it emerge that the minister's visit had been a courtesy call following the death of Vassall's mother. He had been there for fifteen minutes, and had taken along his wife.

Once Vassall's trial was over, media speculation about the minister grew. Galbraith, a steady infantryman in Macmillan's government, tried to restore his reputation. On 23 October, Galbraith went to print in the *Daily Mail* – the rival *Pictorial*'s secret cache of letters, meanwhile, being guarded night and day in a fortified office in Fleet Street. Galbraith wrote:

Some people think he was a great buddy of mine, but in my six years as a departmental minister I have had over thirty officials in my house. I felt rather sorry for him – I felt he had a screw loose.

Vassall would have coffee in the drawing-room while the bag was taken to my study, where I took out those things that needed urgent action. Sometimes he stayed to lunch.

My relations with him were not different from those with other civil servants. The only thing that struck me as strange was his flat. But I believed he had been left money.

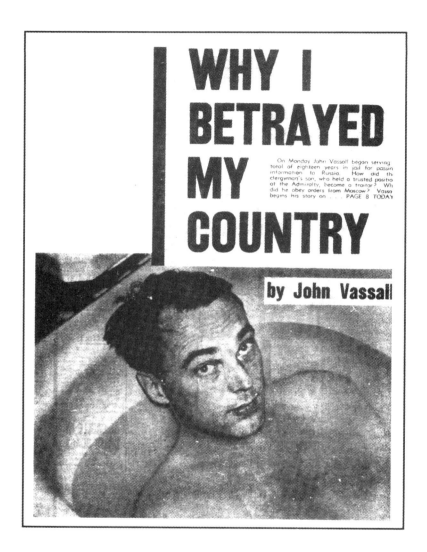

WHY I BETRAYED MY COUNTRY

On Monday John Vassall began serving total of eighteen years in jail for passing information to Russia. How did the clergyman's son, who held a trusted position at the Admiralty, become a traitor? Why did he obey orders from Moscow? Vassall begins his story on . . . PAGE 8 TODAY

by John Vassall

Sunday Pictorial, 28 October 1962

Galbraith's comments only made matters worse. It confirmed the suspicion widespread at Westminster and in the media that Vassall enjoyed unusually privileged access to the minister. The press seized on the contradictions in the article. If he had a 'screw loose', why was he permitted to carry secret documents around the country? The minister's comments merely fuelled the rumours of a sexual relationship between the two men. So much so that seven days later, on 1 November, Galbraith issued a statement through his lawyers declaring that he had not known Vassall was a homosexual. He stressed the point that Vassall had never stayed a single night at Galbraith's Scottish estate.

The media worked hard. Mrs Doris Murray, Vassall's cleaning lady, attracted their inquiries. She proved a sensational witness. In a taped interview with a journalist she insisted Galbraith had visited the Dolphin Square flat alone at least once. Dusting the ornaments on the mantelpiece, she saw the two men enter the bedroom together. They emerged fifteen minutes later. Vassall kept a framed photograph of his former ministerial master in the flat. Fortunately for the Government some of these allegations were too racy for the fastidious 1960s press.

On Friday 2 November, about a week and a half after Vassall's conviction, two Opposition frontbenchers, Patrick Gordon Walker and George Brown, demanded to know how Vassall's homosexuality and high spending had gone unnoticed for so long. Peter Thorneycroft, the Minister of Defence, later (to his amusement) Mrs Thatcher's first Chairman of the Conservative Party, blundered badly, lightly misreading public unease over the spate of spy scandals. 'It is very easy afterwards,' remarked Thorneycroft, 'when a man has put up his homosexual tendencies in defence, to say that you can identify them by just glancing at them. That is an illusion.' When asked about Vassall's expensive flat he replied with more candour than finesse: 'How many of us are living above our incomes in London squares?' There was an audible gasp of disbelief even from his own backbenchers. Thorneycroft claimed that the matter had been blown out of all proportion but he had himself unwittingly done some of the blowing. 'I really think some restraint ought to be exercised in public comment on these matters.'

The press became more determined than ever to arrange a ministerial funeral.

Days later, the *Sunday Pictorial* revealed its letters. Serializing Vassall's explicit life-story, illustrated by provocative photographs of the spy reclining semi-naked in bed, the newspaper primly proclaimed it had passed vital documents, which implicated a minister, to the Government. The letters from Galbraith were handed to an internal inquiry looking at the security implications.

But the *Pictorial* struck a cruel blow at the Government by sending an identical package to Hugh Gaitskell, the Leader of the Opposition, and his deputy George Brown. The following Tuesday, George Brown told the Commons that letters which he had just received 'indicated a degree of ministerial responsibility which goes far beyond the ordinary business of a minister'. There was consternation on the Tory benches when they realized Labour had been handed such explosive ammunition. Gaitskell calmly observed that he could not believe the Conservatives had not been passed documents by the press when they were in Opposition.

The next day, the *Daily Mail* led with 'Postcard to a Spy':

Amid the pile of correspondence is a postcard sent during a holiday abroad to Vassall by a leading figure. The same person wrote a letter to Vassall. His wife also sent a note of some length. The discovery of the picture postcard from abroad does not mean that there was any sexually improper relationship. It does indicate, the Opposition believes, a friendliness which one would not expect to exist between a clerk and a senior colleague.

What masters are English newspapers of the verbal wink! The 'leading figure' was not named. He did not have to be. Galbraith's fumbling attempts to clear his name had focused the spotlight even more keenly on his relationship with the homosexual spy. Later that day Sir Charles Cunningham, heading the internal inquiry, published the celebrated letters under the heading: 'The relationship between Vassall and those for whom he worked'. The decision to publish, sanctioned by Macmillan, meant the battle to keep the Government clear of the Vassall affair had been lost. Galbraith had to go.

The following day the newspapers printed the letters, the *Daily Express* running them under the banner headline: 'My Dear Vassall'. Within hours Galbraith had resigned. The internal inquiry had found no evidence of any impropriety in the minister's relationship with his clerk, but, in his resignation letter to the Prime Minister, the minister conceded:

> It is apparent to me that my accustomed manner of dealing with officials and others who serve me has in the circumstances become an embarrassment to you and the government. For this reason alone I feel that my only proper course is to tender my resignation.

The resignation failed to stop a rot so widely enjoyed. The *Express* carried a new set of allegations: Lord Carrington, First Lord of the Admiralty and Galbraith's former ministerial boss, was accused of having known about the presence of another spy in his department when the Portland spy ring was exposed, a full eighteen months before Vassall's arrest.

Then a *Daily Sketch* journalist had dinner with Conservative MP Peter Tapsell. Even today, exactly what was said that night is the subject of much debate, but what is clear is that Macmillan was rocked by the report he received of the meeting. He went to the Commons on 14 November to announce the reasons why he had set up an independent tribunal into the affair. What Macmillan said was a sensation: 'One of the staff of the paper [the *Daily Sketch*], had been told by a member of the police, or the security service, he was not sure which, that had Vassall not been arrested on 12 September it had been his intention to join Mr Galbraith in Italy and that Vassall then intended "to do a Pontecorvo" [a reference to the British nuclear physicist Bruno Pontecorvo who had defected to the Soviet Union in 1950]. That had the clear implication that my Hon. Friend either intended to defect to Russia or to assist Vassall to do so. It was also said that my Hon. Friend the former Civil Lord was believed to have spent holidays with Vassall before.'

Indeed, one postcard Vassall sent to Galbraith from Italy, which had been printed in the newspapers the previous week, was signed 'With memories of Italy', underlining the suspicion that they had enjoyed holidays together. Vassall, who was let out of prison to appear at the tribunal, denied this and insisted the message referred only to his own memories.

Macmillan, according to his memoirs, was also prompted to set up an independent tribunal by the press's behaviour. Their conduct was 'terrible, without any sense of responsibility. They want sensation.' Macmillan seems to have noticed this rather late. Lord Radcliffe, an eminent judge, presided over the hearing, only the fourth of its kind since the war. By agreeing to an independent examination of the security implications of the affair, the Prime Minister had yielded to pressure from the Opposition and the press, but even in the heat of scandal, Macmillan showed his guile. There was a sting in the tail. He cleverly included in Radcliffe's brief the powerful role played by the press. 'I have a feeling that the time has come for men of propriety and decency not to tolerate the growth of the spirit of Titus Oates and Senator McCarthy,' he told a packed Commons.

The Opposition smelt a rat. Macmillan had set up the tribunal, they warned, to save the Government's reputation, rather than improve national security. What would happen if journalists failed to reveal their sources? Patrick Gordon Walker, Labour's Defence Spokesman, commented that Macmillan had made the prosecuting speech just before the whole matter went *sub judice*. Walker called the Prime Minister 'a very shrewd adroit politician'. Indeed he was. With the tribunal set up and the issue *sub judice*, a lid was effectively put on further speculation and rumour.

Radcliffe's tribunal, which took evidence in public and in private for two months, had a moment of bitter farce when Mrs Murray, Vassall's charwoman, in her best clothes, was pressed about the time she had seen Galbraith disappear into the bedroom with the spy. Under the gaze of Lord Radcliffe she admitted she did not even know what Galbraith looked like. The tribunal's report was published on 25 April 1963 and exonerated Carrington and Galbraith. The First Lord of the Admiralty, Carrington, had been grossly slandered by the press, said the report, and Galbraith was cleared of any complicity in Vassall's espionage or his homosexual activities. The former Civil Lord of the Admiralty was 'not remiss in failing to suspect from his knowledge of Vassall that the latter was a security risk'.

However, after summoning several journalists in the first weeks of 1963, the tribunal was highly critical of the press. The seeds were sown for months of bitterness between the Government and Fleet Street. Two journalists were sent to prison for refusing to reveal their sources: Brendan Mulholland of the *Daily Mail* preferred a six-month spell behind bars to disclosing, among other things, who had told him the spy was called 'Aunty' in his office. Reginald William Foster of the *Daily Sketch* was jailed for three months for refusing to reveal the source of his claim that Vassall bought women's clothing in the West End. Little of this was central to security, and disrespectful suspicion grew that the tribunal had been set up to punish the press.

Another journalist, Desmond Clough, also of the *Sketch,* narrowly escaped imprisonment for refusing to reveal the source of his claim that it was thanks to Vassall's spying that 'Russian trawler fleets managed to turn up with uncanny accuracy in the precise area and on the right date for secret Nato sea exercises' – an allegation the *Sketch* had printed the day after Vassall's conviction, 23 October. He was saved from prison when an Admiralty press officer came forward as his source.

Galbraith, who had kept public silence since his resignation, had been on the backbenches privately protesting his innocence. Exonerated by the tribunal, he gained undisclosed damages from Beaverbrook and Associated Newspapers. Although he was restored to the government in May 1963 as Parliamentary Secretary in the Department of Transport, a promotion from his previous job in the Scottish office, he never fulfilled his early potential. His marriage was dissolved in 1974. He remained a backbench MP, suffering from ill-health until his death in January 1982, a few weeks after receiving a knighthood. The Tory Establishment's loyalty to its own is remarkable.

Vassall served ten years for his spying, mostly at Maidstone prison in Kent. After his release in 1972 he went to a monastery to write his glutinous autobiography, published by Lord Longford's publishing house, Sidgwick and Jackson, in 1975. They lost track of him several years ago.

The journalists' appeal against imprisonment was rejected in the House of Lords on 6 March 1963. Resentment lingered on in Fleet Street, but the two jailed reporters were back behind their desks before – the whirligig of time bringing in its revenges early – their services were required to report the disgrace of Profumo, and the resignation of Macmillan.

JOHN PROFUMO – 1963

'The car needs oil in the gearbox, by the way'

Oh what have you done, cried Christine,
You've wrecked the whole party machine!
To lie in the nude may be terribly rude,
But to lie in the House is obscene.

Anon.

As dusk fell on a warm Saturday evening at the beginning of the 1960s, Viscount Astor and his weekend guest, the Secretary of State for War John Profumo, both in dinner jackets, took a walk in the grounds of Astor's Cliveden estate. At the pool they found a beautiful nineteen-year-old woman swimming naked. Her male companion had hidden her swimsuit. Spotting a towel by the edge, she swam to it and wrapped it around herself in the water, then climbed from the pool to retrieve her costume. Playfully, Astor and Profumo intercepted her but the laughing teenager easily eluded them. As the other guests arrived from dinner the floodlights were switched on. The scene – two prominent middle-aged Tories caught, frolicking with a girl, in a sudden blinding light – could serve as a metaphor for the era.

According to the poet Philip Larkin, 1963 was the year sexual intercourse began. It was the year to which this incident led: the year in which Harold Macmillan's government faced a welter of accusations involving call-girls, Russian spies and society orgies; the year in which a senior judge thought himself obliged to ask an eminent doctor to examine the penis of a famous (and unnamed) politician.

Many have since seen the Profumo affair as a flagship scandal, emblematic of post-war moral decline. The press descended to new depths in its hunt for sensation but never lacked material. In a Commons speech Harold Wilson, Leader of the Opposition, depicted a government enmeshed in 'the London underworld of vice, dope, marijuana, blackmail, counter-blackmail, violence,

156

and petty crime'. Squalid attempts at cover-up led to the trial at the Old Bailey of the socialite Stephen Ward. His subsequent suicide saw a government stoop – and fail – to save its skin. Five months later, Harold Macmillan resigned, exhausted and ill. Tarnished by the scandal, the succeeding administration, Sir Alec Douglas-Home's, fell the following year. Profumo had hastened the end of thirteen years of Conservative government. By finally lying to the House, he had committed what some branded the most heinous sin of all.

John Profumo (Jack to his friends) was born in 1915 of aristocratic Italian stock. Educated at Harrow and Oxford, he entered Parliament as Conservative member for Kettering in 1940, lost his seat in the Labour landslide five years later but was re-elected for Stratford-upon-Avon in 1950. Within two years he was a junior Transport minister. Profumo, whose family fortune was estimated at £9m, married the maturely handsome 37-year-old actress Valerie Hobson.

His circumstances seemed ideal: rich, clever, sociable, with a successful wife and (soon) a son, Profumo quickly rose to become Secretary of State for War in 1960. A year later the Cabinet minister, now 46 and tipped for the usual higher things, accepted (with his wife) a weekend invitation to Lord Astor's grandiose Cliveden estate in Buckinghamshire.

It was that Saturday night, 8 July 1961, that Profumo and Astor took their fateful stroll by the pool. The naked girl was called Christine Keeler, escorted by Stephen Ward, who had hidden her costume. Ward was a noted society osteopath who, in return for treating Lord Astor's back, had use of a cottage in the grounds of Cliveden. Profumo was mesmerized by his lady guest. Astor introduced Profumo to Ward.

Christine Keeler was living at Ward's London flat. Three years earlier, aged sixteen, the dark-haired and beautiful young woman had fled working-class life in Wraysbury, in search of the bright lights and perilous excesses of London. Working as a topless dancer in a Soho cabaret club, she had met Ward and a fellow showgirl, seventeen-year-old Mandy Rice-Davies, who had abandoned her Birmingham council estate for the lure of the capital.

On this particular weekend Keeler was Ward's guest. Astor now invited both to join his own house-party. Profumo took Keeler on a tour of the house. It degenerated into a chase through the bedrooms. Sex, the first element of the scandal, was now in delightful prospect. And so to the second element: espionage...

The next morning a presentable Soviet naval attaché, Colonel Eugene Ivanov, joined the party. Keeler told the *News of the World*: 'Now I liked Ivanov. He was a *man*. He was rugged with a hairy chest, strong and agile. But somehow when we decided to have a water piggy-back fight, it was Jack Profumo's shoulders I climbed on.' Profumo raced Astor and Ivanov across the pool, and won by breaking the rules and walking in the shallow end. 'That will teach you to trust a Minister of the Crown,' he told the others. By Sunday Profumo was planning to break rules of a more important kind. He had asked Keeler for her telephone number.

Ivanov, the balding minister's rival for Keeler's attentions, drove the flirtatious teenager back to London where she was staying with Ward at his Wimpole Mews flat. When they arrived they drank a bottle of vodka. According to Keeler, the burly Russian 'suddenly leant forward and kissed me. Before I knew

Cartoon by Cummings, 7 June 1963 (courtesy of *Daily Express*)

what was happening, I was in his arms. He was a wonderful lover, so masculine. He left not long after and I felt a tremendous warmth about him: he was not the sort of man to do that sort of thing, and I could see he was sad to have weakened.' As she put it to the *News of the World* in spangled and penitential prose: 'We left serious discussion and I yielded to this wonderful huggy bear of a man...'

John Profumo took only days to follow up his encounter with Keeler. Within a week he had arranged their first 'screw of convenience', as Keeler later called them. Their couplings took place at various venues – in Ward's flat; once in Profumo's Mini Minor; and once, while his wife was in Ireland, in his home. But she says: 'It had no more meaning than a hand-shake or a look across a crowded room.' Profumo showered her with gifts and money, to buy her mother a birthday present. Later this was described in Lord Denning's report as a polite way of paying for her services. This was probably unfair. Profumo was smitten.

Keeler was not. Profumo had no idea he was sharing his mistress's bed with the Russian colonel. 'Unlike Jack, Ivanov was a party boy and loved to take me to the bright spots, wining and dining me. Jack never took me anywhere, except for drives all over London, and even then he was so anxious to be discreet that he used to borrow a big black car from Mr John Hare, the Minister of Labour.'

At this point MI5 intervened. Ward had been in contact with the security services since at least the beginning of June 1961 – a month before the Cliveden party. British Intelligence had singled out Ivanov as susceptible to Western temptations. As a high-ranking naval attaché at the Russian Embassy, Ivanov would have been a big catch if he had defected. A meeting between Ivanov and Ward was engineered by Sir Colin Coote, editor of the *Daily Telegraph*. Coote was a friend of both Ward and Sir Roger Hollis, head of MI5, later to be accused by Peter Wright of being the 'fifth man' in the notorious Soviet spy ring. They had lunch at the Garrick club.

Ward was a sensitive and intelligent man, a talented artist who had sketched members of the royal family, and, in a sardonic way, a social hanger-on. Whether or how far he lived off the earnings of the girls he introduced around, is uncertain. He was probably more of a friend than a lover to girls like Keeler; he enjoyed involvement with the rich and famous and liked to please them. He seemed to be drawn by the glamour of espionage.

MI5 wanted Ward to spring a 'honeytrap' on Ivanov, once he had fallen for Christine Keeler. Some observers have speculated that Ward was helping Soviet intelligence too, but there is no evidence for this. 'In the beginning, I was spying with Stephen Ward, delivering stuff to the Russian Embassy, but I didn't really know what I was doing,' Keeler alleged – to incredulity – in 1994.

MI5 learned about Profumo's month-long affair. Fearing it would compromise their honeytrap operation – and embarrass a Cabinet minister – Hollis warned the Cabinet Secretary, Sir Norman Brook, who called Profumo into his office on 9 August, to pass on the warning. The minister left and scribbled to his mistress the note which would later incriminate him.

> Darling,
>
> In great haste and because I can get no reply from your phone – alas something's blown up tomorrow night and I can't therefore make it. I'm terribly sorry especially as I leave the next day for various trips and then a holiday so won't be able to see you again until some time in September. Blast it. Please take great care of yourself and don't run away.
> Love J.
> PS I'm writing this 'cos I know you're off for the day tomorrow and I want you to know before you go if I still can't reach you by phone.

Profumo was infatuated. Despite the warning, he saw Keeler for another four months. It ended in December 1961, when Keeler refused to leave Ward's flat to let Profumo set her up in a discreet *pied-à-terre*. 'There was that amazing evening when Jack was round, and an army colonel showed up suddenly looking for Stephen. I had to introduce him to the War Minister. The colonel couldn't believe it. Jack nearly died,' was how Keeler described one close shave at Ward's flat.

MI5 began to realize that their honeytrap was unlikely to work. Ward's MI5 case-officer said: 'It is not easy to assess Ward's reliability but we believe he is probably not a man who would be actively disloyal, but that he is so under the influence of Ivanov that it would be most unwise to trust him.'

Profumo last saw Keeler in late 1961. The scandal blew up in early 1963. When it broke, Keeler was still living at Ward's flat, as was her friend Mandy Rice-Davies (after a brief affair with the notorious slum landlord Peter Rachman). After Profumo, Keeler had alternated between two West Indian lovers: Lucky Gordon, a jazz singer whom she had first met buying marijuana for Ward, and Johnny Edgecombe. The two black lovers fought over her in October 1962 in an all-night club in Wardour Street. Gordon's face was slashed. Keeler had briefly moved to Brentwood to live with Edgecombe, but before long she was back at Ward's flat in Wimpole Mews.

On 14 December 1962, the sound of gunshots shattered the silence in the quiet mews. Edgecombe, distraught that Keeler had left him, had tried to woo her back, but when she denied him entrance to Ward's flat he blasted the front door with bullets. The incident received minimal coverage in the press, though there had already been rumours about Keeler's involvement with Profumo. The police treated the shooting as attempted murder.

Ward was rattled and told Keeler to pack her bags. Keeler turned for help to one of Ward's patients, a solicitor, Michael Eddowes, who suspected that Ivanov and Ward were conspiring to compromise Profumo. Eddowes met Keeler and heard that Ward had asked her to find out from Profumo when the Germans were given atomic secrets.

A week later Keeler repeated the same story to another audience: Paul Mann, a journalist, and John Lewis, a Labour MP. Lewis met Keeler a week later and secretly tape-recorded a conversation in which she repeated many of her allegations. Lewis passed the information on to Colonel George Wigg, a poisonous Labour MP with a special interest in defence matters. Wigg had recently received a mysterious phone message: 'Forget the Vassall case; you want to look at Profumo.' He was also said to have a grudge against Profumo, who had bested him in the house.

The journalist Paul Mann persuaded Keeler to take her evidence to the press. She met a *Sunday Pictorial* reporter in late January, 1963, showing him the handwritten note from Profumo which she had astutely kept, and was offered £1,000 for her story: £200 in advance and £800 on publication. She repeated her story. The *Pictorial* was cautious – already in the dock before a parliamentary committee examining the role of the press in the Vassall affair (see pp.154–5).

As negotiations with the paper continued, Ward tried to kill the story by tipping off the Government. Profumo was persuaded to threaten to sue if anyone published. On 28 January Profumo, having failed to get MI5 to stop the story on security grounds, saw the Attorney-General, Sir John Hobson, and denied any affair with Keeler. He repeated the denial to the Solicitor-General, Sir Peter Rawlinson, and the Chief Whip, Martin Redmayne. Though sceptical, they were willing to accept the denial, to protect the Government.

The newspaper insisted on securing Keeler's signature before they would publish. Ward put her under pressure not to sign and she agreed, but only after he had promised to compensate her for the lost newspaper fee – a figure 'five' was mentioned. When Ward's solicitor handed over £500 she was furious, having expected, she claimed, £5,000. Ward convinced the nervous *Pictorial* that her story was a pack of lies, and they dropped it. Keeler, enraged by Ward's desertion, made a series of accusations about her old friend to the police. One of them was procuring call girls for his rich clients.

Macmillan, his government already battered, was told the whole seedy story when he returned from a trip to Italy in February. He decided to do nothing. He wrote:

Profumo had behaved foolishly and indiscreetly, but not wickedly. His wife . . . is very nice and sensible. Of course, all these people move in a selfish, theatrical, bohemian society, where no one really knows anyone and everyone is 'darling'. But Profumo does not seem to have realized that we have – in public life – to observe different standards from those prevalent today in many circles.

Does that mild and tolerant response seem naive, foolish or even enviable in the longer perspective?

On 8 March things started to happen: not in a Fleet Street rag, but in the obscure but authoritative weekly newsletter *Westminster Confidential*. Replacing a dull story about exchange rates the newsletter led, in prose dark with hint and half accusation, with a dramatic tale of sexual misdemeanour in high places . . .

'That is certain to bring down the Government,' a Tory MP wailed – 'and what will my wife say?' This combination of tragedy and tragi-comedy came from the efforts of this MP to check with a newspaperman on the story which had run like wildfire through Parliament . . .

One of the choicest passages was from a letter signed 'Jack', on the stationery of the Secretary for War. The article went on:

> . . . the allegation by this girl was that not only was this minister, who has a famous actress as his wife, her client, but also the Soviet military attaché, apparently a Colonel Ivanov. The famous actress wife, of course, would sue for divorce, the scandal ran. Who was using the girl to 'milk' whom of information – the War Secretary, or the Soviet military attaché? – ran in the minds of those primarily interested in security.

Profumo decided not to sue because, he said, the newsletter had a small circulation. On 10 March George Wigg, who had been secretly compiling a dossier on Profumo's relationship with Keeler, took it to Harold Wilson. But the new Labour leader advised caution. Wigg was persuaded to keep his powder dry. Another opportunity arose only days later.

On 14 March Johnny Edgecombe came up for trial at the Old Bailey charged with the attempted murder of Keeler during the shooting incident at Ward's flat. Yet the principal witness had disappeared. Rumours spread that Keeler had been got at. The following day the *Express* chanced its arm. Under the banner headline 'War Minister Shock' it claimed Profumo had offered his resignation for 'personal reasons'. Directly beneath was another article under the headline 'Vanished', and a picture of Keeler. The stories were not explicitly linked. Lord Denning, in his later report on the affair, wrote: 'The *Daily Express* told me that the juxtaposition of the two stories... was entirely coincidental and supplemented it with reasons. Accepting this to be so, it had nevertheless unfortunate results.'

On 19 March the case of the journalists jailed for refusing to reveal their sources to the Vassall tribunal was debated in the Commons. This was Wigg's chance (though barely 'in order' but safe from the laws of libel) to raise the allegations against Profumo:

Here was a set of rumours that gained in strength, consumed men's reputations – might in fact have destroyed them – and which here infringed on the security of the State. But are we quite sure that the same thing is not happening again? There is not an hon Member in the House, not a journalist in the Press Gallery who, in the last few days, has not heard rumour upon rumour involving a member of the Government Front Bench. The Press has got as near as it could – it has shown itself willing to wound but afraid to strike. This all comes about because of the Vassall tribunal.

In actual fact, these great Press Lords, these men who control great instruments of public opinion and power, do not have the guts to discharge the duty that they are now claiming for themselves. That being the case, I rightly use the Privilege of the House of Commons – that is what it is given me for – to ask the Home Secretary who is the senior member of the Government on the Treasury Bench now, to go to the Dispatch Box – he knows the rumour to which I refer relates to Miss Christine Keeler and Miss Davies and a shooting by a West Indian – and, on behalf of the Government, categorically deny the truth of these rumours. On the other hand, if there is anything in them, I urge him to ask the Prime Minister to do what was not done in the Vassall case – set up a Select Committee so that these things can be dissipated, and the honour of the Minister concerned freed from the imputations and innuendoes that are being spread at the present time.

Wigg was supported in his demand by a leading Labour frontbencher, Richard Crossman – although at least one of their Labour colleagues, the eccentric, fox-hunting Reginald Paget, disagreed: 'What do these rumours amount to? They amount to the fact that a minister is said to be acquainted with an extremely pretty girl. As far as I am concerned, I should have thought that was a matter for congratulation rather than an inquiry.' Barbara Castle did not agree and raised the disappearance of Keeler. Henry Brooke, the Home Secretary, was outwardly dismissive:

I do not propose to comment on rumours which have been raised under the cloak of Privilege and safe from any action

at law. The hon Member for Dudley (Wigg) and the hon
Member for Blackburn (Castle) should seek other means of
making these insinuations if they are prepared to
substantiate them.

Privately the Government was alarmed. That night Macmillan
required Profumo to repeat to the Commons the following
morning the denials he had made in private. After sunrise
Profumo was summoned from his bed and quizzed again by the
two law officers, Iain Macleod, Leader of the House, the Chief
Whip and William Deedes, Minister without Portfolio (and future
editor of the *Daily Telegraph*). Unrepentant, Profumo insisted he
was innocent and that the word 'Darling', with which that as yet
unpublished letter began, did not amount to an admission of
adultery.

A couple of hours later, at 11 a.m. on Friday, 22 March,
Profumo delivered his disastrous personal statement. Unusually
for a Friday, the House was packed.

I understand that in the debate on the Consolidated Fund
Bill last night, under the protection of Parliamentary
privilege the hon gentlemen, the Members for Dudley
(Wigg) and for Coventry East (Crossman) and the hon lady,
the Member for Blackburn (Castle), opposite, spoke of
rumours connecting a Minister with a Miss Keeler and a
recent trial at the Central Criminal Court. It was alleged that
people in high places might have been responsible for
concealing information concerning the disappearance of a
witness and the perversion of justice. I understand that my
name had been connected with the rumours about the
disappearance of Miss Keeler. I would like to take this
opportunity of making a personal statement about these
matters. I last saw Miss Keeler in December 1961, and I
have not seen her since. I have no idea where she is now. Any
suggestion that I was in any way connected with or
responsible for her absence from the trial at the Old Bailey is
wholly and completely untrue. My wife and I first met Miss
Keeler at a house party in July 1961 at Cliveden. Among a
number of people there was Dr Stephen Ward, whom we
already knew slightly, and Mr Ivanov, who was an attaché at

the Russian Embassy. The only other occasion that my wife
or I met Mr Ivanov was for a moment at the official
reception for Major Gagarin at the Soviet Embassy. My wife
and I had a standing invitation to visit Dr Ward. Between
July and December 1961 I met Miss Keeler on about half a
dozen occasions when I called to see him and his friends.
Miss Keeler and I were on friendly terms. There was no
impropriety whatsoever in my acquaintanceship with Miss
Keeler. Mr Speaker, I have made this personal statement
because of what was said in the House last evening by the
three hon Members, and which, of course, was protected by
privilege. I shall not hesitate to issue writs for libel and
slander if scandalous allegations are made or repeated
outside the House.

Even as Profumo was speaking the press were closing in on
Christine Keeler, whom they found in Madrid a few days later.
Keeler, who was by now running scared from the powerful forces
which had been unleashed against her, told the *Daily Express*:

> What Mr Profumo says is quite correct. I have not been in
> his company since December 1961. He was always very
> pleasant and on one occasion I met his wife, Valerie Hobson,
> at the swimming pool down at Cliveden. She was charming
> and we chatted for quite a while.

The indefatigable George Wigg never believed a word of
Profumo's statement. The night before Keeler's denial on
Monday, 25 March he appeared on the *Panorama* television
programme and bluntly stated that Ward and Ivanov were security
risks. This outraged Ward who met Wigg the next day. Wigg left
the private meeting convinced that Profumo was a liar. He
reported the conversation to Wilson, who asked him to write a
report of the meeting. An edited version was sent to Macmillan –
who did not, however, see it for about two weeks. Meanwhile,
Profumo had issued writs against *Il Tempo Illustrato* and *Paris
Match*, both having published allegations that he and Keeler had
been sexually involved.

Henry Brooke, the Home Secretary, held a meeting the
following day with the head of MI5 to discuss Ward's explosive

encounter with Wigg. It seems MI5 instructed the Commissioner of the Metropolitan Police to find evidence to bring any kind of criminal charges against Ward in a covert attempt to silence him. This was an arguably disgraceful move. As Philip Knightley and Caroline Kennedy, authors who have studied the affair in depth, point out, the police investigate crimes not individuals: to pursue someone to see what crime he might have committed is highly unusual.

> . . . yet the investigation of Ward's social and business activities was just such a 'fishing expedition' – as the wide variety of charges eventually brought against Ward confirms. It was as if someone had said, 'We want to prosecute Stephen Ward for a criminal offence. Go and find one that has a chance of sticking.'

The police began questioning Ward's friends and patients, many now frightened away from his clinic by the adverse publicity. On 23 April they stopped Keeler's friend Mandy Rice-Davies leaving for Spain where she was planning to marry her Spanish boyfriend. She was charged with possessing a false driving licence. The magistrates fixed bail at the exorbitant level of £2,000, prompting speculation that they were acting under pressure from above. The police told her that even if she managed to pay they had plenty of other potential charges to keep her in the country.

After Rice-Davies had spent ten days on remand in prison the two policemen on the case, Chief Inspector Herbert and Detective Sergeant Burrows, came, she says, to see her: 'Mandy, you don't like it here very much, do you? So you help us and we'll help you.'

She knew what she had to do: implicate Stephen Ward. She refused. Rice-Davies' case came up on 1 May , she was fined £42, and left for Spain. On her return she was arrested and charged with the theft of a TV set, a charge later dropped. Her passport was confiscated. For bail of £1,000 she was released on condition she reported to the police station on the same day Ward went to court in July. Tactics such as these persuaded her to testify.

Ward was beginning to despair. Friends were deserting. Lord Astor refused to let him keep the Cliveden cottage. On 7 May he went to see Tim Bligh, the Prime Minister's Parliamentary Private

Secretary, and asked whether the investigation might be politically motivated:

> You see the facts as presented in Parliament were not strictly speaking just like that . . . I feel I should tell you the truth of what really happened . . . [Profumo] wrote Miss Keeler a series of letters . . . I don't know whether you have any feelings about this, whether there is anything you can do. I know myself here that there is a great deal of potentially extremely explosive material in what I have told you.

Bligh considered this attempted blackmail. He told Macmillan, who questioned Profumo again, but Profumo stuck to his story. An increasingly frantic Ward began reeling off letters to the Home Secretary, to his own MP, Sir Wavell Wakefield, and finally, on 20 May, to Harold Wilson, repeating his complaints about the police inquiry and his claim that Profumo had been lying. Brooke, the Home Secretary, sent a terse reply: 'The Home Secretary has asked me to explain that the police, in making what enquiries they think proper, do not act under his direction.'

Wilson took it more seriously. He passed a copy of Ward's letter to the Prime Minister. On 29 May Macmillan and Wilson met. Macmillan agreed to set up an inquiry under Lord Dilhorne. The pressure was building up again; two Labour MPs put down questions to the Home Secretary about what information he had received from Ward.

On 4 June Profumo was recalled from holiday in Venice to appear before the Dilhorne inquiry. This time he told the truth. Unable to face cross-examination at the independent inquiry, he admitted to Macmillan's PPS and the Chief Whip that he had lied. He resigned the same day not only as a minister but as an MP. His letter of resignation, and Macmillan's reply, were published the following day:

> Dear Prime Minister,
>   You will recollect that on 22 March, following certain allegations made in Parliament, I made a personal statement. At that time rumour had charged me with assisting in the disappearance of a witness and with being involved in some possible breach of security.

So serious were these charges that I allowed myself to think that my personal association with that witness, which had also been the subject of rumour, was, by comparison, of minor importance only. In my statement I said that there had been no impropriety in this association. To my very deep regret I have to admit that this was not true, and that I misled you, and my colleagues, and the House.

I ask you to understand that I did this to protect, as I thought, my wife and family, who were misled, as were my professional advisers.

I have come to realize that, by this deception, I have been guilty of a grave misdemeanour and despite the fact that there is no truth whatsoever in the other charges, I cannot remain a member of your Administration, nor of the House of Commons.

I cannot tell you of my deep remorse for the embarrassment I have caused you, to my colleagues in the Government, to my constituents and to the Party which I have served for the past twenty-five years.

Yours sincerely,
Jack Profumo

Macmillan, ever the showman, responded by the implied rebuke that he had not even read Profumo's letter.

Dear Profumo,
The contents of your letter of 4 June have been communicated to me, and I have heard them with deep regret. This is a great tragedy for you, your family and your friends. Nevertheless, I am sure you will understand that in the circumstances I have no alternative but to advise the Queen to accept your resignation.

Yours very sincerely,
Harold Macmillan

It is now commonplace to observe that it was lying to the House which sealed the War Minister's fate. But had he been candid, would he have been likely to have survived? 'Lying to the House' was the simplest charge, of course, and colleagues would have found it an easier argument than entering the debate on public versus private life. But our view is that Profumo was finished if found out, knew it, and – having nothing to lose – tried lying. This approach has not always failed in politics.

This time, though, it did. Profumo's career was over. But the scandal went into overdrive. Sensation was boosted by the fact that 5 June was not only the day on which Profumo's resignation was made public, but the first day in another trial: that of Keeler's other, West Indian boyfriend Lucky Gordon – charged with assaulting her outside the flat of a friend on 17 April. Keeler arrived at the trial in a chauffeur-driven Rolls-Royce.

The court case made wonderful copy. Papers could report what was said with impunity. Asked why she had sent the defendant £5 to pay a fine, Keeler replied: 'I would say Gordon was blackmailing me on this particular occasion.' A letter was then passed to the judge but remained unread in public. Gordon conducted his own case and made a series of allegations against Ward. 'He is known as a crank and he is a crank. He gets his delight from seeing people get aggravated.' And he accused Keeler of having given him VD, provoking an outburst from her where she sat in the public gallery. Gordon's three-year sentence was quashed on appeal.

On 7 June Ward was interviewed by Desmond Wilcox on the TV programme *This Week*:

> The key point for me to clear my name was to indicate that I had not encouraged the relationship between Miss Keeler and Mr Profumo . . . I was disturbed about certain parts of it and, as tactfully as possible, I had informed the Security Service. I wanted to make it absolutely clear that I hadn't encouraged it and knowing that I had a friend in the Soviet Embassy, I think I was rightly disturbed about it.

The following day he was arrested on the charge of 'on diverse dates between January 1961 and June 1963 having knowingly lived wholly or in part on the earnings of prostitution at 17 Wimpole Mews W1'.

Profumo's resignation had made headlines around the world. This was 'the sordid side of London's high society'. Stories abounded, most famous of which was the tale of the mysterious 'man in the mask' who, it was said, frequently turned up at Ward's orgies. The story first surfaced on 8 June in the *Washington Star*, in an interview with Rice-Davies.

At Scotland Yard's request Mandy cut short a continental holiday last month and came back to Britain. Newspapers said she was helping to uncover a top people's call-girl ring involving dozens of girls. Mandy herself said on June 1: 'I can say that probably a number of well-known people will be involved'. Mandy has talked of one gay little party she went to where the host who opened the door wore nothing but his socks. 'Then,' she said, 'there was a dinner party where a naked man wearing a mask waited on table like a slave. He had to have a mask because he was so well known.'

Who was the man in the mask? Rumour alternated between a Cabinet minister and a senior Royal. The story was first published in Britain by the *Express* on 21 June 1963. They quoted another guest:

. . . As the 'slave' handed (us) cocktail snacks the guests abused and reviled him. He was obviously enjoying it. I was told by the host that the man arrived first at the party. He undressed and put on a mask before the other guests arrived. The host revealed his true identity to me. I could hardly believe it. I left after a few minutes.

Three days later the *Mirror*'s front page read 'Prince Philip and the Profumo Scandal'. Under the headline was a denial of the 'foul rumour' linking the Queen's husband to the affair. The identity of the man in the mask still excites speculation today. Lord Denning later devoted a whole subsection of his report to this sub-plot:

There is a great deal of evidence that there is a group of people who hold parties in private of a perverted nature. At some of these parties, the man who serves dinner is nearly naked except for a small square lace apron round his waist such as a waitress might wear. He wears a black mask over his head with slits for eye-holes. He cannot therefore be recognised by any of the guests. Some reports stop there and say that nothing evil takes place. It is done as a comic turn and no more. This may well be so at some of the parties. But at others it is followed by perverted sex orgies: the man in the mask is a 'slave' who is whipped: that guests undress and indulge in sexual intercourse one with the other: and indulge in other sexual activities of a vile and revolting nature.

Cartoon by Cummings, 8 June 1963 (courtesy of *Daily Express*) with headlines from the *Daily Express*, 6 June 1963, and *Daily Mirror*, 24 June 1963

Denning goes on, breathlessly:

My only concern in my inquiry was to see whether any
Minister or other person prominent in public life was
present at these parties; for, if he were, he would, I should
think, be exposing himself to blackmail.

And yet another whirlwind whipped along Fleet Street towards
Westminster. This involved an alleged affair between a minister
and a duchess: the Duchess of Argyll, involved in a famous
divorce case. A Polaroid photograph of the naked Duchess
engaged in a sexual act with a man was passed to the judge. The
snapshot excluded the head, though only the head, of her aroused
and enthusiastic lover. Rumours spread as to the identity of the
mystery man: a Cabinet minister, it was said. Ward, the rumours
added, had been involved in bribery to keep the MP's name out
of the trial. Denning went to the unusual lengths of persuading
the unnamed minister to submit himself to a medical examination
of his penis by a Harley Street consultant. Bernard Levin
commented:

. . . Even in years so copiously provided with material on
which madness could feel fat, there was one episode which
stands out from the decade, and still stands out, as a
monument to the willingness of man to suspend the
operation of reason . . . how it came about, almost exactly
two-thirds of the way through the twentieth century, and in
a country as advanced as Britain, that a judge should have
been obliged to ask a doctor to examine the penis of a
politician, is something so extraordinary, and in many ways
so significant, that it deserves examination as detailed as that
which the Minister underwent.

Iain Crawford remarks in *The Profumo Affair* that 'the scandal had
now reached the point at which almost anything could be said
about anyone; provided it was sufficiently scabrous it was certain
of wide circulation'. Mervyn Stockwood, the Bishop of
Southwark, attacked both the newspapers and the news:

Things have happened in Britain in recent weeks that have
left an unpleasant smell – the smell of corruption in high
places, of evil practices, and of a repudiation of the simple

"Ladies and Gentlemen, Miss Chris—"

Cartoon by Giles, 11 June 1963 (courtesy of *Daily Express*)

decencies and the basic values. The smell is so intensified in its unpleasantness by the squalid biographies in a particular section of the Sunday Press that thrives, no doubt with considerable financial gain, on sexual scandals. The time has come to clean the national stables.

Stockwood did not explain whether he wanted to suppress the sin, or the reports of it. The reverend prelate contrived both to have his cake of piety, and to eat it.

High on the list of commentators' questions was how Profumo managed to maintain the lie for so long. It had become apparent how long various members of the government had known about the letter, which was finally published on 9 June. Macmillan's knowledge of events made his own position awkward. Speculation began about his leadership. Ministers scrambled to distance themselves from any knowledge of their former friend's private diversions. Lord Hailsham, a likely contender for Macmillan's job, was vitriolic. On the BBC's 'Gallery' he said:

> It is intolerable for Mr Profumo in his position to have behaved in this way, and a tragedy that he should not have been found out – that he should have lied and lied and lied.

Lied to his friends, lied to his solicitor and lied to the House of Commons.

Almost a lone voice, Sir Reginald Paget called that a 'virtuoso performance in the art of kicking a friend in the guts'. He added: 'When self-indulgence has reduced a man to the shape of Lord Hailsham, sexual continence involves no more than a sense of the ridiculous'.

Defensive at the charge of muck-raking, the press homed in on the security implications of the affair. The *Sunday Mirror* published as early as 9 June Rice-Davies's revelation that 'on more than one occasion – as Jack left Christine at the flat where she stayed, Eugene Ivanov, the handsome young Russian naval attaché, walked in. In fact it was something of a standing joke among us.'

Allegations that the Government had treated questions about security too lightly emerged when, on 13 June, Michael Eddowes, the solicitor who had questioned Keeler after the shooting incident, issued a press statement claiming he had warned the Prime Minister. He had submitted his report on the security aspects of the affair to Special Branch as early as 29 March, but nothing had been done. It was through Eddowes that the alleged inquiry about when Germany had got the atom bomb first hit the news-stands. In her paid 'Confessions' in the *News of the World* on 16 June, Keeler confirmed that someone, not Ivanov, had asked her to find this information out from Profumo.

On 11 June under the headline 'It *is* a Moral Issue', *The Times* commented:

Everyone has been so busy assuring the public that the affair is not one of morals, that it is time to assert that it is. Morals have been discounted too long. A judge may be justified in reminding a jury: 'This is not a court of morals'. The same exemption cannot be allowed in public opinion, without rot setting in and all standards suffering in the long run. The British are not by and large an immoral nation but through their pathetic fear of being called smug they make themselves out to be one . . .

. . . It remains strange that not a single member of the Government resigned when the affair broke in March and

[Profumo] did not himself resign.

There is no hiding place from the tidal wave of overthrow and disaster.

Whether in the next few days some heads fall or none, damage has been done. It may be a caricature for the *Washington Post* to say that 'a picture of widespread decadence beneath the glitter of a large segment of stiff-lipped society is emerging'. But the essence of caricature is to exaggerate real traits.

There are plenty of earnest and serious men in the Conservative Party who know that all is not well. It is time they put first things first, stopped weighing electoral chances, and returned to the starker truths of an earlier day.

Popularity by affluence is about played out, especially when it rests on so insecure a basis. Even if the call had metaphorically to be for 'blood, sweat and tears', instead of to the fleshpots, they might be surprised by the result. The British are always at their best when they are braced.

When this dreadful prose was quoted at Lord Hailsham on the programme 'Gallery', he snapped back bitterly: '*The Times* is an anti-Conservative newspaper with an anti-Conservative editor.' On 17 June the affair was debated in the Commons. Harold Wilson piously attacked Macmillan's failure to act earlier.

This is a debate without precedent in the annals of this House. It arises from disclosures which have shocked the moral conscience of the nation. There is clear evidence of a sordid underworld network, the extent of which cannot yet be measured . . .

. . . After the Vassall case [the Prime Minister] felt that he could not stand another serious case involving a ministerial resignation, and he gambled desperately and hoped that nothing would ever come out. For political reasons he was gambling with national security.

Other attacks on Macmillan came from his own side of the House, most notably from Nigel Birch MP:

I must say that [Profumo] never struck me as a man at all like a cloistered monk; and Miss Keeler is a professional prostitute. There seems to me to be a basic improbability about the proposition that their relationship was purely platonic. What are whores about? [*turning to Macmillan*] What is to happen now? We cannot just have business as usual. I myself feel that the time will come very soon when my Right Honourable Friend ought to make way for a much younger colleague. I feel that ought to happen. I certainly will not quote at him the savage words of Cromwell, but perhaps some word of Browning might be appropriate:

> . . . let him never come back to us!
> There would be doubt, hesitation and pain.
> Forced praise on our part – the glimmer of twilight,
> Never glad confident morning again.

There was a delicacy to these razored words not likely to be found today.

Macmillan, though cruelly damaged by the affair, managed to survive. A three-line whip, and the prospect of a rout in any election, enabled the Prime Minister to limp on before resigning just ahead of the autumn Party Conference, Lord Hailsham resigning his peerage to throw his hat into the ring. More lasting was the damage to the public perception of the governing class and to the image of the Conservative Party. Perhaps some of the cynicism engendered remains to this day beneath the surface, waiting to be triggered by new scandal.

On 21 June, Macmillan announced that an inquiry would be conducted by Lord Denning. The Denning Report, published on 26 October 1963, was a best-seller, with 4,000 copies sold in the first hour. Many thought it a whitewash which laid the blame for the scandal largely at the feet of Ward. Denning has also been criticized because, in the words of Philip Knightley and Caroline Kennedy, 'he showed more interest in the sex and rumour part of the affair than in the security, which was his brief'. But then which is more interesting? 'Many of the witnesses said that he quizzed them on salacious and irrelevant details . . . sending the official stenographer out of the room when he thought that she might be embarrassed by the evidence.'

Denning's evidence remains unpublished, a Cabinet secret – obviously, for reasons of national security.

And in the end it was on Ward that the fury turned. Ward's eight-day trial at the Old Bailey in July attracted huge international media attention. A New Zealand newspaper was fined for indecency merely for reporting it. There were moments of pure farce. Court Number One erupted in laughter when Mandy Rice-Davies delivered the most quoted one-liner in English judicial history. It was put to her that Lord Astor denied friendship with her. 'Well, *he* would, wouldn't he?' she replied. Once, the judge mistakenly addressed her as Marilyn Monroe.

The judge, Sir Archie Pellow Marshall QC, delivered a 'hanging' direction. He told the jury of eleven men and one middle-aged woman that Ward had been deserted by his friends: 'There are many people of high estate and low who could have come forward and testified . . . One would have thought from the newspapers that this country has become a sink of iniquity. But

Cartoon by Trog, 14 july 1963 (courtesy of *Private Eye*)

you and I know that the even tenor of family life over the overwhelming majority of the population goes quietly and decently on.'

The judge's comments were too much for the ruined fifty-year-old osteopath to bear. On the night of 3 July, with the summing-up only half completed, Ward swallowed an overdose of sleeping draught. He went into a coma from which he never recovered. With Ward now unconscious at St Stephen's Hospital, and after four and a half hours' deliberation, the jury returned their verdict. Ward was found guilty on two charges of living on immoral earnings. Sentence was never passed. He died on 3 August.

Shortly before his overdose, Ward, having seen his character systematically torn apart, had turned to one of his few remaining friends, the *Express* reporter Tom Mangold, and said: 'This is a political revenge trial. Someone had to be sacrificed and that someone was me.' He killed himself in the Chelsea flat of a friend, Noel Howard-Jones. His note read:

> Dear Noel,
>   I am sorry I had to do this here! It is really more than I can stand – the horror, day after day at the court and in the streets. It is not only fear, it is a wish not to let them get me. I would rather get myself. I do hope I have not let people down too much. I tried to do my stuff but after Marshall's summing-up, I've given up all hope. The car needs oil in the gearbox, by the way. Be happy in it. Incidentally, it was surprisingly easy and required no guts. I am sorry to disappoint the vultures.
>   I only hope this has done the job. Delay resuscitation as long as possible.

The *News of the World* commented, with posthumous valour, that Ward was 'a cornered rat' with 'a fiendish smile', 'utterly depraved' with dirty hands 'now with ugly little marks on them'. 'Now he is dead,' wrote the journalist Peter Earle, 'I'm not surprised. I had known for a long time that he was a coward.'

Profumo disappeared from political life and threw himself into charity work for which he was given a CBE in 1975. He remains independently wealthy, and married to Valerie Hobson.

Shortly after the Ward trial, Keeler, who had failed to attend Lucky Gordon's trial, was jailed for six months for contempt of court. She now has two sons from two marriages, both annulled, and lives in South London. She survives on the proceeds of her 1989 autobiography, *Scandal*, which was made into a film. It is understood that John Profumo saw the film incognito.

Mandy Rice-Davies has not spoken to Keeler for thirty years. She has written a string of novels, acted in films, opened two nightclubs in Israel, and is on her second marriage: to the millionaire businessman Ken Foreman. When Matthew Parris met her she said he was the first Tory politician she had ever met, winked, then giggled.

George Wigg remained an MP until 1967, when he was made a life peer. He became chairman of the Horse Race Betting Levy Board, and later president of the Betting Office Licensees' Association. He was acquitted of charges arising from kerb-crawling in Marble Arch, in pursuit of prostitutes. He died in 1983.

There were six mourners at Ward's funeral and only two wreaths. One was from his family. The other had contained 100 white carnations and was from Kenneth Tynan, John Osborne, Annie Ross, Dominick Elwes, Arnold Wesker, Joe Orton and Penelope Gilliatt. The card on it read: 'To Stephen Ward, Victim of Hypocrisy.' You cannot apologize to the dead and nobody in British public life seems to apologize anyway, but there are people alive today (not Profumo) who wronged Stephen Ward badly. Some indication of remorse would have been refreshing.

Matthew Parris sent Mr Profumo this account of the events, in draft, in case there was anything incorrect or unfair. He replied on 29 June 1995:

> ... Since 1963 there have been unceasing publications, both written and spoken, relating to what you refer to in your letter as 'the Keeler interlude'. The majority of these have increasingly contained deeply distressing inaccuracies, so I have resolved to refrain from any sort of personal comment, and I propose to continue thus.
>
> I hope – indeed I believe – you will understand and acquit me of discourtesy.

Indeed. Writing for *The Times*, Matthew described the night a good-looking young Bulgarian diplomat tried to seduce him when he was a 25-year-old Foreign Office official in 1976. As he went on to become a Tory MP, the story might have been interesting. Fortunately the diplomat had dreadful breath. Upon the smallest things destinies can turn.

REGINALD MAUDLING – 1972

A Civilized Man, a Whiff of Greed

It is to Reggie Maudling that we owe the Commons Register of Members' Interests, which was set up during one of the nation's habitual moral panics about 'sleaze waves'. This one, involving allegations over the business activities of Maudling and two other MPs, began in the early 1970s.

Reginald Maudling was Home Secretary in 1972 when – appearing to set an unusual standard for honourable conduct in ministers – he suddenly resigned. The Prime Minister, Edward Heath, had begged him to remain in the Government while Scotland Yard mounted an investigation into allegations of corruption against one of the Home Secretary's former business associates, John Poulson. But as the overall head of the Metropolitan Police, Maudling insisted on going. The *Daily Express* wrote in July 1972: 'His resignation as Home Secretary was a gesture without parallel in recent politics.'

As events unfolded, the resignation began to look less surprising. It took five years to resolve the affair and though Maudling escaped criminal charges, he did not escape censure. By that time anyway, with Labour in power, it was too late. He

Sun, 19 July 1972

died eighteen months later, never unambiguously implicated in any wrongdoing, never wholly exonerated. A faint whiff – if not of corruption – of greed, hung about his name. It still does.

This was a pity. Maudling was an unusually civilized and intelligent politician, and life could have turned out very differently. After Merchant Taylors' School and Merton College, Oxford, a spell at the Bar, and active service with the RAF, Maudling became one of R. A. Butler's 'backroom boys' at Conservative Central Office after the war. In 1950 he entered Parliament for Chipping Barnet. He was a Cabinet minister and Privy Councillor within five years and a 45-year-old Chancellor of the Exchequer in 1962.

With Labour winning the 1964 election and Edward Heath securing the Tory leadership, Maudling decided to concentrate on his business interests – or, as he put it, 'a little pot of gold'. His own hopes for the leadership of his party had been dashed and a certain disillusion set in. In 1965 he took a consultancy from the well-known Labour supporter and Wilson hanger-on, Eric Miller, Chairman of Peachey Property Corporation. Keen to avoid paying income tax, the former Chancellor of the Exchequer waived his £5,000 annual remuneration. Instead, Peachey bought the freehold of his country house and rented it back to him for £2 a week. In October 1977 Miller, whose financial affairs were under investigation, would shoot himself on the patio of his South Kensington home.

But Maudling grew richer. Already a Lloyd's Name, he accumulated several directorships, putting his annual income beyond £20,000 – four times a ministerial salary. He had a house in Hertfordshire and a Regency home in Chester Square, Belgravia. He wanted more. In his 1978 memoirs he remarked that politicians 'cannot reasonably be expected to neglect their interests and those of their families'. In particular he sought a position for his eldest son, Martin, who had recently graduated from Oxford. His involvements with Dunlop and Kleinwort Benson were lucrative but unspectacular. Maudling's downfall was his move into the booming property market.

In 1966 the Yorkshire architect John Poulson, by then vividly active in town hall corruption, walked into Maudling's life. Poulson had secured the services of the backbench Labour MP Albert Roberts, but wanted a political heavyweight to front the overseas branch of Poulson's new company, International Technical and Construction Services. Maudling fitted the bill.

Poulson's strategy worked. With Maudling's help he snapped up a lucrative contract from the Maltese government for a hospital on the island of Gozo. A former Chancellor does not come cheaply. Poulson made an £8,000 annual covenant (worth £27,000, a tidy sum in those days) to Mrs Beryl Maudling's favourite theatre project in East Grinstead, the Adèle Genée. He also made Martin Maudling a director of one of his companies; and the Maudling family acquired shares in the Poulson empire.

With Maudling, Poulson had struck gold. He decided to share his political ambassador with one of his friends: the Tory MP was sent to work for the corrupt (as it later emerged) Real Estate Fund of America, headed by the 39-year-old American financier Jerry Hoffman. Maudling persuaded at least two foreign banks to invest in Hoffman's venture. He waived his fee in return for 250,000 shares in the company. Maudling wisely severed this involvement in July 1969. The following year the company crashed with debts of £4 million. Hoffman was sent to jail for two years by an Illinois court.

When the Tories came to power in 1970, the new Prime Minister, Edward Heath, made Maudling Home Secretary. He immediately resigned all his remaining directorships. But the storm was gathering. Poulson was in deep financial trouble. He had over-extended, and neglected to pay his taxes. In 1972 the 62-year-old architect filed for bankruptcy. At the sensational hearing which followed, Poulson revealed, among much else, the existence of his £8,000 covenant to Mrs Maudling's pet theatre.

Maudling went straight to the Prime Minister. In a long intimate conversation at 10 Downing Street on the evening of Monday 17 July 1972, he warned his leader that if the police asked for an inquiry into Poulson's bankruptcy he would have to resign. He could not contemplate the embarrassment of the police having to question their political master.

His fears were realized the following day. The Attorney-General Sir Peter Rawlinson's report arrived at 12.30 p.m. on both Heath's and Maudling's desks. Events followed the course the two men had agreed the previous evening. The Home Secretary wrote his resignation letter over lunch. After twenty years on the frontbench, he said: 'I think I can reasonably claim a respite from the burdens of responsibility and the glare of publicity, which inevitably surrounds a Minister and, inexcusably, engulfs the private life even of his family.' But there was no mention of the fact that Maudling and members of his family owned shares in Poulson's companies or that his son Martin was a director of one.

Heath, in a rare public outburst of warmth, replied: 'I profoundly regret your going now and I hope that it will not be long before you are able to resume your position in the public life of this country.'

When Maudling's resignation was disclosed to an astonished Commons, even political foes such as Labour's former Home Secretary James Callaghan, and the Liberal leader Jeremy Thorpe, reflected the confident view of most MPs: that Maudling would be cleared of any improper conduct. *The Times* was perhaps closer to the mark. The paper's editorial warned: 'A leading political figure who goes into business puts the stamp of his reputation on those with whom he associates, and he owes a particular obligation to satisfy himself that he is dealing with sound business.'

The first arrests arising from the Poulson investigation were made in June 1973. The following March, Poulson himself was convicted of corruption and jailed for seven years.

Two other MPs had also been involved with Poulson. John Cordle, the Tory MP for Bournemouth East, and Albert Roberts, the Labour MP for Normanton, had helped the discredited property developer gain business in West Africa, Spain and Portugal. Neither was ever charged, but the feeling that they should have been more open in their business dealings, and the hint that Maudling in particular should have known what sort of a man he was collaborating with – and that he possibly did know – hung in the air. Allegations of sleaze led the new Labour government to set up the voluntary Register of Members' Interests when they came to power that year, 1974.

In October 1976 the DPP announced an end to any further prosecutions. With the criminal investigation over, the *Observer*, among other voices, asked what action would be taken against Maudling and the two other MPs who had helped Poulson. James Callaghan, now Prime Minister, offered an inquiry to look at procedure for the future rather than past events. The outcry, particularly from his own backbenchers, caused a climb-down within 24 hours. A select committee of ten MPs was established. It would examine the role of Maudling and the other MPs in the Poulson collapse.

Its report, published on 15 July 1977, unanimously accused Maudling and Roberts of conduct 'inconsistent with the standards which the House is entitled to expect from its members' by not declaring an interest. It alleged that Maudling's resignation letter had been 'lacking in frankness' when it said his only payment had been Poulson's charitable covenant to the East Grinstead theatre and failed to mention his shares in Poulson companies, and the fact that his son was a director of one firm.

John Cordle came off worse. A damning piece of evidence against the Bournemouth MP was a letter he had written to Poulson after the architect had complained about the MP's work rate. Stung by the criticism, the Tory backbencher had penned a detailed reply. The picture he presented of his energetic efforts to earn his consultancy fee (£5,628 over six years) made sour reading. The committee felt Cordle's conduct amounted to 'a contempt of the House'. Having served as an MP for nineteen years, he resigned on 22 July before the report was even debated. He said he wanted to avoid an 'acrimonious and divisive debate'. Cordle had been, according to Poulson, not 'even a minnow'.

The Select Committee report was debated in the Commons on 26 July 1977. Both Maudling and Roberts, who survived as an MP until 1983, spoke in their own defence before leaving the Chamber, as custom dictated. In a highly charged debate, Edward Heath, now an influential backbencher, stoutly defended his former Cabinet colleague. He chose to criticize the committee instead, for suggesting that Maudling had misled him in his resignation letter.

The House Leader, Michael Foot, warned MPs not to succumb to a 'liberal form of lynch-law . . . Of all mobs the most objectionable is the sanctimonious.' The Commons voted 230 to 207 to adopt the inoffensive motion to 'take note' of the report. By a majority of 320 they rejected a move to expel Maudling from the Commons and by a margin of 227 to suspend him for six months without pay.

For someone who had plainly acted, at best, very foolishly, and in the opinion of some, corruptly, Reginald Maudling still commanded much affection and respect. This was due to his high reputation as a moderate, thinking Conservative and a pleasant, intelligent colleague, 'clubbable', and bright. Looking older than his sixty years, he told reporters after the vote: 'It must be the end of the matter . . . for God's sake, after five years.' It was. He died eighteen months later.

He was all out of tune with the new Thatcherite certainties gripping a party preparing for government. But he also seemed wise: thoughtful and undogmatic in his discourse and in his political responses. It is not unusual to find that men, who have been touched both by power and also by some kind of public disgrace, show towards the end a sort of frankness, an impatience with certitude, and a weary humanity.

There was a telling moment not far from the close of Maudling's life. The portly and discredited figure was on his feet in a debate about the ailing British car industry, complaining that 'it takes a German worker one day and a half to build a car, whereas it takes his British equivalent more than three days . . .' Maudling was interrupted by a growl from the Labour MP Dennis Skinner: 'An' 'ow long would it tek *you*, fats?'

LORD LAMBTON and LORD JELLICOE – 1973

'Surely all men patronize whores?'

Within three days in May 1973 Edward Heath's government lost two ministers, both implicated in call-girl scandals. In 48 hours Lord Lambton went from ministerial cars and red boxes at the Ministry of Defence, to questions about drugs at Scotland Yard. Lord Jellicoe, one of the best-liked members of the Cabinet, stood down after being linked with a Scotland Yard inquiry into a 'top people's vice ring'.

Antony Claud Frederick, Viscount Lambton was elected MP for Berwick-on-Tweed in 1950. When his father, the 5th Earl of Durham, died in 1970, he disclaimed the title to remain in the Commons. He was given ministerial responsibility for the Royal Air Force.

In the early summer of 1972 Lambton was making regular use of a high-class call-girl service. His favourite was the 26-year-old Norma Russell. What the popular newspapers were to call their torrid encounters took place at her Maida Vale flat. Other prostitutes often accompanied Norma to satisfy the minister's lively tastes. Marijuana lent an added exoticism to the scene. At first Lambton covered his tracks by using a bogus identity, 'Mr Lucas', but he became careless, and dispensed with precaution. So careless did he become that one evening he paid her £5 by personal cheque. Miss Russell seemed unlikely to shop him. 'I vote for the Tories. They are my best clients,' she later said.

In November 1972 Norma married Colin Levy, a 28-year-old heavy drinker with a criminal record for dishonesty. The marriage stayed on an even keel until March 1973 when, after a domestic dispute, Colin Levy went abroad. His wife told the police he had gone on a drugs-buying run. She also let slip that one of her clients was Lambton. The police pounced when Levy returned, though they found no drugs. Levy, however, implicated Lambton in drugs and prostitution. The police passed the information on to the Serious Crime Squad which was investigating a high-class London vice ring. They in turn passed the information on to MI5, who told the Home Secretary. Edward Heath was informed. The Prime Minister, aware of Macmillan's failings only ten years earlier, ordered MI5 and the police to co-operate in securing any evidence.

Meanwhile, Colin Levy was planning to cash in on his wife's connections. Levy and an accomplice hid cine-equipment and a microphone (the latter up a teddy bear's nose) in his wife's bedroom to capture the minister *in flagrante delicto*. On 5 May they offered the film show to the *News of the World* for £30,000. The pictures were not good enough so the newspaper installed its own equipment in the flat. On 9 May Levy used a tape recorder to capture a conversation about drugs between Lambton and Norma.

The following day, a *News of the World* photographer hid in the wardrobe behind a two-way mirror and took pictures of the minister cavorting on the bed with Norma and a black prostitute. Inexplicably, the newspaper shelved the story and returned the evidence to Levy. He tried and failed to sell it to the German magazine *Stern*. The *Sunday People* was next on his list. Levy demanded £45,000. The *Sunday People* offered £750, with a further £5,250 if they published the story. Reluctantly, Levy agreed. The newspaper gave the material straight to the police.

Norma Levy then embarked on the course which was to prove fatal to Lambton. She told her story to the well-connected wife of the man who ran the upmarket London nightclub Eve, where Norma plied her trade. The woman contacted James Prior, the Leader of the House of Commons, through a mutual friend who happened to be an old business acquaintance of the minister's. They met Robert Armstrong, a senior civil servant (later to become Cabinet Secretary), in the incongruously dignified surroundings of the Privy Council Office.

Prior doubted 'if the room had ever witnessed a more bizarre yet intriguing story'. His discoveries were conveyed to the Prime Minister. On 22 May, hours after Prior had emerged from the Privy Council room, Lambton resigned from the Government and Parliament. His statement was frank and devoid of self-pity. 'This is the sordid story,' he wrote:

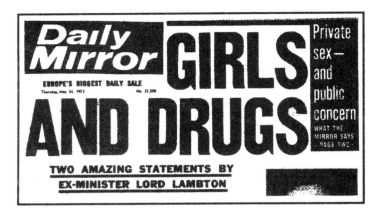

Daily Mirror, 24 May 1973

There has been no security risk and no blackmail and never at any time have I spoken of any aspect of my late job. All that has happened is that some sneak pimp has seen an opportunity of making money by the sale of the story and secret photographs to the papers at home and abroad. My own feelings may be imagined but I have no excuses whatsoever to make. I behaved with incredible stupidity.

Lambton was later to comment that he couldn't think 'what all the fuss is about; surely all men patronize whores?'

The following day, 'a day of sensation' (*Daily Mirror*), it was revealed that Scotland Yard was investigating a 'top people's vice ring'. Within hours of Lambton's resignation statement, the Attorney-General announced that the former minister was to be investigated for drugs offences.

Senior Scotland Yard officers carried out summonses for the possession of cannabis and amphetamines. Lambton, in a second statement that night, said: 'The police appeared to believe I was a heroin addict and asked to inspect the veins on my arms and legs. I consented. They were unmarked.' The press latched on to the fact that the minister stripped to his distinctive red flannel underwear. They searched his house. 'I willingly complied and showed them at once a small parcel of soft drugs that I had confiscated from a friend many months ago. They also found barbiturate pills which I have had, on and off, on prescription for fifteen years. If I had any sense of guilt I had ample time to hide the pills. I made no attempt to do so.' He later pleaded guilty to two charges of possessing cannabis and amphetamines. He was fined £300.

But the Yard's inquiries into the vice ring had uncovered the name of another senior member of the government. The name on the secret dossier which had been handed to the Home Secretary, Robert Carr, was George Patrick John Rushworth, the 2nd Earl Jellicoe, DSO, MC, godson of King George V. Since 1970 Jellicoe had been Leader of the House of Lords. It was alleged that on five or six occasions in the past year he had used call-girls from two agencies which advertised in the *Evening Standard.*

Jellicoe, twice married, took the prostitutes for dinner. After the mints came sex in his London flat. The day after Lambton's resignation the Prime Minister, Edward Heath, had asked Jellicoe if he knew anything about the case; the truthful reply had been 'No'. But Jellicoe, a Cambridge man, felt honour-bound to return to the Prime Minister the next day to tender his resignation. The PM accepted – mainly because he could not now truthfully deny knowledge of Jellicoe's indiscretions.

It was one of the few examples of unextracted honesty in the story of modern political scandal. It is also an odd reflection on Edward Heath, who in his later years radiates a mellow and indulgent 'seen it all before' mood, that he reacted as he did. It is unlikely that the oddly tolerant Margaret Thatcher – for all her 'Victorian values' – would have asked for Jellicoe's resignation. But the Profumo affair had been traumatic for the political class of the day. The country and its media were experiencing a wave of moral edginess not dissimilar to that which gripped Britain at the turn of the century.

On Jellicoe's revelations, Lambton commented: 'The way things are going it will soon be clear that Heath is the only member of the Government who doesn't do it.' Lambton also gave a startling television interview to Robin Day. He admitted to taking drugs, a habit he had picked up in Singapore, but he added: 'Taking opium in China is different to taking it in Berwick-on-Tweed.' Asked by Day, 'Why should a man in your social position and class and personality have to go to whores for sex?', Lambton answered: 'I think that people sometimes like variety. I think it is as simple as that and I think that impulse is probably understood by almost everybody. Don't you?'

Official papers released in January 2004 by the National Archive in Kew disclose that Lambton told MI5 he had thrown himself into a 'frenzied' round of vigorous 'gardening and debauchery' to get over losing a legal battle over his father's title. A blurred picture was also published for the first time of Lambton and a half-naked Norma Levy lying in bed, both apparently in a state of post-coital languor. It was taken by her husband, Colin, through a peephole in the wardrobe.

Lambton, married to his wife Belinda for thirty years, was the father of five; Jellicoe had a distinguished war record and had been awarded the *Croix de Guerre*. There was some public sympathy for both, especially Jellicoe. The *Daily Express* commented:

> In this modern so-called permissive age a splendid [parliamentarian] and junior minister have been cast into the wilderness . . . Can we really afford to discard men of talent, wit and patriotism because their personal lives fall short of blameless perfection?

Jellicoe told a secret security inquiry he locked his red boxes up in a cupboard when the women visited and started using call girls because of his 'exceptionally heavy burden of work', including preparations by Britain to welcome thousands of Ugandan Asians expelled by Idi Amin. He unintentionally blamed 'Ugandan discussions' many years before *Private Eye* used the term as a thinly veiled code for sexual misdemeanours of the great and not so good.

Edward Heath was forced to set up an inquiry. The Diplock report, delivered within two months, expressed satisfaction that there had been no compromise of security in either case. If Jellicoe hadn't resigned, said the report, he would have been allowed clearance for secret material. The same was not true of Lambton. The committee concluded:

> We do not suggest that Lord Lambton would consciously commit indiscretions when in his normal state of mind; but we think that there would be a real risk that he might do so in a mood of irresponsibility induced by drugs . . .

Ten years later, Lord Lambton was to return to the theme of double standards for politicians and the public. Commenting on the Cecil Parkinson scandal he remarked: 'I felt very sorry for Parkinson. I felt sorry for him because he had full attention on him and I know what that's like. But to tell you the truth, I couldn't quite see what he had done.'

Lambton ducked out of the public eye for many years, retiring to a peaceful villa in Sienna in Italy. He wrote a string of novels.

His daughter appeared as 'Miss Whiplash' in the 1986 film *Sid and Nancy*. We contacted him and asked for his reflections on the affair. 'I was rather sad I had to give up politics,' he said, 'I never think about the past any more. It is not worth regretting.' On the procession of Tory ministerial scandals in the 1990s, he commented: 'I think it is rather a pity when they hang on to office when they know they have to go. For me it seemed the right thing to do. Life is much more pleasant here.'

Lord Jellicoe went straight from the Cabinet into the boardroom, where he threw himself with vigour and success into business and industry. He soon collected a raft of directorships including Sotheby's, Smith's Industries, Warburgs, Morgan Crucible, Tate & Lyle and the Davy Corporation, serving as Chairman of the last two. He was also Chairman of the British Overseas Trade Board and the European Trade Council. For some years Chairman of the Council of King's College, London, Jellicoe became Chancellor of Southampton University in 1984. It is perhaps fair to say that the establishment always liked and respected Lord Jellicoe, sympathized with him in his brush with scandal, and never dropped him.

He told us he had never been ambitious politically. 'I had great respect for Mrs Thatcher but I very much doubt whether I would have survived long in a Thatcher Cabinet.' Did he regret having relinquished office without a struggle? 'My name is not Norman Lamont,' he replied.

JOHN STONEHOUSE – 1974–6

Not Lord Lucan

The perpetrator of probably the most elaborate attempt by any Member of Parliament in history to fake his own death, and even assume a new identity, John Stonehouse was the Labour MP who fooled most of the people for some of the time. When the BBC gravely announced his marine demise off a Miami beach, after a massive search by the US coastguard, the former Cabinet minister was sipping cocktails in a topless go-go bar on the other side of the United States. The smooth Stonehouse had left behind a distraught wife, a 25-year-old daughter, a mountain of debts, and a 27-year-old mistress, Sheila Buckley. His former Commons secretary was packing her bags to join him for a new life in New Zealand.

His carefully stage-managed disappearance, leaving his clothes behind on the beach, assumed the air of farce a few weeks later when he surfaced in Australia. Police in Melbourne were disappointed to discover that they had only captured a fugitive former British Cabinet minister; they thought they had landed the rather more interesting Lord Lucan.

John Stonehouse was born in Southampton on 28 July 1925. His father was a leading trade unionist, his mother a former mayor. He went to Taunton School and by the age of sixteen was an enthusiastic member of the Labour Party. After brief spells in the probation service and the RAF he studied for a degree course at the London School of Economics. He was elected to Parliament at the third attempt in 1957 in Wednesbury (later Walsall North), benefiting from the resignation of the pro-Suez Right-winger, Stanley Adams. As Harold Wilson's young Technology Minister he served in the Ministry of Aviation and the Colonial Office before reaching the Cabinet in 1968 as Postmaster-General. He was sacked two years later for allegedly misleading the Cabinet about a telegraphists' strike.

After Labour lost the 1970 election, still an MP, he devoted his energies to making money. He developed a network of twenty companies which only survived by creative accounting. In 1974 the Department of Trade began an investigation into his business empire which had debts of £1 million.

Rather than face a long investigation, Stonehouse, who had salted away £100,000 in Swiss bank accounts, chose another course: he faked his death. He tricked a local hospital into giving information on two recently deceased constituents, Joseph Markham and Donald Mildoon, by telling the Registrar he had money for their widows. The caring constituency MP called round to see the two grieving women to offer his condolences. By the time he had left, their Member of Parliament had obtained enough information about their husbands to assume elements of their identities.

In November 1974, the newly re-elected Stonehouse, who had been passed over for high office in Wilson's new government, left for Miami. Soon afterwards, immigration officers would be waving through a Mr Joseph Markham whose passport photograph showed him in an open-necked shirt, glasses, hair swept back, and a wide grin to distort his features.

On 19 November he went to Miami's Hotel Fontainbleu and carefully befriended the 65-year-old woman beach attendant. She readily agreed to look after the dashing Englishman's clothes while he swam in the warm Atlantic Ocean. He never returned for them. The following day he was reported missing, presumed drowned, and made the front page of every major newspaper.

Stonehouse had, in fact, gone to a disused building and picked up a hidden suitcase containing money, travellers' cheques, credit cards, fake passports and spare clothes. He flew to San Francisco and Hawaii and telephoned his lover in Hampstead who was relieved to hear that the plan had worked. By the end of the month he was in Melbourne. But his undoing was a suspicious 22-year-old bank clerk who spotted the fugitive MP withdrawing large cash sums as Markham and depositing them up the road as Mildoon. The police were informed.

Convinced that he was Lord Lucan, the police put Stonehouse under surveillance and raided his flat. Three days later a detective read about Stonehouse's disappearance from the Fontainbleu Hotel and remembered seeing a box of the hotel's matches in the suspect's room.

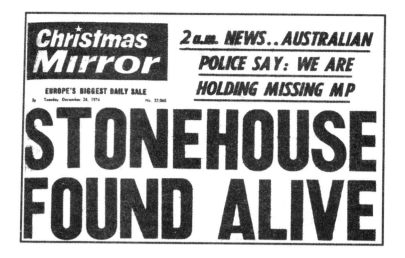

Daily Mirror, 24 December 1974

Photographs of Lucan and Stonehouse were immediately wired from London. On Christmas Eve 1974 the runaway was arrested. Stonehouse's sense of self-delusion at this time seems evident. He later wrote in his autobiography: 'Markham/Mildoon was arrested as an illegal immigrant and the world of Stonehouse was thrust back into the reluctant shell of my body.'

The news was flashed to London at 2 a.m. in time for the Christmas Eve newspapers. 'Stonehouse Found Alive' said the *Daily Mirror* which broke the news to his wife, who was too stunned to speak. Their daughter Jane told reporters: 'We have a lot to talk about at the moment.' The shock was almost too much for his eighty-year-old mother, Rosina: 'It can't be true. I don't believe it . . . surely my boy is dead . . . drowned?'

As Stonehouse was questioned by the police, his wife and mistress boarded separate flights to Melbourne. Meanwhile the papers, which had been speculating that the flamboyant MP might still be alive, found evidence of the collapse of his many companies. Only days before Stonehouse's arrest, the Prime Minister had been forced to deny damaging allegations that the MP, when a Cabinet minister, had been named as a Soviet spy by a Czech defector in 1969.

The embattled MP argued that he had been a man of honour – honourable on the grounds that he had left his wife of 26 years huge insurance sums to collect after his death. Mrs Stonehouse was unimpressed. She returned to Britain within hours, declared that her husband was mad, and started divorce proceedings.

In London the newly elected Leader of the Opposition, Margaret Thatcher, was making the most of the Prime Minister's embarrassment. Wilson agreed to let a Select Committee consider the errant MP's position. There was no precedent for expelling MPs for absence from duty, even by feigning death, and Stonehouse rejected a request to return to answer the committee's questions: 'It would be exceptionally dangerous to my psychological health,' he said.

Stonehouse was extradited in July 1975, requests for asylum having been rejected by Botswana, Kenya, Mauritius, Tanzania, Bangladesh and Canada. Even Olof Palme, the Swedish Prime Minister, would not help his former friend. Throughout this time the electors of Walsall North went unrepresented. No by-election could be called – the MP refusing to resign and being, after all, not dead. But by the time he was extradited his local party had already chosen his intended successor. In October 1975 Stonehouse made one of the most bizarre personal statements to the House in memory. He rehearsed the defence he would later use at his trial: that he was a disillusioned idealist fleeing from humbug and hypocrisy.

In March 1976 his local party demanded his resignation. He refused. Making the most of appearances in the Commons, he provoked angry scenes in April when he alleged widespread official corruption. Tory MPs guffawed. Then he quit the Labour Party, reducing its Commons majority to two, and joined the fledgling English National Party whose chairman, Dr Frank Hansford Miller, triumphantly proclaimed: 'The renewal of England begins today.'

At the 68-day Old Bailey trial, Stonehouse – red rose in his buttonhole, St George's flag in his hand and pleading not guilty to 21 charges of theft, fraud and deception – repeatedly clashed with the judge. He mounted his own defence. Spouting conspiracy theories at every opportunity, he failed to impress the jury who did not accept that the charges were 'politically rigged' against him or that a 'national sickness' had led to his prosecution.

Mr Justice Eveleigh, after several bruising encounters with the disgraced politician, declared: 'You did not simply decide to disappear because you were oppressed by business burdens. You decided to do so in comfort, and it is clear to me that self-interest has been well to the fore. You aimed to get rich quickly. You falsely accused other people of cant, hypocrisy and humbug, when you must have known all the time that your defence was an embodiment of all those three.' Stonehouse was convicted on eighteen counts and sentenced to seven years' imprisonment. He appealed, and lost. His mistress Sheila Buckley walked free from the Old Bailey, having been given a two-year suspended sentence on five charges of theft.

In Wandsworth prison Stonehouse suffered two heart attacks and was released from jail in 1979 after only three years. He was physically broken, and bankrupt. The ever-loyal Sheila Buckley was there to greet him. They married in 1981 at a secret ceremony at Bishop's Waltham and later had a son. Stonehouse eked out a living as a writer, disappearing from public view. He died in relative poverty in 1988.

JEREMY THORPE – 1976–9

'Sponger, whiner, parasite': But Was Scott Lying?

I met Jeremy Thorpe in the summer of 1995 (writes Matthew Parris). I had called on him to discuss the story which follows, and was shown in by his wife Marion. She seemed a refined woman, young for her years. Their house in Bayswater had the worn, interesting and friendly feeling that comes with taste, money and an absence of pretension.

Mr Thorpe waited at the top of the stairs to greet me. He walked with difficulty. Thorpe has been ill for many years with Parkinson's Disease, and people had told me I would be shocked at how he had deteriorated. I was not shocked, having expected this; I was more surprised at how sharp, amused and amusing he was, how closely engaged with modern politics, and how interested in it all he remained. Surrounded in his study by walls crowded with photographs, mementos, including a framed cigar from Churchill, cartoons and pictures from his years in politics, he showed me to a chair.

Jeremy Thorpe's physical deterioration is undeniable: he shakes badly, speaks impossibly quietly and indistinctly, and is unsteady on his feet, but you only have to look into his eyes to see a man always half a step ahead of you in his mental grasp. He was a little more mannered, a little more gentlemanly and more charming than I had expected. You could see how, all those years ago, he had swept the Liberal Party off its feet.

Mr Thorpe's wish in seeing me was not to 'agree' or authenticate any part of what follows, but to draw my attention – and, through me, the reader's attention – to what he has always maintained was the fundamentally dishonest and often fantastic nature of accounts which circulated at the time and which I quote below. He wanted me to be clear throughout that what appeared in many contemporary versions was heavily reliant upon statements made by Norman Scott, whose good character was later questioned by the judge and whose version of events Mr Thorpe has always flatly denied. He drew my attention to his statement, delivered at Bath police station on 3 June 1978, which is printed in full on pp.214–21.

Few twentieth-century scandals rival the Profumo affair, but the humiliation of Jeremy Thorpe comes close. Here, too, was a Privy Councillor and a kiss-and-tell lover. Here, too, money changed hands, new allegations appeared daily and alleged security lapses and foreign spies were thrown in for good measure. Here, too, was a story beginning with obscure and apparently unconnected court cases and ending with a sensational trial at the Old Bailey.

But this time, the kiss-and-tell lover was another man; and this time the Privy Councillor was accused of plotting the lover's murder. Jeremy Thorpe, wit, dandy, epigrammatist, and arguably the Liberals' greatest hope since Lloyd George, was charged with incitement and conspiracy to murder Norman Scott. He was acquitted but his career was ruined. The ink had dried on the 1967 Sexual Offences Act, but twelve years on homosexuality was barely tolerated, and this respected politician's choice of partner made it worse: there was public and press revulsion against the young man one judge called a 'spineless neurotic character'. Judges' pronouncements these days seem to have lost that rippling moralistic quality.

A few days before the trial, the voters of North Devon delivered their own verdict: at the 1979 election Thorpe was thrown out. After his acquittal he still hankered for a return to public life but he was never forgiven by his party.

Yet he was a man of remarkable abilities and born to politics: both father and grandfather were Tory MPs. Aged six, he developed a tubercular condition which confined him to a spinal carriage for more than six months and left him with constant back pain. After Eton, he was at Trinity College, Oxford, where in 1951 his smooth tongue and sharp mind made him a formidable President of the Union.

After starting as a barrister, the 26-year-old Thorpe ran a storming campaign, his first, for the rural Tory stronghold of North Devon in the 1955 election. He lost, but bounced back with a stunning Liberal victory in 1959. At thirty, the energetic bachelor MP was one of the youngest and most dashing of the debilitated 1959 intake. He knew all the best people. Bizarre rumours later grew that he had been considered a potential best man at Princess Margaret's wedding to Antony Armstrong-Jones in 1960 and that MI5 had made inquiries and seen to it that Thorpe was passed over: but there is no evidence for this. Far from being a close friend, Thorpe was not even invited to the wedding. He had not expected to be, he said. It seems the story may have been confused with another one involving similar allegations but a different individual.

One weekend, the young MP escaped Westminster for a friend's riding stables in Oxfordshire. It was here he first encountered an attractive, slightly effeminate, twenty-year-old groom, known then as Norman Josiffe. The young man had spent early adult life in and out of psychiatric clinics. He suffered delusions of grandeur, later changing his name to Scott so he could pretend to be a relative of

Lord Eldon, whose family bore the same name. Norman Scott was to become quite famous in his own right.

It was the autumn of 1961, the story runs. The young man was easily impressed by the sophisticated MP, but Thorpe, too, was much struck. Scott said his father had been killed in an air crash and his mother had unaccountably vanished. Thorpe told Scott that if he was ever in trouble he could turn to the MP for help. Over the next fifteen years Norman Scott was regularly in trouble.

Scott made the next move, and within weeks. Now 21, he turned up at the House of Commons with his Jack Russell terrier, 'Mrs Tish'. The dog was denied entrance and waited at the Anti-Vivisection Society in Whitehall, while Scott related his woes to Thorpe. He was unemployed and penniless, he said: sacked from the stables after being accused of stealing a horse.

This, anyway, is the version of events which has become famous. Thorpe, however, reminded me of a courtroom exchange which was to occur years later, during his final trial. George Carman, Thorpe's QC, was cross-questioning the prosecution witness, Norman Scott. Thorpe's solicitor, Sir David Napley, reported the exchange in his autobiographical *Not Without Prejudice*:

> 'Why did you say Mr Thorpe was a friend of yours when all you had ever done was speak to him for less than five minutes?' asked George
>
> 'Because I had had the therapy at the hospital,' said Scott. 'I was going through a delusion, and I had these letters. I was using them to say that I had a relationship with him already . . .'
>
> 'You were saying you had a sexual relationship with Mr Thorpe before you went to the House of Commons?'
>
> 'Yes.'
>
> 'Quite obviously, that was not true?'
>
> 'No, it wasn't.'
>
> 'You were suffering from a delusion?'
>
> 'Yes.'
>
> 'And you had suffered from other delusions, had you not?'
>
> 'Yes, sir.'
>
> The full significance of these exchanges seemed to have been lost on the public.

The 'letters' to which Scott referred were apparently from Thorpe – but not to Scott. They were to Scott's boss, Brecht Van der Vater, and reading them had suggested to Scott that Thorpe had homosexual tendencies. Thorpe's correspondence with Scott never became an issue in the case.

At the Old Bailey trial, the jury heard Scott say how Thorpe drove the young man and his dog to his own mother's house, Stonewalls, in Oxted, Surrey. What was said to have occurred there has probably condemned Thorpe in the public mind as much as any controversy about murder. It is important to note, here and throughout, that Jeremy Thorpe never gave evidence, and has said little more than that most of what was alleged was untrue. Norman Scott's story received great currency, but it should not be taken as an undisputed history. It was wholly denied by Thorpe in his statement. Scott's story went thus . . .

On the way to Stonewalls the MP suggested Scott should pose as a cameraman going with him to Malta the next day. After dinner, Scott retired for the night to the guest bedroom. Thorpe appeared with a homosexual novel, *Giovanni's Room*. Scott was not left much time for reading. Thorpe returned minutes later and sat on the bed, in dressing-gown and pyjamas. 'He just began talking to me about how I looked so ill, that things would be all right . . . he said I looked like a frightened rabbit. He decided, I suppose, from then on that I was his frightened rabbit and he just hugged me and called me "poor bunny" . . . he got into bed with me. He was hugging me.'

Thorpe left the room and returned with a towel and a tube of Vaseline. He laid the towel on the bed, rolled Scott over and buggered him. Afterwards the MP got up, patted Scott's thigh and left. 'I just lay there with my dog. She was on the bed. I picked her up, brought her into my bed with me, and just lay crying.' The following morning Thorpe, the perfect host, came into Scott's room and asked whether he liked his eggs fried or boiled.

. . . That is Scott's story. It is worth reminding ourselves that it was always central to Scott's credibility that he appeared through-out the long affair as a victim rather than fellow-homosexual. It may also have been important to Scott's fragile sense of self-worth. In addition, there was no great age difference between the two men, and since Thorpe consistently denied the incident, little thought was ever given to how far, if it were true, Scott might have led him on. It is also fair to point out that this was not the only time Scott had made detailed allegations of a sexual nature. As far as the previous occasion (referred to above by David Napley) was concerned, he was later to accept that the allegations were a delusion.

Eighteen years after these alleged events, the court heard that Thorpe took Scott back to London, where he gave him money to rent a flat in Draycott Place, near Westminster, and letters authorizing him to buy clothes on his account from his tailor, outfitter and shoemaker. This has always been denied by Thorpe. He recalls that Scott's allegations became 'increasingly wild'. Once Scott claimed that the MP had bought him Cartier cufflinks. But Cartier's told Thorpe's solicitors he had never purchased anything from them. Thorpe thinks there may have been some confusion with a pair of Cartier cufflinks belonging to his father, which went missing.

The MP did, however, make many efforts to help his friend. Through contacts he found him the first of a succession of jobs. In his hasty retreat from the stables Scott had lost his national insurance card. Thorpe applied for a replacement and stamped it for several months. Technically, Jeremy Thorpe had become Norman Scott's employer. Thorpe did more. For Christmas, he took Scott to the Devon home of May Collier and her husband James, the prospective Liberal candidate for Tiverton. Thorpe instructed solicitors to inquire whether Scott was owed anything from the estate of his deceased father and though he could not fund Scott's ambitions to study dressage in France, Thorpe placed advertisements in *Country Life* to help him find work.

If Thorpe had not yet sensed how unreliable Scott was, he did in February 1962. Scott was accused of stealing a suede coat from a woman, Ann Gray, he had met in a psychiatric clinic. Thorpe insisted to the police, who wanted to interview Scott, that this should take place in his office at Westminster, telling them he was 'more or less' Scott's guardian. Impressed, they dropped the case.

Perhaps to get Scott out of London, Thorpe found him a job in Somerset tending horses. Days later, he wrote to him there. Fourteen years on, the disclosure of this letter did more than anything else to bring about his resignation. Known as the 'bunnies letter', it was used, too, as evidence at the Old Bailey.

My Dear Norman,

Since my letters normally go to the House, yours arrived all by itself at my breakfast table at the Reform, and gave me tremendous pleasure.

I cannot tell you just how happy I am to feel that you're really settling down, and feeling that life has something to offer. This is really wonderful and you can always feel that whatever happens Jimmy and Mary [Collier] and I are right behind you. The next thing is to solve your financial problems and this James Walters [my solicitor] and I are on to. The really important point is that you are now a member of a family doing a useful job of work – with Tish – which you enjoy. Hooray!! Faced with all that no more bloody clinics. I think you can now take the Ann Gray incident as over and done with.

Enclosed another letter!! [reply to *Country Life* ad] I suggest you keep them all – just in case – but will you send back the photo? Thank the guy but say you are fixed up.

Bunnies can (+ will) go to France. In haste.

Yours affectionately,

Jeremy

I miss you.

By April 1962, Thorpe's solicitor was uncovering holes in Scott's story. His dead father was alive and well and living in Orpington. He was a hospital worker. His vanished mother had not moved from her address in Bexleyheath. And she did not take kindly to the MP's interest in her son. 'She is vicious about you . . . as being largely responsible for the rift between her son and herself,' Walters reported.

Scott did not stay long in jobs. Thorpe's earlier affection rapidly cooled. In May an exasperated Thorpe sent a terse note back to one of Scott's new employers, disclaiming any responsibility for the young man, and passing on his parents' address. Scott, lonely on a Somerset farm, could not accept this.

In September Mrs Tish, Scott's terrier, had to be put down after killing some ducks on the farm from which Scott was sacked. His mother begged him to forget Thorpe, but he returned to London, where Thorpe ignored him. Rejected, Scott confided in a woman friend that he wanted to kill Thorpe and commit suicide. She informed the police, who visited Scott at the cheap hotel near Victoria station where he was staying.

At Chelsea police station he made a statement. He wanted, he said 'to tell you about my homosexual relations with Jeremy Thorpe, who is a Liberal MP'. Incredulous, the officers summoned a police doctor. An undignified examination confirmed (in his view) that Scott practised anal intercourse. Scott handed over two letters from Thorpe, including the fateful 'bunnies' letter. In themselves they proved no crime on the MP's part, and the police took no action – filing them, just in case.

Scott began a precarious existence, trying to resume his equestrian career in Northern Ireland. He claims he would return to London so Thorpe 'could screw' him but there is no other evidence for this, and in 1963 the MP refused to pay a bill from his Bond Street outfitters for silk pyjamas Scott had bought on Thorpe's account. Seeking psychotherapy, Scott blamed Thorpe (who he still maintained was his guardian) for his homosexuality and fecklessness. He started to call himself the Honourable Lianche-Josiffe and elevated his 'dead' father to a peer of the realm. He also threw in a young wife, killed in a tragic road accident.

All the while, Thorpe's political future was brightening. At the 1964 election he was returned with an increased majority. Scott contacted him again. He had the chance of a job in Switzerland. Thorpe gave him the money to go. Scott hated Switzerland and left before his luggage had arrived. Thorpe agreed to try to retrieve his luggage, but would have no more to do with him. Scott went to Ireland, writing to Thorpe's mother, Ursula, in March 1965:

> For the last five years as you probably know, Jeremy and I have had a 'homosexual relationship'. To go into it too deeply will not help either of us. When I first came down to Stonewalls that was when I first met him – though he told you something about the TV programme and Malta. This was all not so true. What remains is that through my meeting with Jeremy that day, I gave birth to the vice that lies latent in every man.

He sounds depressingly like Lord Alfred Douglas in penitential mode. He goes on to describe a later meeting with her son.

I think that was the day I realised that Jeremy did not care for me as a friend but only as a — — Oh! I hate to write that!! It upset me terribly and I was rather sick because, you see, I was looking for a friend in the real sense of the word.

Badly shaken by the letter, which his mother posted on to him, Thorpe turned to his best friend in Parliament: 43-year-old Peter Bessell, the Liberal MP for Bodmin. A Congregationalist lay preacher who amazed his Cornish constituents by campaigning in a Cadillac, Bessell was a card, a slick business-man, and an adventurous (heterosexual) lover. Admitting to Thorpe his affair with his secretary, he had also led his comrade into believing he too might have homosexual tendencies. Thus he gained Thorpe's confidence.

Bessell suggests in his book on the affair, *Cover-Up*, that Thorpe was a disaster waiting to happen. He recalls observing Thorpe at a nearby table in the Members' Dining Room in the early 1960s, in 'animated conversation' with a fair-haired youth. Anyone, he says, could have spotted what was going on.

Norman Scott had black hair. Thorpe denies the entire incident, which he says Bessell invented. He points out that only MPs are allowed in the Members' Dining Room at the Commons.

Bessell claims he was next invited by Thorpe to join him for lunch at the Ritz hotel. He handed him Scott's letter and asked him to find Scott in Dublin and shut him up.

Bessell arranged a breakfast meeting at a Dublin hotel with Scott, who arrived late. 'His appearance surprised me. Tall and emaciated with a shock of unruly black hair, he looked considerably more than his 24 years. Tidily but inexpensively dressed, there were deep shadows under his eyes as though he had not slept. He was even more nervous than I had expected . . . when we shook hands I noticed his palm was damp.' Continuing the conversation in a taxi, 'it was not cold. Yet he sat huddled in the taxi shivering'.

Bessell told Scott (untruthfully) that the letter to Thorpe's mother was 'akin to a blackmail attempt'. Scott claims Bessell also told him he had an extradition order in his briefcase signed by Sir Frank Soskice, the Labour Home Secretary. Scott promised to cause no more trouble. This was not surprising as Bessell had undertaken to send him regular retainers. Over the years he received some £700. Bessell says he was often reimbursed by Thorpe, whom the payments were aimed to protect. Scott embarked on a series of failed careers and relationships, increasingly blaming Thorpe for his failures. In August 1968 he received £75 from Bessell to set up as a male model.

Thorpe's political career was going from strength to strength. In 1967 he became Leader of the Liberal Party. He married Caroline Allpass the following year, and they had one son. Bessell wrote that Thorpe still saw the Scott affair as 'a black cloud hovering over him . . . at night he sometimes dreamed it would destroy him.' Thorpe says this is a flight of fancy on Bessell's part.

In 1968, with Thorpe's national profile ever higher, Bessell's business ventures collapsing, Scott's modelling ending in failure and the virtually unemployable young man again demanding his national insurance card, Thorpe began to panic. A plan to ship Scott to America had foundered because the US Embassy had refused him a visa.

Bessell claims the Liberal leader called him into his Commons office and demanded a final solution: 'Peter, we have got to get rid of him . . . It's no worse than shooting a sick dog.' Thorpe was also alleged to have tried to persuade a university friend, David Holmes, a merchant banker who was godfather to his son, to organize the killing. The plot was shelved when the extraordinary news came through that Scott had got married and his wife was pregnant. It was May 1969.

Some time that summer, Scott telephoned Thorpe's cottage in Devon to demand help in retrieving his national insurance credentials. Thorpe's wife, Caroline, answered. She told Scott she knew nothing of this and could not help him. Scott rang Bessell, threatening to sell his story to the papers. A temporary national insurance card was arranged. Scott's marriage failed and by 1970 there was talk of a contested divorce in which Thorpe's name was bound to come up. The murder plot allegedly resurfaced.

Scott left his wife and baby and moved to Wales, apparently expecting Thorpe to foot the bill. No money was forthcoming. Scott poured out his sorrows to an elderly postmistress. Distressed, she wrote to her Liberal MP, Emlyn Hooson, asking him to tell a 'senior party figure' to honour the promise he had made, and pay Scott. Hooson passed the letter to David Steel,

Liberal Chief Whip. A secret inquiry was set up under the Liberal peer Lord Byers, at Thorpe's suggestion.

When he was cross-examined, Scott won few friends, crying, according to Hooson, 'like a jilted girl'. He flounced from the room, declaring that Byers was 'a pontificating old sod'. Later he claimed that leaving the Palace of Westminster he was accosted by a mysterious stranger who said: 'We know all what you've been saying in there, and if you carry on as you are doing, we will kill you.'

At the Byers inquiry, Scott had said the police interviewed him in 1965 when he went to the Commons armed with a gun. Thorpe focused his defence on this lie, presenting evidence from the Police Commissioner supported by the Home Secretary, which proved no such interview had taken place. The Byers inquiry found no evidence of wrongdoing or a relationship with Scott. Thorpe emerged as the victim of a spiteful and unbalanced blackmailer.

The matter seemed to be closed. Scott thought otherwise. He went to Gordon Winter, a freelance journalist. 'I was deeply in love with Jeremy for three years,' his testimony went. 'He discarded me like a cheap tart.' Winter hawked his story round Fleet Street but it was thought too hot to publish. Mirror Group Newspapers bought it and locked it away in a safe. Winter also typed up a 74-page report detailing the allegations, which he passed on to Pretoria. The journalist was a South African spy.

In 1973, his wife Caroline having been killed in a car accident, Thorpe married Marion, the Countess of Harewood. A former concert pianist, she had previously been married to the Queen's cousin, the Earl of Harewood. The Liberal leader was riding high in the opinion polls. Then to his horror Scott moved into his North Devon constituency and became a saloon bar bore, relating his incredible story to any of Thorpe's constituents who would listen to him.

In 1974 the Liberal leader had a lucky escape. Builders refurbishing Bessell's London office discovered letters and photographs. One was Scott's 1965 letter to Thorpe's mother. The builders handed them straight to the *Sunday Mirror*. It was not a good choice. Though the paper already had Scott's confessions on file, Deputy Chairman Lord Jacobsen was a friend of Thorpe's. He decided that 'since the letters hinted at blackmail and had come into the hands of the *Mirror* in dubious circumstances they should be returned to Thorpe'.

In the same year, the embattled Heath government struggled to form a coalition. Thorpe alarmed members of his own party by agreeing at the instigation of Edward Heath to a meeting at Downing Street immediately after Heath had lost the February 1974 election. Heath wanted to discuss the possibility of a Liberal–Conservative coalition. At this meeting Thorpe told Heath that while we knew who had lost the election, we didn't know who had won it. The talks are thought to have been vague with no firm offers made, though it was said there were thoughts on Mr Heath's part of the Liberal leader becoming Heath's Foreign Secretary. Thorpe says this never arose in their discussions. No doubt to Pretoria's disappointment, the plan came to nothing.

Scott, living on the outskirts of Dartmoor and upset that his confession to Gordon Winter had not borne fruit, was now talking to all who would listen.

In 1975 an assassin was purportedly found to finish him off. The Old Bailey heard that Thorpe's banker friend, David Holmes, through two associates, George Deakin and John Le Mesurier (all three were eventually acquitted) paid Andrew Newton, an airline pilot, £5,000 for the contract. The money had allegedly been siphoned off from political donations. Newton would receive another £5,000 when Scott was dead.

The execution of the contract, if contract it was, turned into a farce. Newton went to Dunstable instead of Barnstaple. He eventually caught up with his target in October 1975. Scott, with Rinka, his Great Dane, got into Newton's car believing he had been sent to protect Scott from a mysterious hit-man, who would be arriving soon from Canada.

At this stage it was not difficult to persuade Scott he was a marked man. In August he had been arrested, ostensibly for not paying a £28 hotel bill from nine months earlier, and subjected to intensive questioning not about the hotel bill but about what documents he held which might incriminate Thorpe. MI5 had asked the Devon and Cornwall Constabulary to look into the security implications of Scott's allegations. They may have hoped to bring a charge of blackmail against him. It is not known whether MI5 were acting at political instigation.

Newton drove Scott and Rinka to a secluded spot on Exmoor. His driving became erratic as he feigned tiredness. Scott offered to take over. Stopping the car, Newton produced a 1910 Mauser and shot the Great Dane. He then turned the gun on the terrified former model, warning, 'It's your turn next'. Then he turned the gun away. Either it jammed or Newton pretended it had. Cursing, he leapt back into the car and sped off, leaving a sobbing Scott trying to give Rinka the kiss of life.

The press bided its time. A short piece appeared in the *News of the World* about the death of the dog and the arrest of Newton. Fleet Street was serving notice on Thorpe that they knew a bigger story must break, and could wait for it.

They did not wait long. In January 1976 Scott appeared in court in Barnstaple on charges of defrauding the DHSS. The normally empty press and public gallery was packed with journalists. Scott astounded the magistrate by claiming he was being hounded because he had once enjoyed a sexual relationship with the leader of the Liberal Party. It cannot have been what the magistrate expected.

With the allegations made in court, they could be reported under protection of absolute privilege. The lid was off. Thorpe denied any homosexual affair. He met the then Prime Minister, Harold Wilson, who mentioned the matter, and introduced what was later to be treated as a huge red herring, but now looks credible: Thorpe, he said, was the victim of a South African conspiracy. Agents from BOSS (Pretoria's Bureau of State Security) had plotted to use Thorpe to discredit Wilson's government, which needed Liberal support.

For Fleet Street the conspiracy theory grew when Cyril Smith, now Liberal Chief Whip, resigned claiming he had been kept in the dark. Other Liberal MPs expressed tepid support for their leader, privately jockeying for position in a future leadership race.

In the Commons, Wilson repeated his claim that Thorpe was the victim of a South African smear campaign. Thorpe was still denying homosexuality. The *Sunday Times* (March 1976) gave him the benefit of the doubt as a man 'whose word has proved reliable throughout a long career in public life'.

That month, the alleged hit man, Newton, reached court for shooting Scott's dog. The trial date, 16 March, is significant: the same day Harold Wilson resigned as Prime Minister. Temporarily that deflected press interest. Newton, sentenced to two years for a firearms offence alone, protected Thorpe by claiming it was he, Newton, who was the victim of Scott's blackmail attempts. This did not stop Scott repeating his allegations. David Steel, meanwhile, had discovered that Thorpe's banker friend Holmes had been paid £20,000 intended for the Liberal Party.

Steel, it was said, asked for Thorpe's resignation, but Thorpe refused. Thorpe does not recall being placed under such unequivocal pressure at this stage, remembering only that he made it clear throughout that he would decide for himself, in his own time. Steel, in his book *Against Goliath*, says he spoke to Thorpe in early March. 'I told him . . . he ought now to resign the leadership . . . Jeremy must have been surprised to receive such advice from me but he was so buffeted by everything he showed neither surprise nor resentment. He simply refused, saying he was not going to be brought down by a lot of panicky colleagues.'

Now Fleet Street uncovered evidence of the retainers from Bessell to Scott. Bessell, who had emigrated to America, vehemently denied they were for Thorpe's benefit. Then, in April, this key witness turned. Bessell, desperately in debt, sensed there was big money to be made. He sold his story to the *Daily Mail*. Scott smelt money too, and found a solicitor. On 1 May he issued a summons against the Commissioner of the Metropolitan Police, Robert Mark, to retrieve the two letters he had handed over in 1962. One was the 'bunnies' letter. Thorpe's solicitors promptly applied for both too.

On 6 May the *Mail* printed Bessell's story under the headline: 'I told lies to protect Thorpe.' Bessell maintained that payments to Scott had been to protect Thorpe. Thorpe wanted Scott killed: hence the botched dog-shooting incident. Still issuing denials, Thorpe was losing what remained of his Party's confidence. Fellow Liberals were beginning to ask in public why their leader was not suing. Richard Wainwright voiced the question on radio.

Scott, as the letters' recipient, won custody of the originals. Thorpe, as author, was entitled only to a copy. With his noted solicitor, Lord Goodman, he grimly read over his words of fourteen years earlier: words soon to be in Scott's hands again. The letters were embarrassing but not conclusive. On the advice of his solicitor Thorpe decided to pre-empt Scott by publishing them himself in the *Sunday Times*, who agreed to make no adverse comment, and to publish Thorpe's explanation too. Thorpe

212 *Great Parliamentary Scandals*

denied any sexual relationship and denied involvement in the retainers or the dog-shooting.

The letters appeared in the *Sunday Times* on 9 May 1976. The following morning, T-shirts were on sale in Oxford Street with the slogan 'Bunnies can and will go to France'. Thorpe, staying the weekend with Clement Freud, the MP who had remained most loyal, heard it gently suggested by his friend that it might be time to go.

He had no alternative. On 10 May he handed his bitter resignation letter to David Steel, Acting Chief Whip. The letter blamed the press for a 'sustained witch-hunt', singling out fellow MP Richard Wainwright: 'a party colleague has now taken to the air publicly to challenge my credibility,' he wrote.

> Loyal Liberals . . . deserve better of us than the continued spectacle of a party wrangling with itself with more concern for personality than policy. You will know that, from the beginning, I have strenuously denied the so-called Scott allegations and I categorically repeat these denials today.

Liberal MPs were censured by future Speaker George Thomas for 'showing disloyalty just when their leader needed it most'.

With Thorpe on the backbenches there followed eighteen months of calm. It was shattered by the release from prison in April 1977 of would-be assassin Andrew Newton. He walked straight into the offices of the *Evening News,* which paid £3,000 for his story: 'I was hired to kill Scott.' The *Sunday People* stumped up a further £8,000 to take secret photographs of him collecting his £5,000 fee from businessman Le Mesurier, ostensibly payment for the murder attempt.

Thorpe then blundered. He held a press conference to deny any connection with a murder plot. He admitted that even if he had had 'a close, even affectionate' friendship with Scott it had been non-sexual. Grilled by a BBC correspondent about whether he had ever had a homosexual relationship Thorpe tartly replied: 'If you do not know why it is improper and indecent to put such a question to a public man you ought not to be here.' Thorpe had put his sexuality back on the agenda.

His fortunes now fell fast. The police began inquiries, travelling to California to interview Bessell. In return for immunity from prosecution Bessell, never one to waste a commercial opportunity,

THE TIMES

Mr Thorpe resigns over 'plots and intrigue'

The Times, 11 May 1976

gave an 11,000-word statement heavily implicating Thorpe. The statement – which (in a move which was unusual to say the least) two investigative journalists, Messrs Penrose and Courtier, had helped him write – formed the best part of Bessell's book on the affair. He was offered £50,000 serialization rights by the *Sunday Telegraph*, a third of it being paid in advance. The balance was payable after Thorpe's *conviction*. If Thorpe won, Bessell would receive only a further £8,000.

In agreeing this extraordinary 'no lose, no fee' clause the *Telegraph* was unwittingly sealing the fate of the prosecution. In retrospect it is almost incredible that a newspaper could have contemplated such an arrangement. Some would argue that it could amount to a conspiracy to pervert the course of justice. Those who regard press methods in the 21st century as unusually unscrupulous might cast their minds back to this dirty deal, nearly three decades ago.

Bessell's immunity package covered civil or private prosecutions arising from any trial. An eminent lawyer described it as 'surely the widest terms of immunity that any prosecution witness had ever been given in Britain'. Newton, who had peddled his story for £11,000, was given similar immunity from prosecution for murder, attempted murder, conspiracy to murder, or perjury during his previous trial.

The police now warned Thorpe's solicitors privately (an unusual courtesy) that their client would be charged within days, along with his supposed henchmen, Holmes, Le Mesurier and Deakin, with conspiracy to murder. Christopher Murray from the solicitors Kingsley Napley, acting for Thorpe throughout this trial, sought an urgent meeting at the Commons with David Steel, and warned him. Two days later all four presented themselves, by prior arrangement, at Minehead police station.

Thorpe had already volunteered a written statement some two months beforehand. It follows in full, and encapsulates the gist of the MP's whole defence:

Statement of John Jeremy THORPE handed to
Chief Superintendent CHALLES on 3rd June,
1978.

I have been informed by my Solicitors that
it has been indicated that the current

investigation broadly covers three main areas.
The first is whether I had ever been involved
in a homosexual relationship with Norman
JOSIFFE, also known as Norman SCOTT, which
might form a motive or a wish on my part to
eliminate him, cause him injury or put him in
fear. The second is whether I had been a party
to any conspiracy to kill or injure him or put
him in fear and the the third whether I had
paid, or authorised any payment, to one NEWTON
or any other person pursuant to or following
upon any such conspiracy, or to SCOTT in
respect of the purchase of certain documents
or otherwise.

In October 1977, I made a statement to the
press in this regard. I now wish to reiterate
and confirm as accurate what I said in that
statement save as to certain minor details
which are dealt with in the body of this
statement, and also to add the following:—

As to the first allegation, I wish, with all
the emphasis which I can command, to deny that
I was at any time engaged in any homosexual
relationship with SCOTT whatsoever, or that I
was, at any time, a party to any homosexual
familiarity with him. I described in my
earlier statement and have here confirmed the
circumstances under which I met SCOTT. I
believed that he was a person who was
desperately in need of help and support in
that he was in a suicidal and unbalanced
state. The action which, in the circumstances,
I followed was attributable solely to what I
saw as my duty having regard to the conditions
under which he approached me and in the event
my compassion and kindness towards him was in
due course repaid with malevolence and
resentment.

Although he never so informed me, I formed
the opinion, at an early stage, of the limited
number of occasions when I was in his
presence, that he was a homosexual and that he
was becoming too dependent upon me.
Accordingly, I made immediate arrangements for
him to be accepted into a family near Tiverton
with whom he was to spend Christmas, having
explained to them the reasons why I believed
he was in need of help. However, after only a
few weeks in their house they decided that his
highly neurotic and unbalanced state was too
disturbing an influence in the household and
he was asked to leave.

At about January 1962 SCOTT was still in an
unsettled state and in need of funds to enable
him to establish some means of supporting
himself. He had informed me that his father
had been killed in an air crash in South
America and I suggested that it might be
possible to obtain some compensation for him
in respect thereof. Accordingly, I requested a
Solicitor friend to initiate some enquiries in
this connection. In due course he informed me
that the story told by SCOTT was quite false.
In fact his father was at that time a hospital
porter living in Bexley Heath in Kent, ~~as was
his mother.~~ where his mother also lived. (JJT)

I arranged to see SCOTT again and saw him
whilst he was working at Hawkridge in
Somerset. I told him in strong terms of my
disgust, not merely at the manner in which he
had misled me, but more particularly having
wasted the time and energy of the Solicitor. I
told him there was nothing further I could do
to help; he became highly excited and
emotional. The meeting itself lasted no longer
than a quarter of an hour.

Subsequently, he sought to see me again in 1963 expressing contrition and asking me to allow him to meet me and seek my forgiveness. I arranged to meet him and did so publicly on the terrace of the House of Commons, at which meeting he again became highly excited and emotional, but before leaving suggested that I owed him some duty to support him financially which I refuted in forcible terms. With hindsight I now realise that my proper course would have been to refuse to see him. It was evident from our last meeting that he resented my disinterest in him and was likely to ^try to cause trouble. I was on the horns of ^a dilemma. I foresaw no problem in resisting any demands which he might make upon me or disproving falsehoods which he might utter against me. However, I suspected that the allegations at which he was hinting, although without the slightest foundation, were such as would involve, as in the event they have, baring my soul in public, which could have, however unfairly, serious political implications and repercussions for me and the Liberal Party. As a result, I misguidedly agreed to see him and did so on one further occasion, which I think was at my flat. I agreed to this meeting in the belief that it was better to avoid public discussion and that I could convince him that his grievances were wholly unjustified and fanciful. In the event I was wrong and his feelings of being rebuffed by me led to a series of public accusations, as is now well known. There is, as I have repeatedly asserted, not a vestige of truth in the allegations which he has made.

As to the second allegation, I wish with no less emphasis entirely to refute any suggestion that I have at any time been a

party to any conspiracy to kill or injure
Norman SCOTT or to put him in fear, or that at
any time I had any knowledge of or believed in
the existence of any such conspiracy. Quite
apart from the fact that any desire or
willingness to kill or cause physical harm to
any person is wholly alien to my nature, as
many would be prepared to confirm, the
circumstances which existed at the time when
it was subsequently suggested that such a
conspiracy may have existed, are wholly
inconsistent with the pursuit of the alleged
objective of such a conspiracy.

As I have mentioned above, there was a period
of time when I was understandably concerned at
the political implications which would result
from the wild and unfounded allegations which
it seemed probable Norman SCOTT would publish.
As I have further explained, my disquiet in that
connection was in in no way attributable to my
having in any way been involved in any
homosexual relationship with him whatsoever,
but because I foresaw that the mere necessity of
truthfully denying such an association might
raise, as a matter of public question, my own
private matters wholly unconnected with SCOTT
which, in my view, I could claim to be private
to me alone.

It has been suggested in a recently
published book that the time the alleged
conspiracy was conceived and embarked upon was
in the Spring of 1975. By that time SCOTT had
ensured in a variety of ways, including a
statement in the course of an inquest in 1973,
that his allegations had been widely
disseminated and although fully known by the
press and the major political parties, wisely
ignored by them.

The worst that SCOTT could falsely allege had been revealed. Far from this having adversely affected either me or the Liberal Party politically, which had been my fear, the party under my leadership had increased its vote in two elections in February and October 1974, from two million to six million and five and one third million respectively and I had increased my own majority in my own constituency from 369 to 11,000 and 6,700 respectively. Against this background, it is manifestly ludicrous to suggest, either that I any longer considered that any public reliance would be placed upon the utterances of SCOTT or that any measures were needed to deal with him, least of all the wholly unthinkable approach of conspiring to achieve his death, injury or otherwise. It appears that NEWTON was responsible for causing the death of SCOTT's dog and may have made an abortive attempt upon the life of SCOTT. I do not pretend to know the truth of this matter and I can only reassert that which I have already said that not only did I have no need to take any part in any such project and did not do so, but I had no knowledge whatsoever of it and was not and would not, under any circumstances, have been willing to allow any such plot to be pursued had any hint of suggestion come to me about it.

Finally, in relation to the third allegation, I wish vigorously to refute any suggestion that at any time I had knowingly been a party, either directly or indirectly, to the payment of any money whatsoever to NEWTON or to SCOTT for the purposes alleged. The press have reported that a payment of £2,500 was made indirectly to Norman SCOTT in February 1974 for the delivery of certain

letters and documents which had passed between
him and others, not including myself. I
understand that it is claimed that a sum of
£5,000 has been paid to NEWTON subsequent to
the incident involving the death of SCOTT's
dog and after his release from prison and that
the second sum had been disbursed from monies
provided by one Jack HAYWARD. I had no
knowledge whatsoever of the purchase of the
letters in question until the early part of
1976 when the fact was first publicly revealed
in the national press. I immediately expressed
and continue to express, both my surprise and
indeed my horror that anyone could have
thought it necessary to embark upon such a
course. The letters had already been widely
circulated and indeed had been seen by my
parliamentary colleagues in 1971 and nothing
whatsoever was to be gained from their
purchase or to be lost through their
publication. I have no personal knowledge
whatsoever of any payment to NEWTON of the sum
of £5,000 or otherwise and at no time made any
arrangements for any such payment. It is
correct that Mr. HAYWARD paid to me personally
two sums of £10,000 each to be used by me in
any way which I thought appropriate in
relation to campaigning expenses. In fact, by
reason of other donations at the relevant
times it became unnecessary to have recourse
to those two sums. There had been grave
difficulties at one stage in raising
sufficient money for the expenses for the
Liberal Party's election campaigns and I
accordingly resolved that, since Mr. HAYWARD
had made it quite plain to me that, not being
an adherent to the Liberal Party, he was not
making these monies available to the party but
to me personally, I would not cause them to be
paid into the Liberal Party funds where they

would be soon defrayed. I, therefore, made
arrangements for the sum of £20,000 to be
deposited with accountants and to be ~~ehld~~
held$^{(JJT)}$ as an iron reserve against any
shortage of funds at any subsequent election.
At no time, however, have I ever authorised
the use of these funds for any payment of the
kind alleged to either SCOTT or NEWTON and any
suggestion that I may have done so is entirely
without foundation.

I have, in consultation with my legal
advisers, given long and earnest consideration
as to whether I should amplify the firm and
precise general denials set out above. They
are conscious, as am I, of the fact that those
who have in the past been minded to put
forward false assertions against me have, from
time to time, varied the detail of their
account in order to adjust it to such hard
facts as, from time to time, have emerged.
Having regard to the unusual way in which
these current allegations have emerged there
is a real danger that if specific details
relating to matters which can be proved are
made known at the present time, they may in
the course of the investigation become known
to or deduced by those minded to further the
allegations, with consequent re-adjustment of
their version. In these circumstances, I have
been advised that whilst it is right and
proper that I should re-express the denials
which are contained in this statement, it is
neither incumbent upon me nor desirable to add
anything further.

> (Signed) Jeremy Thorpe.
> June 3rd 1978

He now indicated before questioning under caution at Bath
police station, that he would refuse to answer questions because

of the likelihood that his answers would be leaked and prejudice matters. On each subsequent question he indicated that his answer was the same ('ditto'). The exchange was duly leaked and *Private Eye* dubbed him 'The Ditto Man'. At Minehead he was formally charged with conspiracy and incitement to murder.

In October 1978 an unrepentant Thorpe appeared at the Liberal Party Conference. A furious David Steel, the new Liberal leader, escorted his disgraced predecessor to his seat amidst a mixture of embarrassed silence and applause, as the platform party contemplated their shoes.

Thorpe's appearance at the conference dominated the next day's headlines. With an election only months away his local party loyally re-selected him to fight the seat he had first won twenty years earlier. Thorpe succeeded in delaying the trial to enable him to fight the election. Only one Liberal MP, John Pardoe, from a neighbouring seat, set foot in the constituency to support Thorpe during the campaign. From early on it was clear the struggle was impossible. Public meetings were a disaster. Many were attended by a handful of party workers and his loyal Marion, outnumbered by the press. Auberon Waugh, who was writing a book, *The Last Word,* on the trial, put up as a candidate for the 'Dog Lovers' Party'. On 3 May, Thorpe's 6,700-odd majority was swept aside, the Tories romping home by an 8,473 margin. It was a bad result, though other Liberals had disappointing results too, John Pardoe also losing his seat. It is worth reflecting that even then, charged with conspiracy to murder, Thorpe, who despite this had been re-selected as Liberal candidate, received some 23,000 votes. Subsequently he was elected President of the North Devon Liberal Association. He is to this day President of the constituency's Liberal Democrat Association.

When the result was announced, Thorpe's supporters turned on the press in Barnstaple's Queen's Hall with shouts of 'scum'. He bowed out yards from the magistrates' court where Scott had pointed the accusing finger three years earlier. Quietly, as he left the hall, Thorpe said: 'The gap was much wider than I thought.'

Five days later, on 8 May, Jeremy Thorpe went on trial at the Old Bailey before the 69-year-old judge Mr Justice Cantley and a jury of nine men and three women. Charged with conspiring to murder Norman Scott, and inciting David Holmes to murder

Norman Scott, he pleaded not guilty to both charges. His old friend Bessell was the chief prosecution witness. Thorpe and his solicitor, David Napley, had engaged a rising star, George Carman QC. The case helped make Carman's reputation as a barrister. He shredded Bessell's credibility as a businessman, MP and husband. He reminded the jury that Bessell had at various times suggested different locations for his alleged discussion with Thorpe of a murder plot. He had said the incident took place in Thorpe's flat, or in a room in the Commons. Carman showed Bessell a photograph of himself face to face in conversation with Thorpe at the time he was claiming they had been talking on the telephone. It was odd, said Carman, that Bessell could be confused about so key a meeting. And he exploited the fact that the defence witnesses had cashed in with newspaper contracts before the trial and would have even richer pickings if Thorpe were convicted.

The demolition succeeded. The judge in his summing-up called Bessell a 'humbug'.

Carman ruthlessly took apart Norman Scott too, who was painted in court as an unstable liar and blackmailer. 'I will not have myself destroyed in this way,' the one-time male model protested. The judge was harsh. Summing-up for the jury, he labelled Scott:

> a crook, an accomplished liar ... a fraud. He is a sponger. He is a whiner. He is a parasite. But, of course, he could still be telling the truth. It is a question of belief ... He is a spineless neurotic character addicted to hysteria and self-advertisement ...

The following day, as the *Daily Mail* ran the words: 'PARASITE WHINER SPONGER CROOK LIAR' in a mammoth headline down its front page, the jury was locked safely away in a secret hotel to consider its verdict. The defendants, including Jeremy Thorpe, had to spend the night at Brixton Prison while the jurors deliberated – a practice which had arisen since the suicide of Stephen Ward. A handcuffed Thorpe was driven away in a police van, lying on the floor under a raincoat. At the prison he was stripped and medically examined. Complaining of a stomach upset, he was moved to the prison hospital. The prison authorities could not confirm whether this was usual practice for stomach upsets.

The jury quickly rejected the incitement charge which had been based solely on Bessell's word. For some jurors the £25,000 he was guaranteed by the *Sunday Telegraph* represented the equivalent of five years' salary. On conspiracy they initially took a straw poll. It was tied at six all. By the end of the first day four more had come over to Thorpe's side, but Mr Justice Cantley wanted a unanimous verdict.

By day two, only one was holding out for a conviction. Their arguments varied in sophistication. One juror thought Marion Thorpe had suffered enough. Carman had told them earlier that they must not suppose a not guilty verdict was a certificate of innocence awarded by the jury. 'In law, it means the prosecution has failed to make out its case – no more and no less.'

The jurors filed into court number one at 2.34 p.m. on Friday, 22 June 1979. Thorpe and his co-defendants had just finished a lunch of smoked salmon, beef and German hock supplied by his friend Clement Freud in a guarded room at the Old Bailey. Freud had provided a choice hamper on the first day, and added a bottle of chilled hock. In response to friendly representations from the warders, a second bottle of hock was included this time.

Thorpe was led into the dock and stood still, staring straight ahead as the not guilty verdicts were read out. He blinked, motionless, then tossed the three cushions which had supported his back high over the glass partition. Smiling, he embraced his wife from the dock. On the steps outside he gave a politician's victory salute to the ten-deep crowd.

The judge felt the jurors, like Marion Thorpe, had suffered enough during the 29-day trial and released them from further jury service for life.

The following day the *Daily Telegraph* said that Thorpe, while exercising his undoubted right not to go into the witness box, might have been better served 'had he explained the whole course of his behaviour publicly and on oath'. The *Daily Mail,* however, believed such reticence enabled Thorpe to emerge as 'statesmanlike'.

Many supporters in North Devon were ecstatic. The following Sunday a service of thanksgiving was held in a church near Thorpe's home where an eccentric vicar had offered to celebrate the acquittal. The plan backfired, not only because of the ribald publicity and a denunciation from the local archdeacon, but also because the Gay Liberation Front promised to send coachloads of members to attend.

The church was not as full as expected, much of the congregation being from Fleet Street. The vicar thanked God for the 'ministry of his servant, Jeremy, in North Devon'. 'The darkness is now passed and the time of light shines. This is the day that the Lord hath made!' He likened Thorpe's acquittal to the Resurrection.

In 2002 Norman Scott resurfaced, contributing to a Yorkshire Television documentary and speaking in January 2003 to the *Observer*: 'If I do say so myself I was a very good-looking young man but I was terribly naive . . . I was in financial difficulties . . . he coerced me and somehow we ended up having a relationship.'

Scott claimed Thorpe had kept his national insurance card. He believed there had been a number of attempts on his life. 'I was so vilified it was as if I was on trial. I felt the Establishment had won.'

Thorpe broke a 23-year silence, bitterly attacking the documentary as a show that repeated old claims from an unreliable witness. His friends added that it was unjust to an old, sick man, who was physically incapable of speaking for himself.

Jeremy Thorpe has survived everything, and did not, as I spoke to him, sound resentful or unhappy. But he was so wide-ranging in his knowledge, so interesting on modern politics and so engaging on the politics of his own era, that I could not help reflecting how bitter it must be, as a still young man, to find your life and career suddenly frozen – freeze-framed in a merciless spotlight trained upon a single episode, a single relationship, a single story – and to have to spend the rest of your life with the camera focused on that scene. What for others is ephemeral becomes for you permanent: a record stuck in its groove. Others' lives move on; other careers blossom; other players rise and fall, enter and quit the stage: but you are left endlessly going over the history of a few short months whose names, events, *dramatis personae* – whose every aside, sub-headline, solicitor's memo or reported rumour – becomes familiar, worn by repetition, the fixed furniture of your mind, and the hidden thought in the minds of all those you subsequently meet.

I am sorry Jeremy Thorpe did not try to have Scott murdered. I would have.

HAROLD WILSON – 1976

The Lavender List

Enoch Powell once observed that every political career ends in failure. Simone de Beauvoir wrote that if only we will wait long enough we shall see all our dreams turn to ashes. Perhaps determined to prove both of them wrong, Harold Wilson quit while he was still winning, but Powell, de Beauvoir and the British press foiled his plan. Because he had quit, they assumed that he could not have been winning. 'I wonder what he meant by that?' as Clemenceau remarked when told that an arch rival had died. The search for skeletons in Wilson's cupboard began.

It is time to admit that the search has largely failed.

Yet the surprise resignation of Harold Wilson on 16 March 1976 still excites speculation. The KGB, shady business deals, an MI5 plot to discredit his Labour government, a close friendship with his powerful private secretary Marcia Williams . . . all have been blamed for his abrupt departure from 10 Downing Street at the relatively young age of sixty.

An early retirement needs no such explanation, and if Wilson had not been crippled by illness after retiring he might have proved it, by having more fun; but skeletons in the cupboard make good newspaper copy and the conspiratorial air he acquired in his later years encouraged the world to speculate that the cupboard was not bare. They still do.

In April 1974, two months after his narrow General Election victory, had come the Labour Prime Minister's first brush with controversy. Wilson became embroiled in what was to become known as the 'slagheap' affair.

Harold Wilson, 58, had been the undisputed leader of his party since 1963. Since 1956, the masterful Marcia Williams, his private and political secretary, had been his eyes and ears. She was invaluable to him. Her enemies alleged – they still do – that she rigidly controlled access to her boss. Wilson, an accessible but overworked man, needed a bouncer at his gate. Williams, a forceful but loyal woman, accepted the role. A good servant takes the flak, rather than blaming his master. If Williams was the dragon guarding Wilson's cave from even Cabinet colleagues, the dragon was under orders, following him through his earlier career and then into No. 10.

Harold Wilson was elected Labour MP for Ormskirk in 1945 and for Huyton from 1950. Only two years after being elected an MP, he became the youngest Cabinet minister since Pitt when he was made President of the Board of Trade at the age of 31. This was the clever young Oxford economist who had helped with the Beveridge Report in 1942: the cornerstone of the post-war welfare state. A year after becoming Party Leader he became Prime Minister. Out of office in 1970, he returned to 10 Downing Street in 1974.

His reputation being that of a whizz-kid number-cruncher, a meritocrat and a consolidator, it was hard to place him on the Right or the Left. This assisted his rise, but deprived him of a natural constituency. Wilson was itchily suspicious, but not without reason. He once said: 'I am running a Bolshevik revolution with a Tsarist Cabinet.' This attitude, and the complete trust he was able to put in Marcia Williams, explained her hold over him better than the whispers about their personal relationship.

Marcia Williams had taken a history degree at Queen Mary College in London's East End. She was unswerving in her loyalty which she has never, in even the slightest degree, compromised. Even right to the end of his life, and beyond it – she never blabbed. There are really very few males of whom this could be said.

One of the most powerful aides ever to have graced Downing Street, her book on the first two Wilson governments, *Inside Number 10*, was later to meet with her boss's approval. She, at least, was still inside Number 10 in the final chapter. Few others made it through. The Northampton High School girl looked after him, and he looked after her. She was made a CBE in 1970.

Only three months into his new Government in 1974, Wilson rewarded the 42-year-old Marcia, a trusted ally for much of his career, with a life peerage as Lady Falkender. Of course the whisperers, for whom the ancient folk-image – of a scheming, ambitious woman behind the throne of the apparent boss –

remains irresistible, believed they saw her own pretensions beneath this honour. A note which Wilson wrote Williams at the time strongly suggests that she was a reluctant peer. She has, since then, taken little part in the Upper Chamber, due, to some extent, to ill health and a great deal of responsibility in Wilson's last years.

The then Mrs Williams's elder sister, Peggy Field, worked for Wilson's dutiful wife Mary for a short time in 1969, and again in 1974–6. Her brother, Tony Field, had managed Wilson's Commons office (unpaid) in 1972. It was Field who caused the first of Wilson's problems.

Tony Field had left the Bath and Portland Cement Company in 1967 and bought a gritstone quarry site in Ince-in-Makerfield, Lancashire, and (later) a slag heap in Wigan. He set up his own company, J. Taylor's Slag, and began selling off the slag. Marcia, her father and her sister became directors of this company. By 1973, when the slag was exhausted, Field approached land agents in Liverpool for advice on the sale of the land at Wigan, and they introduced him to Wolverhampton insurance broker Ronald Millhench, who owned the neighbouring land. Millhench claimed to be an admirer of Wilson's. He agreed to buy. The sale yielded a large but perfectly legal profit for the Field family – some £250,000.

Exactly one year later Wilson was back in Downing Street.

It was a brief honeymoon. During the election campaign the *Guardian* broke the story of the sale, and raised questions about land speculation. At the time, nobody picked the story up.

Then, a month later, the *Daily Mail* resurrected it. The profit for the Williams family caused much comment, many figures, some of them exaggerated, flying around.

The innuendo was that the family's association with No. 10 had assisted them in the deal. The paper claimed to have been shown a letter addressed to Millhench, purportedly from Wilson. The letter, dated 16 March 1973, states 'Tony [Field, the vendor] and I feel sure that you are quite capable of carrying our Ince-in-Makerfield deal through with efficiency and discretion. Accordingly, I have passed everything over to him.' Some have since suggested that the fact that the letter was an amateurish forgery should have been obvious to any experienced eye.

The same day it was alleged that Tony Field had written in August 1972 on Downing Street notepaper to Warwickshire

County Council on behalf of a man called Victor Harper. Harper, another land agent who turned out to have been an undischarged bankrupt, had cooperated with Field in the latter's business dealings. The two stories became tangled, with Field's name and that of his sister constantly in the press. Despite innuendoes in Tory papers, no one was so incautious as to allege a direct link to Wilson or Marcia Williams, for which there was no evidence. Nor did anybody quite explain how the fact (if it had been a fact) that a Prime Minister was taking an interest in a land deal could have enhanced its profitability.

One view is that, far from being the arch wheeler-dealer he was alleged to be, Tony Field was a bit of a blunderer who got out of his depth with a couple of the Del-boys of his era, hoped to make money, never gave proper consideration to the dangers arising from his association with No. 10, but meant no harm. His dealings look, in retrospect, more incompetent than sinister. The implication that Williams ended up a rich woman was wrong. She never did. Fame, for her, has not made life easier or brought material wealth. A number of others in this book make very similar reports. Those who have suffered the glare of the public spotlight are commonly (and irrationally) assumed, thereafter, to be rich. Often they are struggling to keep a family. 'This has been *very* hard to cope with,' says Lady Falkender. But to say that, of course, did not suit the mood of the hour, or the *Daily Mail*.

And the Prime Minister's attempt to defend Field on 4 April 1974 was ill conceived. Wilson said his secretary's brother was involved in 'land reclamation' not 'speculation'. In fact, this was not so far wide of the mark – the land was reclaimed for industrial development. But it was an unwise remark. Few believed it. Newspaper cartoonists delivered their own verdict on the 'slagheap' affair. Downing Street appeared in the popular press festooned with 'valuable reclamation site for sale' boards.

Between 3 and 11 April, the national press devoted 6,000 column inches to the affair. Nixon's visit to London on 7 April – he was in trouble himself – served only to heighten the conspiracy theories gripping Fleet Street. Wilson believed the media were intent on his downfall.

Speculation continued until 22 April when Millhench, who kept a signed photograph of the Prime Minister on his desk, was

Cartoon by Mac, 3 May 1976 (courtesy of *Daily Mail*)

arrested and charged with forgery and the theft of notepaper from Wilson's office. He owned up. In November 1974, Millhench was jailed for three years. Wilson, Williams and Field had all issued libel writs, but, after Millhench's arrest, did not pursue them.

Recollections of the slagheap affair (at the start of Wilson's second term) have paled by comparison with what came at the end: the row over his resignation honours. Once again the (now) Lady Falkender's powerful position at Downing Street animated press speculation.

When the much leaked, much delayed and much attacked Resignation Honours List finally appeared on 27 May 1976, there was an immediate outcry. Some 100 Labour MPs signed a motion dissociating themselves from the list. It was alleged that it had been compiled in advance, ready for the day the Prime Minister announced his resignation on 16 March 1976.

Falkender says this allegation is wildly inaccurate. She says the resignation took the whole Downing Street machine by surprise, and very little had been planned or premeditated. There could have been no advance planning in any case because of the need for strict secrecy about the resignation. By her own account the episode looks more like cock-up than conspiracy.

Normally one of the most closely guarded Whitehall secrets, some of the more contentious names leaked. This was not least because the Political Honours Scrutiny Committee, while approving the personal political honours which fell within its remit, grumbled, semi-publicly, about some of the names outside the remit. Two of the three members let it be known that they were astonished that 'their reservations over at least half the list were ignored'. James Callaghan, the new Labour Prime Minister, was forced to set up a leak inquiry even before the list was finally published.

Two months later, on 26 May 1976, the 'Lavender List' – it was written, people said, on Lady Falkender's favourite lavender notepaper – was finally published.

She was entertainingly exasperated on the subject. 'I've *never* written on lavender notepaper. I wouldn't dream of writing on lavender notepaper.'

Falkender said that, in the excitement and confusion surrounding Wilson's surprise resignation, his draft list was scrawled out on the basis of many hurried consultations and conversations. By the time it was needed – urgently – for a preliminary meeting, the list had been amended so extensively that, on glancing at it, Wilson thought it too much of a mess and handed it to Lady Falkender who offered to rewrite it quickly and legibly. 'I grabbed the nearest piece of paper,' she said, 'which was pale pink, not lavender, and rewrote Harold's list neatly.'

Her own view is that when (on later consideration) some names on the list emerged as embarrassing or unwise choices, some of those around Harold Wilson decided 'to pin it on me'. That the draft list had been in Falkender's handwriting on unofficial paper – whether lavender or pink – helped the story stick. 'Lavender list' alliterates memorably.

This version has the ring of truth. If an aide like Falkender were really intent on masterminding an honours list in order to sneak in honours of her own choosing, the last thing she would do, surely, would be to handwrite it on to feminine notepaper, as she did?

But the story stuck. The showbiz flavour was said by some to reflect the recent interest taken in the theatre and the arts by Lady

Falkender. It included an OBE for Mike Yarwood and peerages for
the showbusiness brothers Sir Lew Grade and Sir Bernard
Delfont. But Falkender has never been famously interested in
showbusiness, and hardly moved much in these circles. Wilson, of
course, loved to. His links with the film industry and entertainment business went back many years to his days as President of
the Board of Trade in Attlee's government. He admired Mike
Yarwood's work, and enjoyed the company of showbusiness
people.

A former colleague was quoted anonymously as saying: 'At one
stroke [Wilson] damaged the House of Lords, the honours
system, the Labour party, the Jewish community and himself.'
There seemed to be a degree of anti-Semitism in the hints
dropped that some of the names on the list were Jewish. 'These
were not my personal friends, not my choices,' expostulates
Falkender. 'It was my *job* to meet these people as they were part
of Harold's world. I did not choose to do so, nor did they become
my personal friends. They were part of his world in which I
worked.'

Even more controversial was the knighthood for James
Goldsmith, the chairman of Cavenham Foods, honoured for
services to 'export and to ecology'. Sir George Weidenfeld, a
distinguished publisher, respected in the political salons and a
long-standing patron of current-affairs publishing – but also, it is
true, Wilson's friend and publisher – was given a peerage.
Honours like his were, taken individually and in themselves,
uncontroversial. Peggy Field, Lady Falkender's sister, received an
MBE – but she had worked for Mary Wilson, and Downing Street
staff are often honoured. Wilson's personal doctor, Sir Joseph
Stone, became a life peer; but there are many precedents for
honouring personal doctors. What started tongues wagging – and
once they wagged, they wagged about everybody on the list – was
the presence of a few distinctly odd names. It was the cumulative
effect which shocked the Westminster Establishment.

Sir Joseph Kagan, Labour Party supporter and benefactor and
manufacturer of the Prime Minister's distinctive Gannex
raincoat, who became a peer, later served ten months in prison for
theft and false accounting. Eric Miller, treasurer of the *Socialist
International* and millionaire chairman of Peachey Property
Corporation, gained a knighthood, but shot himself the following

year. The former business associate of Reginald Maudling had faced an official investigation into his finances.

The furore over the Honours List was all the more fierce because only twelve years earlier Wilson had announced an end to the awarding of hereditary titles. He had also tried to end automatic honours for civil servants. In 1966, he had declared: 'The position now is that the basis of selection will be public service.' The contrast between Wilson's early egalitarianism, and his behaving, then, as a fount of patronage, sharpened the attacks. Wilson had not enamoured himself with the Left by accepting the Garter from the Queen.

Marcia Williams hit back, claiming critics were snobbish and anti-Semitic. There is no doubt that a vein of anti-Semitism could be sensed beneath some of the criticism. 'It was a sanctimonious protest by the unimaginative half of the establishment,' she said.

On 2 June Wilson released a statement defending his judgement. Lord Shackleton, who had chaired the Scrutiny Committee, recalled Wilson saying something like: 'Anyway it wasn't my list.' Lady Falkender said this was exactly the sort of protest Wilson would have made, but that it has been misinterpreted if the suggestion is that the list was hers. He was lobbied very hard, she says, by friends and colleagues in the Labour Party. There were long-time supporters and patrons to reward. He had 'debts of honour and service to repay, within the Party'. She recalls that he came under a good deal of pressure from old colleagues. 'It's unfair to Harold,' she added, 'that the idea should be left that he himself was insisting on some of those names.' She stood right outside most of this, she said. It was 'Harold's world, not mine.'

A fair summary of Falkender's view is to say that she saw the honours episode as rushed, erratically judged and badly handled; and accepted that some of the appointments were ill considered. But the explanation, she thought, lies in the shortage of time at a confused period, coupled with external pressures and Harold Wilson's strong wish to repay debts of friendship. However, it suited some to blame her, and it made a marvellous story for the press.

Wilson returned to the backbenches. He was wounded by the hostility. His memoirs never reached beyond 1978, and his mental faculties diminished early. Much has been said of the disease which caused this, but Falkender also thought that a massive operation for cancer of the colon, four years after his resignation, hit him very hard, and he never entirely recovered. He died in 1995, after years of deepening premature senility through which he and his wife, Mary, continued to depend on Falkender's help.

The BBC's former political editor, John Cole, suggests in his memoirs a reason for Wilson's resignation: that early intimations of premature senility persuaded him to quit. Once, towards the end, says Cole, tears were seen to fill the PM's eyes as he was reminded that an undertaking he had given had slipped his mind. Falkender agrees there may have been something in this. 'He did start to get worried about Prime Minister's Questions, and he got less quick – though we all do. I think that worried him.' But she dates his sharpest decline to the operation he had four years after resigning. 'It destroyed him.'

While not subscribing to the wilder conspiracy theories which the Wilson entourage sometimes entertained about the hostility of the outside world, Falkender was baffled by the relentless and (sometimes) apparently coordinated nature of the attacks he suffered from the press and others. '*Why* did it go *on*?' He had 'more than his fair share'. She said that in preparations for his memorial service, John Major was exceptionally sympathetic and thoughtful. Mr Major will know what Harold, Mary and Marcia went through with the press.

His folksy and fireside television manner, with its hint of concealed 'ordinary man's' Methodist rectitude, though at first it endeared him to many voters, caused much of the nation to grind its teeth when the promise implicit in his premiership, of a new start for Britain, was never fulfilled. Tony Blair should have taken note.

Wilson's relationship with Falkender was presented as strained if not strange by Bernard Donoughue, the former head of Wilson's policy unit, in *The Heat of the Kitchen*, published in 2003. Donoughue wrote that on one occasion as Prime Minister, Wilson called from an Oxford payphone and asked him to drive to her house and 'pull the telephone wires out of the wall to stop her speaking to the press'. Another time, recalled Donoughue, 'In my hearing Marcia threatened to "destroy" Wilson, tapping her handbag ominously.'

Donoughue also claimed Wilson had to be prevented from carrying out a secret plan to disappear in a snowstorm on election night in February 1974, a scheme that echoed John Stonehouse's disappearing act and reeked of the paranoia of the later Wilson years. Under the plan, the Labour leader, fearing humiliation at the hands of Ted Heath and the Tories, intended to switch hotels after the close of the polls and board under the cover of darkness his official Heathrow-bound plane to a small Bedfordshire airstrip then vanish by car to a secret hideaway. Wilson had an old road map, said Donoughue, and moved from Liverpool's Adelphi hotel to the less salubrious Golden Cross but was persuaded to go back to the Adelphi when it emerged the Tories were doing poorly. When Donoughue, wondering how he would travel back to London, told Falkender, she described it as a 'schoolboy behaviour' and said: 'You will be on the plane to London, like everybody else, including him.'

Joe Haines, Wilson's press secretary, alleges in his memoirs, *Glimmers of Twilight,* that Wilson's personal physician, Dr Joe Stone, offered to 'dispose' of Falkender in 1975 when she supposedly threatened to destroy Wilson by revealing their affair.

Haines claims that Wilson (who knew nothing of the doctor's suggestion) recounted how Falkender had summoned his wife, Mary, and told her: 'I have only one thing to say to you. I went to bed with your husband six times in 1956 and it wasn't satisfactory.' Falkender has always vigorously denied a sexual relationship with Wilson – when questioned about it by an embarrassed Matthew Parris, she responded: 'Spit it out. Are you suggesting I slept with him? That is untrue. I never did.' She has also rejected the notion of a murder plot as 'outrageous' and out of character for the late doctor.

Wilson's period of power coincided with the surfacing, in a way we could no longer avoid, of the signs of massive post-war failure in our economy. Also surfacing was a gap between the promise and the performance of the welfare state; some began to doubt this great national enterprise, and to begrudge its cost. Dimly we were being made aware (and it was to become a cliché) of nettles which needed to be grasped. But we were not ready to grasp them and our Prime Minister, beneath his apparent confidence and control, reflected our own hesitation. Did Harold Wilson not become for us an unconscious proxy for our own rage and disappointment at ourselves, as a failing post-imperial nation?

The observation may seem a strange one to make, in a book about scandal, but one of the reasons parts of Britain looked so hard for evidence of wickedness in Wilson and his entourage was that much of the nation and almost all of its press really wanted him to emerge as villainous.

Whatever the explanation for his final resignation, rumours and whispers about Harold Wilson will keep pundits guessing long after they have forgotten to credit him with winning four General Elections. In a way it serves him right. Wilson was determined in his later years to see conspiracies in unremarkable events. When he resigned, the world repaid the compliment.

MAUREEN COLQUHOUN – 1979

Undaunted

'The day hasn't yet arrived when an MP can be unseated by a gossip columnist,' Maureen Colquhoun declared defiantly in 1977. But an alliance of gossip columnists and hostile forces within her local Labour Party proved a deadly combination. Britain's first 'out' lesbian MP, and the only woman to have a chapter in this disgracefully politically incorrect book, lost her seat at the 1979 General Election. It is interesting to note that some of the lonely crusades she initiated, and which wrecked her career, are now quite fashionable. She was rather brave, although many contemporaries thought her ridiculous and some found her threatening. Where all agree is that she was imprudent. In her five years as MP for Northampton North, Colquhoun had waged a feminist war from within what remained essentially an exclusive gentlemen's London club: the House of Commons.

Maureen Colquhoun arrived at Westminster after the February 1974 election nonchalantly carrying a 'Shop at the Co-Op' plastic carrier bag instead of a briefcase: a portent of things to come. Forty-five and still living with her husband Keith, a journalist to whom she had been married for 25 years, she had three grown-up children. She had won her marginal seat with a majority of 1,538. The following year, the Tribunite MP left her husband for another journalist. This time it was a woman: Babs Todd, a British Council officer who was also a director of *Sappho*, a magazine for lesbians. At first this move was known mainly to friends. But Colquhoun was an irrepressibly open politician: fierce in her beliefs, impatient to advertise them, and loath to compromise. Like Margaret Thatcher, she was not a woman to build bridges with those who opposed her. Unlike Thatcher, she never took care to keep in with her natural allies: in Colquhoun's case, the Left. Step by step, she was to antagonize Right, Left and Centre. There was something admirable about Colquhoun's utter disregard for protecting her own back.

In February 1976 Colquhoun asked the Speaker, George Thomas, to refer to her as either 'Maureen Colquhoun' or 'Ms Colquhoun'. At the time this appeared a wildly defiant request. No Honourable Lady had ever made it before. The Speaker was flummoxed. He wrote back: 'In the interests of the House, I think I must continue to use some form of prefix, but I will endeavour to slur it in such a way as to reduce, if not entirely eliminate, the audible distinction between "Mrs" and "Miss".' The press publicity was predictable.

Even Labour MPs – many of them – were scornful. Political correctness had not yet reached Westminster. Colquhoun was making a stand in an era in which the page seven topless model in the *Star* was still called the 'Starbird'. Newspapers turned on her and she was dubbed 'Trendy Ms Colquhoun' and 'Thoroughly Modern Maureen'. 'When a Ms Is As Good As a Male,' giggled one paper.

Colquhoun had drawn attention to herself. More circumspect parliamentarians, stung by the reaction, would have lain low for a while. The following month, in March 1976, Colquhoun held a housewarming party with her new partner Babs Todd at their East London home. By less than straightforward means, Nigel Dempster got hold of one of the invitations which on 15 April he cheerily described in his widely read *Daily Mail* column as picturing 'two entwined females' labelled Maureen and Babs. Their home was immediately besieged by reporters.

Ms Colquhoun protested to the Press Complaints Council. Dempster appeared before the PCC, trumpeting the public's 'right to know'. The PCC sided with the MP and ruled that the *Mail* had harassed her and her partner. *The Times* commented on 8 December 1976: 'The methods used to obtain information from her were a gross intrusion into privacy, and harassment of a serious kind.' But the paper added that her private life was relevant as she had taken a public stance on feminist issues. Reports of her decision to leave her husband and move in with Ms Todd were in the public interest, the newspaper argued.

Timider folk would have avoided controversy for a while. Colquhoun, however, was now campaigning on issues such as abortion, the decriminalisation of cannabis and prostitution. She earned the epithet 'loony feminist'. She was ridiculed for demanding that the word 'female' be removed from rail tickets.

Just when a period of silence was most called for, Ms Colquhoun moved to hammer into her parliamentary coffin perhaps (after her open homosexuality) the most significant nail of all. Her local Labour Party, especially its Left-wingers, were convulsed when Colquhoun, who had a high immigrant population in her constituency, appeared to side with Enoch Powell in the controversy over his 'Rivers of Blood' speech. 'I am rapidly concluding,' she said, 'that Mr Powell, whom I had always believed to be a racialist before I went into the House of Commons, is not one.' Labour was in government at the time and this attack appeared to side with the Tory Right. Labour members, she charged, had closed their ears to what Powell had to say 'and I think sometimes they ought to listen'. She attacked her colleagues for demonizing Powell rather than addressing the issues. 'The real bogeymen are in the Labour Party, who use soft words and put no money into solving the problems of poor blacks and poor whites in inner cities,' she said later.

Time started running out for this volcanic dyke when in December 1976 she punched a car-park attendant in a fracas over a complimentary parking ticket. The middle-aged MP – a 'cheery butch battleaxe', commented one journalist, of her photograph – confronted the attendant when he slammed the parking barrier down on her car as she tried to leave. 'He was totally insulting...

I bonked him one' (words have changed their meaning). 'And he also hit me, which he later denied,' Colquhoun wrote later in her memoirs, *A Woman in the House.*

It did not take the press long. On 5 December the *Sunday People* published the story on its front page under the headline: 'Woman MP socked me.' They ran a photograph of the attendant holding what would have been the wrong side of his allegedly damaged face.

The inevitable dreary succession of Tory councillors in Northampton offered to pay the car-park attendant's legal fees if he sued. In the Commons chamber, Tory MPs clutched their faces in mock pain when they saw her enter, or rise to speak. Colquhoun was inundated with letters from sympathetic Northampton car owners who had encountered the allegedly belligerent parking attendant before.

Anything Nigel Dempster could do Northampton North Labour Party could do better. In the days when local Labour Party witch-hunts were widespread, their MP had invoked the wrath of certain members who accused her of being 'too middle-class' and snubbing the general management committee. Colquhoun then threatened legal action against anyone making unsubstantiated allegations, but a small group concentrated in one ward was already plotting to unseat her.

She complained in the national press, 'The Park ward seems to have taken over this constituency.' It proposed a motion that 'in view of her recent statements and public behaviour, Mrs [*sic*] Colquhoun is no longer acceptable as the representative in Parliament of Northampton North Constituency Labour Party, which therefore states its intention not to adopt her as the candidate at the next General Election.' In the *Guardian* she vowed to fight the 'bent rule-book infiltrators' from the ward.

In September 1977, after a fierce battle ('I have been dealt a mortal blow,' she told the press), Colquhoun was de-selected. Accused by local party members of an obsession with 'trivial' concerns such as women's rights, she was reproached for her spat with the car-park attendant, the Powell remarks, and her widely mocked campaign for all train passengers to travel first class. After she was de-selected by 23 votes to eighteen she admitted to reporters what had been plain for years, but what she had avoided admitting in terms which would have made an easy tabloid headline: that she was a lesbian. The local party chairman denied they had dumped her because of this. He said: 'Her sexual behaviour is not the issue.' Opposition to her had arisen around 'a lot of small things which amounted to larger things when added up'.

But the world knew better. The previous month, her local party secretary, Mr Pat Garrett, told the *Daily Express*: 'This matter hasn't been raised officially but the publicity did upset people and certain party workers felt that it might lose votes.' Weeks later Norman Ashby, party chairman, came clean to the *Sunday Telegraph*: 'Maureen got in on the supermarket vote as a solid wife and mother. This business blackened her image irredeemably.'

At Westminster Colquhoun's lesbianism embarrassed rather than angered MPs. 'I found a lot of support within the House. But it came mainly from heterosexual MPs – not the homosexual ones, for the obvious reasons that they felt threatened by my frankness. Men can now be real friends knowing I'm an absolute lost cause,' she later said. Undaunted – every chapter in her story begins 'Undaunted'! – she returned to her causes with a vengeance, introducing bills to protect prostitutes from victimization and to install more women on to public bodies. Both failed.

Her marriage to Keith, who with rare good sense has always refused to respond to journalists' questions about the matter, was dissolved in 1980. Colquhoun altered her *Who's Who* entry to include Babs alongside her husband: an amendment which broke new ground, perturbing the publication's editors.

A group of feminists now set up the Colquhoun Action Committee to challenge her de-selection. The National Executive Committee held an inquiry. She won. She was reinstated: the second MP ever to be reinstated by Labour's NEC, after Bessie Braddock. It was all in vain. She lost the 1979 General Election to Tony Marlow, a staunch supporter of the leader (Margaret Thatcher) whom Colquhoun described as a 'man with tits'. There must be something about the water in Northampton North: Marlow fast became an equally colourful and independent member, boasting a mistress, numerous children, and an extraordinary range of opinions, from the anti-European Right, to the authoritarian, to the libertarian.

Although Ms Colquhoun will go down as the lesbian who lost Labour Northampton North, the swing against her was smaller than that suffered by plenty of other MPs who lost their seats. She was not bitter. She wrote: 'I felt no sense of loss. Just a sense of relief. I was glad to be rid of Northampton and that the electorate had freed me of my Northampton Labour Party opponents for ever.' She went on to become information officer with Gingerbread, the charity for single parents. She did not retire from politics and became a councillor in her home borough of Hackney in 1982.

The rows continued. A long-running dispute between the council and the unions NALGO and NUPE led to Colquhoun, the vice-chairperson of the Housing Committee, being locked out of a local housing office. It did not stop residents turning up for her regular surgery and the former MP was forced to offer interviews in the snow-covered street.

She remained a Hackney councillor until 1990. By 1984 Colquhoun had given up hopes of returning to Westminster as an MP. Colquhoun, who now has six grandchildren, went back instead as a researcher for a Labour MP. She still works at Westminster today on a part-time basis: she has worked with two MPs and in recent years has been arranging parliamentary seminars on the way the House works. The rest of the time she spends in her Lake District home with her partner Babs. She describes their relationship, now of over 25 years, as 'more respectable than most heterosexual ones'.

She recalls that when she was being pilloried over her sexuality, she found support in some unexpected quarters – and not from expected quarters. She never got the support she hoped for from the Left. One or two women MPs were remarkably cool. Only one MP wrote a kind note: Jeremy Thorpe. 'Jeremy told me it was times like these that you knew who your friends were. I was very touched as he was himself in great trouble.'

JAMES DUNN – 1980

A Sleeping Pill and an Unusual Shopping Spree

Some Labour ministers took the 1979 election defeat harder than others. Only two months after losing his chauffeur-driven ministerial car, James Dunn was caught red-handed on a shoplifting expedition only 500 yards from the Commons.

On 27 July, Dunn, who had been a junior Northern Ireland minister in James Callaghan's government, went into the Army & Navy store – the MPs' nearest department store – in Victoria Street. He stuffed two ties, two armbands and a sweatshirt, worth £15.13, into a plastic carrier bag and left by the front door. Two store detectives set off in hot pursuit. They saw the 53-year-old MP for Kirkdale, Liverpool, slip into a stationer's and remove a map worth 60p. When they apprehended him Dunn asked his captors, 'Can I have a quiet chat, and I will tell you all about it?' Unimpressed, the store detectives turned the hapless MP over to the police.

The case came to court on 12 May 1980. Dunn, an MP for fifteen years, told the Inner London Crown Court that he had panicked when he saw the store detectives staring at him. He said: 'I immediately associated one of them with some of the men I had had to deal with in Northern Ireland.' The 'father of four' admitted taking the goods, but pleaded not guilty to theft, his defence being based on his claimed state of mind at the time of the incident. He told the court that flying to Ulster, sometimes twice in one day, had exhausted him. Often he spent less than an hour and a half in a week at his homes in Liverpool and London.

He had suffered a heart attack in 1978 and was also on anti-depressants. The evening before the offence he had attended a late-night debate. He had drunk five half-pints of beer in a Commons bar. A sleeping tablet had given him a fitful night's sleep. The following morning, when he went on his illicit shopping expedition, he could not, he said, remember precisely what happened.

That this last claim at least may indeed have been the case, the judge found herself inclined to accept. The errant MP, she agreed, was 'acting entirely out of character, which was attributable to [his] appalling state of health'. The jury found Dunn guilty, and the judge conditionally discharged him for a year, and ordered him to pay £100 costs.

Dunn defected to the SDP in 1981 but lost his seat in the 1983 General Election. He died two years later. If he had been a Tory, and if the year had been 1995 instead of 1979, we should have accounted the episode evidence of a 'growing wave of sleaze'. As it was, however, the affair was little noted, quickly over, and seen for what it was: a small, isolated, personal tragedy.

ALLAN ROBERTS – 1981

'*Nein*, it is Rover!'

A seedy gay nightclub in Berlin's red light district. Whips. Men in SS uniforms. Studded dog collars. Torture chambers. The Labour MP, the late Allan Roberts. Allan had a terrific sense of fun.

The Left-wing bachelor had a track record for living it up. In 1978, the year before his election, neighbours had demanded his eviction after a string of outrageous parties at his aptly named Shady Lane home in Manchester. In February 1981 the ginger-haired former social worker struck again.

Roberts's antics in Berlin's Buddy Club made the front pages after a *Private Eye* investigation. The *News of the World* reported that the MP for Bootle had donned a studded dog collar for the late night visit and had been whipped so severely he had required hospital treatment.

Roberts wisely refused to talk to the *News of the World*, but admitted he had been involved in a 'drunken spree' at the club. He explained to his constituency association that he was so inebriated he had fallen over, had a slight accident, and required one stitch. But *Private Eye* tracked down the doctor who had administered emergency medical treatment to the MP. 'I declined to administer any sutures as the swelling was so great that additional damage could have been caused,' he said. Roberts had discharged himself the next day without paying the £110 bill.

Questioned later, Roberts went on the offensive, denying any involvement in bondage. As to the unpaid hospital bill, he told his local party: 'I thought there was an arrangement between the NHS and Germany.' The bill had, in the end, been paid by Charles Irving, then the Tory MP for Cheltenham, who happened to be in Berlin himself on official business. Charles, who died in 1995, was the kindest of men and escapes our attention in this book.

The *News of the World* hit back the following week. It printed a signed statement from one of the MP's six companions at the club, detailing the night's events. A man wearing an SS uniform had asked Roberts, a leading supporter of CND, his name. He was not satisfied with the answer, Allan. '*Nein*,' he barked, 'it is Rover.' He then attached a dog lead to the studded dog collar already in place around the MP's neck. He dragged the MP for Bootle around the floor and, egged on by dozens of other baying S&M enthusiasts, repeatedly whipped Roberts, who (the testimony continued), bleeding from the wounds, screamed: 'That was beautiful, baby.'

Private Eye alleged that the painful weekend in Berlin had been organized by the 'Motorcycle Leather Club'. The club was an 'Interpoof' organization which had branches throughout Europe. The magazine probed some of Allan's other social outings. It regaled its readers with a party at the American Embassy in London from which the MP and some of his friends were ejected. One of them stood on a bar and denounced Ronald Reagan for being anti-gay.

Private Eye also recalled a speech Roberts had given to Manchester City Council. For once the flamboyant MP eschewed his usual arm-waving technique and kept his right hand planted firmly in his jacket pocket. The reason became clear at the end when a particularly excited supporter ran up to shake his hand. Dragging the MP's right hand free, his jaw dropped. A set of handcuffs was dangling from Roberts's wrist. During his swift exit his only audible words were 'f—ing key . . .'

The press, who tried and failed to 'out' Roberts (Allan never admitted to being gay, let alone a masochist) resorted to attacking his Left-wing views. In 1981 he was dubbed 'Afghan Roberts' when he described the newly installed Soviet regime in Afghanistan as the 'lesser evil' after a controversial fact-finding visit to Kabul with two other Labour MPs, including Ron Brown (see pp.285–90), in 1981. He opposed what he called Neil Kinnock's 'witch-hunt' against the Militant Tendency and supported the Left-wing Eric Heffer in his leadership bid.

In 1984, Roberts was awarded libel damages against the *News of the World* and *Private Eye* over allegations that he was being investigated by the police for sexual offences. He invested the money in a constituency office and a share in a London East End pub.

Despite the constant stream of bad publicity, Roberts received a unanimous vote of confidence from his local party. When he died after a long battle against illness in March 1990, he commanded a 24,447 majority – one of the biggest in the Commons.

The adverse press attention never damaged his parliamentary career and he went on to become a respected member of Labour's front bench Environment team. Politically he remained an outspoken defender of gay rights.

Music-hall nights at his pub were enjoyable. Allan was jolly company, funny, bright, and a generous host. In his flat afterwards there would sometimes be marijuana, sometimes just alcohol. Allan would have made an odd addition to Tony Blair's new Labour Party. There was an unmistakably degenerate strand in his personality and a wild side to his life, but he was kind to men and women he could help, sponsor, shelter or give part-time work to. He burned the candle riotously at both ends, and finally burned himself out.

NICHOLAS FAIRBAIRN – 1982

'Everything which is not dull becomes scandalous'

So protested the late Sir Nicholas Fairbairn. Sir Nicholas was certainly never dull. The press were fascinated by him – and Bernard Levin was unapologetic: '. . . when the lamp-posts outside a man's home are thick with the bodies of ladies mad for his love, or at the very least for his double-breasted waistcoats, he must expect more than a passing interest in the matter to be shown, if only by the envious.'

Fairbairn not only expected attention, but sought it. His daughter Charlotte has described to the *Daily Mail* some of the clothes he created for himself: 'A see-through negligée top, with a huge black cross beneath it, and white flared trousers'. He was, she adds 'stubbornly fond of a waistcoat made up from the skins of two antelopes'. At his house in Roupell Street, panels had been painted showing Lord Whitelaw as a bullfrog, Lady Thatcher as a heron and Lord St John of Fawsley as a toad climbing up a slippery pole.

He was also an inveterate lecher, who once remarked, 'What is a skirt but an open gateway?' Being chauffeured to his daughter's wedding he talked loudly to her of gonorrhoea. 'Charlotte was familiar with the range of her father's interests, the driver less so. "He was trying hard not to listen, but he obviously heard. He ended up taking the wrong route and we were late to church."'

Judged by the later Tory spate of ministerial resignations, Fairbairn, once Scotland's Solicitor-General, got off lightly. Few ministers would expect to survive today if their teenage daughter was reported to have discovered their divorced Dad's lover hanging from a lamp-post outside the family's London home. The bizarre stunt claimed in newspaper reports may never have happened quite like this, but there was undoubtedly a suicide bid, in 1981: a cry for help from the 47-year-old Fairbairn's 34-year-old lover.

Mrs Thatcher, however Victorian her own values, was unmoved by the ensuing scandal. It was a 'private matter' (though it dominated the front pages for days) between 'two single people'. She had no intention of intervening.

Fairbairn discovered weeks later that MPs were less forgiving when he, as a minister, dared to breach one of Parliament's hallowed rules. Scotland's most powerful law officer spoke to a newspaper about a controversial rape case before he told Parliament. This time there was no forgiveness and he was forced to resign.

MP for the vast and beautiful constituency of Kinross and West Perthshire, Fairbairn dwelt in a castle. He entered Parliament in 1974. An able if erratic speaker, an often brilliant advocate, and at home with the hangers and floggers (though neither himself) on the Right of the party but never with the Mother Grundys, he got on well with Mrs Thatcher, who overlooked his flippancy. Fairbairn's *Who's Who* 'hobbies' changed each year. One entry read: 'drawing ships, confounding whips and scuttling drips'; another: 'debunking bishops, serving Queens' (real ones; he loathed homosexuality) 'restoring castles, entertaining knights and befriending pawns'. An earlier entry said 'making love, ends meet, people laugh'. He did.

The Chief Whip had known about the 'lamp-post' allegations (some reports said iron railings, others an overdose of aspirins) within hours of the suicide bid in the early hours of 26 October 1981. He chose not to burden Mrs Thatcher with the news until it was just about to break, two days before Christmas. There was a clamour for Fairbairn's resignation. It was the topic of conversation at Christmas lunches throughout the land, though perhaps not at Chequers.

Pursued by the press, the spurned lover, a former House of Commons secretary, denied hanging from anything – saying she 'wouldn't even have had the energy to climb up a lamp-post'. The love affair, she claimed, had started in 1974 when the colourful laird of Fordell Castle in Fife was still married to his first wife, the Honourable Elizabeth Mackay. Fairbairn had wooed her, she said, with red roses, passionate love letters and proposals of marriage.

The Scottish Solicitor-General pulled up the drawbridge on his castle to wait for reporters to leave. They didn't. So he emerged, arrayed in a blue and white dressing gown, to tell the press it had been a happy relationship. But it was the lady, not he, who was the

RAPE ROW LAW CHIEF IS SACKED

MRS THATCHER sacked her flamboyant Scottish law officer Nicholas Fairbairn last night.

Daily Mail, 22 January 1982

ardent suitor. She had demanded his hand in marriage, not the other way round.

He labelled the press 'vicious, priggish and pseudo-priggish' (an elegant distinction) but reserved most venom for Colonel Michael Mates (see pp.313–7), the MP for Petersfield, who had been accused by some MPs of being the 'fourth-form sneak' who tipped off the press.

The lady survived her suicide attempt and Fairbairn survived the lady. It was then that he pushed his luck too far. There was an outcry when he tried to justify the decision not to prosecute three Glasgow youths for rape. The mistake was to make his case (that there was insufficient evidence) in the *Glasgow Daily Record* the day before he was due to make a statement to the Commons.

As well as a discourtesy to the Commons – a hanging offence among MPs – his comments prejudiced any possible private prosecution. Such was the outrage that an emotional apology in the House was not enough. He resigned the next day. Having stuck by her errant minister thus far, Mrs Thatcher summoned him to 10 Downing Street. One report claimed Fairbairn was handed a copy of his resignation letter and a pen, and told: 'Sign this.' Fairbairn showed loyalty, claiming afterwards that she was 'probably the warmest and kindest human being that those who have met her have ever encountered'.

Nicky Fairbairn was one of the most gifted Queen's Counsel of his generation. His style was flamboyant. He designed for himself the extraordinary tartan trousers and waistcoats he wore at the Commons. He was seldom out of the limelight for long. In October 1982 he was cited in the divorce case of Alasdair MacInnes, an investment consultant. He had enjoyed an affair with MacInnes's wife, Suzanne, whom he affectionately called Sambo and married the next year. But the headlines 'Top Tory stole my wife' infuriated him.

The following month he delivered a coruscating attack in *The Times* on what he saw as the hypocritical moral crusades of the press:

> Scandal may be good copy, but it adds nothing to the integrity of our institutions. I do not think they were any worse, indeed I think they were probably much better, when those who ruled us were known and seen to have healthy sexual liaisons with many mistresses and lovers.

Acknowledging his well-wishers earlier that year, Fairbairn thanked one of the great train robbers for a gift he had sent.

He could rarely resist putting two fingers up to the conventional tut-tutters, and the trait endeared him to many, and enraged a few. During the Commons debate on salmonella in eggs (Mrs Edwina Currie, a junior Health minister at the time, had started a national alarm – a false alarm, some believed – about the bacteria) Fairbairn reminded Mrs Currie that she had once been an egg and added that members on both sides of the House regretted its fertilization.

His opinions were unspeakable, his behaviour objectionable, and he drank far, far too much. A former Chief Whip remarked that a whip's test of the viability of a ministerial appointment was 'whether, when the chap's in the *wrong*, other chaps, who know he's in the wrong, can still be found to defend him in the House. When Nicky was in the wrong, other chaps stayed away.'

But he took punches on the chin, seldom whined and never sued. And even near the end there were moments when his wit could wither an opponent, his logic slice an argument, or his rhetoric soar. Speaking of her father, Charlotte remarked: 'There was nothing to stop Papa. It was almost as if he did it deliberately. He had a self-destructive element, which became apparent when his creative side was frustrated.'

He is dead now. It appears he cut his daughters out of his will in a death-bed codicil signed in shaking hand, 'F of F' (Fairbairn of Fordell). He died in February 1995, his liver having given up the unequal struggle. Close to death he took the opportunity to denounce his would-be successor, the Tory candidate John Godfrey, a London-based banker: 'He's a clone. I don't think he knows anything about Perthshire or Scotland. He is totally irrelevant.' Mr Godfrey lost the election. The *Daily Mail* later reported that Fairbairn had fathered a son, whose existence had been kept secret, nine years before his death.

There were few in the Commons – but, to be fair, there *were* a few – who did not think the place poorer for the loss.

CECIL PARKINSON – 1983

'Is there no flaw?'

'In some ways, he seems too good to be true,' it was said in *The Times* of Cecil Parkinson in October 1981. The remark was without irony. 'Tall, handsome, charming and likeable . . . the perfect constituency MP, intelligent without being intellectual, self-made, brilliantly supported by a politically committed wife – is there, one wonders, no flaw?'

There was. The fifty-year-old Chairman of the Conservative Party had a 34-year-old mistress, Sara Keays, who was to become pregnant. The story which follows relies heavily upon her own account. The (now) Lord Parkinson has written little about the affair, and does not comment on it; but he would have his own perspective on the story.

Fixed now in the public mind is the focal chapter of that story, though much had gone before and much was to follow. The chapter started in June 1983, as the Tories won a General Election, and ended in October, as Parkinson was all but torpedoed off the Conference platform.

'Golden boy' is a cliché, but apt, for the political persona was a cliché. Very much the golden boy of early 1980s Tory politics, Cecil Parkinson had organized Margaret Thatcher's 1983 General Election landslide. As Mrs Thatcher and her Party Chairman waved to their ecstatic supporters from an upstairs window at Conservative Central Office, no one would have guessed anything was wrong. But only hours earlier, on 9 June, as the country went to the polls, Parkinson had made a startling confession.

Thatcher, already convinced that victory was in the bag, had just offered her favourite minister any Cabinet job he wanted in her next government. The Foreign Office was Parkinson's for the asking. His reply was the last thing she expected. Parkinson, married for 27 years, with three grown-up daughters, admitted to having a 'serious personal problem'. He said: 'I'm not sure I should be in your Cabinet at all.' Mrs Thatcher listened in unaccustomed silence as Parkinson explained that Sara Keays, his Commons secretary since 1971, was carrying his child.

In his autobiography, Parkinson wrote: 'Mrs Thatcher was immensely sympathetic, not at all censorious.' She agreed to his becoming Trade and Industry Secretary. As to the baby, 'she said she was sure that as sensible people we could sort it out'. She could not have been more wrong.

Even as they spoke, Colonel Hastings Keays, soon to be a proud grandfather, fired the first salvo in a guerrilla war which was to end with Parkinson's dramatic capitulation at 2.00 a.m. on 14 October 1983 at the Tory Party Conference.

Parkinson left Blackpool with his loyal and formidable wife, Ann, by his side, only hours before Mrs Thatcher was due to address the party faithful and bask in the glory of June's election victory. The theme of her speech was to be 'rejoice'. Press photographs of the Parkinsons returning to London identified their companion as a detective. In fact it was a young man – Parkinson's special adviser – whom few would have recognized at the time: Michael Portillo, not yet an MP.

Parkinson, a self-made millionaire, had been forced to pay a bitter price by Keays for at least twice breaking his promise to marry her. On Friday, 14 October, *The Times* published a sensational statement from the jilted Keays. She said that when she had broken the news of the baby to Parkinson he had asked her to end her pregnancy. 'I was not aware that political expediency was sufficient grounds for an abortion,' she told *The Times* . . .

However, the reader is hearing only one person's account of the story: that of Sara Keays. We hardly have Parkinson's. Imagine how many different accounts could be offered, all true, but each from a different perspective, of a discussion between a man and a woman about the possibility of an abortion.

Nor must Parkinson's silence be interpreted as implying that he has nothing to say. In conversations not only with him, but with a number of others mentioned in this book, the view that 'least said soonest mended' was often encountered. It is felt that where one has been guilty there is more to be lost than gained through joining a debate about just how guilty one has been; or which accusations are wholly and which only partly true. British MPs have a genuine dislike of what looks like special pleading: they have to put up with so much of it from others.

There is also an emotional horror of returning in one's mind to a period of anger and shame. Some people approach their recollections in a way which is almost pathologically post-traumatic. . . . But to return to the story, and begin at the beginning.

Cecil Parkinson had travelled far from a humble start as the son of a Lancashire railwayman. He was born in 1931 and educated at the Royal Lancaster Grammar School and Emmanuel College, Cambridge. He met his wife, the independently wealthy Ann Jarvis, in 1955, they married the following year, and at the same time he joined the Conservative Party. Earlier, he had inclined to the political Left.

He qualified as a chartered accountant in 1959 and went on to become a director of several companies in the 1960s and 70s. He founded Parkinson Hart Securities in 1967. By now a millionaire, he owned homes in Hertfordshire, Pimlico and Cornwall. He entered Parliament in 1970 as MP for Enfield West, moving to nearby Hertsmere after boundary changes.

One year later, on 2 June 1971, the 23-year-old Sara Keays walked into the 39-year-old MP's life when she became a Commons secretary. Keays claims the affair began soon after: 'It was not a mere "dalliance", a "sad and silly blunder", but a long-standing, genuine love affair.'

In March 1974, according to her widely publicized book on the affair, *A Matter of Judgement*, serialized in the *Daily Mirror* and described, rather surprisingly, in a review by the late Lord Goodman as 'this unpleasant and unnecessary book', Keays had started to work for Parkinson. She says she tried to quit the job but that Parkinson refused to let her. This, she wrote, marked a fundamental change in their relationship. She said they were very much in love, and spent more and more time together.

Parkinson enjoyed a rapid rise within both party and Government. After a period as junior Trade minister, he became Party Chairman in 1981, joining the Cabinet. His closeness to the Prime Minister earned him a place in her War Cabinet during the Falklands conflict.

Parkinson and his mistress separated when Keays went to Brussels to work for Roy Jenkins in July 1979. When she returned briefly to London on 27 October they met up, according to her book. He proposed, she says. She accepted. Yet there was no ring, nor wedding date. Parkinson, outwardly still happily married to

Ann, explained to Keays (she wrote) that timing was everything. He could not afford, at just this point, to jeopardize his soaring political career.

At the end of 1980, Ann Parkinson became seriously ill, and went into hospital for surgery. One of their daughters, Mary, got into difficulties with drugs. This was no time to leave his wife and family. But he and Keays did not stop seeing each other when she came back to work in the Commons. In January 1981, his car was stolen from outside her mews house in Southwark. Disaster was only narrowly averted. His two distinctive red ministerial boxes were in the car. Although the car was returned, Parkinson had to tell the Home Secretary, William Whitelaw, of its inconvenient position. According to Keays, Whitelaw replied: 'There but for the grace of God go a great many of us.'

Those who read or hear Keays's descriptions of their affair will form an insistent impression that Parkinson was the pursuer: an impression based, not least, on her reports that he was repeatedly promising to marry her. This impression, of one individual as victim and the other as huntsman, is really quite central to the moral perspective of the picture which has arisen in many minds. It is overwhelmingly based on Keays's account.

In September 1981, Parkinson was a surprise choice as Party Chairman. He fast proved a highly effective salesman for his party. A year later he was faced, as Chairman, with a cruel dilemma: how cruel, few can have known.

Keays had political ambitions of her own. She had stood unsuccessfully as a candidate in Southwark council elections. She came close in October 1982 to securing the Conservative nomination to fight the seat of Bermondsey at the General Election. Then the Tory selection process for Bermondsey had to be repeated when the sitting member, Bob Mellish, died. A by-election was called, and the candidate who had beaten Keays for the seat resigned, unable to fight a by-election.

It fell to Conservative Central Office to advise Bermondsey Tories whether to select their runner-up – Keays – as candidate, or to re-open the selection. As Party Chairman, Parkinson's judgement was critical. He decided that in the new circumstances Bermondsey should re-select. They did, choosing a young man called Robert Hughes (see pp.326–7). We may surmise that Parkinson would be damned if he did act to 'install' Keays in

Bermondsey, and damned if he didn't. She may have felt that Parkinson had scuppered her chances. He may have felt that he was rescuing her from a wretched campaign. We remember what befell another candidate in that by-election, Peter Tatchell.

Yet their affair drifted on until May 1983, when she became pregnant. She told him on 21 May. A June General Election was looming. In her book she said that Parkinson, in calling for an abortion, threatened never to see her again if she had the baby. 'I was appalled. So that was how he really felt. His talk of marriage had been a sham. He did not love me and probably had ceased to love me a long time ago.'

Keays turned for support to her family in Marksbury near Bath. It was agreed to deliver an ultimatum to Parkinson. Her father, the Colonel, intervened. Throughout this affair the Colonel was a colourful figure, his interventions as dramatic as they were unexpected. He now sent a letter by courier to the Prime Minister. How Mrs Thatcher took this extraordinary missive we do not know. Keays says that Parkinson telephoned her on election day; she wanted him to marry her; he told her (she says) that he had now discussed the affair with the Prime Minister, who was offering him the Cabinet post of Trade and Industry Secretary, in addition to his Party Chairmanship role.

On 11 June, two days after the election, Colonel Keays received a telephone call from Parkinson. He assured him 'he intended to do the right thing by Sara and that he intended to look after her and the child'. Colonel Keays was unenthusiastic about this statement.

On 5 August Parkinson went on holiday to the Bahamas, after paying £5,000 into his pregnant mistress's bank account. The press had by now got hold of the story. On 23 August *Daily Mirror* reporters chased the five-months-pregnant secretary through London demanding to know if Parkinson was the father. So hot was the pursuit that Keays and the reporters were involved in a minor collision.

Parkinson, with time to reflect in the Bahamian sunshine, resolved to stay with Ann. On his return Keays says he telephoned her and in a heated conversation accused her of trying to blackmail him into marriage. They agreed that all further dealings should be conducted through solicitors.

THE TORY MINISTER AND THE EX-SECRETARY

Cartoon by Jak, *Daily Express*, 8 October 1983 (courtesy of *Daily Mail*)

Keays demanded that Parkinson tell the Prime Minister of what Keays said was his change of heart about marriage. On 2 September, Colonel Keays wrote to Mrs Thatcher and warned her 'that a public scandal must be regarded as imminent'.

The countdown to the biggest parliamentary scandal to trouble Mrs Thatcher's reign had begun. At this stage (after the election victory but before the Party Conference) the election-night conversation between Parkinson and Mrs Thatcher had not leaked out. But there had been some vague speculation. This intensified when, on 14 September, Parkinson suddenly and surprisingly resigned as Party Chairman. The unknown John Selwyn Gummer took over with the Party Conference only three weeks away. We may surmise that Parkinson and the Prime Minister felt that the publicity likely to surround the affair would make his Central Office job impossible. Those who seek an explanation of the origins of John Gummer as a national figure need look no further. God, it may seem, looks after his own.

On 5 October, while lawyers for both parties were trying to agree a joint statement, *Private Eye* delivered its own interpretation of a rapidly moving story. 'Why was Cecil Parkinson asked to step down as Tory Party Chairman? I can assure readers that it had nothing to do with his marital difficulties which have recently caused raised eyebrows in Tory circles.' The magazine went on to break the story that his secretary, Sara Keays, was pregnant.

Keays telephoned Parkinson and said: 'If you don't do something about it, I will. You've got until midday to decide whether or not you are going to issue a statement and if you won't then I will.' It was their last exchange. It was the most awkward moment imaginable for her threatened torpedo, which was to come nine days later in her statement in *The Times*.

Parkinson's own pre-emptory statement at 11.45 p.m. on 5 October, in time for the next morning's newspapers, was dramatic:

> To bring to an end rumour concerning Miss Sara Keays, and her family, I wish, with her consent, to make the following statement. I have had a relationship with Miss Keays over a number of years. She is expecting a child, due to be born in January, of whom I am the father. I am of course making financial provision for both mother and child.
>
> During our relationship I told Miss Keays of my wish to marry her. Despite my having given Miss Keays that assurance, my wife, who has been a source of great strength, and I, decided to stay together and to keep our family together. I regret deeply the distress I have caused to Miss Keays, to her family and to my family.

The only other statement that night was from Downing Street, in which Mrs Thatcher said she regarded the issue as a 'private matter'. It was plain she saw no reason for her favourite Cabinet minister, tipped as a future leader, to stand down.

Within minutes, gangs of reporters were camped on Parkinson's doorstep, and on the doorstep of the Keays family home in Marksbury. Holed up inside, the pregnant Sara Keays read with increasing frustration each day's press coverage of the affair. Parkinson was enjoying a wave of sympathy for having 'come clean'. Keays was being portrayed as bitter, clinging and vindictive.

The much-read John Junor in the *Sunday Express* wrote a column which was decidedly sympathetic to Cecil Parkinson.

Even Mary Kenny in *The Times* was unforgiving towards Keays. 'Men who tell the truth and face their responsibilities are, in my view, far more worthy of public office than men who take the easy way out. I trust Cecil Parkinson more for having done the brave thing.' Parkinson, buoyed, he wrote, by 16,000 supportive letters against only 46 demanding his resignation, seemed to have survived.

Sara Keays was enraged. She thought Mrs Thatcher's advisers were orchestrating a campaign of misinformation against her.

> A week after his statement he was emerging as the unfortunate victim of a scheming woman who had tried to trap him into a marriage by 'deliberately' becoming pregnant . . . it seemed not to have occurred to a single commentator, certainly not to any of his colleagues, that he had acted selfishly. No one had commented on what was being done to me . . . I had to put a stop to these accusations for my child's sake as well as my own. I had to refute the rumours that I was promiscuous and had had a casual affair with Cecil.

Whatever their differences now, Keays had learned something from her former lover about the art of timing in politics. Her long, detailed statement to *The Times* was released to coincide with Mrs Thatcher's rousing end-of-conference speech. Parkinson was due to take his place at the PM's right-hand side.

Keays wrote:

> Press comments, Government pronouncements and the continued speculation about this matter have put me in an impossible position. I feel that I have both a public duty and a duty to my family to put the record straight.

She detailed Parkinson's alleged broken promises and pledge to divorce. The baby, she said, had been conceived in a relationship she felt was leading to marriage after he had proposed, in 1979, an offer she says he had repeated.

Her statement was immediately flashed to the Imperial Hotel in Blackpool, where Parkinson was staying only a few yards from the Prime Minister's suite. As he walked the short distance to her room he knew it was over. They spoke for fifteen minutes. No decision was made. But it was plain that Keays would not fade into the background. He knew he had to go. He had no choice. Mrs Thatcher spoke to a subdued conference that afternoon. One section of her triumphal Leader's speech had been rewritten.

Daily Mirror, 15 October 1983

Instead of eulogizing Parkinson's achievements as mastermind of the election victory, she said: 'We do not forget today the man who so brilliantly organized the campaign.' But she did forget to mention him by name. There was a warm and sympathetic cheer from the hall. The underlying feeling among representatives and MPs was of bafflement.

Parkinson had already left Blackpool for Hertfordshire. When he surfaced the next day, the mobile multitude of journalists and photographers was camped outside. 'Just before I left for the office,' he says, 'I received a telephone call from a friend who was the editor of a popular daily newspaper. He advised me not to say a word, not even "good morning", to his jackals or to anyone else's. I suggested if he felt like that, perhaps he could take his away. He replied that as long as other people's were there he could not move his!'

Two days later Parkinson escaped to Portugal with Ann. There was little respite. They were discovered on a golf course by the press. A slim Mrs Parkinson took a full swing at the ball and was congratulated by photographers. She replied sweetly: 'Perhaps I am stronger than I look.' She had supplied the next day's headlines: '"I am a very strong lady" says Ann Parkinson.'

On New Year's Eve 1983, Sara Keays gave birth to Flora – 8lb 3oz. Parkinson was informed of this by two *Daily Mirror* reporters. He did not visit, but in a statement wished his daughter, for whom he was providing financially, 'peace, privacy and a happy life'.

Since then something has been made of Parkinson's separation from the child. Few commentators seem to have asked themselves whether an absent parent might not be concerned mainly for the child's privacy and peace. Visits to the child would (whenever the press found out) be given prominent coverage in the newspapers. Parkinson may feel that, with the relationship broken down and with constant media interest, the child could easily become a battleground. He has suggested as much when talking to Anthony Clare in the radio programme 'In the Psychiatrist's Chair'. The girl is disabled and the publicity would be cruel and confusing for her.

Parkinson retired to the backbenches. He never faced any serious threat from his constituency association. For years newspaper rumours would circulate claiming he was on his way back into government. But Mrs Thatcher, under pressure from the whips, decided there could be no return until the voters in his constituency had delivered a verdict. On the eve of a Cabinet reshuffle in August 1985 she rang him to explain that she did not feel able to appoint him until a General Election. She was giving new jobs to Douglas Hurd and Leon Brittan.

'I was expecting nothing, Margaret,' Parkinson replied, 'but may I offer one word of advice? Brief the press that I stay out of the Cabinet *now*, to get that story out of the way in tomorrow's papers. Then the following day's story will be Douglas's and Leon's.'

'Oh Cecil,' she replied, 'I'd never have thought of that. *That's* why I want you back.'

And she undoubtedly did. Despite gossip at the time about his continuing ambitions, the evidence is that it was Mrs Thatcher who believed he could recover. Parkinson lost confidence that he could. This was not just realism on his part (though it was realistic). It was also an emotional reaction. Though a self-made man who had always worked doggedly for his success, it is fair to say that until then Cecil Parkinson had been used to winning. He had that air about him. He never gave the impression of someone who knew what it was to hit the kerb. Unlike (for instance) Jeffrey Archer, he had no experience of being broken, crushed, or knocked down, and crawling back from the wreckage. Parkinson is not emotionally well adapted to large reverses.

Still, Mrs Thatcher kept trying on his behalf. When Parkinson was returned in 1987 with an 18,000 majority, an increase of over 3,000 – he was judged to have served his penance. He took the relatively junior Cabinet post of Energy Secretary and two years later became Transport Secretary. Mrs Thatcher was pushing.

He managed both jobs with his customary fluency and ease, but Cecil Parkinson never recovered the electric touch. He was never again seen as a contender for the leadership. He resigned from the Cabinet on the same day as Mrs Thatcher. He stood down at the 1992 election and was elevated to the House of Lords.

He says little about the affair. Keays, who was given a significant financial settlement but remains unreconciled to her former lover's behaviour, has spoken often since. She addressed a conference on single motherhood. The sight of Sara Keays lambasting Tory wives for turning a blind eye to their cheating husbands' infidelities raised an eyebrow or two.

Parkinson does briefly break his silence on his relationship with Keays in his memoirs, *Right at the Centre*. Whereas she devoted an entire book to the subject, he devoted seven pages – to what he called 'The Keays Affair'. It shed little new light on one of the most widely talked about scandals at Westminster of recent decades.

It is perhaps worth observing that one curious moral does seem to emerge from the affair: that in media eyes the greatest modern sin is not to get divorced. Men who divorce to marry their secretaries, mistresses or constituents (and more than one successful modern Tory has done so) seem to provoke less moralizing than men who, after being unfaithful, return to their wives. Nor, for instance, was there ever much media interest in the original Mrs Thatcher, Denis Thatcher's first wife.

It is an open secret that Parkinson would have been Mrs Thatcher's choice for Foreign Secretary if he had been divorced from his wife. After all, recent Foreign Secretaries have been twice-married, though in vastly different circumstances. When Parkinson left the Cabinet, he was replaced by Nicholas Ridley, who had left his wife and later married his secretary. The ratio of divorced to undivorced Cabinet ministers altered from 10:11 to 11:10. An intriguing victory for modern morals.

Cecil Parkinson did not, it seemed, want to marry Sara Keays. But the media hardly appear to have noticed that this choice was probably not open to him anyway. He could not have divorced Ann, who was blameless. She would not have divorced him.

Flora Keays, now an adult, has never met her father. Keays has never married. Parkinson is still with his wife. Those who like to believe that even supermen have feet of clay, those who like to believe that pride comes before a fall, and those who like to believe that Hell hath no fury like a woman scorned, have all enjoyed the confirmation of the proverbial wisdoms which the tale of Cecil Parkinson and Sara Keays provides.

KEITH HAMPSON – 1984

An Accidental Brush with Scandal

As the naked male go-go dancer strutted his stuff on the stage of a Soho nightclub, Keith Hampson enjoyed a late-night drink before meeting his wife at a party. But unknown to the Tory MP for Leeds North-West, the man standing beside him on the night of 3 May 1984 was an undercover police officer on 'routine surveillance'.

Earlier, Hampson, the Parliamentary Private Secretary to the then Defence Secretary Michael Heseltine, had been drinking with colleagues in a pub near Conservative Central Office on the fifth anniversary of the Tories' 1979 election victory. He downed five pints of his favourite brew, then went back to his office to work on a speech for Michael Heseltine. He nicknamed the beer 'brain damage'. This may explain the tone and content of Mr Heseltine's speeches, whatever it may do to account for Mr Hampson's subsequent behaviour. He was due to meet his wife later on.

After completing the speech he decided to kill a few hours in Soho. By chance he went into the Gay Theatre in Berwick Street which features non-stop male strip shows. Inside, smoke filled the club, the music was throbbing, and a male stripper, Luscious Leon, was dancing naked on the stage.

Hampson's attention was captured by a woman – or was it a man in drag? – standing nearby. Hampson couldn't tell. He bent forward for a closer inspection. In the process he accidentally brushed the thigh of the man standing next to him. The man was an undercover policeman acting as an *agent provocateur*. The woman was a police colleague.

The phrase 'accidentally brushed' was Hampson's. The policeman claimed a left hand was placed on his buttock, while his groin was grasped by the right. The subsequent court case turned partly upon whether the PC's evidence was believed, but others asked what – were this evidence true – the constable

263

thought he was up to, getting himself into these situations. Hampson was arrested for indecent assault and led from the club. The club manager, Russell McCleod, had seen it all before. He would have been well advised to warn his clients that the club was a regular haunt of plainclothes police.

Forty-year-old Hampson kept quiet about the arrest. He did not tell Heseltine – in his case rather like keeping a secret from God. But when a crime reporter on the *Sunday Telegraph* started asking questions, Hampson consulted his boss, then resigned as Heseltine's PPS. His wife supported him, testifying that her husband was perfectly heterosexual.

Marcus Fox, a senior Tory and fellow Yorkshire MP and steady, as ever, in everything but a crisis, proclaimed that he was 'staggered that he (Hampson) was in a place like that'.

Hampson blamed the incident on personal stress and alcohol but the manager of the club made Hampson's plight worse when he claimed that he was a regular client as were three or four other MPs.

A few days later, Hampson was charged with indecent assault. With the party split over whether or not he should resign as an MP (so causing a by-election), he decided to tough it out. He opted for trial by jury.

In October he appeared before Southwark Crown Court, the prosecution basing their case on the disputed police evidence. For the defence, character witnesses such as Lord Tonypandy, former Speaker of the Commons, impressed the jury. The judge told jurors that to suggest Hampson was a homosexual was 'absurd and unthinkable'. He urged the jury to remember that the 'history of mankind is littered with debris of men who have acted more stupidly than anyone else would have thought possible at the time'. After five hours the jury had failed to reach a verdict.

A week later the Attorney-General, Sir Michael Havers, announced that because of the widespread publicity and exceptional circumstances there could be no retrial. A verdict of not guilty was recorded.

Many had assumed at first that all was lost. But for every case cited as evidence that it is best to go quietly because to struggle only makes it worse, there is another suggesting that one should fight every inch of the way. Hampson was adamant throughout that the charge was false; so those of us who questioned whether

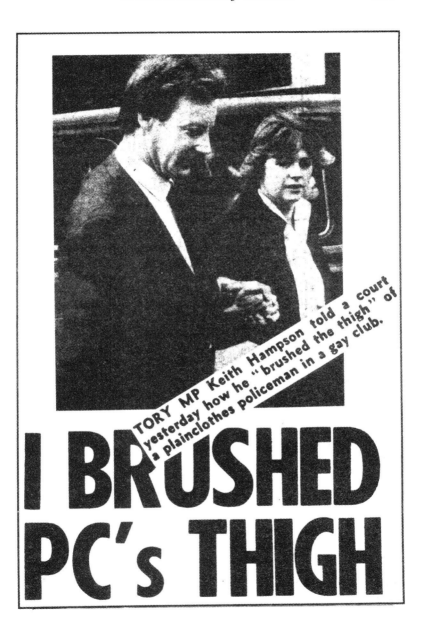

TORY MP Keith Hampson told a court yesterday how he "brushed the thigh" of a plainclothes policeman in a gay club.

I BRUSHED PC's THIGH

Sun, 19 October 1984

the behaviour alleged – in the place where it was alleged – should anyway have led to a prosecution, were denied the opportunity to support Keith by such an argument, probably to his considerable relief.

Keith Hampson came perilously close to going under, survived, and his reputation has largely recovered. Bristol University and Harvard educated, a former personal assistant to Edward Heath and a clever, clubbable and liberal Tory, Hampson lost the Leeds North-West seat in 1997. He co-ordinated Michael Heseltine's bid for the Tory leadership in 1990.

JOHN MAJOR – 1984–8, 2002

'Spicier than we guessed – John Major and Edwina Currie'

Many political scandals are depressing affairs: unedifying and grubby, they lower the spirits and spoil our hopes for humanity. Somehow this one was different. It was positively thrilling. It delighted the world, putting a spring into people's steps for a few days as we repeated what fast became a popular mantra: 'Of course it's Norma I feel sorry for.' Little that John Major achieved as a political leader contributed so obviously or so fast to the sum total of national happiness as the one achievement he had tried so skilfully not to advertise. 'John *Major* and Edwina *Currie*? Well, who would have guessed!' we trilled, in mock horror.

Out of a clear blue sky, unsuspected by the press and as stunning to their friends as it was amazing to the wider public, came not the greatest but perhaps the most perfect little parliamentary scandal of modern times. 'I don't believe it!' became the new way of saying 'I do.' For it was true. National astonishment was complete. For some days after the story broke in September 2002, millions of us could do no more than shake our heads and grin.

A bespectacled former Prime Minister who had himself rejoiced in the adjective 'grey', lampooned by satirists as a tucker of his shirt inside his underpants and a chaser of peas around his plate, Mr Major's greatest passion was assumed on all sides to be cricket. A shy and unconsummated flirtation with a Commons librarian might just about have been believable – but to have enjoyed a sizzling four-year affair with one of the most audacious women MPs at Westminster? It was positively delicious.

The affair had long been finished by the time Major became Prime Minister but its potential to damage him would have been immense. As PM he had used a Conservative conference to launch his ill-fated 'Back to Basics' campaign ('evil', stated Currie), immediately interpreted as a blast on the Tory trumpet for a return to traditional morality; but he was hiding a secret which would have blown his leadership and his whole political career sky high.

For remember the background. During Major's premiership, minister after minister was forced to resign over their extra-marital affairs and sexual peccadilloes as the salivating media pack sunk its sharp teeth into David Mellor, Steven Norris, Tim Yeo, Uncle Tom Cobley and all. The Prime Minister himself, genuinely happily married to Norma and father of two grown-up children, would have provided a spectacular finale to the fireworks display, a real rocket of an affair.

Yet nobody spotted the fuse and nobody lit it. This was the Great Parliamentary Scandal that never was, remaining a well-kept secret until both had left the House of Commons and frontline politics. We had to wait until Saturday 22 September 2002, when *The Times* landed on doorsteps with a scoop which framed the shock in a sober ten-word headline that riveted the nation: 'Edwina Currie: diaries disclose four-year affair with John Major'. *The Times* was serialising Currie's diaries, about to appear in book form.

Mrs Currie, married to an accountant and the mother of two daughters, was an outspoken Health minister in Margaret Thatcher's administration. Her gift for publicity had first become evident when she had waved a pair of handcuffs in front of a cheering audience at a Conservative Party Conference during a debate on law and order.

The post of Health minister may not sound high-profile, but everything Mrs Currie did became at once high profile. Or, as we now know, almost everything.

She had finally been forced to resign as a minister when her theatrical but important warning about salmonella in eggs sparked one of the first in a now regular series of modern political health scares. She had never been shy of the headlines: that was both her talent (she was a brilliant communicator) and her problem (colleagues distrusted it). That she knew anything sensational which she had not already turned into a sensation would not have occurred to Currie-watchers. But now she was publishing news she had kept under wraps for eighteen years. Giving her former lover the codename 'B', she described an affair that had begun in 1984 and smouldered on until 1988.

'And then B came along,' she recalled, 'and he was so bloody nice and so attractive, and so quiet in public that it was a challenge to unearth the real person. And to seduce him? Easy!' After one three-hour sex session, she told her lover: 'That was some going!' Currie concluded: 'He may have been grey to the world but he was a very exciting lover.' The pair met every two weeks or so for sex at her London flat, swapping winks, nudges and glances in the Commons, only to rendezvous later. 'I wish my flat was filled with one big man in his underpants,' she said, adding: 'Non-political spouses don't understand our love affair with politics and simply mutter that we asked for it. I remember B saying his wife was the same. But the brotherhood of politics – and of the Commons – does create intimacy and exclusiveness.'

Currie described intimate moments, of how in the bath he asked her if she believed in God. 'We were like teenagers exploring the world together,' she said.

Some observers believed the disclosure explained the mystery of the apparent delight Major's wife, Norma, took when Currie lost her seat in the 1997 Labour landslide that was also sweeping her husband out of No. 10. In the Prime Minister's Huntingdonshire home a puzzled Sheila Gunn, John Major's press officer, watched with surprise as Norma clasped her hands and yelled 'Yes, yes!' at the TV set as reports came in of Labour's capture of Edwina Currie's Derbyshire South constituency.

Until the very public airing of the story, Mrs Major must have hoped it had been successfully buried. In a statement quickly rushed out, the former Tory leader said that his wife had known of the affair for many years. He went on to express his regret in an unfortunate phrase that had not been meant to sound ungallant, but which enraged Mrs Currie. 'It is the one event in my life of which I am most ashamed,' he said. 'I have long feared it would be made public.'

There was now no hope of a dignified silence as Currie toured the television studios expressing her affront and publicising her book. There was plenty to talk about, and in both the diaries and the subsequent interviews she held little back. Starting when Major was a junior whip in Margaret Thatcher's government, the affair finished after he entered her Cabinet. 'I ended it by writing to John,' Currie said, adding that his promotion to the post of Chief Secretary to the Treasury in 1987 meant he would have needed to give his bodyguards the slip every time they wanted to meet: an exciting thought, though chief secretaries do not have bodyguards.

She had written her note ending the affair in March 1988:

I wrote to B on Thursday night saying that's it, no more; posted it Friday morning, so he won't have seen it yet, maybe not till Tuesday. Because it isn't quite the fun it was – he has changed. It was best when he was restless, hiding himself, lacked confidence; he told me about his family, his early background, about being out of work, nearly being killed in an accident, all the deep things you only tell your soul. He wrote only once, back in 1984 before we started, apologising for something he'd said thoughtlessly: 'I wouldn't hurt you for the world'. Once, unguarded, he answered when prodded, 'I think you're lovely,' but that was it.

According to the diaries her feelings for him lingered for a time after he became PM in 1990, 'dominating her life'. She was hurt that Major never mentioned her in his memoirs, complaining that she appeared to have been forgotten. Her pain at being overlooked in his memoirs was almost certainly matched by his pain at not being overlooked in hers: there were 104 mentions of him in her book, plus seven entries for Norma.

Mrs Currie gave the impression that not being mentioned in Major's book was the last straw. If so, this will not be the first time that an editor's shears have done more damage than intended. Your authors understand that Mr Major's notes for his autobiography included at least one story about Currie; it was harmless, amusing and kindly meant. At some point during successive edits of an over-long text the story disappeared, probably because it was not interesting enough.

Currie protested that neither revenge nor money were her motives. 'If I really wanted a lot of money, if I really wanted revenge or whatever, I'd have done it when he was Prime Minister, wouldn't I,' she said during an interview blitz. 'It was about time that, in every sense, the history books were written accurately . . . I was part of the making of a Prime Minister.' Whatever may be thought about Currie's love for publicity, and though she did make a tidy sum from her memoirs, there is much to be said for that protest. It is undeniable that if she had timed her revelations differently she could have made a fortune, and a big name for herself in British history. The tremendous discretion she showed for so many years, as a potentially epoch-making story steadily lost its financial value, may suggest that she really did hesitate to hurt him when she could have hurt him most. The deluge of (often male) wrath that descended on her when she did publish overlooked, rather unjustly, how far she had gone to protect Major, and for how long. Major had been fortunate rather than unlucky in the way she had handled the affair.

Currie's claim that she was unmotivated by bitterness, however, is harder to sustain. She had been forced to resign as a junior minister (over the salmonella affair) the year she stopped seeing him, and her diaries hardly hide her sense of betrayal when as Prime Minister in 1990 he failed to give her a job. True, she was offered the post of minister for prisons after the 1992 election, under the man (Kenneth Clarke) who as her Secretary of State had proved unable to protect her during the salmonella scare; but she had believed that by then she deserved a Cabinet post.

While Major refused any comment beyond his initial statement, his family and friends waded in. His elder sister, Pat Dessoy, said her views on Currie were unprintable but 'everyone

I know who has met her says the same thing: "she's a total cow".'
David Mellor, forced to quit Major's cabinet when his own
extramarital affair was exposed, also turned on Currie. 'Basically,
she sold John Major down the river for cash, like a cheap little
trollop,' he said. Lady Archer, whose husband Jeffrey was in jail
after perjuring himself, remarked: 'I am a little surprised, not at
Mrs Currie's indiscretion but at a temporary lapse in John
Major's taste.'

Currie hit back. He was cold, she now said, adding for good
measure that her former lover was 'one of the less competent
Prime Ministers'. 'The true version, which is not very pleasant, is
that he was never much good at anything, except convincing
people he was capable.'

The affair offers one of the great what-ifs of contemporary
politics, a game of speculation over how earlier disclosure might
have changed the course of history. For once without
overstatement, Currie said: 'A lot of newspapers have said that
history is going to have to be rewritten and I think that is right.' If
the liaison had been made public before the 1990 Tory leadership
election, would Major have succeeded Margaret Thatcher? Very
unlikely, leaving Conservative MPs to choose Michael Heseltine,
perhaps, or Douglas Hurd as Thatcher's successor. Made public
during his fragile but near-seven-year tenure of 10 Downing
Street, would he have survived the ridicule and charges of
hypocrisy? Again very unlikely. Would Major have been more
vulnerable when he faced Neil Kinnock at the 1992 election?
Undoubtedly. If not removed then, would he have survived later
challenges, such as that from John Redwood? Perhaps not. We will
never know. What is certain is that John Major was very much a
more interesting leader than any suspected; or interesting in
different ways.

Knowledge of the Currie affair would almost certainly have
scuppered Major's successful legal action in 1993 against the *New
Statesman* and *Scallywag* magazines when both alleged he had
been unfaithful to his wife. If the adultery had been known,
speculated lawyers, the outcome could have been very different.
Claire Latimer, the Downing Street caterer who was falsely
named as his lover, wondered whether Major had used her as a
'decoy' and permitted the rumours to get into print to hide what
would have been a more politically damaging exposure. 'Now I

can hold my head up high,' said Latimer, 'and say it was nothing to do with me . . . I've been planted to hide a story, which is the most extraordinary thing to me when you work in a place like Downing Street.'

Currie, who has remarried, is now a successful novelist and broadcaster. Her novels include *A Parliamentary Affair*, in which the leading characters are remarkably similar to this unlikely duo. It is a raunchy tale of a four-year affair between a married female MP and a married government whip. Nobody raised an eyebrow when it was published some years before Mrs Currie's disclosure; nobody thought to wonder.

Fact really did prove stranger than fiction.

HARVEY PROCTOR – 1986

'You haven't murdered anyone, have you?'

Harvey Proctor MP never did anything more shocking than spank people – and willing victims at that, for he paid them for their pains. Today his behaviour would not come to court. In 1987, however, the affair was a celebrated scandal. Though taken with as much amusement as shock, it wrecked his political career.

Harvey Proctor, a Conservative MP since 1979, was popular in his Basildon (later Billericay) constituency for his hard-line views on 'new' Commonwealth immigration. In fact his opinions, sometimes Right-wing, sometimes libertarian, could not be as crudely pigeon-holed as the media suggested – he voted consistently for such liberal causes as reform of the mental health act, homosexual rights, penal reform and freedom of information

– but he was described as being 'one of the Thatcher praetorian guard'. Such over-simplifications served to shield him from censure in Billericay, where palms are hairy and Proust is hardly read. But they also deprived him of support or sympathy in the liberal press and among fellow MPs on the ideological Left, when his own colourful lifestyle hit the news. As the whispers about Proctor's sexual behaviour grew at Westminster and in Fleet Street, so did the support he always maintained from his Essex constituency association.

Proctor would not see it like this, but my impression was that Right-wingers among his Tory officers persuaded themselves that their MP was the victim of a liberal conspiracy to discredit him, and believed in him all the more fiercely. Gradually, an unbridgeable gap yawned between the two sides – political and private – of his life. It was a chasm into which he eventually tumbled.

In September 1981 Proctor, educated at state schools and a graduate from the University of York, had his first brush with scandal. He had always enjoyed a tempestuous relationship with Terry Woods, his long-standing boyfriend. Woods became furious when, after he had walked out of Proctor's small Fulham flat, the MP refused to let him return. Woods spoke to journalists in Dublin, prompting a *News of the World* story.

Private Eye's exposure of Proctor's homosexuality was followed by the national press. They pursued him on a parliamentary visit to Finland, *News of the World* journalists checking in, incognito, to his hotel there and telephoning him in the middle of the night to see whether he was alone. Although a conscientious MP, he had only a modest majority (5,180) and could not afford a scandal. He dismissed the stories Woods had prompted as a 'campaign of political character assassination'. His constituency party, inclined to believe their independent-minded MP, backed him.

The problem seemed to be that though Proctor and Woods were genuinely fond of each other, Woods would often drink too much and lose control of his tongue. Proctor, however, who had known Woods since 1973, was unwilling to lose his friendship or turn him away. Woods was married with two children, though he separated from his wife. He did not return to live with Proctor until much later (1988) but saw him often. He was to feature in this story again.

Five years later, in 1986, a series of lurid allegations in the *People* proved harder for the bachelor MP to shake off. The newspaper and Proctor had been snarling at one another over the MP's successful libel action against them after they had (wrongly) alleged Mrs Thatcher was refusing to call Proctor 'my hon. friend'.

That summer the *People* printed a huge story, over three pages, about Proctor's proclivities. A male prostitute said that Proctor would play the headmaster. 'I would have to pretend to be a pupil who had done something wrong. He said I must call him Sir at all times and must not answer back. He took me into the bedroom and told me to put on a pair of white shorts.' Then the spanking sessions took place. The MP was gentler in bed, according to the newspaper. The young man in question had moved in with Proctor for a while, the paper alleged. Proctor denied this but said the man had stayed in his flat for a few days, at his mother's request, to study for his exams.

The MP, who had moved to the safer Tory seat of Billericay after boundary changes, was accused by the *People*, the following Sunday, of using a rent-boy network. A gay massage parlour boss was procuring youths for the MP at £35 a time, according to the newspaper, which alleged that youths would take part in sex games at Proctor's flat and that the politician would spank them 'while he watched by-election results on television'. Given the direction of subsequent Tory fortunes at by-elections, it is surprising the practice did not become more generalized.

At this time, Proctor refused to comment on sexual allegations, saying that his private life was his own business and did not interfere with his parliamentary or constituency work. He later told friends that what was published was usually a mixture of truth, half-truth, and falsehood. He lacked the funds to gamble on libel actions, which he feared would degenerate into confused disputation over half-truths, damaging him regardless of whether he won the individual arguments.

But of course failure to sue only whetted the newspapers' appetite for new stories. Friends would telephone Proctor after encountering men in gay bars or clubs showing photographs of the MP and asking whether anyone knew him. The *People*'s next scoop was sensational. They ran it as a 'splash' story for six weeks running.

One of the *People*'s informants was a young man whom Proctor says journalists had been hunting for some time. He was an eighteen-year-old rent boy, who had told Proctor he was 21 (the age of consent for gay sex at the time). He was allegedly called Max, though nobody was ever sure of this, and he cannot now be traced. Armed with the *People*'s hidden tape recorder, he had visited Proctor and, under the pretence of chatting about the MP's life and desires, gathered the evidence the paper wanted. 'Max' was paid by the *People*. Wired for sound, 'Max' assured the MP that he was over 21 (this could be heard on tape.)

These stories were proving a serious embarrassment to some Billericay Tories, who were facing a General Election within eighteen months. Their chairman, Frank Tomlin, was no fan of the MP. Proctor has claimed that, unlike most of the Billericay Conservative Association, Tomlin was embarrassed by his MP's views on immigration, which he did not share. He now demanded an explanation. His wife, Proctor's agent, agreed.

The *People* sent six reporters to Billericay in the run-up to the Executive Committee meeting which had been called, in October 1986. The journalists repeatedly contacted members of the Executive Committee, and managed to secrete a tape recorder into the meeting, with one of Proctor's opponents who sat at the front. After a stormy meeting Proctor won the day by thirty votes to ten. The Tomlins resigned, as did the deputy chairman and the treasurer.

Proctor announced he would not be suing the *People* because of the prohibitive costs involved. The newspaper, regarding this as an admission of guilt, turned over their dossier to the vice squad. Reading the early edition of the paper late on a Saturday night, the MP immediately telephoned Scotland Yard to offer to give evidence. For the time being, however, the police made no effort to talk to him. But Proctor discovered they were making inquiries of a number of other people.

The next story – which appeared in the *Daily Mirror* – concerned Proctor's recent jaunt to Morocco. The headline read: 'Naked Arab under MP's bed'. At the Ali Baba hotel in Agadir it was alleged that a naked young Moroccan man had been forced, with Proctor's help, to escape discovery by hiding under the bed in Proctor's room. A journalist seems to have extracted this story from a friend of Proctor's. Proctor protests that the 'youth' was in fact 25, and not naked at the time.

With a General Election only months away, the MP again attracted the attention of the press. Or rather, Terry Woods did. Woods, an art dealer, once again found himself on the wrong side of Proctor's front door in the early hours of the morning. He was wearing only underpants.

By now the interest of the Metropolitan Police was aroused. In April 1987, several months after receiving the *People* dossier, detectives swooped on Proctor's flat in a dawn raid. The raid was led by Chief Superintendent Marvin of the Serious [*sic!*] Crimes Squad. Interestingly, whenever the police went to Proctor's flat there was always a media circus in attendance, and this was no exception. The press had been tipped off and were waiting to watch a grim-faced Proctor leaving his flat at 10 a.m. to accompany detectives to Fulham, then Cannon Row, police station. At this point Proctor's solicitor resigned his case.

That Saturday night, Proctor went to a Tory cheese and wine party in Billericay. He was cheered by most of those present, but the loyalty of the MP's local party was now being strained to the limit as indications grew that a third General Election might not be far off. Feelings in Billericay were divided. One member said: 'The papers say Harvey's a racist one minute, then the next minute they say he's slept with an Arab boy in Morocco. They can't have it both ways, can they?' Others suggested that have it both ways was exactly what he had done.

Another homespun Billericay expert commented: 'I was in the navy during the war and I can spot a homosexual at 50 feet; Harvey Proctor is not one of them.' Throughout, Proctor commanded intense loyalty among many. In March 1987 his local association had given him an overwhelming vote of confidence by 220 votes to 62.

The police raided his flat again, early in the morning. He was not there (the police apparently thought he had 'escaped') but with his brother, where he watched, on Breakfast TV, the police and press surrounding his flat.

Proctor understood that 'Max' had until then always refused to give the police a statement. But after the April raid they had told him that Proctor was to be prosecuted regardless, and that 'Max' must not 'pervert the course of justice'. Max now agreed to make a statement.

PROCTOR IS GUILTY: RENT BOY TELLS OF SPANKING

New sex scandal rocks the Tories

Star, with additional headlines from *Daily Mirror*, 5 March 1987

On 11 May, the same day the Prime Minister announced a 9 June election, the police decided to prosecute on four charges of gross indecency. Proctor was due in court on 20 May – during the election campaign. On Saturday 16 May he finally bowed to the pressures and announced his intention not to stand again. That morning, when he forewarned his association officers of his decision, many, even the men, were in tears. Perhaps they had reason. Billericay Conservatives chose Teresa Gorman to replace him.

Until now Proctor's response to allegations had been a refusal to talk about his sexuality to the press, insisting he had not committed any criminal act. He had believed throughout that those with whom he slept had been 21 or over, and had always checked. His legal advice, however, was that some of his contacts had been under-aged, and (unlike the law on heterosexual sex) a belief that they were not under-aged was no defence. Proctor had been under a misapprehension.

Shorn of what he had always supposed would be a defence, Proctor had no alternative but to plead guilty. He admitted to four counts of gross indecency (in private, in his own flat) with two under-aged rent boys (it was said that they were seventeen and nineteen) whom he had believed to be 21. He listened impassively at Bow Street Magistrate's Court as allegations were recounted, with no detail, however embarrassing, spared. The age of consent for homosexuals was then 21. None of this behaviour would be likely to be prosecuted today.

Until the court case, the MP had consistently denied the allegations, famously issuing a statement in which he described them as a 'tissue of lies'. When he pleaded guilty to the charges Billericay Tories were dismayed. One association office-holder remarked: 'All Proctor's denials were a tissue of lies.' Proctor told Matthew Parris later that he pleaded guilty because the police threatened to go on digging for more allegations, and, after nearly two years of continuous harassment, he had had enough.

Proctor's solicitor, the late Sir David Napley, said the youths were willing partners. He attacked the press for paying people to give evidence in the pursuit not of justice but of higher newspaper sales. Sir David said: 'He has not only brought this terrible shame and despair on himself, but on his colleagues and constituents.' Proctor was convicted and fined £1,450 with £250 costs.

Later, Chief Superintendent Marvin retired from the

Metropolitan Police and retailed his story to the *Sun*. Over three issues of the *Sun* Marvin wrote about three cases, including his investigations into Russell Harty. One of his 'revelations' was that Proctor was involved in a call-boy network at the House of Commons. Proctor said this was simply not true. Another was that when he raided Proctor's flat he found a blackmailing message on Proctor's telephone answering machine. It was implied that this was a justification for prosecution – because as an MP Proctor had opened himself to blackmail.

Proctor gave his own version of this story. Months earlier, he said, one of the police witnesses had tried to blackmail him, offering to withdraw his evidence in return for cash. Proctor had tape-recorded this threat and handed it to his solicitor, keeping a copy in his own flat. It was this that the police raid 'found' among his legal files, through which they delved.

The night before his trial began, Harvey Proctor appeared calm, even cool, anxious only at the possibility of a prison sentence. His main concern seemed to be for his elderly mother, who was stuck in their home in his ex-constituency. He gave the impression that they did not have much money. Harvey displayed remarkably little outward fury towards the newspapers. He seemed to feel that, though what they had done was disgraceful, he should have expected it, and half had.

After the trial was over, the police, who had systematically leaked details of Proctor's life to journalists, continued their briefings. An unnamed police source arranged an impromptu meeting with the press at which he gave further details and opinions concerning the case – which had already been decided – calling the MP a 'Jekyll and Hyde' character. All this was duly printed.

Proctor ended his relationship with his constituency where he had built up a 14,615 majority, where he and his mother lived, and to which he seemed devoted. There were few tears for him in the newspapers, even in the more sober titles, and criticism of the methods of the tabloids was muted in this case by widespread disapproval of Proctor's politics.

At Westminster, however, Proctor gained a measure of support within the Parliamentary Conservative Party. A number of MPs, disturbed by the nature of his entrapment, rallied round. After all, they said, Proctor's telephones had been tapped; he had covered the first three pages of the *Sunday People* six Sundays running; at least one rent-boy had been hired by journalists, and wired up with hidden tape-recorders before entering Proctor's flat; two trespassing reporters had barged into his Billericay house, which he shared with his mother, then in her late seventies, demanding to know where he was; every detail of his bedroom games had been broadcast; and the onslaught had continued for more than eighteen months.

This constant coverage had become unbearable to a back-bencher with no ministerial ambitions. None of the leading players in the spate of subsequent scandals, even David Mellor (see pp.295–304) or Tim Yeo (see pp.321–4), was to endure such sustained, hostile coverage.

So colleagues' sympathy towards him was understandable, but two questions sprang to mind. One was: if Proctor had been so traduced, why had he not taken up his grievances in the press or through the courts? Proctor's reply (and it is wholly convincing) is that litigation can be ruinous and he had no capital. The experience he had gone through had given him an unreasoning horror of journalists, a fear that he would be misrepresented again, and a suspicion (in which he was right) that newspapers are restrained in attacking each other's methods. There was also an overwhelming sense of wanting to turn his back on a period of sustained terror, anger and humiliation. Harvey retains all these feelings to this day.

The second question is: why was he not more open about his sexuality from the start, or at least once it became clear that the press were on to something in which there was a large element of truth? Harvey's insistence that his private life is no business of the press is very deeply felt and has been consistent. He would sometimes go further than 'no comment', however, and describe allegations as lies. His justification to friends has always been that newspapers said many things about him, some true, some half-true and many false. It was not for him to disentangle these. It was better to advise that the picture as a whole was wrong.

This is disingenuous. With hindsight Harvey would have been better to start with 'no comment' and stick rigidly to it. He would like to review a period of his life in which he was often close to panic, and see it as though he had acted with more consistency than he did. But it is hard not to sympathise with his plight. Proctor told London's *Evening Standard* that he had contemplated suicide after the court case. 'I equipped myself with pills, but I did not even try to swallow them.'

Mrs Proctor, under great emotional stress, turned once to her son and asked: 'I just don't know what's going on, can you just answer me one question – you haven't murdered anyone, have you?' 'They could not have been more invasive of my privacy and hers if I had murdered somebody,' Harvey said.

One of the reasons Proctor kept the respect of the Tory Party hierarchy at Westminster was that, despite his sometimes eccentric politics, he never played fast or loose with the whips, who always knew where they stood with him, and were able to rely on his vote. Privately, the whips defended him fervently. A group of sixteen Tory MPs and ministers, notably from the Left as well as the Right and including Michael Heseltine, Tim Yeo, Neil Hamilton and Tristan Garel Jones, then the Deputy Chief Whip, invested a total of £80,000 in the new business venture to which Proctor turned, with what capital he had (£20,000) on leaving the Commons: a high-class men's shirt shop, *Proctor's Shirts and Ties.*

A second followed. *The Spectator* printed a cartoon in which Proctor's shop bore the sign 'Shirtlifters will not be prosecuted'. Gritting his teeth, Proctor bought the original, and displayed it in his shop in Brewer's Lane, Richmond. Proctor keeps in touch with figures on the Tory Right. Neil Hamilton (see pp.355–67), the Thatcherite former Trade minister, came to the rescue when Proctor was attacked in the shop by queer-bashers. Hamilton, a regular customer, exchanged blows with one assailant who was eventually chased down the street by the minister's even more formidable wife, Christine. Hamilton's nose was broken in the fracas. His wife was unhurt. The two assailants were jailed.

To this day Proctor remains close to his friend Terry Woods. Their friendship is still deep, but press intrusion into their lives – it is occasionally resumed, even today – has been traumatic for both, and for their relationship. 'One must plod on. After a while you can put up a front to people who are being beastly. You get accustomed to feeling everybody is against you, so when you come across someone who isn't, well, you are so baffled you are not sure how to react.'

After this chapter in his life was over, Proctor said that since the age of fourteen he had always wanted to be a backbench MP, and a good constituency member; and that he believed he had achieved that. He was still receiving letters of support and good wishes from former constituents.

Proctor was adamant that he could never be accused of hypocrisy, and that this charge, at least, had never been levelled against him in the press. He said that he had never been asked publicly whether he was a homosexual, and nobody could accuse him – and nobody did – of letting private life interfere with professional duties. It never involved constituency or constituents. He would never confirm what went on in his flat, he said, or with whom. He would simply not discuss his private life with the press. 'Nor will I today.'

His mother, Mrs Hilda Proctor, died just before this book first went to print. Proctor's, as the shop was called, closed some years ago. The former MP is now manager of the Duke of Rutland's ancestral seat, Belvoir Castle, and lives with Woods in a large country house in the grounds of the 18,000 acre estate near Grantham, Lincolnshire. Tracked down by the *Daily Mail*, Proctor said: 'I do hope you don't mind but I really don't wish to talk about myself any more. Life has moved on. This is a new chapter in my life.'

KEITH BEST – 1987

'By the skin of his teeth'

One of the claimed successes of 1980s Thatcherism was the £4 billion sell-off of British Telecom in 1984. So enthusiastic for the plan was the 34-year-old backbench Tory MP Keith Best that he bought six times more shares than the 800 he was entitled to. After their value doubled he sold them. Best might claim to have uttered for Fleet Street the cock-crow to the dawning era of 'Tory sleaze'. It was only a cheep. His shares sold for £6,240.

At first, nobody noticed. Keith Best had narrowly overturned a Labour majority on the Isle of Anglesey, promising his bemused constituents that he would learn Welsh. He worked hard and was popular with his Tory association. By the run-up to the 1987 General Election he may have forgotten his little flutter with Telecom. Having served as PPS to Welsh Secretary Nicholas Edwards, the energetic young MP's dream of ministerial office looked close to fulfilment, for Tories from Wales are in short supply. His appointment to the Welsh Office would have been a popular move: Best was a bright, likeable and articulate government member.

It was now, however, that the *Labour Research* magazine started to sift through the 51,000 pages of BT share applications to check whether any MPs had broken the rules. Keith Best's application was there. So was Lander Best's. And Keith Lander Best's. K.L. Best MP had used three variations of his name, together with four addresses, including his widowed mother's. He had used four bank accounts across the six different applications.

Labour called for his resignation and arrest when the story broke on 1 April 1987. His Welsh constituency party stood by him. John Biffen, the Leader of the Commons, berated Labour's 'sanctimonious and distasteful' demands.

Best had not used false names, merely variations, and the wording in the prospectus was unclear. Best's explanation was that he had made multiple small BT applications (individuals were limited to only one) because, with the offer likely to be heavily over-subscribed, he wished to ensure that he did not miss out if, as expected, the bids were scaled down. Colleagues were sceptical, but the Director of Public Prosecutions was reluctant to prosecute.

Though Best had assured his constituents this was a single indiscretion in an otherwise blameless career, the press had been busy. The *Observer* soon revealed that he had made four applications in the Jaguar cars sell-off. These were legal.

Days later, after consultations with the whips' office, the normally bouncy MP, for once crestfallen, announced that he would not stand again at the imminent General Election. In the belligerent mood of the hour, his climbdown brought no respite.

Labour's Brian Sedgemore, an enthusiast for investigative work in the financial world, called the resignation 'political expediency at the expense of the integrity of Parliament'. Neil Kinnock, the Labour leader, said he was 'waiting to see if we get a sermon on moral values from Mr Norman Tebbit in the next few days. He has fallen strangely silent.' The media then focused on Best's eager, but legitimate, purchase of shares in TSB, British Aerospace, British Gas, Cable and Wireless, Britoil and Enterprise Oil.

Labour Research had discovered another MP with more BT and British Gas shares than was normal. Eric Cockeram, the Tory member for Ludlow, claimed his grand allocation was for his grandchildren. He admitted to 'the right motive but the wrong method . . . I may have committed a technical breach about which I am of course very concerned.' Under pressure, Cockeram announced on 10 April that he would not be standing in the forthcoming election. On 29 April the CPS confirmed they would not be prosecuting.

Keith Best was not so lucky. His public pledge that the profits from the BT venture would go to charity cut little ice. Four months after his party was returned to government he went on trial in October 1987 at Southwark Crown Court, pleading not guilty to 'dishonestly attempting to obtain more shares than his entitlement'. Once, he wept in the witness box. He was found guilty on three charges of attempting to obtain BT shares by deception, and fined £3,000 with £1,500 costs. A four-month prison sentence was quashed and the fine increased to £4,500. But not before Best had spent an uncomfortable weekend in the hospital wing of Brixton prison.

At the Monday morning appeal, the judge, announcing his decision to release Best, said that it was 'only by the skin of his teeth that this appellant escapes gaol'. Richard Caborn, a Labour Trade spokesman, called the decision 'appalling'. Best's mother, Peggy, said at the time: 'This will completely finish him.' It finished the Conservatives in his Anglesey constituency, now renamed Ynys Mon. Plaid Cymru captured the seat in 1987 and held on in 1992 and Labour's Albert Owen won in the 2001 election.

But Keith Best, genuinely public-spirited, seemed irrepressible. Promising to donate his winnings to charity proved more than public relations. Best began working for the National Children's Home and Prisoners Abroad, campaigning for the release of jailed

Britons abroad. His rehabilitation seems to go from strength to strength. Best is now the head of the Immigration Advisory Service. He has stood unsuccessfully as a Tory candidate in local government elections and in 1997 was elected constituency Chairman of the Vauxhall Conservative Party, but laughed at rumours that he was seeking a second parliamentary career. At the 1992 election, his wife, Elizabeth Gibson, stood as the Conservative candidate in Birmingham Hodge Hill, a safe Labour seat. Her agent was Keith Best.

He had few enemies in the Commons. Most regretted his downfall, but few imagined he could have expected otherwise. Still, his £3,120 profit proved rather modest by comparison with the (perfectly legal) windfalls which were later to come the way of senior management in the utilities then being privatized.

At the time, almost nobody would have supposed he had any future in government, the Conservative Party, or public administration. We would have advised him to seek new fields. But walking away – or keeping your head down – is not always the answer: a certain shameless buoyancy can work miracles in public life.

RON BROWN – 1988, 1990

'A bit daft but at least he's daft on behalf of us'

Ron Brown presents a problem for any directory of parliamentary scandal. The problem is how to file him and where to start. A fervent admirer of the reviled Colonel Gaddafi and the Soviet regime in Afghanistan, he outraged the Commons by swinging the mace and, unlike Michael Heseltine, dropping it.

Then there were the hotly denied reports of sex in the Commons shower, but not with his long-suffering wife and secretary, May. An appearance in court followed his highly publicized break-in at his former mistress's home when he was caught brandishing his swag: two pairs of ladies' knickers. Sam Galbraith, the Labour MP and brain surgeon, is reputed to have said, 'There is nothing I can do for him professionally.'

Brown's pedigree at his election as Labour MP for Edinburgh Leith in 1979 gave some hint that his parliamentary career might prove stormy. In 1972 he was sacked as an electricity board fitter for leading an unofficial 24-hour strike in sympathy with the striking miners. A prominent councillor, he was suspended for three months from the Labour group on Lothian Regional Council for defying the whips over spending cuts.

His maiden speech in the Commons signalled the style of things to come. Traditionally maiden speeches are non-controversial affairs, but Brown ranted about Margaret Thatcher declaring a 'class war'. In 1981, to the fury of the Labour leader, Michael Foot, he visited Afghanistan after the arrival of the Soviet tanks. Worse was to come. He appeared to endorse the new regime by posing for photographs next to a tank.

He was twice expelled from the Commons for calling Nicholas Fairbairn (then Solicitor-General for Scotland) a liar and for waving a 'Hands off Lothian' banner. By now the antics of the Honourable Member for Edinburgh Leith provided daily copy for newspapers keen to seize on Michael Foot's battles with his 'loony Left'.

When Brown was suspended from the Commons for the second time the Labour Chief Whip, Michael Cocks, was taking no chances. He locked Brown in a room until Black Rod arrived to escort him off the premises.

In 1982 Brown made his mark on Mrs Thatcher's visit to the Holiday Inn at Glasgow by lunging at her, yelling: 'You're not welcome here.' He was fined £50 for a breach of the peace. The tabloids had another field day.

In 1984 he flew to Libya for secret talks with Colonel Gaddafi. Public opinion was outraged. It was only months since the murder of WPC Yvonne Fletcher, shot outside the Libyan embassy.

The last leg of Brown's ignominious journey to expulsion from his party began on Monday 18 April 1988, during a debate on the hated poll tax. The headlines the next day featured Brown picking up and promptly dropping the ceremonial mace. Brown denied he was drunk: 'I'd only had a pint of Younger's Tartan. The bloody thing was heavier than I'd expected.' His offer to have it repaired by the Amalgamated Engineering Union, which sponsored him, failed to assuage Labour MPs whose assault on the Government had been hijacked once again by their maverick colleague. The union replied by withdrawing its sponsorship from Brown.

The following day Brown provoked uproar in the Commons when he ten times refused to read the apology he had agreed earlier with the Speaker, Bernard Weatherill. For six minutes the Commons descended into farce as Conservative MPs made unpleasant noises while the Labour leader, Neil Kinnock, sat white with fury. Don Dixon, Labour's Deputy Chief Whip, signalled furiously at Brown to read the statement. 'I didn't write this rubbish,' he yelled back. 'Mr Speaker, since you want a grovelling statement, I am not going to read it. I don't accept it, all right?' Three times the Speaker ordered him to leave the Chamber. Once again a whip took matters into his own hands. The burly Don Dixon bundled Brown out.

The following afternoon, Brown was suspended from the Commons for twenty days and ordered to pay for the repair of the mace. The Shadow Cabinet withdrew the party whip from him for three months. Neil Kinnock went on record with a denunciation of the 'louts and loudmouths' of the Party's Left wing.

On 19 May, the day Brown's suspension from the Commons came to an end, the Parliamentary Labour Party met to consider the Shadow Cabinet's decision to withdraw the whip. During the stormy meeting which followed, and to Brown's rage, the Labour MP Michael Martin, now the Speaker of the House of Commons, questioned Brown's sobriety when he brandished the mace. The PLP backed Kinnock but his victory was spoiled when a popular Left-winger, Tony Banks, resigned as a whip in protest.

Brown's next appointment with scandal came the same night. Bill O'Brien, a Labour MP, told the press he had seen Brown dash out of a Commons shower 'with only his mace visible'. Brown's researcher, Nonna Longden, denied she had run after him screaming: 'I want your baby! I want your baby!' Brown said Longden had wandered in by mistake. Protesting innocence, he told reporters: 'I may be bonkers but I wasn't bonking. Because I drop the mace, I also drop my trousers?' He denied having an affair with Longden: 'I can assure you that at my age, 47, I have sex weekly – very weakly according to my wife . . . My credentials certainly leave something to be desired – that's why I keep my trousers up.' A few weeks later he denied reports that Longden was pregnant by him: 'It would be physically impossible . . . A doctor can examine me if he wishes. These operations do work, don't they?' But Nonna Longden would return to haunt him.

In June of the same year Telford magistrates issued a warrant for his arrest. The warrant had been requested by a solicitor, John McMillan, who thought Parliament had been too soft on Brown after the mace incident. The MP, facing a private prosecution under the 1971 Criminal Damage Act, made the front pages again when the Edinburgh Sheriff's Officer claimed Brown hit him when he served him with the summons. Brown denied it. The Director of Public Prosecutions halted McMillan's case.

The following week, Brown's constituency party passed a vote of censure on him for the affair with the mace. A similar motion on his voting record as an MP was narrowly defeated.

In January 1990 he was back in the dock. At Lewes Crown Court he denied charges of theft and causing £800 of criminal damage at Nonna Longden's flat in Charles Road, St Leonards, on his way back from the TUC Conference at Eastbourne.

Brown admitted that a three-year affair with his researcher Longden had ended the previous March. Longden claimed that after she had rejected Brown's pleas for a reunion he had turned up blind drunk at her flat. She beat a hasty retreat with her new boyfriend. Brown promptly went berserk in her flat. When the police arrived, he had fled, leaving behind a trail of destruction. The spurned lover had left a testament to his undying devotion: the word 'love' scrawled in lipstick on a smashed mirror.

Brown, under police interrogation, denied having returned to resurrect the love affair, but insisted he had gone back to retrieve politically sensitive documents and tapes. The mirror had been broken, he claimed, as he ducked to avoid objects being hurled at him by the man who had replaced him in Nonna Longden's affections. When the police searched him they found hidden under his raincoat two pairs of ladies' knickers and some jewellery.

After a six-day trial he was acquitted of theft, but found guilty of criminal damage and fined £1,000 with £2,500 costs and £628 compensation. Brown interpreted this as a 'moral victory' and

MYSTERY OF NAKED MP AND GIRL IN COMMONS

By SIMON WALTERS

A LABOUR MP claimed yesterday he saw mace-throwing Lefty Ron Brown walk naked from a mass-only Commons bathroom—and heard a WOMAN'S voice inside.

Former miner Bill O'Brien said fiery "Red Ron" came out of a cubicle in the plush ground-floor MPs' bathroom.

"The only thing that was visible was his mace," said Mr O'Brien.

He added: "I heard a female voice and a male voice, but whether they were coming from a radio or not I don't know.

"The voice said the word 'Ron', but I did not see a woman."

Other MPs who rushed to investigate said they also heard "voices" coming from Mr Brown's cubicle.

The story sparked a Tory demand yesterday for a full inquiry by Commons authorities into "an abuse of the facilities."

LAUGH

But last night Mr Brown shrugged off the story, saying: "It's a great laugh—but it is totally untrue.

"I wasn't even in the changing room.

"I can assure you that at my age, 67, I have sex weekly—very weakly according to my wife.

"I'm guilty of many things, but not dropping my trousers.

"I'm sure most women would run a mile if they saw me like that—I have not much to show.

"My credentials certainly leave something to be desired—that's why I keep my trousers up.

Mr O'Brien, MP for

Normanton, Yorkshire, said he was bathing in the bathroom at 4.45pm on Thursday night.

Only hours earlier, Mr Brown had been kicked out of the Parliamentary Labour Party for damaging the ceremonial Commons mace.

Mr O'Brien, 59, said he was getting dressed when Mr Brown came out of a cubicle and asked for a towel.

He added: "What startled me was hearing voices in there.

"I could identify a female voice or voices. Whether or not he had a radio in there I don't

MP Brown . . . "sex weakly"

Continued on Page Two

Sun, 21 May 1988

celebrated with his wife, May, at his side, showering reporters with champagne on the courtroom steps. Up in Edinburgh, watching the spectacle on television, his local party secretary and friend, Bill Axon, said: 'People here think he's a bit daft but at least he's a bit daft on behalf of us and they are prepared to forgive him.'

He spoke too soon. Brown's constituency party turned against him for the last time and asked the Labour leadership to re-open the selection process. A delighted Neil Kinnock was quick to grant the request. Ignoring Brown's protestations of a 'shamocracy', the party passed a formal vote of de-selection on 5 April 1990. A typically defiant Brown hit back. 'Ron Brown is a fighter. Ron Brown believes in the Leith motto and that is to persevere. What have I done except be a thorn in the flesh of some people? When I get a chance I will sock it to them.'

He got that chance on 24 July 1991. Along with three Labour MPs, the fiery Scot visited Terry Fields MP, serving sixty days in jail for non-payment of poll tax. Against prison rules, Brown smuggled in a tape recorder, interviewed the prisoner-MP, and played the tape to journalists waiting outside. On tape, Fields embarrassed Neil Kinnock by claiming many long-serving Labour MPs were so disillusioned with him they could resign.

Typically, Brown appealed against de-selection, fighting all the way to the Court of Sessions, Scotland's supreme civil court, and losing. At the 1992 General Election, he was forced to stand as an independent. He trailed home, second from last, with only 4,142 votes. The official Labour candidate won comfortably, with 13,790 votes. Uncharacteristically, Mr Brown accepted defeat.

In December 1994 *The Times* revealed that Brown had a long association with Oleg Gordievsky, the former KGB controller in London. Brown passed on information about his Labour colleagues which he claims the Soviet spymaster could have read in 'the *Beano*'. But unfortunately Brown never realized that Gordievsky was, in fact, a double agent. Brown now fears that his insights on the Labour Party were more useful to Margaret Thatcher as Gordievsky was probably passing on most of the information to MI5.

Brown still lives in Edinburgh with his wife. When last encountered he was doing the Edinburgh 'knowledge' to become a black-cab driver. Hopefully, this venture will be more successful than his previous foray into the world of work. Brown applied to become the steward at an upmarket Hong Kong golf club. The scruffy working-class former MP was deemed inappropriate for the task of pouring gin and tonics for English expatriates. Perhaps he should re-apply now that the territory has reverted to the People's Republic.

PADDY ASHDOWN – 1992

Paddy Spoilsport: Top MP
Refuses to Deny All

The Paddy Ashdown scandal was a five-minute wonder and a model for students of damage limitation, but it earned the Leader of the Liberal Democrat Party a sobriquet which he will never live down: 'Paddy Pantsdown'.

The former Royal Marines Captain, only days before the 1992 General Election, activated his ejector seat in the nick of time. Rather than give Fleet Street the opportunity of breaking the story of his short-lived affair with his former secretary, he went public at a dramatic press conference at Westminster. It was a classic spoiler operation which took the wind from the newspapers' sails.

Tricia Howard had been separated, but not yet divorced, from her husband. In 1987 she fell for the Yeovil MP who was destined to become leader of the Liberal Democrats. He was supposedly happily married to Jane. They had two children. Had rumours spread at this time, it is questionable whether Ashdown's bid to assume the leadership of his party would have succeeded.

But it did succeed, the following year. In 1990, with the affair long since over, Mrs Howard was in the throes of divorce. Fearing his own name might come up, Ashdown consulted his solicitor, Andrew Phillips, about the affair. The lawyer wrote an *aide mémoire* and locked it in his safe.

Two years later, in late January 1992, reporters from the *News of the World* were camped outside Tricia Howard's Wiltshire home. After refusing their lucrative offer for her story of the affair, a distressed Tricia Howard called her former lover. Fifty-year-old Ashdown in turn rang Andrew Phillips. The solicitor checked his safe – and discovered the worst. The document he had written two years earlier was missing. His London firm, Bates, Wells and Braithwaite, had been burgled two weeks earlier, but the solicitor had not noticed at the time the disappearance of such a sensitive document.

That document was held at the time by Simon Berkowitz, a 45-year-old painter and decorator. A few days earlier Berkowitz had arranged a secret assignation with a *News of the World* reporter in the booking hall of Victoria Station. For £5,000 he had offered him documentary proof that Ashdown had enjoyed an affair with his former secretary. His price eventually rose to £20,000. The *News of the World* refused to pay but went straight to Tricia Howard.

Deeply embarrassed, Ashdown's solicitor gained an instant injunction against the newspaper, the rest of Fleet Street, and the other news media, preventing publication of the document. Because its circulation arose from a criminal act, Phillips assured his client, it would be protected by the full force of English law, and would give at least a breathing space.

It was correct legal advice, but Ashdown, a veteran observer of many encounters with the press, knew better than to rely on it. He called a late-night conference with a handful of his closest advisers. Having broken the news of the affair to his wife, he had her support in making a complete revelation at a press conference.

In the event he was rushed into it – before, even, he could warn Liberal Democrat colleagues. The *Scotsman* was not covered – and could not be – by the English injunction and ran the story on Wednesday 8 February. National newspapers were still silenced by the injunction.

Ashdown was forced to hold a hastily convened press conference at Westminster, and an impromptu one outside the front door of his home with his wife Jane 'standing loyally by his side'. 'Paddy Pantsdown' was the *Sun* headline. It was in common use by hecklers until he retired from the Commons in 2001 and even – occasionally and affectionately – among supporters.

There was instant and unreserved support from John Major and Neil Kinnock. The Liberal Democrats were riding high in the polls and might hold the balance of power after the election. John Major and Neil Kinnock would be the only beneficiaries of a scandal involving the Liberal Democrat leader but both the Tory and the Labour Party were anxious to avoid any suggestion they were involved in dirty tricks. Mr Major, as we now know (see pp.266–72), will have been pondering further reasons for silence.

Tricia Howard, knowing media interest in her would not disappear immediately, decided to pre-empt it. She read a

Sun, 6 February 1992

y eggs at the
sponta-
neous public demonstration.

The following day, Berkowitz was charged with stealing and handling the document. He was joined in the dock by his former wife, Maria Watson, who was charged with handling. Berkowitz, a former member of the Conservative Party, denied that his crime was politically motivated. His ex-wife agreed, memorably: 'Sure Simon was a Tory. But first and foremost he looked after himself – that's why he admired Maggie Thatcher so much.' Berkowitz was sentenced to two and a half years for handling but was acquitted on the theft charge. He asked for scores of other offences, including other burglaries of solicitors, to be taken into account.

Ashdown's personal popularity increased in the aftermath of the scandal. 'It says more about the British people than it does about me,' he commented. Toy manufacturers cashed in on this new twist to his 'action man' image by producing a range of best-selling Paddy Ashdown dolls in full army fatigues. Tricia Howard declined a complimentary model from the manufacturers.

Never overlook the virtue of those who have saleable stories to sell, but refuse to sell them. Tricia Howard could have sold her story to the press for £30,000–60,000. She forwent that sum in the cause of one small but notable decency.

Max Clifford, the publicist who acted for (among others) Antonia de Sancha (see pp.295–300) said he would recommend the Ashdown case as required reading for any politician keen to learn how scandal is best handled.

And as for (the now) Lord Ashdown's solicitor, Andrew Phillips now sits in the upper chamber as Lord Phillips of Sudbury.

DAVID MELLOR – 1992

'If you can dish it out, you've got to be able to take it'

Few modern ministers have dished it out more brutally than David Mellor. Few have taken it with more chutzpah.

In political ethics, this affair presents a dilemma of gripping intensity. David Mellor's behaviour was at the same time wholly reproachable, yet irrelevant to the ministerial post he held. Such was his talent and expertise that when he left office a whole area of national life lost a formidable ally. Such were his antics that even his friends despaired of recommending any other course.

Not least among this Cabinet minister's contributions to cultural life, during his brief but colourful stint as Heritage Secretary, was to acquaint the English with a new word: shrimping. Not least among the disappointments which have arisen since is the discovery that Mr Mellor and his friend may never have shrimped. She now says the story, along with the story that he made love in a Chelsea strip (the apparel of the football team Mellor follows), was invented.

'To shrimp' is a term imported from the United States. It describes the Putney MP's alleged penchant for having his toes sucked by his partner: a passion also indulged, it was alleged, upon the Duchess of York, though not by Mr Mellor. Thanks probably to both, it was included for the first time in *Chambers's Encylopaedic English Dictionary* after becoming probably the best remembered allegation concerning Mellor's unlucky affair with actress Antonia de Sancha. When Mellor was finally forced out of office and on to the backbenches the *Sun* summed up his fall from grace with one of its punchier headlines: 'From Toe Job to No Job.' The nation remains in some confusion as to whether Mr Mellor was alleged to have sucked his friend's toes, or *vice-versa*.

David Mellor was elected in 1979. Arrogant, rude, capable, ambitious, entertaining, quick-minded, sharp-tongued, liberal in his thinking and brutal in debate, Mellor was a man of steady and humane judgement in public affairs, yet often unbelievable insensitivity and self-defeating impatience in personal and political relationships. He both impressed and infuriated, often at the same time.

He also became a friend and ally of the man who was to become Prime Minister: John Major, a fellow Chelsea Football Club supporter. There was no surprise when Major created a tailor-made job for him after the April 1992 election: the first Secretary of State at a new Department of National Heritage. Responsibilities included the press, broadcasting, heritage and the arts. There were high hopes for Mellor: probably the Cabinet's only genuine aesthete, one of whose boasts was the possession of the largest classical music collection on CD in South London. But Mellor was also Parliament's most articulate authority on football. In his new job he was quickly dubbed Minister for Fun.

And Mr Mellor was having much more fun than many of us realized.

A key part of the Heritage portfolio was the media. In July Mellor, educated at Swanage Grammar School and Christ's College, Cambridge, commissioned Sir David Calcutt, the eminent lawyer, to produce a report into press freedom. Mellor, whose own doubts about state interference with the press had never been a secret, and never changed, was under political pressure to reduce unwarranted intrusion by the press into individual privacy. He warned the press barons they were 'drinking in the last chance saloon'. Unbeknown to all of us, least of all himself, he was about to provide trebles all round.

David Mellor was 43 and married with two children. On Saturday 18 July 1992, he received a tip-off that the *People* newspaper was to splash a story the next day about his affair with the 31-year-old actress, Antonia de Sancha. Her telephone in the Finborough Road flat in West London where she lived and where he frequently visited her, had been bugged. Her landlord had co-operated in this with journalists, who had been tipped off about the story after Mellor had been recognized. Within weeks, the press were publishing photographs of the room, with a mattress on the floor.

Mellor immediately rang the Prime Minister to offer his resignation. The offer was refused. John Major reassured his old friend that he had his full support. He stood by Mellor the next day and publicly made clear that there was no question of any conflict of interest: Mellor would handle the Calcutt Report.

It is worth making clear that Miss de Sancha was not accused of having tipped off the press, or assisted in any way in the first 'scoop'. She too was – at least at first – a victim. And now she was under siege. The press uncovered her single most memorable film role: her portrayal of a one-legged prostitute who has sex with the pizza delivery man in the soft porn film, *The Pieman*. Photographs of bottoms, and of Miss de Sancha, taken from the film, graced many tabloid front pages.

Antonia de Sancha's story of the media circus in which she became involved makes extraordinary reading. Cast into the wilderness by the man she claimed had declared his love for her, she chose to enlist the services of the near-legendary freelance publicist, Max Clifford, who presumably stood to gain a cut of her earnings from the affair. She made a shrewd appointment. She later told Julia Langdon in a *Guardian* profile that the Chelsea strip story had been made up during a conversation with Clifford (she says he suggested it; he says she did; he 'laughs uproariously' at the suggestion that he knew the story was untrue, and denies it). Clifford told me the coincidence of Derek Hatton's claim some years ago that he made love in an Everton strip is no more than that: a coincidence. Clifford advised Hatton too.

From Antigua, taking a respite from the affair, de Sancha said she rang Clifford to try to break off the deal whereby he was to represent her. He said, 'Calm down, it's all right. I've just had a call from Los Angeles and Jack Nicholson wants you to play Catwoman.' He had suggested to her, she says, ('to keep the story hot') that she pretend to be pregnant and resting in Antigua while deciding whether or not to keep the child. Julia Langdon adds, 'Max Clifford laughed when this was put to him. "Really," he said, "I don't remember saying that!"'

On her return from Antigua, de Sancha says, she found her 'Chelsea strip' story had been sold to the *Sun*. 'I thought, I just don't think I can do this. It was like it wasn't me doing it.' . . . 'Max stormed into the room and said: "Antonia, tell her [a woman reporter from the *Sun*] about the Chelsea strip" . . . It was just awful, awful, awful. I'd have to look them in the eye and say "Yes, it's true."'

The toe-sucking story, de Sancha told Langdon, 'was complete and utter garbage'. Although she admitted her mistake in going

Sun, 25 September 1992

along with these stories, 'she did manage to stop some others. She did not, for example, allow her PR adviser to promote the story that she was pregnant with Mellor's child – to be followed later by a miscarriage. And she refused to make a video on how to suck toes. "I hate feet."' Clifford has not recognized any such account of events.

At this point the minister was forced to admit the difficulties this was causing his marriage of almost twenty years to his obviously devoted wife, Judith. On the steps of the National Heritage Department the following day he appealed for privacy for his family, especially his two young boys.

There were also difficulties in his relationship with his father-in-law, Professor Edward Hall. Two days after the *People*'s story, Hall attacked Mellor in the media. 'If he'll cheat on our girl he'll cheat on the country.' The next day there were allegations that Mellor had responded with a threat that Hall would never see his grandchildren again. Judith Mellor stepped in to deny it.

Two days later came a small but critical mistake in the Mellor campaign for survival. Having appealed for privacy, he arranged a photo-call at the home of his parents-in-law. A smiling Mellor posed with Judith, the boys and the in-laws. They stood at the gate of Professor Hall's property before disappearing inside for a cosy family lunch. Those who live by Saatchi & Saatchi die by Saatchi & Saatchi. Britain cringed.

Yet still he seemed likely to survive. The scandal had broken in the summer when Parliament was not sitting. He did not have to appear at the Dispatch Box. And it was universally agreed that he was doing a good job as Heritage Secretary. The Prime Minister and most Conservative MPs backed him, resentful of the media furore. There was also widespread anger at the way the *People* had netted the story, aided by the bugging devices secretly installed at de Sancha's flat.

By an unlucky coincidence, the following Friday the BBC broadcast Mellor's *Desert Island Discs* on Radio 4 – recorded five days before the controversy erupted. The programme had an unusually high audience in Fleet Street. Nor were journalists disappointed. Mellor told his interviewer, Sue Lawley: 'I think one of the great things about politics, you know, is that if you can dish it out, you've got to be able to take it. It never does you any harm.' Mellor also revealed a gift for unwitting irony: 'The sad thing about politicians is that they often give the impression that they want to stay for ever. They have to be dragged kicking and screaming off the stage.'

This storm, too, he weathered. The worst he had to endure through the summer was the revelation from North Petherton, Somerset, that a bespectacled potato called 'David Mellor' had won a vegetable look-alike competition.

On Monday, 7 September, the *Sun* began the serialization of de Sancha's story. No details, or alleged details, were spared. There were photographs of the mattress on the floor where the couple first made love – a replica of the bottle of cheap white wine which he always brought to woo her, in the foreground. There were the cheap red silk bedclothes. And there were, of course, the famous disputed accounts of how Mellor was said (by de Sancha) to enjoy being given a 'toe-job'.

Mellor was reduced to a laughing stock as readers of the *Sun* feasted on de Sancha's story about Mellor's penchant for dressing up in his beloved Chelsea soccer strip – centre-forward – for his 'sex romps with the leggy de Sancha' (who loathed football). The *Sun* even mocked up a photograph of the tubby MP in his favourite number nine shirt. It guaranteed Mellor a permanent spot in soccer terrace folklore. His name was sung out for months by rival football fans.

Herself the object of ridicule, anxious to be taken seriously, and by now a hot, not to say exotic, media property, Miss de Sancha was seldom off the television or radio. But still the Prime Minister stood by Mellor who, he insisted, would oversee the Calcutt Report. 'I am not one of these people,' Mellor said, 'who will change my views merely because I have been getting a bit of stick myself.' The Tory Chairman, Sir Norman Fowler, assured Mellor there was no pressure from the backbenches for him to quit.

Three days after the *Sun* started its serialization, the *Daily Mail* printed allegations about Mellor's friendship with an investment businessman called Elliot Bernerd. He had loaned the politician a chauffeur-driven Mercedes during and after the recent General Election.

Still David Mellor survived. Then fate struck another blow, this one fatal. The Mellors' family holiday at the Marbella home of Mona Bauwens, daughter of one of Yasser Arafat's main funders in the Palestine Liberation Organization, became front-page news. Bauwens had started a libel action against the *People* over its stories. Unluckily for Mellor it reached the High Court on 14 September, just when his fight for ministerial survival was at a critical stage. The four-week holiday at the six-bedroom villa had begun the day before Iraq invaded Kuwait. Internationally isolated, the PLO were almost alone in supporting the invasion.

The press tore into what they saw as the minister's lack of judgement with headlines such as 'I had Mellor – for tea' and 'Mr Mellor's Mona Tea-ser.' Bauwens, who was suing the *People* because it had cast her in the role of 'social outcast and leper', was mortified. The first day's reports made her want to 'throw up'.

The *People* had hired the formidable libel lawyer, George Carman, who described the Mellors' holiday as 'politically insensitive and possibly insulting to the families of British citizens . . . Marbella has sand, sea and sunshine and if a politician goes there and, in the honest view of some, behaves like an ostrich and puts his head in the sand and thereby exposes

his thinking parts, it may be a newspaper is entitled to say so.'
After a week-long trial the jury was split 6–6. The *People*'s editor
hailed it as a 'terrific victory'. He demanded Mellor's resignation.
Bauwens never went for a re-trial, despite her immediate
statement that she wished to. Mellor was not giving up without a fight, though. Bolstered by
advice from Sir Tim Bell, Margaret Thatcher's favourite advertising
man, he toured the television studios on the night of 23 September
1992, the night after the trial ended, hoping to salvage his
reputation. 'Undoubtedly I behaved foolishly,' he told the world,
'and I have never made any secret of that – but I think that to a lot
of people in this day and age that was not a resigning matter.' He
repeated his defence that he still had the backing of the Prime
Minister, who had told him the Bauwens holiday was within
ministerial guidelines. 'Who,' asked Mellor, 'decides who is to be a
member of the British Cabinet – the Prime Minister or the editor
of the *Daily Mail*?' It did not take long to find out the answer.

Earlier in the evening the minister had insisted on going ahead
with a long-standing engagement to address the Newspaper Press
Fund's annual reception, attended by many of the editors who
were baying for his blood. It was a brave and stylish performance.
Mellor thanked the press for asking him along: 'I was going
through a quiet patch so it was good of you to invite me tonight.'

With the morning came unhelpful tidings from Sir Marcus
Fox, Chairman of the backbench Conservative 1922 committee.
Fox was not hopeful about the outcome of the 1922 meeting
scheduled for that afternoon. For those anxious to discover how
backbench opinion is moving in the Tory Party, Marcus Fox had
always been a useful weather-vane. Mellor called the Prime
Minister and told him he was quitting. Initially reluctant, Major
finally agreed. David Mellor's Cabinet career was over.

His Commons resignation speech was reported by Matthew
Parris in *The Times* the following day thus:

The fun – *Mr Mellor: A Personal Statement* – was scheduled
for 11 a.m.: a civilised time for a lynching . . . Just before 11,
Mr Mellor arrived for his ritual humiliation. Tory numbers
had doubled. They had come for the usual show: pale figure
of minister – head bowed – old school tie – restrained regrets
concerning own folly – delicate references to nature of folly

– heartfelt thanks to colleagues for support during difficult time – sit down – 'hear hear' from all sides – shoulder-patting from pals – dignified exit, to kindly buzz of 'poor David', 'there but for the grace of God . . .' etc from outwardly mourning, inwardly sniggering colleagues.

By 11, the Tory benches were full: a charcoal waste of Tories, one of whom has a new wig. From backbenches, where he was a stranger, Mellor rose. Something within him said 'stuff the lot of you'. The speech was not an outburst: more of a shrug of the shoulders, a brave grin, and two fingers fidgeting to make a rude sign.

'Having become heartily sick of my private life myself,' he said, 'I cannot expect others to take a more charitable view.' It was an eccentric statement, by degrees chatty, defiant, funny, menacing and bitter: but devoid of self-pity. His colleagues had come to reward a show of regret. But of regret there was little, so sympathy was tinged with bemusement.

A fortnight of total cock-up ended yesterday with just one resignation: a man agreed on all sides to be good at his job.

The behaviour of 'certain tabloids', Mellor had said, had made him wonder whether 'one was living in Ceaucescu's Romania or John Major's Britain'.

Mellor's father-in-law could not conceal his glee. 'It was inevitable. We all get our just deserts, don't we?'

The next day a short letter appeared in *The Times*:

Sir,

        In David Mellor we had a secretary of state committed to and with a deep understanding of the arts. Could we not have allowed him to get on with his job?

It was signed by many of the leading lights of British music, opera, theatre and television.

Any chance of an early return to government vanished in November 1994 when the *News of the World* uncovered a very different affair. David Mellor had fallen for an attractive and talented viscountess, Lady Penelope Cobham, a past adviser at the Heritage Department, and an energetic member of many public bodies. 'I know this sounds a bit Mills and Boon,' he told a hostile press, going on to insist that this was a romance, whereas the affair with de Sancha had been a fling. Developments since seem to bear Mellor out, but it was a distinction the beleaguered couple never had much chance of persuading the press to feature. 'Mellor: new mistress' was about the limit of it.

The press wolves now circled David and Judith Mellor's Putney home, waiting to be fed. Mellor, who had said he would seek a divorce, agreed to step outside for the cameras. It was a disaster. In a friendly exchange with reporters on his way to post some letters he quipped: 'It's no big deal.' He had written the next morning's headlines.

The Mellors were under immense pressure. The MP railed against the media, in the media. Judith Mellor even rang a breakfast-time TV studio to insist she was not the distraught abandoned wife she was being painted as. Even this backfired. With Mr Mellor standing behind her, she asked the TV presenter if he wanted her husband back on the phone. 'Do *you* want him back?' the presenter asked. 'I'll have him back,' she laughed. It was virtually all the media reported. It was in any case too late: Mellor's and Lady Cobham's plans to marry were soon on public record.

The ex-minister's constituency remain loyal. And he has had a last laugh. Having long before told *Desert Island Discs* there was 'life after politics', Mr Mellor seems to be proving it. Far from 'toe job to no job' he has a broadening career in writing and broadcasting. The world continues to hate him, envy him and seek him out.

David Mellor is a brilliant communicator but a lousy self-publicist. Wittingly or unwittingly he had encouraged the world to see him as a sex-cheat and a rat. Certainly he had provided the evidence for both charges. But an uncensorious study of his political and media career provides evidence of another side to his character: Mellor's work in home affairs, heritage and the media added up to a focused, sustained and principled effort in the public interest, conducted with energy and intelligence. This was widely overlooked in the desire to criticize his adultery. Well, the adultery was punished. And the era lost one of the few politicians able properly to champion the arts.

David Mellor is now earning vastly more than he did as a minister; more than most of the newspaper editors who helped to bring him down. It is also possible that he is having more fun than when he was minister of fun. And within a few years his former post was occupied by an Arts minister with no known interest in the arts, or sport. Perhaps that was safer.

NORMAN LAMONT – 1993

'Je ne regrette rien'

No single incident in Norman Lamont's long career qualifies him for a place in a book of great parliamentary scandals. The clever, but not always wise, former Chancellor is notable, rather, for a spectacular series of small parliamentary blunders. His story is worth recounting in some detail here for the light it sheds on the media's power to turn caricature into virtual reality.

'Accident-prone' is a wonderful media cliché. It tends to prove self-reinforcing since, as minor accidents are occurring in most people's lives for most of the time, the evidence is seldom hard to gather – *if* you try to gather it. Once the impression settles around the person of any politician that he is 'accident-prone', endless small stories confirming it can be found, and become newsworthy as evidence of a famous characteristic in this man. The caricature takes shape and sharpens, and the virtual reality grows. Just ask former Tory Chairman Jeremy Hanley.

Not that Lamont did not from time to time assist his caricaturists. The often and widely predicted downfall of one of history's most 'accident-prone' Chancellors of the Exchequer was attended by no more than an hilarious succession of minor misfortunes. First impinging on the popular consciousness as the only politician ever to conceal a black eye by wearing sunglasses on *Any Questions*, he seldom disappointed the newshounds. And yet he is a capable and often prescient man, so why the mutterings and whence the caricature? Lamont would recognize the word 'louche'. The murmur was never far from bar and smoking room assessments by fellow Tories of our colleague. It well encapsulates both the criticism, and what his friends would see as the unfairness of the criticism, for it is pointedly unspecific.

When you examine the record, nothing disgraceful emerges. There has never been any hint of real dishonour in the conduct of his career. Lamont is more honourable a politician than some of his less beleaguered contemporaries. But . . . that puffiness under the eyes, that morning-after look. The *Sun* put it best, the day after his fall: 'For years, bad publicity . . . has dogged Norm like a bad smell.'

There were embarrassing allegations over an unpaid credit card and hotel bills. There was what was (somewhat inaccurately) reported as the use of taxpayers' money to evict a self-styled sex therapist, 'Miss Whiplash', from the basement of his London home. Perhaps less forgivable to the underlying public sentiment which hardened against him, there was a series of unhappily timed remarks, often reported quite out of context, during a long and (for many) hideous recession.

In October 1991 he declared: 'The green shoots of economic spring are appearing once again.' In fact they were. But they did not appear to most ordinary people at the time. Lamont was 'singing in the bath,' he said, shortly after Britain had been forced out of the European Exchange Rate Mechanism in circumstances which appeared to most a humiliating fiasco in which billions had been staked unsuccessfully to prop up the pound sterling. That it was made in an ambiguous context is quite forgotten. Lamont put it like this later: 'The remark about singing in the bath was made the week after Black Wednesday, in Washington DC. I was there for the IMF Conference and gave a press conference about the G7 meeting and the Russian economy. It was a very nice day and I had just been for a walk in the sunshine in the Embassy garden. A reporter asked me, "Why are you looking so well today?" I replied that I didn't know but that it must be the case because my wife had complained that I had been singing in the bath. The remark was at the end of the formal proceedings and was nothing to do with economics.'

The 'singing in the bath' remark was never (he has insisted) meant as a comment on exit from the ERM; even if it had been, subsequent economic news was to vindicate any bathroom song. But this did not make the report welcome at the time.

Millions, including hard-pressed Tory voters, already remembered – and would not forgive – an earlier remark: 'rising unemployment and the recession . . . has been a price well worth paying' for getting inflation down. This was no more than a frank, if brutal, statement of an arguably successful policy. Those who call for more candour from our politicians should look at what the press and public do to politicians who offer it.

Lamont, elected MP for Kingston-on-Thames at a by-election in May 1972, became Chancellor after organizing John Major's leadership campaign in 1990. Born in Shetland during the war he was part of the Cabinet's 'Cambridge mafia', his university contemporaries including John Gummer, Michael Howard, Kenneth Clarke and Norman Fowler. After a stint at Conservative Central Office he joined the merchant bank N. M. Rothschild. When Mrs Thatcher won the 1979 General Election he was brought into the Government for the first time.

In July 1985 Lamont, 43, married to a strong-willed woman, Rosemary, and with two children, hit the headlines for the first time. He surprised a Radio 4 studio audience by appearing in a pair of dark glasses. They barely concealed the Trade minister's shiner. Lamont told friends he had walked into a door. The other story was that he had been thumped when he made a late-night call at the Bayswater home of Olga Polizzi, the eldest daughter of Lord Forte.

Richard Connolly, also 43, a wealthy art dealer, was already at the £350,000 home of the glamorous Mrs Polizzi, who had separated from her Italian husband in 1980. Connolly, alleged Nigel Dempster in the *Daily Mail*, laid into Lamont. 'I was very angry with this man, who is a member of the Government. I was so angry that I chased him down the street and caught up with him in the next street. I won't tell you exactly what I did to him but he would have difficulty passing it off as an accident with the filing cabinet.' By the time he returned to the Commons, a plaster was insufficient to cover his embarrassment. The affair was 'innocent but complicated,' Lamont remarked. It did not seem to bother the oddly worldly Prime Minister, Margaret Thatcher.

Lamont wisely kept a low profile after that until April 1991 when a *News of the World* reporter called at the basement flat of his

Notting Hill home. By now Lamont was Chancellor. His estate agents had let the flat five weeks earlier to Miss Sara Dale. Unknown to the Chancellor she was running a thriving 'sex therapy' business in the basement. Miss Whiplash, as she became known, offered to dress up in a school teacher's mortar board and gown to fulfil her clients' domination fantasies. Whiplash, who also dressed in rubber, denied being a £90-an-hour prostitute, but admitted the newspaper revelations would be 'good for business'. They were not so good for her hapless (and until then unwitting) landlord, the Chancellor, who promised to remove her if the allegations were true.

The following day the *Sun* gave him all the evidence he needed. 'Lamont tart says: "I'm not budging from this house."' She admitted she stripped naked while massaging clients. The paper featured a two-page spread under the heading: 'Welcome to my vice den. The tart in Mr Lamont's house shows it all to the *Sun*.' The story then faded . . . Until September when it emerged that the Treasury had authorized a £4,700 payment towards Lamont's £23,000 legal costs – 'to evict Miss Whiplash', said the papers. Tory Party benefactors paid the rest.

Or so the newspapers suggested. In fact the Treasury payment was made to Lamont's solicitors not for the cost of eviction but for handling press inquiries. Normally media or public inquiries would have been handled by the Treasury Press Office, at the taxpayers' expense. In this case Lamont's personal solicitors took responsibility for inquiries about the Chancellor's affairs and the Treasury recognized this by contributing, for work they would otherwise have handled. As to the 'Tory Party benefactors', Lamont comments: 'The bill was paid by Conservative Central Office. Whether there was an individual or a group of individuals, or no one, I do not know.'

Outcry ensued. According to the media, Lamont was accused of breaching Cabinet Office guidelines that ministers should not accept gifts worth more than £125. He was criticized for not disclosing the financial assistance from Conservative Central Office. Lamont comments: 'I did not do so because it never occurred to me a Conservative MP could register as an interest help from his own Party. There have been many examples over the years where Members in financial difficulties have been helped by their Party.'

"WHAT DO YOU THINK...SEX THERAPIST OR GOVERNMENT CHIEF WHIP?"

Cartoon by Cookson, 15 April 1991 (courtesy of *Sun*)

Lamont raises an interesting point here. Indeed one could go further: it was not, until recently, uncommon for a Tory parliamentary candidate to pay for or contribute towards his own election expenses. Overwhelmingly, his or her local association now funds these. Members who are not financially reliant on their own local officers have an important independence – and the remainder an important dependence – which is of potential interest to press and public. But nobody has ever suggested that this is a declarable interest.

As to the Treasury money, Lamont explains: 'the decision . . . was made by the Permanent Secretary of the Treasury, the Head of the Civil Service and the Prime Minister. It was not made at my request . . . They came to the conclusion that those costs arose out of my public position. For the same reason the Prime Minister decided . . . that it was reasonable for the Conservative Party to help me with the total legal costs I had in evicting my tenant. These costs were way above those that would normally arise in a situation like this . . . [because of the Chancellor's public position] it was necessary to accelerate legal procedures in order to end the ridiculous publicity. I would point out that I also incurred large legal costs because of allegations made over 'Threshergate'. These were completely without foundation. But I had to pay a large bill.'

Given that there was never the hint of a suspicion that Lamont himself was involved in or had even known about Miss Whiplash's business, he was unlucky to attract the publicity he did. But it was hardly damaging, and caused only giggles. A parliamentary aide well placed to know said at the time that all Norman's friends were urging him to relax and treat the matter lightly. 'But he was in a great state about it,' and determined to act. The former Chancellor later remarked that there may have been no 'printed hint' linking him to Miss Whiplash, but 'there were plenty of threats to make such allegations, which is why I had to engage libel lawyers'.

The Chancellor over-reacted. The scent of potential writs excites as well as frightens editors. But it would not be surprising, in light of his experiences so far, if the Chancellor were becoming increasingly defensive. He added: 'All the photos of this woman in my family's house were immensely distressing to my wife and to my children. As a matter of politics as well, the view in Government was that it was essential to end the publicity as soon as possible.'

And what was the *private* view among media folk? The reader may find it immoral, even shocking, that journalists' reaction was one of hilarity that a non-story which some of our tabloid cousins were doing their tongue-in-cheek best to present as an issue of national importance (but which we all knew readers would take with a large pinch of salt) should be causing such a flutter in the Chancellor's dovecote. The media often remind one of a boisterous and undisciplined infant, gazing with amused bafflement at what it has broken in its romps. Most of the press does not believe that its readers really believe what it writes. Most politicians believe they do. This can cause a mismatch between the two groups' attitudes to media behaviour.

After the débâcle of the ERM withdrawal in October 1992, Lamont found himself in a scrape with the press which was really not his doing. The *Sun* reported that the Chancellor had walked out of the Grand Hotel after the Conservative Party Conference in Brighton without paying his bill.

The story was a travesty. It is, after all, hardly credible that a man as easy to find as the Chancellor of the Exchequer would try to do a runner from a Brighton hotel. In fact Lamont had arranged with the hotel that his bill should be sent to him at

Conservative Central Office. The same arrangement was made for many of the guests at the time. The *Sun* (says Lamont) obtained the information that Lamont's bill had not been paid by telephoning the hotel and pretending to be Conservative Central Office, asking for a list of all those whose bills were to be forwarded. 'The list included several ministers but the paper chose to write the story only about myself. At the time the *Sun* ran the story I had not even received the bill. The management of the hotel said the story was completely untrue.'

The *Sun* seemed to have it in for Lamont. The following month the paper announced that he had exceeded his credit card limit 22 times in the last eight years. He was £470 over his £2,000 limit. He had received five warning letters from Access. 'This,' Lamont said, 'is about the only allegation in the newspapers that was broadly true. For some years I simply paid my credit card bills every two or three months in order to save myself the bother of writing endless small cheques. Some people may or may not approve of this. But it seems to me an entirely private matter . . . A much more important question was why newspapers felt it right to obtain access to my own financial records and to publish them.'

Of course by now a familiar dynamic was in play. Once a public figure has attracted a reputation for some supposed defect, any news which remotely embellishes it becomes a good story. An impression grows of 'mounting evidence'. There must be dozens of other MPs who are late in paying Access bills, or who enjoy socializing until the small hours, but with Lamont it had become a story. A Tory Chancellor's unpopularity at a time of economic recession had much to do with the delight the tabloid press and its readers took in Lamont's discomfiture.

The *Sun* now said Lamont had last used his card at an unidentified Thresher's off-licence. It was the cue for the Chancellor to become embroiled in 'Threshergate'. The assistant manager of Thresher's in Paddington, one of the seedier parts of town, claimed to reveal what Lamont had used his credit card for: a bottle of Bricout champagne at a 'recession-busting' price of £15.49 and twenty Raffles cigarettes, at £1.98. Neither Lamont nor his wife smokes Raffles.

The Chancellor disputed the date, and this purchase, at this branch of Thresher's. The Treasury went to the extraordinary and undignified lengths of producing a credit card slip, signed by Lamont, which did show he had spent £17.47 – but on three bottles of wine in the more upmarket Connaught Street branch of Thresher's, near Marble Arch. On 30 November the Thresher's assistant at Paddington admitted inventing the story. It must have been the first time in history that normally staid senior Treasury officials found themselves in the position of showing their Chancellor's credit card slips to journalists.

Tory MPs said that it was proof Lamont was the victim of a smear campaign. 'Maybe the man in the off-licence is a Left-winger,' said John Townend, a senior Tory Right-winger and chairman of his party's backbench Finance Committee. In fact the conspiracy may not have approached such exotic proportions, but Lamont pointed out that 'the management of Thresher's told the economic adviser Sir Terence Burns that Thresher employees were offered money to make up this story, when it was completely untrue'. One newspaper, he added, 'offered a woman, whom I did not know, £100,000 to embellish the story in a further, predictable, way.'

Lamont limped on until May 1993. More serious policy troubles than these dogged him, but the damage done by the note of farce from which no profile of the Chancellor was now free, should not be ignored in any assessment of his final downfall.

Unleashed on voters during the Newbury by-election campaign, and pressed on whether he was proud of his achievements in office, Norman Lamont was reported as delivering his final flippant quip: '*Je ne regrette rien.*' It was reported on television that night. What quickly disappeared from the record (and has now been entirely forgotten) was that the remark came in response to the question 'Which do you regret more: singing in the bath, or seeing green shoots?' Treating the question as frivolous, Lamont replied, 'As Edith Piaf said, "*je ne regrette rien*".'

It was only after the by-election was lost that the media played up the remark, ignoring its original context. Nobody really supposes it damaged the Tory candidate's chances. However, it was turned into a hallmark of the Chancellor's supposedly insouciant attitude to political life and party managers warned John Major that his Chancellor had become a serious political liability. Bitterly – and only hours before he was due to be sacked – Lamont mused: 'I am sure I seem responsible for the sinking of the *Titanic*.' On 27 May, offered the post of Environment Secretary as a consolation,

Lamont walked out of the Government.

The news was relayed to the world not by Downing Street but by 83-year-old Irene Lamont, Mr Lamont's splendidly doughty mother. She had told the *Grimsby Evening Telegraph*. The *Grimsby Evening Telegraph* told the world.

The tabloids celebrated his departure with a series of biting, but none too subtle, obituaries. The *Daily Mirror* ran a front page with a cartoon of a gravestone. Etched on it was 'RIP Norman Lamont 1990–1993.' 'Hooray, Hooray, We're Norm Free Today,' trumpeted the *Daily Star* in one of the decade's least clever headlines.

Chris Moncrieff, the political editor of the Press Association, tried to put Lamont's achievements in perspective in the London *Evening Standard*. He had brought inflation down to a 25-year low of 1.3 per cent, said Moncrieff, but all anyone remembered was that his credit card was overdrawn. He had run John Major's campaign for the Tory leadership but talk of a bizarre sex therapist hogged the headlines. Interest rates were at a fifteen-year low but memories lingered on of an episode which had never happened: the Chancellor being chased out of a Brighton hotel for not paying the bill. 'Where others glide gracefully into the water, Norman Lamont does a bellyflop.' Moncrieff put it well, but as a veteran newspaperman loyal to his trade he did not add what we might: that once the press has decided to present you as a bellyflopper, photographs of your better dives will never get past the picture editor's desk.

The final insult was delivered by the Boundary Commission later that year. It abolished his Kingston constituency and he began looking for a seat to fight at the next election. His increasingly public dislike of the government his party was running may not have assisted him in early and unsuccessful efforts to find one. Questioning the Tory leadership, Lamont described John Major as 'in office but not in power'.

In March 1995 he amazed colleagues and commentators by voting with the Labour Party on a motion criticizing the Government's European policies. In June, after appearing ready to stand himself against the Prime Minister in the 4 July leadership contest, he openly backed John Redwood's challenge. It failed.

But it may be that it is not ambition which drove Lamont, but anger. He would say – and honestly believed – that it was principled objection to some of the Government's central policies.

He sat at the back, arms folded, often pale with fury – in George Eliot's phrase – 'like a malign prophecy'. Emerging from Room 12 on 4 July after having presumably voted against Major, he smiled thinly at waiting reporters and remarked, 'I enjoyed that.' His bitterness on the backbenches was palpable. But after that his approach became more conciliatory and it may be that the Party leadership felt it wisest to get him back on board. At all events, he was selected in 1996 to contest another Tory seat.

Norman Lamont had some reason to be bitter. What would a snap poll of British voters show, for instance, about recollections of 'Threshergate'? With many people a hazy memory of the Raffles and Bricot episode remains, while the fact that the story was finally found to be wholly untrue has never sunk in. And still the image dogs him. On 24 July 1995, the *Sun* reported that, after filling his tank with petrol, he found he had left his wallet behind. To which of us has this not happened? But Lamont made the front page. Of the songs Norman Lamont might choose to sing in his bath, *Je ne regrette rien* is not one. His Kingston upon Thames constituency abolished, at the 1997 election he stood in the relatively safe Tory seat of Harrogate and Knaresborough. Tactical voting helped deliver a Liberal Democrat gain. He accepted a peerage in 1998 as Lord Lamont of Lerwick.

MICHAEL MATES – 1993

'Don't let the buggers get you down'

But they did. Although not in the way Michael Mates, a junior Northern Ireland minister, had expected. The words were engraved on a £20 watch which Mates had given to Asil Nadir at a dinner to celebrate the Turkish Cypriot businessman's 52nd birthday. Nadir's new watch became the most talked-about item of jewellery since Gerald Ratner, the High Street jeweller, labelled one of his own products 'crap'. Mates became the only minister ever to believe he was the victim of a Serious Fraud Office plot. Media interest in the affair evaporated, yet that allegation has never really been cleared up.

Nadir, the founder of Polly Peck, was the subject of a Serious Fraud Office investigation into thirteen charges of fraud and false accounting worth £30 million. Mates had bought the watch to cheer up the millionaire businessman, whose own £3,500 Blancpain watch had been confiscated in one of the SFO's raids; and it was out of indignation against these, says Mates, that he first became involved. Nadir's adviser was his constituent.

Three days later, on 4 May, Nadir jumped bail of £3.5 million and escaped to his sumptuous home at Lapta in his native Northern Cyprus, which has no extradition treaty with Britain. In the rush to flee he left behind many treasured possessions, but he made very sure to take the watch.

For the next three weeks Nadir's business reputation was torn to shreds in his absence by MPs from both sides of the House. Nadir hit back from exile in the orange groves of Lapta and threatened to reveal corruption at the highest level of government.

The corruption revelations never materialized, but on 30 May the watch did. The following day Mates faced the first blow. Nadir praised the minister's 'unflinching help' in the fight for justice. It is not clear that it was Nadir who first broke the story to the press, or that he had intended to embarrass the minister, but that was the effect. Mates was taken aback. Of the watch he declared: 'it was a light-hearted gesture'. And, admitting he had helped put Nadir's case within government, he insisted he had been within his rights to do so while a minister.

Sleaze was already on the agenda. Now Labour MPs demanded to know why a minister of the Crown had been fraternizing with a businessman accused of one of the biggest frauds in history. They soon found out more. The first in a steady series of leaks revealed that Mates, advised by Anthony Scrivener, defence counsel to Nadir, had written three letters to two attorneys-general, questioning the conduct of the SFO.

There was uproar. Labour bayed. Tory MPs were dismayed. The wounds from David Mellor's and Norman Lamont's bitter departures from office were still fresh. Colleagues were puzzled at this choice of friend by a former lieutenant-colonel in the Queen's Dragoon Guards.

Mates, a 57-year-old MP for Hampshire East, had led Michael Heseltine's leadership campaign against Margaret Thatcher. Perhaps surprisingly for an apparently genial ex-military man, a good communicator and a persuasive politician, Colonel Mates was not without enemies on the Tory backbenches. He looked every inch an army officer with his black bushy eyebrows and brusque intimidating manner. But he was in deep trouble.

On 6 June, Michael Heseltine, always a close ally of Mates, admitted he had briefly interceded on Nadir's behalf – after a lunch with Christopher Morgan, Nadir's public relations adviser. But the following day John Major let it be known that Mates's resignation was neither sought nor offered. The following day Major told the Commons that 'his minister was guilty of a 'misjudgement' but it was not a 'hanging offence'.

Richard Ryder, the Chief Whip, was drawn into the fray when he admitted he had been approached by the Nadir camp. But he had summarily dismissed them and told Nadir's advisers to raise their client's case with their constituency MP, Peter Brooke, the Heritage Secretary.

Mates seemed safer. But a week later the affair erupted again when it emerged that the Tories had accepted a £440,000 gift from Nadir, who owed creditors millions of pounds. On 16 June Sir Norman Fowler, the Tory Party Chairman, was forced to concede that any money 'which had been stolen' would be repaid. On 17 June Nadir renewed the pressure by claiming that he had evidence of a Watergate-type scandal.

The allegations, so remarkable that the press tended to treat the affair as bizarre, involved the charge that someone (who, it was never revealed) had tried to involve the judge in the case against Nadir in some kind of conspiracy. MPs, however, and to some extent the media, never entirely came to grips with all this. Easier to handle was the known fact of Nadir's help for the Conservative Party and friendship towards Mates, and the unusual intervention on Nadir's behalf by a Tory minister – Mates.

Tory funding – always a favourite Labour topic – was back on the front pages. Sleaze and corruption dominated the headlines. Colonel Mates was watching the lift from the bottom of the lift-shaft. Elected in 1974, he had spent the Thatcher years in the political wilderness. A minister since 1990, he was determined not to return to it. He fought with tenacity, but on 20 June the steady flow of leaks designed to undermine him became a torrent. Newspapers disclosed that the minister had borrowed a car for his estranged wife from Nadir's public relations adviser. And this was after Nadir had jumped bail.

Support, never warm, was ebbing. But still the Prime Minister, unwilling to be bounced by the press, backed Mates.

On 24 June the *Daily Mail* published the text of the minister's letter to the Attorney-General. Mates was accused in one newspaper of basing this on a draft he had been given by Nadir – an accusation which has since been withdrawn.

The Prime Minister, now conspicuously failing to give public backing to Mates, found his own leadership criticized for failing to rid the Government of another lame duck minister. Mates arrived at the Northern Ireland Office declaring it was business as usual. But the lunchtime ITN news revealed that he had dined at the Reform Club the previous evening with Nadir's PR adviser. Mates declared: 'It proves you cannot trust the Reform Club. It would never have happened at the Garrick.'

It was an error of judgement and a dinner too far for John Major. A meeting was hastily arranged at Downing Street. At 2 p.m. Mates offered his resignation 'with regret' not, he said, because he had done anything wrong, but to spare the Prime Minister embarrassment. At Question Time Mr Major announced that Mates had finally gone: 25 days too late for Tory MPs.

The galloping Colonel, however, had not finished. On 29 June, in one of the most remarkable resignation speeches heard in the Commons, he accused the SFO of improper conduct and exerting pressure on the judge who was to have tried the case. A packed Chamber listened in numb amazement as Madam Speaker, in a series of weird clashes with the MP on his feet warned him nine times to quit the subject because of the *sub judice* rule. But Mates, cheered by Labour MPs revelling in the Government's discomfort, bulldozed on and completed his speech. He has the distinction of being the only MP to have successfully brushed the assertive Miss Boothroyd aside.

Her Assistant Clerk, Donald Limon, scowling under his wig, kept turning to her to hiss that Mates must be stopped. At one point (said Simon Hoggart in the *Observer*) 'the Attorney-General, Sir Nicholas Lyell, could be seen signalling' the clerk to get Mates silenced. He never was.

A few days after his resignation speech, at a prize-giving at his old school, Blundells, in Tiverton, the former minister said: 'Can I say what a relief it is to be on my feet without Madam Speaker present.'

As for Asil Nadir, he no longer wears the watch. Mates confessed afterwards: 'I very nearly never had it engraved. It cost £32, which was even more than the watch. I wish I had sent it to the Prime Minister instead.'

Colonel Mates was throughout doggedly loyal to John Major. He believes the Prime Minister did his best for him. He tells friends that Major's government was more important than his own woes and that, to take the heat off the Prime Minister, it was best for him to pipe down, and go. They remain friends.

There appeared a curious footnote to the affair, when what had been intended as a private conversation between the Prime Minister and the TV interviewer Michael Brunson was published in the *Daily Mirror* after hints emerged that Major had called some of his Cabinet colleagues 'bastards'. As Hoggart writes, that was the issue absorbing the nation, and few noticed Major's reply to Brunson's criticism that he had held on to Mates too long, and should have 'swatted' him. People would have said that Mates had been 'set up', protested the Prime Minister. 'As the Cabinet Secretary [Sir Robin Butler] told me, "It was an act of gross injustice to have got rid of him." Nobody knew what I knew at the time.'

And still nobody does. Mates has enemies and too few colleagues were prepared to stick out their necks for him. Even friends agreed he conducted his defence imprudently. But the suspicion remains that elements to this story never emerged.

At the time of writing he is serving (as a member of the Commons committee which oversees Britain's spies) on an *ad hoc* committee appointed to inquire into Intelligence failures before the 2003 Iraq War. The committee is chaired by the (now) Lord Butler of Brockwell.

STEVEN NORRIS, TIM YEO, UNCLE TOM COBLEY and ALL – 1993–7

Back to Basics

John Major's call to go 'back to basics' at the Tory Party Conference in October 1993 met with a rapturous reception. It came two days after Peter Lilley had been cheered to the rafters for his attack on single mothers on state benefits who leapfrogged to the top of housing waiting lists.

At last the party faithful, demoralized by months of bickering over Europe and Britain's humiliating withdrawal from the ERM, had something to applaud. Major's carefully crafted slogan underlined the party's traditional values by attacking the progressive doctrines of the dreaded 1960s. A Conservative government stood, said Mr Major, 'for a country united around those old common-sense British values that should never have been pushed aside.' The message was easily understood in the constituencies. The Conference warmed to it instantly.

A pre-speech press conference at Blackpool, minutes before the Prime Minister took the floor, had been given by Tim Collins, one of Major's chief spin-doctors. Journalists had seen an outline of the speech. They asked Collins how important the 'back to basics' theme was to the overall message and he confirmed that Downing Street intended it to be a dominant one. Within seconds, journalists were asking sceptical, cheeky, or downright lewd questions about divorce, adultery and waywardness among Major's own colleagues.

John Major is not personally or politically a morally censorious man. At no point did he mention sexual morality. He had probably hoped to centre the 'basics' theme more around basics in education, school discipline, respect for the law, civic-mindedness, cricket, warm beer, ginger snaps and cocoa. But the press saw it differently. If the Prime Minister had needed an early indication of just how differently, Mr Collins could have warned him before he even made the fateful speech. And at Westminster, too, some MPs saw the danger signs of a party, with a long and glorious history of scandal of its own, leading what could so easily be represented as a moral crusade. They were right. The media, anxious to expose any whiff of hypocrisy, lost no time in exploiting what they somewhat fancifully declared to be the new mood of moral self-righteousness at Conservative Central Office. Thus began what was really a kind of undeclared open season on the private lives of Tory MPs. Over Christmas and the New Year the public was fed an almost daily diet of ministerial misdemeanours. Resignations followed, some faster than others.

The first minister to have reason to regret the campaign dreamed up (apparently) by the Downing Street Policy Unit, was Steven Norris, the 48-year-old Transport minister. Norris, married with two children, was revealed as having not one but *five* mistresses.

This bombshell first hit the news-stands during the Party Conference, almost before the Prime Minister's standing ovation had died. Steven Norris had been supposed by many to be living with his wife of 24 years, Vicky, in their cottage in his Epping Forest constituency. But Mrs Norris knew differently. A niece of Cardinal Basil Hume, the head of the Roman Catholic Church in England and Wales, she was by then (says Norris) living in her own house in Berkshire. She knew her husband was a weekday Romeo. He says she knew about all his mistresses.

They did not, apparently, all know about each other. But they soon found out, once the press got the story. Five mistresses were located: a lady surgeon who dated Norris for eight years until 1986; a 46-year-old sales executive who took over from the surgeon but dumped Norris in January 1991 when he told her about mistress number four; a 45-year-old journalist on *The Times* – a divorcée with two children who had actually rented a home to share with the philandering MP; a forty-year-old director of *Harpers & Queen*; and a 29-year-old secretary to another Tory MP, who left Norris on discovering the existence of an earlier mistress, who was to become his wife.

The tabloids called him 'a serial adulterer', and for some weeks the discovery of new Norris mistresses brought on a chuckle at many British breakfast tables.

Mrs Norris formally separated from her husband. She has wisely and with dignity refused consistently to utter a word to the press. Her husband's constituency party had plenty to say. But the congenial and persuasive former car-salesman, who has never moralized about others and who is popular with colleagues, comfortably saw off threats to de-select him in January 1994. Norris kept his ministerial job. Nobody really knows how, but few wished him ill.

Steven Norris has commented that 'what appeared in the tabloids was considerably at variance with the facts, but there is

YES, YES, YES, YES, YES MINISTER!

Norris and his five mistresses

Photograph by Mike Poultney, 10 October 1993 (courtesy of the *Sunday Times*)

no mileage for me in going into it'. On 4 July 1995, emerging from Room 12 at the Commons after voting (for the Prime Minister) in the Tory leadership contest, Mr Norris remarked: 'I owe him one.' Aware perhaps that the Prime Minister does *not* owe him one, he later announced that he would retire at the next election to pursue business interests and subsequently ran as a candidate for mayor of London.

Tim Yeo had a rougher time of it. As families in his Suffolk South constituency were eating their leftover turkey on 26 December 1993, they discovered in the press that the married Environment minister had a six-month-old 'love child' (the word 'bastard' was now effectively cornered by the Prime Minister for use in describing his own Cabinet colleagues). It was Yeo's misfortune that the *News of the World* decided to break the story of Julia Stent's baby on Boxing Day at the beginning of a traditionally quiet news period. This served the paper well. They ran the story almost without distraction, and for nearly a fortnight other papers picked up on this too, featuring it prominently.

There was an instant fuss. Yeo's mistress was a single mother. Journalists were not slow to dig up a quote the minister had once made to a local newspaper after visiting a constituency branch of the marriage guidance group Relate. 'It is in everyone's interests to reduce broken families and the number of single parents; I have seen from my constituency the consequences of marital breakdown.'

This was unfortunate and uncharacteristic. In fact Yeo was not one of those MPs who habitually preached about moral issues. Like Steven Norris he is a liberal and uncensorious man.

Much good it did him. Worse still for party managers, the new woman in the minister's life was a Tory councillor – one of the handful who clung on in Hackney. He had met her at a party conference, but not the 'back to basics' one.

Yeo's wife, Diane, performed the traditional role of a Tory wife and appeared for photographs 'standing by' her man. Yeo had told her in February that the girlfriend, Julia Stent, was pregnant.

John Major immediately pledged loyalty to Yeo, declaring that it was 'a private matter'. Yeo took his wife and two grown-up children for a holiday in the Seychelles. It was unlucky, the holiday having been booked long before, partly as a treat for his son Jonathan, a talented painter who was recovering from

Hodgkin's disease. A decision to go ahead with the trip – made for kindly reasons with family interests in mind and when the last thing Yeo wanted to do was have a holiday – was represented as betraying an arrogant disregard for the gravity of his situation.

While he was away, David Evans, a voluble Tory backbencher, demanded Yeo's resignation. Evans was at least consistent. He had also called for Norris to go. In fact both the Foreign Secretary, Douglas Hurd, and Virginia Bottomley, the Health Secretary, spoke up strongly for Yeo, but it was Evans who got the attention.

When Yeo returned, the press were waiting. The Environment minister made the mistake of hiding from the cameras on the floor of the family car.

On 2 January, elements of his constituency party, which had warmly embraced 'back to basics', were in a state of revolt. A local Tory mayor, Mrs Aldine Horrigan, had written to the Prime Minister expressing her disgust with Yeo. She repeated her demand to the press the next day: Yeo should resign as a minister.

On 4 January, Yeo was summoned to a meeting with the eight officers of his constituency association. He echoed the fateful words of David Mellor: 'The Prime Minister decides who is in his government and not the tabloid newspapers.' He was wrong. The constituency party was about to have an unusual say in the matter.

He was dismissed from the meeting, which lasted six hours. The next morning the officers issued a statement which pledged less than wholehearted support. Yeo, who wanted to fight on, was called before Sir Norman Fowler, the Party Chairman, and Richard Ryder, the Chief Whip. The ministers, faced with this apparent revolt in the constituency, told Yeo he had lost his Prime Minister's support. He resigned the same day.

On 14 January the much larger and arguably more representative Executive Council of the association, comprising some 100 members, voted overwhelmingly in Yeo's favour, many expressing dismay at the statement of the officers' meeting. But it was too late for the ex-minister.

Though a local association has often been instrumental in forcing an MP to resign his seat or not to stand again, this had been different. Officers of the Suffolk Conservative Association nudged their MP not out of Westminster, but out of Whitehall. Rarely if ever has a constituency party taken the decisive role in removing a minister from government.

On 7 January, days after his resignation, Yeo criticized, in the *Daily Express*, the local mayor who had led the campaign against him. 'When I think of what I have done for her. I have campaigned for her in local government elections. And I rescued her husband's business when it was in receivership.'

On Sunday, 9 January, with the 'back to basics' campaign in tatters, the *Mail on Sunday* disclosed that in 1967 the ex-minister had fathered another child while he was at Emmanuel College, Cambridge. He was 22-years-old at the time. This daughter was adopted. She did not know that Yeo was her father. Mrs Yeo had known about the child before they married.

Doubts continued about his future as an MP when he refused to say whether that future would lie with his wife or his Hackney mistress. Some local activists said that losing the seat at a by-election was a price worth paying for getting rid of Yeo. But after spending a week telephoning his local party members one by one, Yeo survived a vote of confidence.

On 19 January Julia Stent resigned as a Hackney councillor – over non-attendance in the previous six months. She can be forgiven for her distraction. On 21 January, Diane Yeo, widely regarded among the press as 'a good thing', told *The Times* she had actually received hate mail for standing by her husband, whom she still loved.

The same day Yeo was pictured entering one of London's more fashionable restaurants, Langan's Brasserie in Mayfair, with his mistress. They stayed for three hours. Again, the tabloids' implication was clear – but unfair. Yeo was trying to act decently towards Stent.

Nobody close to Yeo ever criticized him in the newspapers at the time, and none has since. This had been a 'story' which had resulted entirely from an investigative campaign by a newspaper. It did not result – as so many other stories in this book did – from the actions of an aggrieved party stirring up the media as an act of revenge. We may surmise that Yeo dealt straightforwardly both with his family and with Julia Stent, and never lost the trust of any of them. As we remarked of the Parkinson affair, not getting divorced seems to be the modern sin. Yeo was rather unlucky.

He was not, however, bitter. Some time later, writing in the *Independent*, Yeo attacked the notion that the press could by legislation be made less prurient. 'Newspapers print stories they believe their readers want to read,' he said.

By now the alleged scandals were coming thick and fast. Alan Duncan, the newly elected millionaire MP for the safe seat of Rutland and Melton, had resigned as a parliamentary private secretary on 8 January.

The young Mr Duncan, known as 'Hunky Dunky' at Westminster for his bonsai good looks, had taken advantage of the Tories' right-to-buy policy by arranging for the purchase of a council house adjoining his own in Westminster. It involved a private deal with his neighbour Harry Ball-Wilson, who benefited from a £50,000 tenant's discount.

Embarrassingly to journalists labouring to present Mr Ball-Wilson as the impoverished victim of Tory greed, the old boy was on holiday in Hawaii at the time of the fuss. He also appeared to have been a winner, as Duncan had paid handsomely for, and repaired, a dilapidated freehold with a sitting lifetime tenant in a slow property market: an outcome the MP had always contemplated.

In a different atmosphere the Duncan story might not have warranted mention. It was a telling indication of the hysteria gripping the nation over 'basics' that this was given front-page treatment by the *Daily Mirror*. The newspaper went on to point out that Duncan's own house (which it was his plan to expand sideways) had been the headquarters of John Major's leadership campaign. Duncan's comments, when tracked down on a skiing holiday in Switzerland, were unprintable but may be summarized as a robust expression of the thought that if he were to be indicted for immorality, he could think of immorality which would have been more fun.

The following day, along with the exposure of Tim Yeo's second love child, reports about the previously obscure backbench MP David Ashby provided an irresistible sideshow to the 'back to basics' fiasco (see pp. 345–52).

In an atmosphere of heightened media interest in 'love-children', the investigative zeal of the tabloids 'uncovered' even poor Gary Waller, the harmless and little known backbench Tory MP for Keighley, celebrated (until then) only for his tubby appearance and his dogged four-hour-plus London Marathons. He escaped with his life, his seat, and most of his reputation.

On 23 January 1994, the *News of the World* revealed that the long-time 'church-going' bachelor Waller was the father of a child by a mistress. 'Another Tory Shaker' said the headline, across a graphic of the top of the tower of Big Ben flying into the air. The paper said he had been 'booted off the books of a posh dating agency' for claiming he was single and fancy-free. He had also described himself, said the paper, as 'intelligent, humorous, career-oriented and youthful in approach'.

Had he belonged to the agency? 'Waller: "I did, but I was very, very reluctant. I only took it on on a trial basis."' In fact, far from being fancy-free, 'Waller (48) has a long-term girlfriend *and* a love-child by a Commons secretary.'

The phrase 'So what?' occurred even to hardened journalists at the discovery of this shocker. Waller did not resign. Nobody called on him to. The top of Big Ben did not fly off. And the affair dropped fast from the news. It was only ever a giggle.

Utterly unfunny – but tinged with a dreadful element of black comedy – was the bizarre death a few weeks later of the high-flying young Tory MP, Stephen Milligan. It was sensational.

By lunchtime on Monday 7 February, Vera Taggart, Milligan's secretary, who had followed him from the *Sunday Times* to the Commons when he was elected in 1992, was worried. He had not returned her telephone calls. Forty-five-year-old Milligan had failed to show for appointments in the Commons that morning, which was totally out of character. The energy and intelligence of the new MP for Eastleigh in Hampshire had already been noticed by the Prime Minister and the whips. He had been made PPS to the Chief Secretary to the Treasury, Jonathan Aitken.

Vera Taggart had set off for Milligan's Chiswick home. On arriving there she was alarmed to find milk still on the doorstep. She let herself in with a spare set of keys. She found her boss slumped over the kitchen table. He was naked apart from a pair of stockings, a cord round his neck, a black stocking over his head, and a plastic carrier bag over that. There was also, it was widely reported, a segment of satsuma in his mouth.

Vera Taggart called the police at 4.20 p.m. The Tory Whips Office knew most of the details within thirty minutes. They suspected foul play. The press knew thirty minutes after that. Nobody has ever quite established how. The police blamed Milligan's political colleagues; MPs blamed the police. The story made the BBC evening news, although the details were still sketchy, and the BBC's

initial phraseology was 'in unusual sexual circumstances'.
Milligan's father heard about his son's death from the media.

The BBC later circulated an internal memo which said: 'We
can now say that he was wearing women's clothing, we can say he
had a plastic bag on his head, and we can mention that he was
bound with flex. But on no account mention fruit.'

It emerged that Milligan, a bachelor, had used the £700-a-year
dating agency, Drawing Down the Moon. An inquest later recorded a verdict of accidental death. The Tories were crushed in the
subsequent by-election. Milligan's sexual habits were not an issue.

The tabloids struck again on 8 May. Michael Brown, the
Conservative MP for Brigg and Cleethorpes, was revealed by the
News of the World to have enjoyed an exotic Caribbean holiday with
his alleged twenty-year-old boyfriend. He resigned immediately,
having broken the law, in which the minimum age was later (that
autumn) to be reduced. The *Sun* reported that John Major had
said it was not necessarily a bar to ministerial office to be gay. One
source said: 'Michael had to go because the age of consent has not
yet been reduced . . . Apart from that he did nothing to be
ashamed of. The day when a minister could lose his job simply for
being gay has passed.'

Brown never commented or sued. His sexuality had been an
open secret for years at Westminster and many in his constituency
were aware of it too. A hard-working constituency MP, he was
given support by his party organization in Brigg and Cleethorpes.

At the Tories' next conference, in Bournemouth, he made it clear
(in an interview with BBC Radio 5 Live's 'Out this Week' programme) that he was gay. In doing so he joined Labour's Shadow
Cabinet member Chris Smith, becoming the Commons' second,
and the Conservative Party's first, openly gay MP. The Sunday
tabloids hardly bothered to report the news. Years later Alan
Duncan was to do the same – and was virtually lionized for it.

The next victim of the newspaper feeding frenzy was also
trained in the Conservative whips' office and seems to have taken
Brown's example to heart. Elected for Harrow West in 1987,
Robert Hughes resigned as a junior minister for the civil service
and returned to the backbenches in March 1995. Unbeknown to
his second wife, he had been having an affair with a Commons
secretary. To our disappointment, she was a woman. In 1983
Hughes had stood for Bermondsey against Peter Tatchell. Both

failed to be elected, and Tatchell was spectacularly 'outed' by the press. In Hughes's case the Curse of Bermondsey was longer in coming and took a different form.

'Minister Got His Oates Morning Noon and Night,' declared the front page of the *News of the World* ('full story pages 2, 3, 4 & 5') – the paper to which, after Hughes's resignation, Janet Oates had been persuaded to talk. 'Love-cheat Tory Robert Hughes was ready for sex any time of day or night, his mistress has revealed.' Details followed. It seems that Hughes had first met Oates when she went to him as her local MP for help. She had sought his advice after being assaulted by an ex-boyfriend. Their friendship blossomed. He gave her lunch at the Commons. She gave him a cuddly bear, and more.

The press dug up a photograph of Hughes embracing another lady friend at a Young Conservatives ball in 1993. Perhaps wisely, he had already resigned as a minister at the weekend on 4 March, days before all this hit the news-stands. His sparsely worded announcement gave no details.

The following Monday, a rapidly appointed successor boned up on the questions Hughes was to have fielded. The following weekend Oates went into further details in the *News of the World*. She had threatened to take Hughes to an industrial tribunal after he had dismissed her, she said; he had begged her not to. (Hughes denies this.) The newspaper did its best to keep interest in the affair alive; but it quickly died.

. . . To be replaced, a few weeks later, by perhaps the most questionable in a line of increasingly indefensible press intrusions into MPs' private peccadilloes. 'Tory MP, The Tycoon and the Sunday School Teacher,' said the front page of the *News of the World* on 9 April: 'We expose three-in-a-bed sex session. Exclusive'. It seemed that a hitherto unheard-of MP, Richard Spring (Bury St Edmunds), had invited 'a financial whizzkid and a Sunday school teacher' (in fact an executive in a pension company and his girlfriend, who worked for him) to dinner. None of the three was married.

It seems to have been one of those parties which got out of hand. The woman (felicitously named Odette Nightingale) seemed able to recount events and conversation with quite remarkable recall ('allowing the laughter to die down, he added . . .') and to have reported it all to the *News of the World* ('still shuddering at the memory, Odette recalled . . .') with great promptitude. The unlucky Mr Spring was quoted as having told the dinner party that he found the Prime Minister's wife, Norma, attractive (who didn't?) and considered the Employment Secretary, Michael Portillo, to be equally so. In this opinion he was probably joined by much of Britain, and certainly by Mr Portillo.

The bedroom scene was described in every detail, across many pages of the newspaper. 'All I could think of,' she trembled, 'was "How can I get out of here?"' The door does not seem to have occurred to Miss Nightingale as a possible means of exit.

Mr Spring's exit was swift. He was not pushed: he immediately quit as the Northern Ireland Secretary's Parliamentary Private Secretary. ('As Ulster peace talks near a critical phase, he would have been privy to sensitive information,' squeaked the newspaper.) By now, the press were regularly describing PPSs as holding 'government posts'. This is untrue. A PPS does voluntary, unpaid, political work as a sort of parliamentary bag-carrier for a minister. He or she is privy to almost nothing.

The Times complained it was an outrage for junior back-benchers to be expected to resign in these cases, and blamed both the tabloid press and the Prime Minister – who had (reputedly) now made it the rule that any MP working for or as a minister was to resign at the first whiff of a sexual scandal. The paper said such resignations added credibility to the ludicrous claim that exotic private behaviour disqualified an MP from office and that media investigations into such behaviour were therefore in the public interest. They were not, said *The Times*. Ministers should take no notice of them.

John Major ignored the advice and, after a lull of over a year, yet another obscure minister was driven from office. Rod Richards resigned from the Welsh Office within hours of a salacious report in the *News of the World* in June 1996 over his alleged liaison with Julia Felthouse, a public relations officer twenty years his junior.

Mr Richards, 49, married for 21 years with two young children, had made what we now know to be the potentially fatal mistake of mentioning one's family with any degree of enthusiasm in *Who's Who*. His keen support for 'back to basics' had cheered grassroots supporters in his chapel-going constituency in Clwyd North West. It also spelled doom to his short-lived career as a junior Welsh Office minister. There were perhaps fewer to come to Mr Richards's support because of his reputation for harsh public commentary about his own political enemies. A politician who had said of Labour councillors in Wales 'They're all the same. They're short, they're fat, they're slimy and they're fundamentally corrupt' could not expect – and did not ask for – mercy.

His departure left the Prime Minister with an awkward hole to fill as there were only six Welsh Tory MPs and three ministerial posts to fill.

Mr Richards, unlike some of his colleagues, was uncharacteristically reticent about the affair. His only public remarks on the controversy came as he was chased by a television camera crew, while driving his son and daughter to school. He shouted: 'Get out of my son's way. You will regret this.' His mother-in-law, Elvira Knight, was barely more forthcoming. 'There have been no problems in their marriage. My daughter adores Rod and I always thought it was mutual.'

A week later Julia Felthouse turned the knife in a classic 'kiss and tell' in the *News of the World* when she alleged that Richards had made a final pass at her in his ministerial office as he cleared his desk.

Richards survived a constituency attempt to deselect him. Ray Formston, 75, leader of the Tory group on the local council, who led the anti-Richards campaign, said: 'People have been stopping me in the street and saying it's disgusting. It's not good enough.' His son, Neil, 38, also a councillor, added: 'This is Costa Del Wrinkly. The elderly folk who predominate don't like adultery. This could haunt us up to polling day.'

Rod Richards was not to be the last casualty of 'Back To Basics'. The slogan, cheered to the rafters in October 1993, failed to make its way into the Conservative manifesto. No sooner had the election year begun than another unfortunate backbencher found himself facing the *News of the World* treatment.

The affable Jerry Hayes was better known for his regular television appearances and charity stunts – parachute jumps in chicken costumes – than he was for his role as Harlow's MP, which is a shame. Married for seventeen years, he was a devoted father to his two young children. Their happy Christmas holiday came to an abrupt end on the first Saturday of the new year. At his surgery, the

MP found himself face to face, not with a constituent, but someone he considered (and still does) a friend: Rebekah Wade, then Deputy Editor of the *News of the World* and now Editor of the *Sun*. A young man, she explained, had sold his story of an alleged sixteen-month affair with Jerry Hayes to the newspaper.

The man, Paul Stone, was a 24-year-old trainee tax accountant. His revelations appeared the following day, 5 January 1997, under the headline: 'TORY MP 2-TIMED WIFE WITH UNDERAGE GAY LOVER: INTIMATE LETTERS REVEAL HIS LONGING FOR TEENAGER'. The story ran over five pages.

The *News of the World*'s justification for the story was that the affair allegedly started in 1991 when Paul Stone was eighteen years old – under the homosexual age of consent of 21. (The reduction in the age of consent to eighteen, which Mr Hayes had supported, did not take place until 1994.) The paper added that the letters written by the 43-year-old MP created a security risk. Jerry Hayes was PPS to Robert Atkins, the Northern Ireland minister and 'on an IRA hit-list'.

The paper published letters from Hayes. One said: 'I love you. I miss the magic of your hugs and watching you when you are asleep'. The letters suggested Paul Stone had ended the friendship.

Hayes had told Rebekah Wade that the relationship, although close, had always remained platonic. The young man had even been a babysitter for the children. 'There was always a limit to our relationship', he said, but reportedly admitted some turmoil. 'I didn't understand the feelings I was having . . . I knew these affections for this boy were becoming unhealthy.'

To avoid the press, Jerry Hayes, his wife and children went into hiding in a 'distant part of the UK'. The week, he said later, was 'the worst nightmare you could imagine . . . like having a car accident – everything was in slow motion. For the first two nights I couldn't sleep . . . I'm not going to pretend I didn't have gloomy, suicidal thoughts, but that would have been a spectacularly selfish thing to do.'

Why did the scandal suddenly erupt in January 1997? Some papers suggested it was linked to John Major's New Year launch of a family values campaign in the *Daily Telegraph*. In truth, it was the earliest the story could run. Paul Stone had made up his mind shortly before Christmas that he wanted to go public with his allegations. He went to his local library in Peterborough to look up the telephone number of the publicist Max Clifford – then rang him. Clifford invited him to London and they met in the PR man's Mayfair office on Christmas Eve. Stone says if Max Clifford had refused to take him on he would not have dared approach a newspaper independently.

Paul Stone was paid £30,000 for the story – some recompense for shouldering the indignity of lines like: 'His power, fame and good looks intoxicated me.' For almost a week he was guarded in a Wimbledon hotel. He enjoyed the attention and gave further interviews – including one for the *Guardian* under the headline 'Oh Paul, How Could You?' – a comment his mother had made.

The following week, Hayes's wife, Alison, gave an interview to the *People* saying that her husband was not gay. Paul Stone's claims were sick fantasies, she said. The letters were to give the boy, who had been suicidal, a sense of self-worth.

In a way, few cared whether the allegations were true. In this most modern of sex scandals, the accuser faced greater vilification than the accused. Stone's father – a life-long Tory, whom he had not seen for two years and who did not know he was gay – told the *Daily Mail* 'it's going to take an awful long time before I forgive him for this'. The firm of chartered accountants Stone worked for sacked him, as he half-expected, for 'gross misconduct'. The young man was (temporarily) banned from his local gay pub. Pictures of him in drag in a church hall pantomime appeared in the press. After a week, interest rapidly waned.

The MP survived. There was no question of his constituency failing to reselect him, although he immediately offered to stand down. The Commons too, he found, is a forgiving place. When he went back, he says, he was hugged by half the Labour Shadow Cabinet. Clare Short gave him a big kiss. 'All my chums in the Press gallery were terrific', he added. Although he lost his seat at the General Election, he believed the allegations played no part: the swing of 12.5 per cent against him was about 1 per cent less than that suffered by neighbouring Tories.

Jerry Hayes has built a media career for himself. Paul Stone planned to open a gift shop in Peterborough.

But there was more to come from John Major's dying government. In the end, it could hardly have been worse for the Tories. Two Scottish scandals – an ex-minister's affair in a clinic for alcoholics and an alleged one-off gay encounter involving a senior party official and his researcher – emerged in a campaign that ended with the Conservatives failing to win a single seat north of the border. As Michael Forsyth, John Major's Scottish Secretary, admitted at a press conference while the rubble fell around him, 'I could have planned it better.'

News that Allan Stewart, a Technicolor Scottish Tory in the tradition of Sir Nicholas Fairbairn and member for the safe Glasgow commuter-belt seat of Eastwood, had checked into an alcohol rehabilitation clinic in the borders and formed what was prudishly described as a 'close relationship' with a fellow patient and married mother of four, broke in the Scottish *Sunday Mail* ten days into the campaign. He was dropped from the Government by Mrs Thatcher in 1990 only to be brought back Mr Major in 1990. He lasted until 1995 when he 'presented', as he was later to put it in court, a pickaxe to eco-protesters opposed to the M77 being built through his constituency. Having been fined £200, he found himself back in the spotlight two years on when his affair with a woman known as 'Bunny' to her friends was splashed across the *Sunday Mail*. The following day, a Monday, Stewart announced he would not re-stand in Eastwood. Within a week he collapsed with a nervous breakdown, and was taken to Dykebar psychiatric hospital in Paisley after a noise in his house led to neighbours summoning the police.

Eastwood's 11,000 majority attracted the attention of Stewart's party colleagues, including that of Sir Michael Hirst, leading contender to the Stewart throne. A former MP, he was on the Tory centre-left in a country where the right was in control. A close friend of Major, Hirst was Scottish party chairman and was visited at his Milngavie home by Forsyth, who insisted he take the nomination for the good of the party. The Hirst bandwagon, however, led his enemies to act. Allegations filled the air and it was suggested Hirst had once had a gay 'fling' with Paul Martin, his former personal assistant. Added spice came in the knowledge Martin was once a close mutual friend of former male LSE student and government whip Michael Brown. Indeed all three were implicated in the same story someone sold to the *News of the World*, allegedly for £10,000. In a nasty game of bluff, Hirst was wrongly told a Sunday newspaper had paid £50,000 for incriminating evidence. Some accused Right-wingers; Hirst believed 'the trail of blood' led to the door of Left-wing enemies, the 'scavengers'. According to the *Scotsman*, 'Arthur Bell, chairman of the Scottish Tory Reform Group made senior party officials aware of homosexual allegations against the party chairman that he had known of since 1995.' The Thursday after Stewart resigned, Hirst let it be known he would not stand and wrote a longhand A4 resignation statement.

With only five weeks to go before polling day, Conservative election plans were blown off course by another *Sun* exclusive: 'SCANDAL OF TORY MP'S MISTRESS, 17 – HE TAKES SOHO CLUB HOSTESS CANVASSING'. Piers Merchant, a 46-year-old non-drinking, non-smoking, vegetarian, happily married father of two had been caught on camera kissing a miniskirted girl in a South London park. The paper alleged they had been conducting an affair (Piers Merchant denied this), but, with the election campaign underway, seventeen-year-old Anna Cox had realised the MP would not leave his wife. 'I'm not old enough to vote,' Anna Cox declared, 'but I'm old enough to know when I've been used.'

The timing was fortunate for Labour. That week the Tories had inflicted real wounds over the Opposition's plans for extending Trade Union rights. Then in the space of 24 hours Tim Smith had been forced to resign over cash in brown paper envelopes, pressure had intensified on Neil Hamilton (see pp. 355–67) – and now Piers Merchant had been caught on candid camera. The focus was back on Tory sleaze.

Merchant said he first met Anna Cox (at a Young Conservative meeting) for 'ten seconds' several months before but did not see her again until about three weeks before the *Sun*'s story. She came from a 'nice quiet family' and was a real Young Conservative known to the other local Tory MPs. When the election came she fitted well into his campaign team. 'She was not at all as the papers described her,' he said. Miss Cox told the MP she worked as a secretary in the City. He thought she was in her twenties. As for her job - which the *Sun* made much of – as a £100 per night hostess who drank with male punters in a seedy Soho Club, she had explained that this was a job advertised in the *Evening Standard*. It had lasted four nights and she had left when she found out what type of place it was.

The *Sun* took a different view. They claimed Anna Cox was a confident young woman who rang the newsdesk at least a week before the story appeared, alleging she was already having an affair with a married Tory MP. Feeling 'used', she wanted revenge and knew she would be rewarded for her story. Following several hours of interviews, she took *Sun* reporters to Merchant's London flat and described in detail the interior.

But the paper needed to see them together. After several days, the *Sun* claimed she rang on the Tuesday morning to say she was meeting Merchant at a railway stadon in his Beckenham constituency. A reporter and a photograper raced down there, saw them greet one another, then trailed them as they went delivering leaflets. Eventually, awaiting her return train, she led the MP into a nearby park. Undetected, the men from the *Sun* photographed them kissing. The Sun alleged more, but pictures, if they exist, have neither been published nor privately produced. Later that night she was photographed arriving and leaving his Pimlico flat.

The next day, Wednesday 27 March, the seventeen-year-old was whisked to a hideaway for a photo shoot as the *Sun* polished its scoop. By now Anna Cox was hot property. A fee of £25,000 was allegedly agreed. Sky Television was called in to shoot a video. That evening, the MP was doorstepped outside his home. Piers Merchant stared at the fuzzy black and white prints the *Sun* reporter offered him, and admits he said too much: 'That may well be me kissing her in the pictures, bu I see nothing wrong in that. I am sure my wife will not be the slightest bit concerned . . . You must have a very weird sense of values if you see anything wrong with kissing a girl in the park. Anna is a very dear friend of mine and has been helping with my campaign. But there is no question of us having an affair. I have never made love to her.' As for the night in his flat, she slept on the sofa, he said.

As if to demonstrate how unconcerned his wife was, she appeared alongside him on the doorstep later that evening. Egged on by the photographers, husband and wife kissed in a manner more adventurous than anything pictured in the park the previous day.

The following morning, as the *Sun* landed on doormats across the nation, and parts of Britain giggled at its contents, Michael Heseltine publicly called the whole affair an 'embarrassment'. Piers Merchant should 'consider his position'. John Major stared at the paper and reportedly remarked 'How can people do this sort of thing?'. The party Chairman, Brian Mawhinney, who before the campaign began had told every back-bencher to act 'as if there were a tabloid reporter under every bush' was furious that his advice had been so soon ignored. Tabloid headlines heralded the 'End Of The Piers Show'. Conservative Central Office began briefing against their own MP.

Despite this pressure Piers Merchant held on. The following week 116 constituency members in Beckenham voted to re-select him (he was by all accounts a good constituency member) with only four dissenters. In the General Election, Piers Merchant was returned to Parliament. The 15% swing against him was lower than some of his neighbours.

It was hard not to agree with Auberon Waugh, who said that in backing its MP, we saw 'old England reassert itself: a tolerant, easy-going country with a highly developed sense of humour and little taste for being cowed by puritanical fanatics'.

Six months later, Helen Merchant, the MP's wife, appeared with Anna Cox for an impromptu photocall. Responding to claims in the previous day's *Sunday Mirror* that Piers Merchant and Anna Cox had spent four days together in the north of England, Mrs Merchant said 'Anna is here as a family friend.' Far from conducting an illicit affair, Piers Merchant and Miss Cox were working together on a book about the excesses of the tabloids, they said. But Mr Merchant's decision, announced the next day, to resign from the House of Commons led many to question that version of events.

GEORGE GALLOWAY – 1994

'The honourable member for Baghdad South'

Speaking to a moustachioed middle-aged man sitting a few yards away, the British visitor lavished praise on his host: 'Sir, I salute your courage, your strength, your indefatigability.' George Galloway's fulsome tribute in January 1994 to Saddam Hussein, a vicious dictator responsible for the deaths of hundreds of thousands of people, must go down as one of the most cringe-making political speeches of recent years. It certainly earned the Labour MP public opprobrium and endless jibes that he represented Baghdad South rather than Glasgow Kelvin. Galloway claimed he had been misrepresented – he lauded the Iraqi people not their leader – and that his message had been wrongly translated. Yet the local TV footage picked up by the BBC monitoring centre in Cavendish was clear enough and the English words pronounced with a Scottish accent left no room for doubt about what was said.

Galloway, however, could point to countless speeches in the 1980s attacking Saddam when the tyrant was regarded as a 'friend' of the West in Downing Street and the White House, using British and US munitions to attack neighbouring Iran. The politician described the President of Iraq as a 'bestial' and 'brutal' as he sought to justify his position, pointing out that until after the first Gulf War, Iraq was the only Arab country he had not visited because his support for the communist opposition made him no friend of the Ba'athist regime.

But the Baghdad South tag was to stick, particularly after he emerged from another audience with Saddam nearly a decade later to recount how the dictator had offered him a Quality Street chocolate (Galloway politely declined, he doesn't eat sweets) and admired British double-decker buses rather than discussing politics.

Galloway's championing of the Arab world and relentless cam-paigning against what he regards to be imperialism won him few friends in the Labour leadership, his stunts and trips to Baghdad to fight against sanctions imposed on Iraq alienating the party's hierarchy. He took a young leukaemia victim, Mariam Hamza, to Glasgow for treatment in order to highlight the plight of Iraqis and then used the fund set up in her name to finance his battle.

That the American-Anglo invasion of Iraq in 2003, and his opposition, would lead to a parting of the ways was predictable. Galloway was expelled in October 2003 from a Labour Party he had joined 36 years earlier as a thirteen-year-old after he described Tony Blair and George Bush as acting 'like wolves' by invading Iraq, and was accused of inciting attacks on troops and urging US–UK soldiers to disobey orders. 'This is a politically motivated kangaroo court whose verdict has been written in advance in the best tradition of political show trials,' protested Galloway. He planned to stand for Westminster as an independent with his own party, Respect (named after the Aretha Franklin anthem), and to run for the European Parliament in June 2004. He has picked up an estimated £250,000 from successful libel actions, including £50,000 from the *Christian Science Monitor* after it acknowledged that documents it had relied on to accuse Galloway of taking a small fortune from Saddam were forgeries.

At the time of writing, another legal case was outstanding against the *Daily Telegraph* after it reported that separate documents supposedly found in a bombed-out Baghdad government building showed he had profited from the UN oil-for-food programme. Love him, loathe him, lampoon him but never underestimate him. With his Portuguese holiday home, all-year tan, sharp suits and fat cigars, this MP believes nothing is too good for the workers. When accused of being a 'medallion man', Galloway responded, 'That is the unkindest cut of all. I have never worn a medallion! I've never even worn a *vest*, for God's sake. I'm a Scotsman!'

So let's put it like this. Few MPs at fifty could still pass relatively unnoticed in a provincial disco or a Club 18–30 package holiday, and the sub-playboy image is not thought to sit well with any MP's role, let alone a socialist's. But it has to be said that 'Gorgeous George' Galloway seems to have carried it off. The Scots Labour MP for Glasgow Kelvin, and flamboyant champion of what the tabloid papers called Labour's 'loony Left', could not present a more striking contrast with the man he ousted for his

Glasgow seat, Roy Jenkins, now dead. One imagines that each man's personal vision of Hell probably featured a small cell and the permanent company of the other.

Galloway is not a member of the 'loony Left'. He never joined Labour's Campaign Group. He has never been part of any group. He has made fun of the old Labour-led Greater London Council, calling them a 'greenhouse of exotic pot-plants'. However, he is basically a Left-winger and he is his own man. In Fleet Street, a usefully libel-resistant catch-all term to imply (variously) a louche, pleasure-seeking or startling quality is 'colourful'. The name George Galloway has seldom appeared in a newspaper without it. Yet Galloway is no fool. A combination of cunning, charm and chutzpah has landed Galloway in more hot water, and delivered him from it, than a less brazen character could dare expect. He is sharp, astute and consistent in debate and arguably the best orator of his political generation.

Fixed, perhaps, in many minds is the day in 1987 when – as though one alleged scandal were not bad enough – the MP and General Secretary of War on Want had called a press conference to try to clear his name over allegations of fiddling the charity's expenses. Galloway was insistent that his energies and activities were devoted to the public good. But, straight in to the television cameras, Galloway, married with a five-year-old daughter, was forced to admit instead to a string of sexual infidelities on an expenses-paid charity trip to Greece.

The following day the *Star* was merciless: 'I bonked for Britain.'

Thirty-three-year-old Galloway had become General Secretary of War on Want, one of Glenys Kinnock's favourite charities, at the age of 29, before becoming an MP. His flair for publicity and fundraising matched his ability at self-promotion, and brought a record 26 per cent increase in donations. Within four years his autocratic style of management landed him in difficulty with some of the charity's officers. However, in March 1987 an auditors' inquiry at War on Want cleared him of any impropriety, dishonesty or bad faith over his expenses.

Selected as candidate for what was then Glasgow Hillhead, Galloway went on to record a famous victory at the General Election over Roy Jenkins, ending the latter's Commons career and sealing the fate of his SDP. Fêted on all wings of the Party for

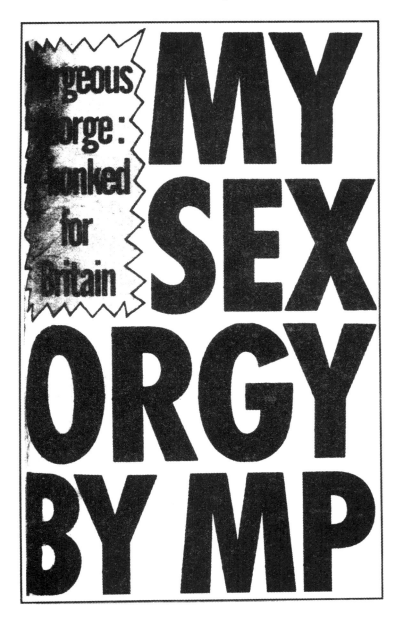

Star, 15 September 1987

the humiliation of Jenkins, Galloway, now a hero of the Labour movement, may have thought his troubles were behind him.

But all was not well at War on Want. Executive members, concerned about his allegedly extravagant expense claims, called in the Charity Commissioners in the summer. They cleared the MP of any wrongdoing but demanded that the charity tighten up its procedures.

Galloway agreed to repay £1,720, including £525 for a *World Marxist Review* seminar, in Athens, on the Ethiopia–Eritrea war. A further £850 was for minicab trips to and from his house. The repayment was, some said, small beer for Galloway. The following month the *Sun* alleged his total expenses were £20,000 in eighteen months. In fact they were for a longer period, and included travel for War on Want to many countries and throughout the UK, and all associated costs. As a bald headline, however, the figure looked dreadful.

In September 1987, BBC Scotland ran a critical programme on the 'colourful' MP's stewardship of the charity. He immediately hit back, issuing a libel writ seeking six-figure damages and called what would prove to be an ill-fated press conference.

Galloway was horrified when a reporter fired a question about alleged sexual infidelities while on the sunny Greek island of Mykonos, after the Athens conference. He may not have been entirely surprised, however, as photographs of him with his girlfriend Lillian had been stolen from her London flat. They had now reached the possession of the press.

The MP hardly hesitated. 'I spent lots of time with women . . . I actually had sexual intercourse with some of them.' He has never, he pointed out, slept with more than one at the same time, or claimed to have, but such subtleties are too deep for Fleet Street where one is a love-nest and two is an orgy. 'Gorgeous George', as he was fast nicknamed the next day, encountered headlines such as: 'My Sex Orgy – By MP'. Sketchwriters made what they could of the fact that the conference had been grappling with the Horn of Africa. By now Galloway's wife, Elaine, was slamming down the phone on reporters.

Declaring himself an 'extremely sad man' after the 'explosion of lurid headlines', Galloway explained the reason for his out-burst: 'I had said I would answer any questions. I could not lie.'

Matters went from bad to worse when it was disclosed two days later that while his wife stayed in Scotland, Galloway was spending time in a one-bedroom flat with a partner, Lillian Grewar, in the East End of London. The 'disclosure', Galloway pointed out, was of something he and Lillian had never hidden. They were lovers for nine years, and had started living together (which they did for five years, until 1992) after he and his wife separated in 1987. There was never any secret, he says.

Galloway brazened it out. He is an intelligent and quick-witted man, a passionate speaker, and politically original and brave. He is also, by common account, likeable company. He received a loyal vote of confidence from his local party the following month.

A month later his future was in jeopardy again. A Channel 4 documentary, 'In the Red', alleged that Galloway and three other MPs – former leading figures in the Dundee Labour Party – were involved in the transfer of funds from three Labour social clubs in the city. The money had gone to the Dundee Labour Party. The clubs were so heavily in debt at the time that they could not pay their rents, said the programme. Channel 4 claimed that £100,000 in the clubs' accounts was not accounted for. Senior Labour Party figures had cashed personal cheques of up to £600 at the clubs. Some had subsequently bounced. Galloway called the programme 'despicable', and again threatened a libel action. He also demanded a police inquiry which, after two years, charged nobody with wrongdoing except the manager of one club, who had made the allegations on the programme.

In early February 1988 his local party executive passed a vote of no confidence which was ratified later the same month by the party's General Management Committee. In Labour's re-selection round the following year he was once again re-selected. Where more timid fellows might have gone to ground, Galloway had raised his profile and won new popularity through his support (to the fury of the Labour leadership) for poll-tax non-payers. At the 1992 General Election he was re-elected with an increased majority.

Asked what he would do with huge damages awarded to him after a successful libel action against the *Daily Mirror*, he replied that he hoped to invest the money in a restaurant in Havana, Cuba – an investment made, he said, 'from the ashes of Robert Maxwell's empire'.

To those who know his part of Glasgow – prim, well-to-do territory where a crèche is a motor accident, sex is what the coal comes in, and there are no rates, only a few wee mace – the irony of its being represented by George Galloway was delicious. There are things, he said, that he regrets, and things he would prefer to forget, 'but it is, and must remain, a free country'.

DENNIS SKINNER – 1994

'The Beast of Legover'

The headline in the *News of the World* of 20 February said it all. For Tory MPs the discomfiture of Bolsover's Labour MP, the famous socialist ranter, puritanical class-warrior, coal-mining hammer of wealth, decadence and privilege whom the sketchwriters had long dubbed 'The Beast of Bolsover', was delicious, a brief respite from the unrelenting tide of bad publicity washing over the Government benches.

Dennis Skinner, scourge of the Tory fat cats and Liberal Lotharios, had been hoist with his own petard. Married to a no-nonsense Northern woman and living in a no-nonsense council house in his no-nonsense coal-mining constituency (and boasting that he would not travel abroad, did not own a passport, and relied upon public transport), Skinner had been having a secret affair with his 47-year-old Commons researcher, in her Chelsea pad. And she was American! And she was teaching him to drive!

For the press there followed a short-lived field-day. Skinner was 'romancing his glamorous Sloane Ranger mistress Lois Blasenheim in her upmarket Chelsea flat'. Her neighbours in Carlyle Square included the Duchess of Portland, Felicity Kendal and Sir David Frost. It was a big leap for the former Glapwell colliery miner who describes his parentage in his *Who's Who* entry as: 'Good working-class mining stock.' The 62-year-old MP had been educated at Tupton Hall Grammar School where he made the grades to go on to Ruskin College, Oxford, which was founded in 1899 for the sons of the toiling masses.

According to breathless tabloid reports, Skinner, who had never himself shied from publicity, would turn up at his lover's home even on hot summer evenings wearing a hat, scarf, and upturned collars on his jacket and shirt – to avoid recognition. He would never (they said) knock at the door, but lurk in the bushes until she let him in at a pre-arranged time.

Newsagents in Skinner's home village of Clay Cross, deep in the heart of his Derbyshire constituency, reported a roaring trade in sales of the *News of the World*. But no one would say whether a copy had been taken by Skinner's 61-year-old wife, Mary, who lived in the couple's three-bedroom semi.

Commons
Mr Angry
has secret
mistress

THE BEAST OF
LEGOVER
NEW MP SEX SCANDAL

News of the World, 20 February 1994

Tory MPs, who had been the butt of Skinner gibes for years, hit back with a vengeance. Philip Oppenheim, a fellow Derbyshire MP, led the charge, saying: 'It is comforting to know that Dennis is human after all, but this does not reflect at all well on his researcher's tastes.' For some time the very sight of Mr Skinner rising to intervene in the Chamber would trigger calls of 'Where's your balaclava?' from the redoubtable Dame Elaine Kellett-Bowman (then seventy years of age), the Tory MP for Lancaster.

All good fun, and it must be said that Skinner asked for it. He gave no quarter and, when his turn came, received none. But the story of a working-class hero and son of the Derbyshire soil was never the whole man. Skinner has always been a rather sensitive chap. He is known by friends in Derbyshire not as a political thug at all, but as the 'bookish' one of the family. The 'Beast' image, which he undeniably enjoys, is something of an alias. And he has been effectively separated from his wife for some years, though they shared an address. Really, he has (in some ways) grown away from his boyhood Derbyshire, though his parliamentary career depends upon his association with it.

And Lois Blasenheim hardly fitted the image (insinuated by the press) of a pleasure-seeking American heiress. She was a rather intense, middle-aged, single woman, living modestly in a tiny flat in Chelsea, who genuinely was Skinner's researcher and secretary, had been for years, works full-time for him and his constituency, and was completely devoted to his beliefs and causes – though latterly, no doubt, to the man too.

Ah well . . . such is the mythology of Fleet Street. A demagogue, who has lived and prospered by a mythology of his own, should not complain when he falls victim to a rival fairytale. One cannot help feeling that the real victim of all this was neither Skinner nor his foes, but Ms Blasenheim.

DAVID ASHBY 1994-6

'They're a bunch of shits'

There follows a story of such stupendous inconsequence that its
inclusion among famous scandals of its era – for famous it was –
serves as more eloquent witness to the craziness of the hour than
any sermonising on your authors' part.

David Ashby's credentials were impeccable. His 1992 election
address stated: 'Married with a family, and therefore under-
stands the needs of families. He is a man of integrity who
believes in traditional moral values, discipline, and effective law
and order.'

In retrospect it was a pity he chose to dwell on such platitudes.
Ashby was a brave MP, a defender of minorities, a hater of
apartheid and an obstinate fighter for traditions of liberal
conservatism which seemed at times beleaguered in the late 1980s.

But it was upon family values that the fateful paragraph in his
election address dwelt. It seemed strange therefore, when the
Sunday Times reported on 9 January 1994, that the MP for
Leicestershire North West had left his wife because of 'a
friendship with another man'. The *Sunday Times* had been talking
to Silvana, the MP's fiery Italian-born wife. Fifty-one-year-old
Mrs Ashby, a staunch Roman Catholic and daughter of a wealthy
Turin food merchant, had met her future husband on a skiing
holiday. They had been married for 28 years. She had spoken to
one of the paper's journalists at the family home in Putney. Her
husband had turned up midway through the interview. It was too
late. She had already given the journalist his story. And whatever
justification he needed. 'I think politicians should set standards,'
she had told him. 'If they are preaching something they should
live by those standards.' Entering, David Ashby silently pointed
the *Sunday Times* man out of the door. He spent eighty minutes
alone with his wife before driving off. He refused to comment. On
the Sunday, the front-page report appeared under the headline:
'Wife's fury over errant MP'. The following day Mrs Ashby
insisted on issuing a statement of her own, setting the record

straight. She and her husband were not separating. Later it was reported that they had separated in 1993.

In a bizarre, impromptu press conference on the gravelled drive of their marital home, Mr Ashby admitted sharing a bed with a man in a French hotel on a holiday over the New Year. Newspapers tittered that it was a 'queen-sized bed'.

His reported reaction was: 'I've been all over the bloody place and shared bloody beds.' Mr Ashby explained he had spent a holiday with a close friend. 'We went to two hotels. In the first one we managed to find twin beds, and at the second one we didn't. It doesn't make any difference. It was much cheaper: it halved the price.' It appeared that the problem may have arisen, he went on, through his friend's use of the words *chambre double*, which does not, as it might seem to, imply two beds in French. The friend, a young doctor, lived in a flat beneath one recently purchased by Mr Ashby in Putney, south London. Ashby was at a loss to understand the media interest. Fellow MPs would understand the arrangement, he said, because he had shared rooms with them on officially funded trips. But he declined to name his sleeping companions. The *Sunday Times* persisted. They printed a further story that Mr Ashby had shared a double bed with a man on a holiday in Goa. This was not true. The paper stated, their hotel was a 'love nest' where few questions were asked.

In the spring of 1994, Ashby appeared to have survived the gossip, but the affair left him bitter about what he called 'the intrusion'. The allegations, he said at the time, he could handle, but the personal intrusion he found wounding in a way he could not put out of his mind. He said one newspaper 'used a pink filter in photographing a bedroom where we stayed'. 'I kept thinking of the McCarthyite question: "Are you now or have you ever been . . . ?" It's the worst experience I've ever faced. It had a profound and devastating effect on me. I can't forget it. It gnaws at you.'

There was surprise at the depth and intensity of the MP's feelings. Most journalists regarded his spot of bother in early 1994 as hilarious rather than serious. What to most of the world is simply a giggle, can be little short of crushing to the individual concerned. But worse was to come. David Ashby chose to sue the *Sunday Times*, the paper which first broke the story.

The paper had apologized for the Goa story but refused to retract the allegation that the MP was a homosexual, a hypocrite and a liar.

Man in Mask

Mr Ashby could not afford to lose the case. Already a Lloyd's casualty, he had three mortgages to pay. The case lasted twenty days. It was a legal, financial and personal nightmare for the MP. Not least because his wife was one of the principal witnesses against him. The couple's only child, Alexandra, 27, a banker, went into the witness box on her father's behalf against her mother.

The case turned, not on whether he was homosexual as both sides doubted that this was any longer defamatory, but on whether he had had an affair, and lied to his wife and to the public in doing so.

Over several days in the witness box David Ashby frequently broke down in tears, admitting depression, worry over his losses at Lloyd's and impotence. He demonstrated in court the unusual device, supplied by the National Health Service, which he used to prevent snoring and help him breathe at night. As he strapped on the contraption, its elephantine corrugated trunk wobbling beneath his chin, some faces in court number thirteen stayed straight only through superhuman effort. The *Daily Telegraph* commissioned artist Julia Quenzler to provide a graphic illustration, reproduced above.

Mr Ashby called in his Harley Street physician to confirm that he was impotent and that the MP had told him he had been unable to have sex with his wife for four years. Dr Lewis Sevitt had prescribed anti-depressants in the hope that it would improve the MP's performance.

Dr Sevitt told the court: 'I would have hoped his medication would have been successful . . . and his interest and ability to make love would have improved. As it was I don't think there was much change.'

As for the bed-sharing episode, Ashby's friend explained that on their carefully budgeted trip to northern France they had dined together and played cards in the lounge of the Château Tilque hotel. Mr Ashby retired first. They had not discussed which side of the bed they wished to sleep on. He did not recall Mr Ashby snoring that night.

Above all Ashby had to rake over in cringe-making detail, his 'marriage from hell' to his wife Silvana who, he said, called him a 'poofter' as a standard insult. He even produced a pair of broken spectacles which he alleged his estranged wife had smashed during a fight.

Mrs Ashby sat with her head in her hands for much of the proceedings, listening intently as the jury heard allegations of her screaming fits, her taunting the MP as 'queenie' or 'poofter', her discovery of him alone in the house with an elderly male friend causing her to throw a tantrum of jealousy, knives and crockery.

He told the court: 'My wife does not have normal reaction.' At this point Mrs Ashby quietly slipped out of Court where she stood outside in the corridor, smoking furiously.

Mrs Ashby, who gave evidence for two days, said that her husband had confessed to her that he was a homosexual when they ended their 28-year marriage. She sounded less certain out of the witness box. Asked if she was convinced her husband was a homosexual she said: 'I don't know, it was up to the jury.'

Mr Ashby, called to the Bar in 1963, was only too painfully aware of the dangers inherent in taking on such a high-profile action. But he exuded confidence in the courtroom to the extent that he regularly interrupted the flow of his QC to order him to pursue a different line of questioning.

Perhaps Mr Ashby's error was to become so (understandably) inflamed by the injustice of the newspaper's libel over Goa, and what he saw as their palpable unkindness, that having cornered and caught them out on this he felt emboldened to pursue them for redress over their wider claims about his sexuality. But there were other grounds for these. The *Sunday Times* launched their secret weapon at the end of the trial. Their last witness was Andrew Pierce, a *Times* journalist (and assistant editor on an earlier edition of this book). Mr Pierce's employers knew he had spoken of seeing Mr Ashby in a gay pub, and now asked him to repeat on oath what he had recounted by way of anecdote. He told the court he had seen Mr Ashby, wearing an anorak, in the Queen's Head in Tryon Street, Chelsea, on 14 December 1991. The Queen's Head is one of the oldest gay pubs in London. 'To my astonishment I saw David Ashby walking towards me. You don't normally expect to see a Conservative MP in a gay pub,' he said. 'He walked up, he was inches from my face. He looked directly at me and I looked at him.' Mr Pierce told the court he remembered thinking at the time, 'I bet he's married and I bet his wife is in the constituency.'

Mr Pierce, a former parliamentary reporter for *The Times*, said he had seen the MP many times in the Commons chamber. That night he was 'walking around the bar, stopping still, looking around, looking at people, looking at some of the customers. It is a pub where, if they want, people can try to seek a partner.'

Warming to his theme, he added that a stranger would have to be blind not to realize it was a gay pub. 'It is by Chelsea Barracks, which makes it very popular,' he said to laughter in court. The bar was wall-to-wall with men wearing 'traditional' gay clothing: 'checked lumberjack shirts, jeans, short hair and moustaches'. There were men canoodling with one another .

'The bar staff are as camp as a row of tents. They call each other dear and love. They have girls' names for each other.' There were gay newspapers lying around. Mr Ashby was still in the pub when Andrew Pierce left.

The jury took four hours to rule by majority verdict against the MP, in favour of the newspaper. After the verdict, Silvana approached her husband and tried to put her arm around him. She managed to kiss the back of his neck, before he pushed her away saying: 'Just leave me.' She walked grimly back to her seat, where she buried her head in her arms.

Outside the court, Silvana insisted: 'I love my husband very much and will always be behind him. It gives me no pleasure to see my husband lose an expensive libel action. I hope that it will not have a terrible effect on him. On numerous occasions I asked him to think twice before continuing with the litigation which I did not believe would be in anybody's long-term interests.'

Mr Ashby retreated to the Inner Temple. His solicitors, Peter Carter-Ruck, put out a statement on his behalf: 'I am deeply disappointed by the decision of the court today. I am very grateful for the kind support of my constituents during what has been a most traumatic ordeal.'

That afternoon he rather bravely returned to his seat in the Commons where he was cheered by his Conservative colleagues.

Ashby later called his wife's court appearance 'unChristian . . . I would never have done that to her.' Despite the impression that he forged ahead blindly with the trial, he said, 'I never wanted it. But I was never truly given a chance to back out.' The *Sunday Times* lawyers would vigorously contest this last statement.

After the trial, Alistair Brett, their in-house lawyer, said he would expect the Editor to see the case as a 'tragic family problem . . . We will have to show magnanimity in our victory'. Mr Ashby faced total costs of £470,000 and financial ruin. He owned two four-bedroom houses, and the Putney flat, and earned around £50,000 a year excluding his fees at the Criminal Bar.

The final nail in the coffin of his political career was hammered in when, in March 1996, he supported a Labour amendment, tabled by Glenda Jackson, to the Housing Bill which would allow homosexual couples the right to inherit the tenancy should their partner die. His vote was decisive.

Characteristically this brave and defiant action was portrayed as a 'betrayal' of his party. The Government later overturned the amendment on the floor of the Commons. It was too much for the burghers of Leicestershire North West so soon after the trial.

The following Friday they exacted their revenge. Two hundred members turned up for his reselection meeting in the aptly named town of Ashby de la Zouch. They listened to their MP since 1983, who had a majority of 979, for 45 minutes. He blamed the press for his plight. 'When the meeting is over tonight, will you be going out and rolling over to let the press tickle your collective tummies? Will you go out and tell them that you have done what you knew to be right and that they can wrap themselves in newsprint and depart to their collective hells?' The applause he received was described as 'polite'. They voted against him. After the result he described the ninety members of his local party who had voted to deselect him, as 'a bunch of homophobics'. 'They are behaving like Smithfield porters – or is that being unfair to Smithfield porters? – love the Queen Mum and bash the queers.' His comments immediately after the meeting were more measured. 'I am absolutely certain I am the only person who could win this seat but being in public life has been very difficult indeed.'

John Kailofer, the vice-chairman of his association, reacted angrily: 'Homophobia did not have a bearing on it. It was his court case when he had been branded a hypocrite and liar, and finally his vote against the Government. But a lot of people have never warmed to David. He has always been fairly arrogant.'

After four hours' sleep, a *Sunday Telegraph* journalist and photographer were on his doorstep on Saturday morning. He called out of the window a cheery hello, invited them in and made them coffee. 'Looking serene, even cheerful', according to the journalist, he admitted to taking 'something very similar to Prozac'. He wanted to assure the Prime Minister that he would not resign in a 'fit of pique' and threaten the Government's perilous majority. 'I am meeting him next week and am happy to do whatever he requests. I would be his driver if that was what was required.'

The paper went on: 'A good-looking young man, Erick Lamothe, a House of Commons researcher, answered the constant stream of phone calls. 'Oh dear, the newspapers would have a field day with this situation wouldn't they?' Mr Ashby said. 'Erick? Have I ever laid a hand on you?' The banter was light-hearted, yet reflective, with echoes of something bitter-sweet. But not of regret.

On Sunday evening he was remarkably candid. He appeared on Radio 5 Live's gay programme, *Out This Week*. He told listeners he was 'proud' to be called a 'gay MP'. 'I couldn't care a damn. I want to be judged as I am, for what I do, and how I'm able to achieve things.' Asked what he thought of his constituency party, he said: 'They're a bunch of shits, aren't they, and we know they are.' As the programme came off air, he relaxed in his seat, beamed, and said; 'I've always wanted to call them that on national radio.'

The remark is revealing. David Ashby had been to hell and back and, in the opinion of some, has been immeasurably improved by the experience. He was still angry: you would not expect him to take a relaxed view of the unkindness he believed has been done to him. But he seemed steadier, more at ease with himself. 'A good man', Alistair Goodlad said, of Ashby in August 1996: high praise from a Chief Whip.

GRAHAM RIDDICK and DAVID TREDDINICK 1994–6

Cash for Questions?

After 'back to basics' came 'cash for questions'. The premiership of John Major, though his personal integrity remained unquestioned, was again nearly swamped beneath a fresh wave of scandals. It began with two Tory MPs accused of selling questions in the Commons at £1,000 a go. For years Fleet Street had suspected MPs of abusing Question Time to line their pockets. The *Sunday Times* 'Insight' team set about proving it.

A reporter, posing as a businessman, offered ten Tory and ten Labour MPs £1,000 each to ask a parliamentary question. The Labour MPs rejected the inducement. Two of the Tories, Graham Riddick and David Tredinnick, nibbled at the bait, in slightly differing ways and circumstances. At the fake businessman's request, Riddick asked a question about a company called Githins Business Resources, Tredinnick about a drug called Sigthin. Crossword addicts may spot what the MPs failed to – both names are anagrams of Insight.

Newspapers were quick to point out that Riddick, MP for Colne Valley and PPS to a junior minister, and Tredinnick, MP for Bosworth and PPS to the Transport Secretary, had both suffered losses in Lloyd's – though this hardly distinguished them from dozens of their colleagues.

On Sunday 10 July, the newspaper broke its 'cash for questions' story. The paper claimed a good old-fashioned scoop. Tory MPs cried foul – journalists had used 'entrapment' methods. But that was before the newspaper released a crucial tape recording.

Tredinnick, an Old Etonian, had angrily denied the allegations and claimed he had refused to accept any money. But on the Monday the *Sunday Times* released the tape of a telephone conversation. Millions of people heard the 43-year-old MP ask for the cheque to be sent to his home. Thirty-eight-year-old Riddick initially accepted the cheque, had second thoughts, and sent it back. Tredinnick has pointed out that he at first refused to see the journalist (Jonathan Calvert) but Calvert told him a fellow MP had specifically suggested he approach Tredinnick – something which would prompt most MPs to give the petitioner a hearing.

Neither MP had ever offended in this way before, and nobody suggested that either was in the habit of asking questions for money. The *Sunday Times* had prompted delinquency rather than discovered it. Nevertheless Richard Ryder, the Tory Chief Whip, acted decisively, determined to avoid further stories about MPs 'clinging to office'. He suspended them as PPSs the same day.

Betty Boothroyd, the Speaker, much alarmed that the honour of Parliament was apparently being sullied in the press, swiftly agreed to an emergency debate on Wednesday 13 July. Riddick threw himself upon the mercy of the Commons. 'Beyond the challenge to my own integrity which I deeply regret, the thing that has mortified me the most is that my judgement may have undermined the general standing of MPs and even perhaps have damaged the reputation of this Parliament,' he said. Tredinnick stayed silent.

MPs voted overwhelmingly to refer the matter to the Committee of Privileges. The Committee, on the direction of Tony Newton, the Leader of the Commons, decided to hold its inquiry – to howls of protest from Labour – behind closed doors.

The All-Party Committee reached an agreed report on 3 April 1995. It concluded that both MPs' behaviour 'fell below the standards which the House is entitled to expect from its Members'. It recommended that Riddick be suspended for two weeks and have his salary docked by £900. For Tredinnick they recommended double that penalty. The House later endorsed these recommendations, after both MPs had apologized to Parliament.

It was an unsatisfactory affair. No sustained defence of the two miscreants was mounted – their friends recognized that silence served them best – but one sensed a groundswell of anger and irritation from many on the Tory backbenches at what they saw as a kangaroo court. Riddick had argued to the Committee that he had returned the money *before* there was any intimation that he had been set up; he had done so, he said, because he felt unhappy about the arrangement. The committee may have taken this into account, but its response was not outlined or explained to the House. This added to backbench unease.

MPs had been furious about the methods used by the *Sunday Times* to ensnare the two MPs: in the case of the Tory benches, angrier almost than they were with their two delinquent colleagues. The Committee concluded that the paper's 'conduct of its enquiries fell substantially below the standards to be expected of legitimate investigative journalism'.

This affair, which left the Prime Minister obliged to take what looked (crudely) like the media's side against members of his own party, kindled sparks of resentment among some of Mr Major's backbenchers. These were later to be fanned by backbench anger at what these MPs saw as Lord Nolan's intrusive and constitutionally unwelcome recommendations.

The overall effect was subtly damaging to Major at a crucial time in 1995. Apart from being Prime Minister of the United Kingdom, a premier is also leader of his or her Parliamentary Party. The two roles are not the same. The leader of a party, like the leader of a gang, has a sort of duty (never quite articulated but deeply felt) to support members of the gang in trouble – even when they are in the wrong. Cases like Riddick's and Tredinnick's – victims of a below-the-belt attack by a rival gang, the media – caused Major's statesmanlike duty as Prime Minister to diverge from his tribal duty as Tory leader. Nolan was later to widen that breach. The importance of the warmth this lost him, among the gang, should not be overlooked.

In 1996, The Press Complaints Commission upheld a complaint by Mr Riddick. The newspaper watchdog said that although the *Sunday Times* had the right to protect confidential sources and to use subterfuge in 'appropriate and special circumstances', the paper had insufficient *prima facie* evidence 'to justify a random attempt to lure MPs to accept payments by a direct invitation to behave improperly – which constituted the particular form of subterfuge used in this case'.

TIM SMITH AND NEIL HAMILTON – 1994–7

'You need to rent an MP like you rent a London taxi'

The 'Winter of Discontent' scarred the Labour party's reputation for twenty years, and there are many in the Conservative party who believe that 'sleaze' could do the same for them. If so, Tim Smith and Neil Hamilton, the one-time minister for business probity whose own affairs did not stand scrutiny, must shoulder some of the blame.

On a European scale their activities seemed small beer: Bettino Craxi, Gianni de Michelis and Bernard Tapie would not have been bought by tea at Harrods, a stay at the Ritz or even the £25,000 Smith and Hamilton allegedly received in £50 notes, stuffed into brown paper envelopes. Smith and Hamilton were greedy – some would say corrupt – but even in Britain their behaviour was not without precedent, as readers of this book will know.

What turned Neil Hamilton, particularly, into a figure of national fury was his refusal to go with good grace. Protesting his innocence, he dug in, to the rage of the media, his opponents and even his colleagues. John Major, then Prime Minister, would go tight-lipped and stony-faced at the very mention of his name. 'The Hamilton affair is the Westminster scandal of the decade because his mates had clubby faith in him, or would not whisper their doubts,' wrote Alan Rusbridger and Peter Preston, the editor and former editor of the *Guardian* who brought the story to light.

The two MPs were unlucky in their choice of enemies: the ever persistent *Guardian* and the vengeful Mohammed Al Fayed. Hamilton fell into a three-year slough of belligerent declarations of innocence, libel cases, alleged evasions and postponed enquiries which culminated, in 1997, in the victory of the white-suited anti-sleaze candidate Martin Bell, in Hamilton's Tatton constituency.

Tim Smith and Neil Hamilton were both bit players in the Thatcher revolution, but there the similarity ends. Smith enjoyed an effortless rise through the Tory squirearchy; Harrow, Oxford and the City. He won a by-election in a normally safe Labour seat in 1977, and though soon defeated returned to the Commons in 1982 as the member for Beaconsfield, the third-safest Tory seat in Britain, beating a Labour candidate called Tony Blair. Within a year he was parliamentary private secretary to a cabinet minister, Leon Brittan; within four he was vice-chairman of the backbench Conservative trade and industry committee.

Hamilton was a raffish, ambitious man, famous for his acerbic wit, penchant for horseplay and dreadful bow ties. With Christine, his formidable wife, who in a less prejudiced age might well have become a Conservative MP in her own right, the couple attracted notice as coming things on the Tory right. Their motto was 'WDTT' – we do things together. Colleagues sympathised with Hamilton when he was named in a BBC documentary on right-wing politics, *Maggie's Militant Tendency*, and backed him in his successful libel case.

Like Smith, he became an officer of the backbench Conservative trade and industry committee.

By the mid-1980s things were going well for both MPs. And their success was shared by a fellow Conservative, Ian Greer, the owner of the largest of a growing band of firms employed by corporate Britain to lobby politicians, 'Ian Greer Associates', or IGA.

In October 1985 Greer signed up a new client, Egyptian millionaire Mohammed Al Fayed. He wanted help. His purchase, the year before, of the House of Fraser chain of shops had attracted the opprobrium of both the British Establishment and 'Tiny' Rowland, the fiendishly energetic and determined owner of the Lonhro corporation and the Observer newspaper. Partly because of pressure from Rowland, the Department of Trade and Industry (DTI) eventually launched an enquiry into the takeover, in 1987.

In a series of meetings, Greer persuaded Al Fayed that he could provide supporters (it was reported) boasting that 'you need to rent an MP like you rent a London taxi'. The quote infuriated Greer, who attributed it to his enemies.

Al Fayed was a demanding client. He wanted to ensure that the Government allowed him to retain control of Harrods, and expected Greer to provide the support of well-placed Conservative MPs. Greer cultivated a group of Tory MPs, later nicknamed 'the Members for Harrods', which included, at various times, Tim Smith and Neil Hamilton, Michael Grylls, who was chairman of the Conservative Trade and Industry Committee, Andrew Bowden and Sir Peter Horden.

Co-ordinated by Greer, the group conducted a campaign of lobbying. House of Commons stationery was kept handy at IGA's offices for the purpose and in at least one case letters were pretyped ready for the MPs' signatures. Though the whole tale is now told as a story of unmitigated abuse, it was common in the 1980s to enlist a lobbyist's help in organizing what we used to call 'a tame MP or two' – or three. Or five.

The exploitation of parliamentary powers was more dubious. Greer's tame MPs tabled questions in the Commons, backing Al Fayed's cause. Smith was the most assiduous. Sitting in the Commons chamber early in 1986, he asked question after question designed to undermine and denigrate Rowland.

In addition to the questions, Smith called a Commons adjournment debate in June 1986 to denounce Rowland. Protected from the libel laws the press reported his remarks. In return for such services Smith earned £10,000 – the first of a string of cash payments from Fayed.

Greer also received £18,000 from Al Fayed, to boost the election campaigns of chosen MPs. He sent his own and others' money to a number of campaigns in marginal seats (including that of Labour MP Chris Smith). Claims that they were payments to the MPs themselves are wide of the mark and have been dropped.

At this point Hamilton enters the plot. Though involved with the Harrods group of MPs from the start, his libel case with the BBC kept him on the political sidelines until 1987. But, according to *Guardian* reports, in June 1987, days before the General Election, he joined the Fayed payroll, receiving an envelope containing £2,500 in banknotes (he denied this). For the next two years (he denied this, too) the payments allegedly continued: Al Fayed claims they totalled £28,000 in cash. Though the details of Fayed's story have varied (at one point he insisted the amount was more like £40,000) he was accepted as a reliable witness by both the *Guardian* and the Sir Gordon Downey's investigation. Hamilton's accounts, as later investigated, showed no trace of the money.

On occasion, Fayed claimed and Hamilton denied, Hamilton visited Harrods to take the money in person; at other times, it was couriered to his home. This money did not pass through IGA. There is no evidence Greer knew of it and he was emphatic that he did not.

Though Hamilton denied that cash ever changed hands (and nothing was declared to the Inland Revenue) Sir Gordon Downey, whose inquiry into the scandal was published in July 1997, reported that 'the evidence that Hamilton received cash payments from Fayed in return for lobbying services is compelling; and so I conclude.' Smith has confessed to receiving cash in envelopes.

Ian Greer was also asked to invite a select group of them to the Ritz Hotel in Paris, owned by Fayed, for a weekend shortly before the 1987 election. He had to cancel the trip when the DTI inquiry was announced but in September Neil and Christine Hamilton took up the offer. The trip later came to symbolize all that was seen as disgraceful about the Hamiltons. Their bill for the week-long stay was £3,602, including £200 a night on meals at the hotel's Espadon restaurant.

Days later, driving back towards Paris, Neil Hamilton phoned from the roadside to ask if they could stay a few more nights. On Fayed's instructions the manager apologized; the hotel was full. Suspicious of the sudden run on rooms, Christine placed another franc in the phone and rang back. She gave a false name and was told the hotel had plenty of rooms. But the Hamiltons soon forgave their host. Fayed treated them to another expense-free holiday the next year, at his castle in the Scottish highlands.

Ian Greer said in his book, *One Man's Word*, that 'there was a shamelessness in the actions of many MPs. In an era when City yuppies boasted of the size of their bonuses, parliamentarians shared tales of their freebies.' Greer described an occasion when Christine Hamilton, keen to join her husband on a tour of America, called to ask first for a free courier ticket on British Airways and then a free upgrade to business class. 'My patience was wearing thin,' he wrote – but he arranged them. When the flight was merged with a TWA one, and Mrs Hamilton risked having to travel economy class, she called again. She ended up with a free limousine at JFK. Christine's actions were not unusual.

What did Fayed's money buy? An oddity of the whole affair is that the money was paid not to ministers, who may have the power to change things, but to backbenchers: lobby fodder. A weakness behind some of the more scandalised reporting has been to overstate the influence bought. Often little was bought, the real victim being not the public interest but the lobbyist's clients. This explains some of the clients' later fury; but it is in the interests of neither the lobbyists, nor the erstwhile client nor the journalist anxious to make his name as an investigative reporter to lay much emphasis on the point. Greer had to reassure Fayed that his money was not wasted.

Greer calmed the tycoon's anxieties as publication of the DTI report loomed. Hamilton wrote a string of vituperative letters to the government ministers responsible (to little effect) and lobbied them in more informal ways. He asked a string of questions in the Commons helpful to Fayed's case, and put an early day motion to the Commons denouncing the DTI enquiry.

Ian Greer was also paying Hamilton (and two other MPs, Michael Grylls and Michael Brown) 'one-off commission payments' as rewards for attracting new business to his lobbying firm. They were recorded in IGA's books. Some journalists have suggested that these were really an undeclared reward for lobbying, and the story has become tangled in the public mind with the Harrods story. We should try to disentangle it. Companies involved included the National Nuclear Corporation

– constituents of Hamilton and already paying him consultancy fees. Greer, Hamilton and Brown also worked with an American tobacco giant. Brown was involved in an (ultimately unsuccessful) effort to forestall a ban on one of its products, Skoal Bandits. Being carcinogenic, the tobacco-flavoured chewing gum was not uncontroversial. Brown received a one-off payment of £6,000. The ever-discreet Grylls was paid a far larger sum.

Meanwhile, Hamilton was rewarded with two 'commission payments', totalling £10,000, not all paid directly. The Hamiltons bought several paintings on a trip to Cornwall, and sent the bill to Greer's offices. They also spent almost £1000 on garden furniture at a London department store and booked tickets to America. Again, Greer footed the bill.

The Ritz trip proved the highpoint of what Hamilton termed his 'mistakes'. In 1988, the Select Committee on Member's Interests launched an inquiry into the burgeoning lobby business. It was an inept affair, itself over-lobbied, and steered clear of examining deficiencies in the Register of Members Interests (an often-bypassed guide to MPs commercial activities established after the Maudling scandal of 1972).

To Fayed's dismay IGA's work had been spotted by the target of the attacks, 'Tiny' Rowland. He denounced Smith as a bought man – neutralising him days before the release of the DTI report. There was no mention of Hamilton, who, with Horden and Grylls, worked frantically to prevent publication of the harshly critical report. They delayed it: the document was referred for further consultation. Finally published in 1990, the report's judgement on Fayed was damning. But he retained control of Harrods.

By 1990 the affair seemed to be settled. Al Fayed had kept his shops. Hamilton, still without declaring his involvement with Harrods, became a government whip (just as Grylls was being reprimanded by the Commons for not declaring commission payments from IGA). In 1992 Hamilton was appointed a minister at the DTI. Imagine Al Fayed's feeling at the news. Tim Smith was the next to take office, as a junior Northern Ireland Minister, in 1994.

In fact, the scandal was just hotting up. Fayed, angered both that his money bought so little and by the Government's decision to refuse him British nationality, revealed his side of the story over 15 months to *Guardian* editor Peter Preston. But only in October

1994, after the European Court of Human Rights rejected Fayed's appeal against the DTI report in September 1994, did his star witness go public.

The *Guardian*'s front page story of 20 October 1994 was sensational. It accused Hamilton and Smith of taking cash to ask questions in Parliament and revealed the details of Hamilton's trip to the Ritz. Primed by Fayed, some of the reporting was accurate – the payments had been made – and the paper made the claim that IGA acted as the conduit.

Tim Smith immediately admitted taking money, and resigned. Hamilton and Greer issued libel writs against the *Guardian*. Hamilton (pluckier or more shameless, depending on your point of view) clung on to his job: according to a note by Cabinet Secretary Sir Robin Butler, Michael Heseltine, the President of the Board of Trade, asked him directly if he had a financial reladonship with Greer. Hamilton's answer was 'no'.

For the embattled Prime Minister, John Major, this was a serious crisis. He dealt with it in an extraordinary way. Major explained to a chamber agog (and packed press gallery) that he had known of Fayed's allegations for three weeks. But, he told MPs, he had refused 'to come to any arrangement'. There were gasps in the Press Gallery. Was the Prime Minister implying blackmail? It emerged that Brian Hitchen, Editor of the *Sunday Express*, had acted as an intermediary between Fayed and the Prime Minister. Stakes were raised when the Prime Minister told the Commons that the Director of Public Prosecutions had been given the minutes of the meeting.

The Opposition was now on the rampage. 'Sleaze' knocked almost all else from newspaper front pages.

Pressure grew on Hamilton. His response, characteristically brazen, was to make light of his difficulties. Emerging from a visit to a school, the formidable Christine by his side, he brandished a biscuit presented by the pupils: 'I must remember to declare it in the Register of Member's interests.' Tories groaned. The Prime Minister was reportedly enraged.

Days later, on 25 October, the MP compounded the mistake by comparing his position to that in which Prime Minister had once found himself, embroiled in a legal battle with a satirical magazine over allegations of an affair with a caterer. The Prime Minister had been exonerated, Hamilton pointed out, but had not felt it necessary to resign in the meantime. Hamilton was sacked the same day. We wondered why he seemed surprised.

His resignation letter made it clear that he had been pushed. 'I think it is sad and deeply disturbing that I have been forced to leave office because of a foully-motivated rumour and a media witchhunt.' Editors who had led the calls for him to go had been recipients of similar hospitality at the Paris Ritz, he said.

Tory heavyweights were by now urging the Prime Minister to set up a committee to examine 'standards in public life'. The Nolan Committee was born. Set wide terms of reference including appointments to public bodies and the assumption of business directorships by former ministers, Lord Justice Nolan's remit was not to judge members on their past conduct, but to decide rules for the future. Major chose the same route as Harold Macmillan (over Vassal) and Lloyd George (over the honours scandal).

Meanwhile Fayed conducted a daily war of words in the press over the conduct of the Government. The DPP had investigated the case for prosecuting Fayed for alleged blackmail over the meeting between Major and Fayed's intermediary. They found no evidence and dropped the matter.

In the Commons, the Select Committee on Member's Interests was investigating Hamilton's Ritz trip. Labour members of the Committee were enraged when Tory members ruled that substantial allegations were *sub judice*. Two years later a note by David Willetts, then a whip and later a minister, was revealed, suggesting that the Committee chairman, Sir Geoffrey Johnson-Smith 'wants our advice' and proposing that he rule the allegations *sub judice*. The note implied Government interference in the supposedly independent committee and, late in 1996, Willetts resigned.

After months of stalling, the committee cleared Hamilton suggesting he had been 'imprudent' not to declare his Paris holiday, but 'understandably' confused by the rules of the register of interests. Labour members voted against the report (as did one Tory) and then walked out in disgust, calling it the 'death knell' of the committee, soon to be made redundant by the Nolan reforms.

Parliament having failed adequately to investigate the scandal, the drama moved to the law courts. At first it seemed obscure rules of parliamentary privilege would prevent Hamilton and Greer's libel actions from coming to court at all. Unwilling to concede, Hamilton made an eccentric attempt to revive a medieval procedure and have the case heard by Parliament. This failed. But at a secret meeting at No. 10 he gained the Government's support for an amendment to the Defamation Bill, effectively amending the British Constitution and allowing the case to go ahead. His ability to do this was a spectacular indication of the Conservative party's continued willingness to indulge the disgraced ex-minister, in retrospect a terrible error of judgement.

Greer and Hamilton wanted to fight because they assumed the case (Greer was suing for £10 million damages) would be fought on the *Guardian*'s initial claim that IGA had been a conduit for cash to Hamilton and Smith – a claim which the paper had difficulty substantiating. The newspaper eventually won because of an exhaustive month-long effort, led by its QC, Geoffrey Robertson, to produce other evidence to discredit the plaintiffs. This included Greer's commission payments, his donations to MPs' election campaigns, more payments to Grylls than Grylls had declared and, most damaging of all, a Cabinet Office memo recording Hamilton's denial to the Deputy Prime Minister. As the evidence mounted, the libel case began to crumble. Witnesses were willing to confirm Hamilton's regular cash payments from Fayed. On Monday 30 September the cases were withdrawn. The two men paid £15,000 towards the *Guardian*'s £400,000 costs. They have disagreed ever since about whose case fell first. Rather ludicrously, both believe they would have won had they fought on alone, without the burdens of new evidence against the other. If this were right, one wonders why their cases fell at all.

The next day, the *Guardian* celebrated, running a banner headline 'A Liar and a Cheat'. Its campaign seemed vindicated. But Hamilton was not finished, the MP for Tatton rowing famously with the editor of the *Guardian*, Alan Rusbridger, on the BBC's *Newsnight*. For the scandal's dénouement, the public had to wait until 1997 and the Downey report.

In the wake of Hamilton's collapsed libel case, and the subsequent resignation of David Willetts over a document acquired by the *Guardian* during the case (see above), the Parliamentary Commissioner for Standards, Sir Gordon Downey, was asked to examine the behaviour of the twenty-plus MPs suspected of having links to IGA. The Commissioner's post was a product of the Nolan enquiry, established at the time of Smith and Hamilton's resignation.

The *Guardian* expressed doubts that Downey's investigation would be any more thorough than its feeble predecessors. But the 67-year-old career civil servant appointed Nigel Pleming to aid him, a rising QC specialising in judicial review. Smith admitted taking cash from Fayed in person, concluding that 'I was very foolish'. Hamilton accepted that he had taken money from Greer and gifts from Fayed but denied that he had received cash payments.

Less well known was that Downey called in at least one key witness, Ian Greer, several weeks before his official questioning for a private chat about the lobbyist's payments to Grylls. He urged him: 'Don't do a David Willetts. It was a great mistake for him to argue his case before the Committee. I would advise you to write a letter to Committee, apologising, and you will get a slap on the wrist.' A parliamentary inquiry designed to shed light on clandestine meetings began with a clandestine meeting.

As the General Election loomed in Spring 1997, Downey prepared to publish his findings. But John Major pre-empted him, dissolving Parliament and calling the election days before publication, a move widely seen as an attempt to suppress politically damaging news. It had the opposite effect: blowing the scandal back onto the front pages.

On 21 March, the *Guardian* published evidence on the case, defying the Prime Minister. John Major dismissed the allegations as 'total and complete junk'. But the *Guardian* had just demonstrated that Tim Smith, at least, had taken £18,000 to £25,000. This turned up the heat on Smith and Hamilton who were both standing for re-election. Tim Smith fell first. After claiming he had the full support of his Beaconsfield constituency association he stood down when it became clear he did not. He has now left public life. Michael Brown, who was mentioned by the *Guardian* as having failed to declare his commission payments from IGA, was later reselected to fight his constituency of Cleethorpes but lost the seat at the ensuing election.

Up in Tatton, Neil and Christine Hamilton denied that Tim Smith's decision to quit had implications for them. The result was perhaps the most extraordinary constituency campaign since

The famous *Guardian* headline:

A liar and a cheat: official

"THIS IS MARTIN BELL FROM THE HAMILTONS FRONT LAWN ...."

Richard Willson's *Times* cartoon (5 November 1997)

In an eleventh hour twist, Martin Bell, who ousted Neil Hamilton as Tatton's MP, agreed to take up his constituent's case that Mohammed Al-Fayed should be interviewed by the Select Committee.

Quintin Hogg fought Oxford on a pro-appeasement platform in 1938. The press descended on the pair, tracking their every move in the Cheshire seat. And rumours began to fly: that Labour and the Liberal Democrats would stand their candidates down in favour of an anti-corruption independent. This was derided as an unworkable stunt, but, to universal surprise, BBC war-correspondent Martin Bell stepped forward. His campaign appeared amateurish, and Bell himself seemed uncertain how to deal with the media – most famously standing, bewildered, on Knutsford Heath as the Hamiltons berated him. The press began investigating Bell's own marital history. Bell's white posters, however, blossomed everywhere. The result was an 11,077 majority for Bell. Hamilton had been trounced.

The Downey report, delayed by the election, was published on 2 July, under a Labour Government. It was more critical of Hamilton and Smith than most had expected. In his first big test, the Parliamentary Commissioner for Standards had carefully captured the public mood. Hamilton's denials were dismissed; his behaviour 'fell well below the standards expected of Members of Parliament'. Smith was guilty of 'a disingenuous attempt at concealment'. And there was a 'strong probability' that Greer, too, had accepted regular cash payments from Fayed. Downey rejected Greer's assertion that Fayed fabricated evidence indicating this.

All the MPs and former MPs investigated by Downey were allowed to respond to his report and their answers were printed as an appendix. Neil Hamilton provided a 22-page response, angrily denying almost all of Downey's charges. Ian Greer also wrote, but, never having been an MP, his response was not published. He was, perhaps understandably, unhappy about this.

Mrs Hamilton accepted invitations onto 'celebrity' editions of two popular reality shows, *Big Brother* and *I'm a Celebrity, Get Me Out of Here!*, and the pair were handed a brown envelope stuffed with used notes when they appeared on *Have I Got News For You*. Standing between the Hamiltons and a TV camera quickly became one of the most dangerous pastimes in Britain; a crew was even on hand when the couple were arrested after college lecturer Nadine Milroy-Sloane made false allegations claiming they were involved in a vile sexual assault. The tearful detention and release of the Hamiltons was captured for the nation by Louis Theroux, who was making a TV programme on the duo at the time. The couple also played up to their roguish image with books: Mr H plumping for *Great Political Eccentrics* and Mrs H *The Bumper Book of British Battleaxes.* The undoubted chutzpah could not mask, however, the damage inflicted by the cash for questions scandal to their own reputation and that of the Conservative Party. Hamilton suffered a crushing High Court libel defeat in December 1999 when he failed to prove that Fayed had told a 'pack of lies' about the former MP's corrupt demands for cash payments, gift vouchers and hospitality in the Ritz. When an appeal was thrown out a year later, the Hamiltons owed an estimated £2m in legal costs. Bankruptcy followed for Neil Hamilton in May 2001, Fayed petitioning against his old foe. The Old Rectory, the couple's home in Nether Alderley, Cheshire, where a life-size cardboard cutout of Mrs Thatcher once greeted visitors, was put on the market at £1.25m.

Recognising the damage done to his party, William Hague singled out Neil Hamilton as one of the MPs who had brought the party into disrepute, when he asked him to stay away from the Tory conference. No matter how much the Hamiltons play up to *The Odd Couple* image, presenting themselves as a game pair who enjoy a laugh, the name Hamilton will remain synonymous with Tory sleaze for some years to come. The scandal serves as a parable of its times.

JONATHAN AITKEN 1994–7

'The simple sword of truth and the trusty shield of British fair play'

Jonathan Aitken's mistake was not just to lie – though he was a more fanciful liar than most in this book. It was to damn the press for excavating his untruths. It made the fall of the millionaire ex-Cabinet minister all the more brutal. 'Jail him – Aitken: serial liar, cheat, coward,' cried the *Daily Mirror* when the end came. 'His marriage is over and he faces a £2 million legal bill. It is not punishment enough. He must be sent to jail . . . He is unfit to mop the floor in a soup kitchen. He is not just a failure as a politician. He is a failure as a human being.'

As a Conservative backbencher (writes Matthew Parris) I thought I knew a different man. Some years after joining Aitken in Parliament, I had my first brush with his beguiling hospitality, intelligence and charm. I was known as a keen long-distance runner, and Aitken, who had entered himself in a charity marathon in his constituency of Thanet South, invited me to join him as a guest runner. 'Come down and stay,' he said, and – on learning that I was training with a fellow-marathoner who wanted to run too – 'bring your friend'.

So my comrade Simon Briscoe and I turned up at his pleasant cottage in Kent, the night before the race, with our running gear. Jonathan was there alone.

We ate a good supper, our protestations that we must abstain from the wine ignored as glasses were filled and refilled. Any thoughts of an early night in preparation for the big race were banished when, after coffee, a tray of cold vodka and caviar was brought in. Abandoning hopes of achieving a good race time, we sat up talking politics with him and drinking vodka, until the small hours. Aitken had nothing to gain from my good opinion or Simon's. He was simply a wonderful host. In the event, all three of us achieved excellent times in the race next morning.

Never since have I found Jonathan Aitken less than the best of company. He was not ingratiating and did not patronize, or trade on friendships. I have no doubt that his conviviality, his fascination with politics and political thought, and his friendly interest in other people, is genuine. Aitken is not, in the accepted sense of that term, a confidence trickster or a fraud. But any review of his glamorous social life, his gradual political rise, his calamitous fall and his ultimate disgrace cannot but conclude that he fooled a great many people in a pretty big way.

I think he fooled himself. He was prey to his own strange claims on our trust and admiration. When caught out, he could hardly believe it. He was very convincing in asking us not to, either.

But perhaps the shadows were always there. I remember Aitken recalling the time when, as a cub reporter on the London *Evening Standard*, owned by his great uncle, he was asked to ghost-write the paper's astrological predictions column for a week while their regular astrologer was on holiday. At the time he was hoping to seduce a young woman whom he knew to read her stars regularly in the *Standard*. He did not tell her of his temporary post, but did find out her star sign. On an evening she had agreed to dine with him he wrote, under her sign in the paper, that women born under this star might shortly spend time with a tall, dark and attractive young man. They should throw off all inhibitions and give themselves to him utterly and at once. She did.

We all laughed. None of us mused upon his character.

The story of the Aitken scandal is almost impossible to tell, because there isn't a story. There isn't really a plot. There is no theme, only a series of episodes, not necessarily related, any one which was potentially shaming and destructive. Apart from his womanizing (he earned Margaret Thatcher's undying hostility by giving her daughter, Carol, the push) only one thread runs through his difficulties: arms.

Fresh out of Oxford in 1970 he was chosen as Conservative candidate for the safe seat of Thirsk & Malton. The candidature was an easier move for the son of an MP, the grandson of a peer, and great nephew of Max Aitken (Lord Beaverbrook), the press baron, than it would have been for many, but the young Aitken was genuinely talented as well as notably good looking. 'Not so much gilded as pure gold,' Roy Hattersley wrote much later.

Over dinner with his constituency chairman, an army general, he was shown, in confidence, a classified report suggesting that Britain was secretly aiding rebel forces in Nigeria. Aitken passed a copy to the *Sunday Telegraph*. He also gave a copy to the Tory

MP Sir Hugh Fraser, a friend and a supporter of the Biafran rebels. As a consequence, Aitken was charged with breaking the Official Secrets Act and tried. In court he attempted to implicate both the general and Sir Hugh, while exonerating himself. He was acquitted, they were embarrassed, and he lost his candidature.

But by the time he was elected, in 1974, Aitken was again being seen as a rising hope. He had become rich (a managing director of Slater Walker, Middle East), he was still good looking and he was evidently talented. He became friends with Prince Mohammed bin Fahd, son of the Saudi King, and his business manager Said Ayas. Ayas was to become godfather to one of his children. In 1979 Aitken married (in preference to Carol Thatcher) Lolicia Azucki, a wealthy Yugoslav-born Swiss economist. It is said that a telephone proposal of marriage to Carol was abandoned in mid-flow when Lolicia who had entered the room, began to throw flower-pots out the window and refused to let him leave until he broke the engagement.

Once in Parliament, Aitken's political rise levelled out. Margaret Thatcher, by then Prime Minister, was not a fan – and Aitken's dinner-table remarks – 'I would not call her open minded on the Middle East so much as empty-headed: she probably thinks Sinai is the plural of sinus' – did not help. He remained on the back benches for eighteen years after his election.

It was at this time that I knew him. Even without office, Aitken managed to cultivate an air of significance, but his taste for plotting against colleagues ('my old standby for many a dirty trick,' wrote Alan Clark in his diaries) was – far from being Machiavellian self-advancement – too often self-defeating: a man acting more in his nature than his interests.

Some say he became involved in British intelligence. He called the claim 'dotty'. He was certainly getting even richer. A convincing salesman, a well-connected link man, and a skilful businessman, he founded a merchant bank (Aitken-Hume) which was to serve as a basis for much of his future financial dealing. Middle Eastern interests were big investors. But there were controversies. Early in the 1980s he negotiated the purchase of the Inglewood Health Hydro in Berkshire, of which he was director. Appearing to be the owner, he did not reveal that the spa had been purchased with Saudi funds. He later sued the *Guardian* and Granada TV's *World in Action* over their allegation that he tried to influence the club's staff to procure prostitutes for Arab businessmen, telling the court during the trial: 'I remember burying my head in my hands and saying to no one in particular, "the *Guardian* have said on their front page that I am a pimp"'. He said his son then asked him 'what's a pimp, Daddy?' Before Aitken's libel case collapsed (of which more later), the defendants, unable to substantiate the pimping allegations, had withdrawn their defences on these.

Using Arab money, Aitken bought a controlling stake in TV-am for more than £3m. He used a front company in a Caribbean tax haven. He did not reveal the source of the money as this would have invited a block on the purchase by the Independent Broadcasting Authority. The truth came out in 1988 and he resigned as a director, expressing regret at putting the 'confidentiality' of his clients 'above the candour that should have been offered'. Anna Ford, a presenter on the station, threw a glass of white wine over his head at a party when she heard about Aitken's behaviour.

While on the back benches, the MP became closely involved with Prince Mohammed's London office. Two of his secretaries worked from there. He arranged to buy a personal airliner for the Prince and was a part-time managing director of his company, Al Bilad UK.

Aitken had also joined the board of BMARC, an arms manufacturing company, as a non-executive director. He was on the board from 1988-1990, for an annual fee of £10,000. Of this more later.

This was a time when Saudi Arabia was a huge importer of British arms, an important export for Britain in an intensely competitive international market. Insistent suggestions have appeared that Aitken was himself involved in the arms trade. He has been equally insistent that, with the exception of BMARC, this is not true. But there is no doubt he was well-connected in the Middle East and trusted by the Saudis. His advice would have been valuable. And with the fall of Mrs Thatcher in 1990, an effective block on his ministerial career was removed.

After the 1992 election, John Major made him Minister of State for Defence Procurement. It is fair to acknowledge that unlike most new ministers, Aitken certainly knew a bit about his portfolio. Arms exports safeguarded British jobs during the trough of a recession, and Aitken had many friends and enjoyed much goodwill in the Middle East. But this argument for the appointment is double-edged. One civil servant was quoted in the press as calling Aitken 'the Saudi Ambassador to Europe'. 'There are people at Westminster nowadays,' said the *Sunday Times* in June 1997, 'who believe Aitken became Defence Procurement Minister to ensure the continuation of Saudi Defence orders.' The *Observer* has since claimed that 'Aitken brokered a £5bn arms deal.' His Saudi associates had stood 'to get more than £750m in commission. No one knows how it was shared out.' Aitken says this was 'wild and mendacious nonsense'. He was involved as a minister in negotiations for the sale of Tornado aircraft, he says 'I have never in my life made a penny out of an arms deal.'

In 1994 he was promoted again, to Chief Secretary, joining the Cabinet. There was no suggestion that he had done other than the rules required, forsaking his outside interests from the moment of his appointment as a minister. Some began to speak of him as a potential leader of his party.

And now that recurring triptych in the Scandalous Nineties, the *Guardian*, the Paris Ritz and Mohammed Al Fayed, struck. In a front-page article published in October 1994, the paper said that while arms minister Aitken had stayed at Fayed's hotel in 1993, and paid FF 8,010 (almost £1,000) for a two-night stay in a 'single, superior class room'. No offence there, you might think. But a copy of the computerized bill was spread across the front page of the *Guardian*. It was unsigned; but a note on the bottom indicated that it had been debited to the account of Aitken's old friend, Said Ayas. Ayas was staying (at the same time) in a fabulously expensive suite at the hotel. Settlement of the minister's bill in this way, it was claimed, might have breached the Questions of Procedure for Ministers guidelines, governing the acceptance of gifts.

The article, which appeared in October 1994, had an involved and (until then) unpublished history. It was a product of conversations between the *Guardian*'s editor, Peter Preston, and Al Fayed. These resulted in a six-month correspondence between Preston and Aitken. The editor wanted to know why the minister's bill was paid by a Saudi businessman involved in a major arms contract.

At first Aitken provided a simple explanation. In his letters to Preston he did not deny that the bill had been debited to Ayas, but said this was a mistake on the part of the Ritz. He claimed his wife had sorted things out with a cash payment to Ayas's account. Had he left things at that, Aitken might still be on the Conservative front bench. But as the letters between Preston and Aitken multiplied, the tale took on the characteristics of a good whodunit. Aitken decided to explain why a woman he said was his wife paid the bill for a hotel room she did not stay in.

His story, contained in the letters, was as follows. On Friday 17 September 1993 he flew to Paris from Poland where he had been on ministerial business, to join Lolicia Aitken and his daughter Victoria, already in Paris, for a family weekend en route to Victoria's new school in Switzerland. Victoria and Lolicia, he said, stayed at a flat belonging to Ayas's daughter while he was booked in at the Ritz. But Aitken was delayed in Poland and on arriving in Paris found that his wife and daughter had gone to Geneva ahead of him, by TGV. So Aitken remained in Paris for a couple of days, jogging and working on book proofs. After taking Victoria to her school, Lolicia Aitken returned to Paris to join her husband. They met briefly. He then departed for Geneva to visit his daughter, leaving his wife at the Ritz. On departing for London the same day, she settled the hotel account with (said Aitken) 'money given to her by me for this purpose'. This was 'some hours after I had left Paris'. As mentioned above, this cash payment was credited to Ayas's account because, said Aitken, the bill had been paid mistakenly by the Saudi businessman.

The story just about hung together. Aitken's correspondence with the *Guardian* was passed to the Cabinet Secretary, Sir Robin Butler, and shown to the Prime Minister.

But nothing in the correspondence explained why Ayas's accounts (furnished to the *Guardian*) showed no cash credit of Fr 8,010 from Lolicia. Aitken needed to explain this. On the Ayas account was a cash credit - from somebody - of Fr 4,257. Perhaps this was the solution? He asked the Ritz to investigate. The hotel's President replied that he had talked to the cashier on duty at the time. 'I am pleased that he does in fact remember the transaction to which you refer. His recollection is that a brunette lady of European aspect, paid the cash sum of Fr 4,257 in favour of the account of Mr Ayas.' Aitken wrote to the Cabinet Secretary reciting this but editing it to omit mention of any figure, ending at the words 'cash sum'.

Sir Robin was thus led to believe that the sum in question was the Fr 8,010. He was satisfied with Aitken's explanation and cleared him of impropriety. And there the matter rested.

Until October 1994. Fayed was now enraged at the attitude of the British government towards him. Using a go-between he communicated his complaints about four ministers to the Prime Minister (see p.361). These included complaints about Aitken. John Major asked Sir Robin Butler to investigate these. But before Butler could complete this work, the Guardian published its claims about 'cash for questions' and John Major faced the Commons.

Seizing the moment, the paper published its allegations. Its case direcdy contradicted Aitken's claim, made in the Commons in response to a question from a curiously well-briefed Gordon Brown, that no part of his bill had ever been paid by Ayas. But Sir Robin, completing his investigations after the *Guardian* had gone public, again cleared Aitken of any impropriety, while acknowledging that there were discrepancies.

The *Guardian* knew about these. It had seen the original of the note from the hotel's president, mentioning the sun of Fr 4,257, and noticed that Aitken had not included the sum in his letter to Butler.

Aitken took the dispatch box at Treasury Questions to defend his reputation. He called for an end to 'this hysterical atmosphere of sleaze journalism'. And it emerged that Peter Preston had made an error of judgement on which Tory critics were delighted to seize. To conceal Al Fayed's involvement he had authorized the use of a fake (or 'cod') fax on Commons note paper, purporting to come from Aitken's private office, to obtain a copy of the Ritz bill.

Abuse what you will, but never abuse Commons procedure. Betty Boothroyd, the Speaker, was furious. She instructed the Serjeant-at-Arms to conduct an investigation. Preston had thrown the Government a life raft. The Tories lost no time in clambering aboard. Lord Tebbitt led the attack, accusing Preston of behaving in a 'scurrilous, scandalous and wicked manner'.

The following day, Preston was summoned before the Commons. Tory MPs had suffered months of media taunts about 'Tory sleaze'. Now, for a moment at least, came their revenge. Eyes bulging and blood pressure rising with righteous indignation, they vented their spleen at the hapless editor of the liberal broadsheet. Roger Gale, Tory MP for Thanet North (Aitken was MP for Thanet South) led the charge, calling Preston a 'whore from hell'.

Fleet Street editors, perhaps not untouched by envy at the *Guardian*'s scoops, laid into Preston with mournful glee. On 1 November, he resigned from the Press Complaints Commission. A few months later, the longest-serving editor on Fleet Street vacated the editor's chair, and moved upstairs.

In April 1995, the national press renewed the attack on Jonathan Aitken. The *Independent* claimed that arms-manufacturer BMARC, of which Aitken was a director, had been exporting to Singapore weapons whose ultimate destination was Iran. The former chairman of the company, Gerald James, alleged that Aitken ought to have known of this project, 'Project Lisi'. Other directors say it was never known to the board that the destination of the arms was Iran. From the dispatch box, Aitken made a biting attack on the *Independent*'s claims, blaming them on 'an unholy alliance between a failed chairman and a failing newspaper'.

Before the Westminster dust had settled on this affair, Granada Television's political documentary, *World in Action*, screened a programme about the Chief Secretary. The contents of the programme, *Jonathan of Arabia*, were heavily trailed in the *Guardian*, and contained allegations about Aitken's involvement with Saudi Arabia and the arms industry. Granada TV refused Aitken's demand for a slot in which to answer the allegations personally, but included quotations from his response. The programme's contents, and the linked *Guardian* article, became the subject of a libel action brought by Aitken.

Returning the media salvo from a studio in Conservative Central Office, with the assistance of an Autocue machine (a first in the history of parliamentary scandal?), Aitken responded, angrily refuting the charges in the purplest of prose: Britain had 'the best media in the world and the worst media in the world. If it falls to me to start a fight to cut out the cancer of bent and twisted journalism in our country with the simple sword of truth, and the trusty shield of fair play, [and the stout armour of Autocue] then so be it. I am ready for the fight.' His words came back to haunt him in the sketches of a thousand cartoonists after his downfall.

The episode had its lighter side. *World in Action* hired a camel (for £1000) and filmed it trudging among dunes near Liverpool, in scenes intended to invoke Arabian imagery.

At the Cabinet reshuffle of 5 July, Aitken resigned from the Cabinet – 'to spend more time with his solicitors,' press wags suggested. John Major wrote him a supportive letter. But within days of his resignation, Aitken faced yet more 'scandal' as the *Daily Mirror* reported an affair (fifteen years previously) with a prostitute, who specialized in sadomasochistic sex. 'My wife long-ago forgave me,' commented Aitken. 'I hope others will follow her example.'

But the story prompted another recollection. In the *News of the World* on 22 June 1997, under the headline 'Four in a bed, whips and an orgy in a gothic mill', 'hooker Paula Strudwick' recalled her corporal punishment sessions with the then MP. 'In the beginning his lovemaking was very gende . . . but that soon changed. Within a few weeks all he was interested in was whips.' She told the paper that one weekend Aitken gave 'strict instructions to stop and collect basketfuls of birch twigs. As soon as I was home, he was on the phone saying 'Soak them in a bath and get them really pliable. I'll be over on Monday at 7pm'.

After resigning from the government, Aitken spent a year of relative obscurity on the backbenches. He issued further writs for libel and aggravated damages against the *Guardian* and Granada in December 1995, when both organizations returned to Aitken's affairs with a story about his involvement in arms companies in the late 1980s.

In June 1996, however, Aitken won an important battle in the effort to return to high office when he was cleared by an all-party committee of MPs of any wrongdoing in relation to BMARC. The Trade and Industry Select Committee found at the end of a twelve-month inquiry that there was no evidence to substantiate allegations over his directorship.

'I feel I have been cleared, exonerated, vindicated . . . I am glad now that we have reached the end of the trail,' announced Aitken. Gerald James, the former chairman of BMARC at the centre of the allegations, was less convinced – telling reporters at the time that 'sensitive papers remain concealed'. And Granada and the *Guardian* pointed out that Aitken's actions had delayed the libel trial until after the General Election. At the election, on 1 May,

Aitken, like most Conservatives in Kent, lost his seat to Labour. The libel case came to court on 4 June 1997, and, at Aitken's request, was heard without a jury. It pitted two of Britain's leading QCs, George Carman and Charles Grey, head-to-head. The case hinged on six allegations: that Aitken had conducted private business with an arms company, Future Management Services; that he had attended a business meeting at the Ritz in 1993 and lied about his bill; that he was effectively in the pocket of the Saudi royal family and financially dependent on them; that he offered to help a company called Astra Holdings sell arms to Iran and Iraq; that he knew BMARC sold a cannon to Iraq; and that he 'pimped' by asking two former employees of Inglewood Health Hydro to procure prostitutes for Arab clients.

The case lasted eleven days. For ten of them Aitken sat in the well of the court (near his mother, who passed the time reading *Country Life*) and his wife. He proved a confident performer, helped, perhaps, by having spent odd afternoons watching George Carman at work in earlier cases. And at first he appeared well ahead on points. The judge soon ruled against the *Guardian* on the first allegation, that relating to BMARC. The defendants backed down, to Aitken's delight.

He began to stumble, however, when questioned about the alterations to his letter to Sir Robin Buder, admitting to 'sharp editing' and 'subterfuge'. And he confessed to a 'small mystery' over the payment of his bill at the Ritz. On the fifth day of the case, asked whether his wife was a brunette (the hair colour of the women seen paying a cash bill at the hotel) he admitted 'she's not – this week'.

'I have,' he declared to the defendants' QC as he finished his testimony, 'been demonised by the *Guardian* and Carmanised by you.'

Still, nine days into the case, Aitken's lawyers thought he had a good chance of winning. Then, everything fell about him. His claims about his weekend visit to the Ritz, first told to Peter Preston in 1994 and repeated in court, were ripped apart.

It was the outcome of weeks of hard slogging through files all over Europe. In the days leading up to the trial, the defendants had discovered that Aitken had admitted to Sir Robin Butler that he had spoken to Prince Mohammed when in Paris. He had previously denied this. A record of his telephone calls from the Ritz also showed that Aitken telephoned the Hotel Bristol in

Switzerland on Sunday 19 September 1993, at a time when Lolicia Aitken was supposed to be journeying back to Paris.

Explaining this away, he dragged his mother-in-law into the story: she had he said, shared a room with Lolicia and had taken the call. But the *Guardian* was suspicious. It sent a reporter to the Hotel Bristol in the hope of finding Mrs Aitken's bill. The building, in the hands of receivers, was shuttered and locked but a caretaker remembered that the basement contained old records and allowed the reporter to spend three days going through them. He faxed back to London printouts of the guest list, reservation dockets and bill payments for the weekend.

On the relevant night, Lolicia had obtained a 80SF discount, 'because of single occupancy'. Her mother-in-law had not shared the room and could not have answered Aitken's call. The *Guardian* lost no time in presenting this information to the court.

When in a hole, why dig? Aitken dug harder. He obtained witness statements from his wife and daughter, confirming his story. His solicitor told the press that the next day, as at Ascot, would be 'Ladies' Day'. But other parts of Aitken's tale also began to disintegrate. No one knew why Aitken's wife paid the Ritz bill in hard-to-record cash; surely a credit card would have been handier? He blamed his wife's dyslexia, telling the court that she could not use cards. A witness came forth to mock this claim. And Lolicia's bill at the Hotel Bristol had been paid by American Express.

Under subpoena American Express provided documents which not only confirmed Lolicia had paid the hotel bill but also showed she hired a car at Geneva airport – Aitken had always said she came by train. British Airways were also able to help. Just before 4pm on Wednesday 18 June, a white envelope was delivered to the court. It contained Budget car hire dockets, showing that Lolicia Aitken had not returned the car in Geneva until Sunday evening, long after she was supposed to have paid the Ritz bill in Paris. And it contained copies of the flight coupons for Lolicia and Victoria's direct flight to Geneva on Friday 17 September. They had never been in Paris.

The case was adjourned for a day, followed by a two-minute session on Friday 20 June which saw Aitken's lawyers withdraw and offer to pay the *Guardian*'s costs in full. The night before, news came that Lolicia Aitken intended to separate from her husband.

The endgame delighted journalists everywhere. To save any 'embarrassment' he resigned as a privy counsellor and vanished in Ayas' private jet, said the press, leading even the *Spectator* to speculate that he might have 'done a Lucan'. Aitken observes that 'I travelled to France on Eurostar, then took a commercial flight to New York.' He reappeared though, at Heathrow, two weeks later – having spent the time with his son at a beach resort in northern California. His Westminster house, just around the corner from the Millbank TV studios, was besieged by journalists. Aitken attempted to satisfy them by walking, for the cameras, to Abingdon Green, across the road from the Commons, after issuing a press release announcing his plans to do so. The walk turned into a scrum. Michael Brunson, ITN's political correspondent, was knocked to the ground, and Aitken was forced to retreat to his house.

The one-time Cabinet minister's fall was complete. But unanswered questions abound. We do not know why Aitken was in Paris – we only know his wife was elsewhere. As the *Spectator* put it: 'Whatever it is that Mr Aitken is hiding, he has, so far, done a pretty good job of it. We are all, the *Guardian* included, still in the dark.'

Aitken was jailed for eighteen months after pleading guilty to perjury, serving seven months before he was released early with an electronic tag around his ankle. For a couple of years after leaving prison, he studied theology at Wycliffe College in Oxford. Having found God and patience, Aitken now sits on the boards of a number of Christian charities. He published *Psalms for People Under Pressure* as well as his autobiography, *Pride and Prejudice*, and, divorced from Lolicia, married Elizabeth Harris, ex-spouse of Richard Harris, Rex Harrison and Aitken's cousin Peter Aitken.

The former politician and ex-prisoner denied squirreling away cash in Swiss bank accounts when, facing huge legal costs, he claimed bankruptcy. Aitken says he had to sell his home, cufflinks, Rolex; everything. Asked what he thought when looking back on the episode, Aitken told an interviewer: 'I feel ashamed about the whole thing. I was arrogant. I made the Sword of Truth speech about scything through the corruption in journalism and society and then, months later, I was sent down. I think about that speech now and cringe. I don't blame anybody but myself and I deserved my punishment.'

It emerged in early 2004 that Aitken fancied becoming an MP again, with reports suggesting that more than 200 Tory members in his old constituency of Thanet South wanted him to stand once more. Aitken claimed that, while renting Ian Fleming's flat in Sandwich to finish his book on psalms, people were coming up to him to shake his hand and slap him on the back. With the disgraced former minister warming to the idea of standing again, Conservative Central Office announced he'd missed the selection deadline by twelve hours, before Michael Howard stepped in to show that this was not merely a procedural bar. The Conservative leader made clear that there was no room for Jonathan Aitken in a post-sleaze Tory Party. Forgiveness has its limit.

ROBIN COOK – 1997

'Your lover or your wife'

To be required to choose between a mistress and a wife has been the fate of many an ambitious philanderer, but to be forced to do so by a spin doctor encapsulated the essence of New Labour and was to be the fate of Robin Cook.

The Foreign Secretary was one of the sharpest Left-wing minds on Tony Blair's front bench and was tipped, not least by himself, to do very well in the new government. He was on his way to Heathrow Airport on the first Friday of August 1997 with his wife of 28 years, Margaret, to fly out for a three-week holiday in the USA when he took a call from the man who later would be described, with some justification, as the real Deputy Prime Minister.

On the other end of the mobile was Alastair Campbell. The former tabloid newspaper reporter turned Downing Street communications supremo was a friend of the Prime Minister and a political appointee granted extraordinary powers to order real civil servants about and dictate to Cabinet ministers. The *News of the World*, said Campbell, planned that weekend to expose Cook's long-running affair with his secretary, Gaynor Regan, and he, the Foreign Secretary, had thirty minutes, half an hour, to decide the 'line to take'. Was it to be Gaynor or Margaret, Ms Regan or Mrs Cook, the Westminster assistant or the mother of his two adult children, his lover or his wife?

Campbell's approach to marriage guidance was certainly swifter, and more brutal, than the counselling service offered by Relate. As a result, Cook asked the airport authorities to be left alone with his spouse in a VIP lounge so the Prime Minister's press secretary would have something definite to tell a Sunday newspaper.

'The holiday's off. The *News of the World* has got the story and I can't see how the marriage can continue,' Cook told his wife Margaret. He had opted for Regan. After complying with the spin doctor's ultimatum, Cook spoke to the Prime Minister. A tearful

Margaret asked: 'He wants you to resign?' 'No, I shan't lose my job,' answered a relieved Cook. After breaking the news to a dumbstruck son, Peter, who had travelled to Heathrow to bid his parents *bon voyage*, the unhappy couple got back into the official car. Instead of jetting to the USA, spending a week in Vermont then a fortnight horse-riding in Montana, they headed home for the last time. The new green suede chaps Margaret had bought Robin remained unused in a suitcase. In Carlton Gardens, Cook's official residence, they sat up late sharing a bottle of whisky as the implications sank in and the storm clouds gathered.

The media delighted in the first sex scandal of the Blair era; the elfin Foreign Secretary being presented as an unlikely Lothario who found himself described as 'cock Robin' in the more scurrilous newspapers. The soon-to-be former Mrs Cook vetoed his proposal to announce merely that they were separating. 'I accept that I have behaved badly to Margaret and she has behaved nobly,' he said in a statement. 'I want to apologise to her for the public hounding that the break-up of our marriage has brought her and the painful manner in which it happened. I would ask that she now be left in privacy.'

Mrs Cook, a consultant haematologist in an Edinburgh hospital, had known about the affair but said she thought it had ended some time before. A letter of condolence from Blair was received; it expressed regret that she had been caught up in a media maelstrom following his spin doctor's intervention, but not sorrow at the marriage break-up. Mrs Cook posted an angry letter back to the PM's Tuscan holiday home, eliciting an anxious visit to her Edinburgh home from Peter Mandelson, who was hoping to smooth things over. He failed.

Meanwhile Cook became for some time a diminished figure in the public eye. A minister who had the potential to be a towering figure in the Government had been humiliated. Both he and Campbell would later dispute the version of events at Heathrow Airport reported here – yet close colleagues of both confirmed the details at the time. Campbell stressed the need for 'clarity' when he spoke to Cook, and the Foreign Secretary did not require the services of GCHQ code-breakers to understand what that meant. Cook, who, with his aide David Mathieson, had just collected Mrs Cook from an Edinburgh–Heathrow domestic flight for the ten-minute drive to Terminal 4, muttered into his phone as his aide and wife discussed the holiday. 'We need a decision,' urged Campbell. 'I understand,' replied Cook.

Mrs Cook's feelings after the break-up of their marriage in such unusual circumstances may best be gauged in *A Slight and Delicate Creature*, an autobiography that settled more than a few scores with her husband. Take this reference in the index: 'Cook, Robin: heavy drinking, weight problems, sexual difficulties.' She accused him of taking six lovers, including Regan, and drinking heavily. She related an incident in 1987 when (she said) he passed out on a hotel floor after drinking a bottle of brandy.

To add to her ex-husband's embarrassment she complained that Tony Blair had 'sold his soul to the devil' to win the 1997 election. Her ex-husband, she claimed, was jealous of Chancellor Gordon Brown, 'hates' Peter Mandelson and suffered 'terrible guilt' at ditching his anti-nuclear, Left-wing principles to climb the greasy pole.

The Tories capitalised on all this. They called for Cook to be sacked, though taking care (with their own record of sexual misadventures still fresh in the public mind) to say less about his marriage than his 'disastrous' spell at the Foreign Office. It was unfortunate for Cook that he had begun his tenure with a speech unveiling what was promised to be a newly 'ethical' foreign policy.

During negotiations over his divorce, and with a steady flow of embarrassing details about his private life dogging him, he protested to his estranged wife: 'So you want to destroy me?' She replied that he could say whatever he liked about Regan but warned him against making unpleasant asides about her. With feeling, the Foreign Secretary is reported to have declared: 'I would be happy if I never had to see or hear or think about you, ever again.'

In April 1998, little more than a fortnight after his divorce, the Foreign Secretary married his mistress in a humble Tunbridge Wells register office some two weeks before the couple had told the press to expect it. Paying £101 for a special licence to marry at 8.30 a.m., an hour before the office normally opened, the couple had slipped out of his official country residence, Chevening, near Sevenoaks, with three guests, driving through back roads to avoid photographers. The best man's main duty was to jump out of the car to open farmers' gates, shooing cows from the road. No confetti was thrown when the couple emerged as man and wife, though surprised building workers spotted the Foreign Secretary, a green anorak over his suit, punching the air in triumph. Whether it was because he had just remarried, or succeeded in giving the press the slip, was unclear.

In office, Cook's authority never wholly recovered from this mess. Demotion to Leader of the Commons after the 2001 General Election was followed by his resignation in 2003 over the invasion of Iraq. Perhaps it was only then, out of government and free to speak his mind, that Cook found his voice.

One mystery remained: how did the *News of the World* discover his affair? Speculation persisted either that the Foreign Office establishment or MI6, resentful that Cook had little time to meet overseas ambassadors and wanted to pursue a foreign policy with his famous 'ethical dimension', had deliberately shopped him.

The truth was simpler, if of little comfort to Mr Cook. He was a victim of political in-fighting within New Labour. Cook was betrayed by an aide to a rival Cabinet minister who, before the 1997 election, had spotted the pair canoodling in a Westminster bar and subsequently tipped off the *News of the World*. The Foreign Secretary was invited out for a drink with one of the newspaper's journalists, ostensibly to discuss world affairs but actually to expose his worldly affair. Whether he expected it to come out one day, we do not know, but flattered by the sudden interest in his work by a newspaper known for good reason in the trade as the 'News of the Screws', Cook accepted. He met the journalist and discussed Europe and international developments, before parting with handshakes. The Foreign Secretary left with his Special Branch bodyguards. In yet another triumph for the security services, he was secretly tailed by the newspaper's motorbike riders to his private flat in Victoria rather than his official residence in Carlton Gardens. Waiting inside was Regan, sitting in the dark with the lights turned out to fool the protection officers if not the more resourceful newshounds.

They stayed there together, and at eight next morning out popped Cook to feed the parking meter on her car before leaving in his official vehicle fifteen minutes later. At around 10 a.m. Regan departed, locking the door behind her, captured by the hidden long lenses of Her Majesty's loyal press.

RON DAVIES – 1998

'I have actually been watching badgers'

'A Moment of Madness' was how the newspapers put it, directly quoting the unhappy Ron Davies. The first resignation from Tony Blair's New Labour Cabinet was also an almost complete humiliation and a personal tragedy.

Proud, some said arrogant, the Welsh Secretary appeared to embody the macho culture of the valleys. He revelled in the beery atmosphere of the House of Commons bars, a hard man prepared to fight his corner when crossed. Twice married with a daughter, the architect of Welsh devolution was seemingly destined to be the First Minister (i.e. the leader) of the new Welsh Assembly he had worked to create. Until, that is, he became the author of his own downfall.

It was on a windy night on 26 October 1998 that Davies suffered what he immediately afterwards called his moment of madness. The curious incident on Clapham Common sent him on a spiral of decline which ended in January 2004 with his final departure, to the indifference of most, from the Labour Party.

According to Davies's version of events, he drove to London from his Caerphilly constituency. To relieve stress following a series of political problems and meetings in South Wales, he decided on a walk on Clapham Common, a huge triangle of park-like greenery in South West London. As he considered the great issues of the day, at 7.45 p.m., Davies fell into conversation – his story went – with Donald Fearon, a Rastafarian. He agreed to go for a drink with his new friend, and perhaps a meal. The pair, Davies and his dreadlocked pal, got into the minister's gold Ford Granada and picked up two other people, a man and a woman, friends of Fearon. The four-strong party drove to a Brixton council estate where, he said, a knife was held to his throat and the group relieved him of his wallet, mobile phone, Labour Party card and conference pass. The shaken MP, when allowed to leave, flagged down a taxi to take him to a police station where he made a statement alleging he was the victim of a robbery.

It is fair to say that this version of events was not met with universal acceptance. What is beyond dispute, however, is that the following morning Davies was summoned to a Downing Street meeting with Tony Blair and a grilling at the hands of the Prime Minister's communications chief, Alastair Campbell. By the afternoon he was gone, Campbell writing a resignation letter for Davies to sign and arranging for the episode to be related to an unsuspecting world via a TV interview with the BBC's John Sergeant. As Davies gave his version of events on film, Campbell was glimpsed peering from behind a door before retreating into the shadows.

Inconsistencies quickly emerged in Davies's account. He originally told the police he was assaulted in a Brixton street and made no mention of Clapham Common. When Davies was told that Brixton was the security camera capital of London and the incident would almost certainly have been recorded, he changed his story. A short walk through Battersea Park with Fearon subsequently also emerged.

The area of Clapham Common where Davies was walking is a gay meeting place. Behind the Windmill public house is a spot where men cruise to encounter other men. The now ex-Welsh Secretary denied he had been seeking a gay liaison. In his resignation statement in the Commons Chamber, however, he fuelled the speculation that was already running. 'We are all different,' he told MPs, 'the products of both of our genes and our experiences.' He added that 'we are what we are' – a phrase journalists at once associated with the popular song 'I Am What I Am' sung by the transvestite hero of a musical comedy, *La Cage aux Folles*, recently popular in the London West End. But Davies denied he was bisexual. He laid the blame for his inexplicable behaviour on his father whom he painted as a bully, a man who inflicted hell on the family.

Rastas and homosexual cruising do not normally mix, Rastafarian culture being widely regarded as more tolerant of exotic substances than exotic sex, so the question on journalists' lips at the time was 'was it sex or marijuana?' The truth, it is now generally believed, was that Davies mistook his man in propositioning Fearon – known as Boogie – on Clapham Common; but that Fearon, spotting an opportunity, agreed to help find a male prostitute. The duo drove to the Brixton estate where he was met by two other men. In a lift Davies was robbed and subsequently received a call trying to blackmail him. At this point he decided to go to the police. Homeless Fearon, one of six people arrested in a police investigation, was charged with the theft of Davies' G-registration Granada but the charge, and with it perhaps the opportunity to discover the full truth, was dropped. It is not known whether Fearon was involved in the robbery in the lift; no charges relating to this were ever brought against him.

As well as his Cabinet seat, Davies was forced to relinquish the leadership of the Welsh Labour Party, despite protesting that he was guilty of 'no illegal behaviour, no improper behaviour whatsoever'. He ran for (and won) a seat in the inaugural Welsh Assembly in May 1999, as he had always intended. But no offer of a place in the Cardiff cabinet was forthcoming from Alun Michael, who had been manoeuvred into the leadership to succeed Davies.

Davies was appointed Chair of the Assembly's Economic Development Committee to keep him quiet but was forced to resign within a month. He issued a public statement admitting he was bisexual and receiving psychiatric treatment for a compulsive disorder which attracted him to high-risk situations.

Two Sunday newspaper reporters were not slow to find evidence of such incidents. They tape-recorded encounters with Davies in a wood near his home in Draethen, South Wales, and the two-page account, including photographs, was published in the *News of the World*. Davies was forced to issue a pre-emptive statement, which went a good deal further than previous denials. Appealing for privacy, Davies said: 'Having discussed the matter with my wife, and in order to put a stop to the intolerable stream of lurid and inaccurate stories, I am left with no alternative but to confirm that I am, and have been for some time, bisexual.' He went on: 'During the last week while walking and bird watching near my home I was approached by individuals who, on two separate occasions, attempted to engage me in conversation of a sexual nature. I ended the conversations and walked away. I now know that these were tabloid journalists who were clearly trying to entrap me. I have always believed that individuals are entitled to privacy. I deeply regret this invasion of my privacy.'

The now desperate ex-Cabinet minister added: 'I am saddened that I have been forced into making this statement and I hope that it will end the continued intrusion into my private life. I hope that I will now be allowed to concentrate on my political work and to deal with the difficult personal issues involved where they belong, within the confines of my family.'

The Labour leadership seized the opportunity to bury a politician who posed a threat, securing his resignation as Chair of the Economic Committee despite a fortnight's resistance from the fast-falling figure.

Still a member of the Welsh Assembly, Davies decided against standing again in 2003. By now married a third time and with a young child, in March of that year he was tracked down by another tabloid to Tog Hill, a beauty spot off the M4 near Bath, where he was found in the bushes with a stranger. The Chair of the Caerphilly Woodlands Trust explained: 'I have actually been there watching badgers since first thing in the morning.' But it was 10 a.m., no time to be looking for these strictly nocturnal animals.

Citing devolution, university top-up fees and the invasion of Iraq, Davies quit the Labour Party in January 2004: 'I am disillusioned,' he said. 'I joined a left-of-centre party which is now right-of-centre which I find myself unable to accept.'

It is difficult not to feel sympathy for a man whose personal downfall was so publicly painful. One of the authors of this book tried to make this point to the *Newsnight* presenter, Jeremy Paxman, just after Davies's downfall on Clapham Common had made the headlines. Your author went on to remark that Davies's tragedy was to be part of a generation of politicians among whom homosexuality was unthinkable: an attitude now almost obsolete. At least two members of the current Labour Cabinet were gay, he added.

'Two?' said Mr Paxman.

Your authour cited the openly gay Culture Secretary, Chris Smith, and the Trade Industry Secretary, Peter Mandelson. Paxman's jaw dropped.

But that's another story.

DERRY IRVINE – 1998

'Lord Wallpaper of Westminster'

He was a medieval galleon in an era when New Labour presented itself as a sleek ship-of-state. Sitting atop his Woolsack it seemed at times as if a preservation order had been slapped on Derry Irvine. The Lord Chancellor had little time for those seeking to hold him to account and, encountering the media coastguard, would blast away with all guns firing. But some of the damage was to his own reputation and that of a government in which he served for six years.

Described as a 'benevolent despot' by a biographer, his unkindest critics called him a clown. Yet none denied his intellectual command, nobody would have called him corrupt in any serious sense of that word, and it was almost refreshing in the 21st century to encounter a politician so careless of what anybody thought of him. It must be said, however, that it was hard to behold the majesty which was this Lord Chancellor without the word 'pompous' springing unbidden to the lips. Lord Irvine of Lairg was good at pomposity, an almost Gilbert & Sullivan figure of unfathomed effrontery who simultaneously shocked and entertained – not least with his largesse at public expense.

The son of an Inverness roofer and a waitress, Irvine had not inherited the common touch. This brilliant barrister had acquired majesty as he made his way via Glasgow, Cambridge and the London School of Economics to the Bar in 1967. Becoming a QC in 1978, by 1981 he was heading the Chambers at 11 King's Bench Walk, which he had set up with a number of other lawyers. Earning vast sums representing City clients, Irvine was even rumoured to have asked to be served a peeled orange on a silver salver every day to avoid the indignity of skinning fruit: a tale of doubtful provenance but illustrative of the way he was perceived.

By the 1990s he was a recorder and deputy High Court judge. Within months of joining Tony Blair's first Cabinet in May 1997, Irvine's hauteur was sprung upon an unsuspecting Britain. 'I can compare myself with Wolsey,' he boasted, declaring himself the true heir of the great Cardinal – his predecessor on the Woolsack, the eminent Tudor who was the power behind Henry VIII's throne.

For Irvine to be Wolsey, Blair must have been Henry VIII, which while an interesting idea remains contestable. Yet Blair *was* dependent upon Irvine to an unusually high degree. As 'Cupid QC' Irvine had brought together Blair and his wife Cherie Booth when he took on both as legal pupils. When Blair was elected as MP for Sedgefield in 1983, it was to Irvine the couple had turned for a loan to help buy Myrobella, a pleasant detached Victorian house standing a little apart from the neighbouring terraces of Trimdon Colliery.

Irvine was an established Labour Party figure before Blair's leadership triumph in 1994. He had advised the high command in the 1980s on how to rid itself of the ultra-Left Militant Tendency and was very much a member of John Smith's Scottish Tendency. After Smith's sudden death, Irvine joined his old trainee's kitchen cabinet, where it became clear he was destined for the Lord Chancellorship.

The Wolsey indiscretion was followed by a spectacular display of political naïveté in a scandal made all the more enjoyable because Irvine seemed genuinely unable to understand what all the fuss was about, let alone show any sheepishness about his self-aggrandisement. In an effort to allay fears – and dash hopes – that Labour would be a tax-and-spend government, the Party in its first two years had adopted tight spending plans inherited from the Tories. These left schools, hospitals and the rest of the public sector complaining they were short of funds. A new Royal Yacht was cancelled. Yet one Cabinet minister seemed unimpressed by the new sense of economy enforced on mere monarchs. Lord Irvine of Lairg began a spending spree.

The official residence of the Lord Chancellor, a grace-and-favour apartment occupied by Irvine and his wife Alison, was given a £650,000 refurbishment. This, it must be emphasised, was no rebuild. The Irvines were simply decorating. In an attempt to turn the clock back to 1834 when the Victorian-Gothic designer Augustus Pugin collaborated with the architect Sir Charles Barry to rebuild the medieval Houses of Parliament following a disastrous fire, Irvine agreed to spend £59,000 on hand-made fleur de lys flock wallpaper. Some £20,000 went on curtains and £90,000 on soft furnishings, with the new carpet costing £100 a yard. Then there were the £16,000 Gothic oak beds and a £14,000 dining table, plus a further £8,000 on crockery to put on it. Another £3,000 bought a Victorian water closet, 'Derry's throne'. And £32,000 was spent on eight mirrors; these would cover up some £2,000 worth of wallpaper. The Irvines visited art galleries in England and Scotland to borrow paintings to hang on their newly decorated walls.

The lavishness of the programme leaked. Cabinet colleagues were as shocked as outraged nurses, teachers and the electorate at large. But Irvine the medieval galleon sailed defiantly on and, in a display of chutzpah that opened New Labour to the charge of having fast become as out of touch as the Tories they succeeded, made for the moral high ground. He declared himself a sort of cultural philanthropist. Called before the Commons Public Administration Select Committee in March 1998 to account for the £650,000 expenditure, Irvine declared: 'It is a noble cause and future generations will be grateful.'

Declining an opportunity to apologise for asking taxpayers to find £300 a roll for his wallpaper, Irvine peered down from his ivory tower: 'You are talking about quality materials which are capable of lasting for sixty or seventy years. You are not talking about something down at the DIY store that might collapse after a year or so.'

The idea of wallpaper 'collapsing' bemused the home-decorating community. Shoppers for plastic garden furniture or reproduction-Victorian loo-roll holders had never expected to bump into the Lord Chancellor pushing a trolley on a Saturday morning, but the affronted popular wallpaper industry spotted the opportunity for free publicity and put the boot in anyway. B&Q announced that its £3.99-a-roll paper was better value than Irvine's £300-a-roll, insisting it was likely to last just as long.

Irvine dismissed the row as a 'storm in a teacup', inadvertently refocusing attention on his £8,000 crockery. He tried to shift the blame on to a House of Lords committee that had approved the refurbishment. Lord Wallpaper's brazen performance, however, was distracting attention from his enormously important political achievements, including devolution legislation for Scotland and Wales and the Human Rights Act.

A steady drip of newspaper stories undermined his authority. Tales of how he would be behind his desk at 5.30 a.m. in order that his duties should not cut into his luncheon and afternoon, did little to help. His unconcealed passion for fine wines made him – for Downing Street spin doctors mindful of his relationship with the Prime Minister – a problem that mere marketing was powerless to fix.

During one dinner party at Chequers, according to a report in the *Spectator*, Irvine demonstrated his belief that the PM remained his junior by loudly and repeatedly declaring in front of other guests the need for 'young Blair to bring us some whisky'. His former pupil pretended not to hear but Irvine turned up the volume and on the fourth, and loudest, intervention that it was 'time that young Blair poured some whisky for his guests', the Premier relented and scurried off for a bottle.

That lack of tact was on show again in February 2001 when Irvine was accused of poor judgement over the so-called 'cash for wigs' affair. He was forced to admit having asked lawyers dependent on him for promotion in the legal pecking order to donate money to the Labour Party, he had sent a letter to some Labour-supporting barristers explicitly requesting 'significant contributions' towards its re-election campaign.

If the Lord Chancellor was cavalier with public funds, he remained canny with his own cash. Alone among Cabinet ministers he took his full rise in 1997 when others agreed to forego an increase under pressure from the parsimonious Chancellor Gordon Brown. Though he earned £184,000 a year towards the end of his reign, according to eye-witness reports Irvine caused a stir in the Tarbet Co-op when an assistant refused to give him the 'divi' on £70 of groceries bought for his holiday home in Argyll and Bute. Irvine, unable to find his Co-op card, first insisted that the worker should write the amount, a princely £1, on his receipt; and was then said to have held up the queue while he went to his car to seek the missing piece of plastic. Irvine found the reports misleading.

Unable to reshuffle his former mentor, Blair reappointed Irvine after Labour won a second Commons landslide in June 2001 but the Lord Chancellor's influence was waning. Irvine was to go in the summer of 2003.

Before then it happened that both authors of this book found themselves at the same table in a Brighton restaurant at a Labour Party conference. As the evening proceeded it became clear that the Lord Chancellor was dining there too, but in an inner room. When the Lord Chancellor's party began moving among the ordinary diners on their way to the exit, one of your authors sprang (alongside a female *Times* journalist) to the door, ahead of the Cabinet minister. Posing as *maîtres d'hotel* and bowing as he passed, the pair mumbled 'Good night, My Lord. We trust you enjoyed your meal.' They were greeted with a gracious nod. There is no other senior politician in recent memory of whom a journalist would have been absolutely confident that he or she would not recognise two long-standing Westminster reporters.

But is the laugh on him – or on them? It is an interesting question.

Judgements on this confident intellect and unashamedly flamboyant figure do not agree. On one hand, the example he set appeared not only ridiculous and rude but seriously damaging to the New Labour project at a time when it was vital for the Prime Minister and Chancellor of the Exchequer to be seen as leading an administration prudent in small things as well as large. Irvine was seen as having put two fingers up both to his own team and to the nation, and having handed easy ammunition to a sceptical or even hostile press.

On the other hand there is something admirable in Irvine's pre-Blairite indifference to the opinion of the mob, his refusal to blur the distinction he saw between the important and the trivial, and his intellectual depth – a rare depth in the Cabinet in which he served.

Tony Blair the moderniser, who had shown great loyalty to his old patron, probably saw both sides; but the moderniser won. Despite objections from his ex-employer, Blair decided to scrap the historic post of Lord Chancellor and so bring Irvine's turbulent political career to a close.

The medieval galleon had been sunk by a sleek ship-of-state – and yet in his way Irvine has the last laugh. Discounting the brief interregnum of Charles Falconer (Lord Falconer of Thornton) whom Blair brought in to wind up the post, Lord Irvine of Lairg goes down in history as England's last real Lord Chancellor.

PETER MANDELSON – 1998, 2001

'The question of resignation does not arise'

According to one of his closest friends, the injustice suffered by Peter Mandelson was so terrible it merited comparison with that of Alfred Dreyfus, the French officer falsely accused of treason and wrongly imprisoned on Devil's Island for five years. The best-selling author Robert Harris unexpectedly cast himself as Emile Zola to Mr Mandelson's Dreyfus when the Northern Ireland Secretary was forced to resign over his relationship with the Hinduja brothers, who had been accused of taking bribes in a corrupt Indian arms contract. Had Mandelson not been forced to quit as Trade and Industry Secretary two years earlier over a substantial secret debt to a colleague under investigation by his own department, he might well have survived the Hinduja affair.

A loan and two passports were, successively, the immediate causes of Mandelson's being forced out of Tony Blair's Cabinet not once but twice within a relatively short period. Behind the double disgrace, however, was a recklessness that had characterised his career. Mandelson seemed addicted to risk. A political radar which had so accurately detected Tory sleaze proved blind to the rocks upon which his own career was wrecked.

Peter Mandelson had been credited, not least by his own circle, with the image-making that took New Labour and its red-rose emblem from the drawing board in 1987 to a smashing election victory in 1997. His reputation was for expert calculation. Observers were baffled at how easily this quick, sharp and hard head could be turned by money and fame. Among the few really vivid members of the Blair government, Mandelson was by turns a shrewd and shadowy backroom plotter, and a social gadfly who flittered between soirees at the best addresses in London.

Some called him the Prince of Darkness. Rupert Murdoch reputedly described him as 'a starfucker'. Alastair Campbell, a fellow expert in political communications, mocked his fondness for the 'fancy dinner party' circuit. Socialite Carla Powell, the wife of Margaret Thatcher's former foreign affairs adviser Charles Powell, took him under her wing, introducing him to a series of celebrities. They included Sean Connery and US lingerie millionaire Linda Wachner in whose private jet Mandelson notoriously enjoyed several transatlantic flights; he also stayed in Wachner's Long Island summer home in August 1998 when Trade Secretary.

His determination to get up with the people who were up was to lead to his downfall. Mandelson set his heart on moving out of his modest flat in Clerkenwell into something altogether grander in West London, near his new friends. The result was a £475,000 house in fashionable Notting Hill Gate bought at the end of 1996. On Mandelson's new mantelpiece was an invitation to the Prince of Wales's fiftieth birthday. A £50,000 makeover directed by fashionable architect Seth Stein gave the house what critics called a soulless, and admirers called a minimalist, aspect. *Vogue* magazine was invited into No. 9 Northumberland Place, a narrow, four-storey Georgian house, where Lord Snowden photographed Mandelson posing in his £1,800 leather armchair, one of the few pieces of furniture in the near-empty rooms.

How Mandelson could afford a house costing more than ten times his salary as an MP was a source of speculation. Campbell ribbed him about where the funds came from. Mandelson, made Minister without Portfolio in May 1997 to act as the new Prime Minister's eyes and ears across government, hinted that the money had been forwarded by his mother following the death of his father.

The source was in fact Geoffrey Robinson, the controversial millionaire Paymaster-General in Blair's first government, who had privately loaned Mandelson £373,000. Whether the loan was asked for or offered unsolicited is disputed; Mr Robinson maintained that Mandelson had requested financial assistance, while Mandelson claimed that Robinson had proposed to advance him the cash on hearing he would eventually inherit £500,000. Certainly Robinson took an avuncular interest in the purchase, and the pair went house-hunting around West London in the Treasury minister's own chauffeur-driven Jaguar.

The two politicians agreed to keep the home loan secret. The paperwork was completed by Stephen Wegg-Prosser, a solicitor and father of Ben Wegg-Prosser, Mandelson's aide. But when Mandelson threw a housewarming party he failed to invite Robinson, an ally of his political foe, Gordon Brown, the Chancellor of the Exchequer. Perhaps both were embarrassed. Mandelson had not even told colleagues such as Tony Blair or Alastair Campbell about his indebtedness. Whenever the younger Wegg-Prosser suggested he should come clean, at least to those closest to him in Downing Street and particularly to a Prime Minister who relied heavily on his advice, Mandelson would shudder and change the subject.

When Robinson was revealed in November 1997 to be the beneficiary of a tax-avoiding offshore trust, Mandelson said nothing. When Robinson's links to the crooked Robert Maxwell drew criticism in February 1998, Mandelson said nothing. Reshuffled to Trade and Industry in July 1998, Mandelson became, as Secretary of State, head of the department which that autumn set its inspectors to work investigating Robinson. Mandelson still said nothing. He had left himself open to charges of a conflict of interest and given his enemies in the Brown camp what Charlie Whelan, the Chancellor's rumbustious press secretary, called a 'thermonuclear device' to detonate under Mandelson.

A hostile biography of Mandelson to be published in January 1999 by the *Daily Mirror* journalist, Paul Routledge, author of an admiring biography of Brown, was to be the trigger. It included two incendiary sentences on the subject of the loan. A proof copy sent to the wrong newspaper office in the House of Commons was read by at least one journalist friendly to the Industry Secretary, who tipped him off.

A panic-stricken Mandelson confessed on Thursday 17 December to Sir Michael Scholar, Permanent Secretary at the DTI, and a shocked Tony Blair was apprised of a 'big problem' by Alastair Campbell two hours before the Prime Minister was due to make a statement to the Commons about the latest military action in Iraq. However when the Cabinet Secretary, Sir Richard Wilson, was asked whether Mandelson had broken rules on conflicts of interest for ministers, he concluded he had not because the Secretary of State had taken no part in the inquiry into Robinson.

The story had still not broken, but it now seemed a case of when, not if, the loan was made public. Mandelson was convinced he would survive; Campbell took a contrary view. Blair, exasperated at his lieutenant's foolishness, rang Mandelson on Saturday 19 December, and urged him to pay off the £373,000 as quickly as possible in the hope of limiting the damage.

Monday 21 December saw Mandelson in Greenwich to inspect the Millennium Dome for which he was responsible. From here he was summoned to No. 10 for a war council with Charles Falconer and Derry Irvine, at that time lawyers to New Labour's inner circle. The Cabinet Secretary had decided Mandelson was sufficiently insulated from DTI inquiries into Robinson. But details of the loan were due to be published the following day in the *Guardian* and *Daily Mirror*. A defence strategy was needed.

Mandelson took to the airwaves that night, ringing the BBC to arrange an appearance on the *Nine O'Clock News* to tell surprised viewers: 'There is no conflict of interest so the question of resignation does not arise.' Tuesday's newspaper headlines were terrible for Mandelson. It got worse. As he toured broadcasting studios, the question was raised of whether he had declared the £373,000 loan from Robinson when he signed a legal declaration on a Britannia Building Society form to finance the rest of the purchase and improvements.

Mandelson described himself and Robinson as 'fairly exotic personalities' but a press that had grown fat on Tory sleaze was in no mood to make an exception now that one of Labour's most controversial ministers was in trouble. That evening, Blair spoke to Mandelson from Chequers and made it clear he believed Mandelson should resign. The pair agreed to sleep on it.

The Prime Minister was gently nudging his adviser and friend to the exit door. If he or Alastair Campbell used the intervening hours to intercede privately with editors on Mandelson's behalf, they were not successful. Mandelson awoke on Wednesday 23 December to yet more bloodthirsty headlines. The *Daily Mail* branded him 'The Master of Deception' and the *Sun* abandoned its now habitual loyalty to Blair to ask: 'So How The Hell Can Mandy Stay?'

A tearful Mandelson agreed the game was up. Both he and Robinson quit. A meeting in the Cabinet Minister's DTI office, called to launch a counterattack, instead prepared his departure. Mandelson's resignation letter started 'I can scarcely believe I am writing this letter . . . ' His disbelief was well-founded: Campbell had composed the text.

Cherie Blair rang Mandelson and invited him and his partner, Reinaldo Avila da Silva, to spend the night at Chequers. 'You will always be part of the family,' she told Mandelson. Her husband, meanwhile, advised his colleague to make friends in the Labour Party if he wanted to return to high office.

On Christmas Eve 1998 the *Sun* pictured Mandelson's head coming out of a turkey's bottom, under the headline 'Stuffed'. Again, Alastair Campbell's normally effective links with friendly journalists seemed to have failed.

The shaming of Mandelson was greeted with barely restrained rejoicing in much of the Labour Party. Never a popular man, the Hartlepool MP was resented for his influence over Blair and the power that relationship gave him. There was wild talk of a new beginning for New Labour, of how Ministers would get on better without his malevolent presence, of how the Government would be more harmonious.

One of the former Cabinet minister's more exalted admirers, Roy Jenkins, declared in January 1999 that Disraeli, Gladstone and Churchill – three of the most admired Prime Ministers of the past 150 years – had placed themselves under more compromising financial obligations and no one had ever thought of asking them to resign.

Mandelson, while not exactly donning sackcloth, struck a more humble tone, saying he would learn from his error and concentrate on serving his constituents in his seat of Hartlepool. The Deputy Prime Minister, John Prescott, seemed so concerned for his plight that he proposed sending Mandelson to South Africa to advise the ANC on a forthcoming election as part of his rehabilitation – only spoiling the plan when he said it should be with a one-way ticket.

Mandelson even developed an endearing, self-deprecatory turn of phrase. In June the now unchauffeured backbencher told the AEEU engineering union conference in Jersey: 'I have only just got out of the habit of jumping into the back of cars and wondering why they don't move off.' But behind the public bonhomie, Mandelson was working frantically to be brought back into government, pleading with the Prime Minister to give him a second chance.

Incredibly Blair did – within a year. He appointed Mandelson Northern Ireland Secretary in an October 1999 reshuffle. Blair was showing loyalty to a figure who had backed him against Brown in the 1994 Labour leadership battle; but to bring him back so swiftly was foolhardy. Another scandal was about to be played out.

To follow it forward, we need to return to 1997, when Peter Mandelson had been made what the press called 'Dome Minister' in June of that year. He thus became the Government's sole shareholder in a £758 million project destined to turn into a personal and political disaster.

Blair had resisted pressure to cancel an expensive folly inherited from the Tories when he put Mandelson in charge. The minister was following in the footsteps of his grandfather, Labour Cabinet minister Herbert Morrison, who in 1951 masterminded the hugely successful Festival of Britain. But Morrison's grandson, who had promised the Dome would 'blow your socks off', first had to raise sponsorship for the various 'zones' which were to fill the space within the gigantic tent.

While doing so Mandelson had been courted by and in turn courted the London-based Hinduja brothers who, through their Hinduja Foundation, donated £1 million to the so-called 'Faith Zone'. The Hindujas were at the same time under investigation in India for allegedly taking £6 million in bribes from a controversial 1986 arms deal between the New Delhi government and Swedish armaments manufacturer Bofors. It was to prove a costly relationship for Mandelson – and to some extent for Blair, who was videoed paying homage at a Diwali party hosted by the brothers. Europe Minister Keith Vaz was also ensnared and suspended from the Commons for a month. MPs found he had not fully declared links to the Hindujas, supplying 'misleading information' and blocking inquiries. Guilty of 'serious breaches' of the MPs' code of conduct, Vaz jumped before he was pushed and quit the Government after the June 2001 General Election.

In 1990, Srichand and Gopichand Hinduja had applied for UK passports but were refused. It was in February 1997, when the Tories were still in power, that the brothers had first expressed an interest in contributing to the Dome. Gopichand reapplied for a passport the following month and in November (by now Labour were in power) was granted one. In February 1998, Srichand reapplied. The same month the Hinduja Foundation made a verbal offer of £1 million to underwrite the Faith Zone, putting the offer in writing in June 1998. According to the junior Home Office minister, Mike O'Brien, Mandelson made a two-minute telephone call to ask if Srichand's passport application would be reconsidered following a change in government policy.

Srichand made a second application in October 1998, receiving a passport in March the following year. When donors to the Faith Zone were announced in June 1999, the Hindujas were on the list. Srichand Hinduja wrote to Mandelson about the prospects of a third brother, Prakash, in May 2000 and the minister passed his inquiry to the Home Office without endorsement.

Mandelson had been stripped of responsibility for the Dome when he resigned over the Robinson loan. It returned to bite him now, in January 2001, when he was at the Northern Ireland Office.

Liberal Democrat MP and compulsive sleuth, Norman Baker, received a written Home Office answer from the immigration minister, Barbara Roche, in the middle of the month confirming that Mandelson had inquired about passport applications by the Hinduja brothers. Mandelson was quoted in the *Observer* newspaper as saying that the applications had been dealt with by his private secretary. Media interest was aroused by what might prove a 'cash for passports' scandal. They scented blood: Mandelson's.

The day of the *Observer* scoop, 21 January 2001, Downing Street echoed the Mandelson line, saying he had made 'no direct contact'; but the Home Office press office mysteriously spoke of Mandelson's 'verbal inquiries'. Downing Street stonewalled the following day and Alastair Campbell stated that when the Hindujas asked Mandelson 'to endorse or support any application, he refused quite properly'. On the following Tuesday, however, the confident rebuttals of No. 10 evaporated and in an embarrassing U-turn under fierce questioning, Campbell admitted he had been wrong. Mandelson had made the call himself. The Northern Ireland Secretary maintained he had misled nobody, telling Channel 4 he had not been asked until then whether he put in the call himself.

But the game seemed to be up. Crucially, Home Secretary Jack Straw, a Cabinet member with no axe to grind against Mandelson, had told No. 10 that Mr O'Brien clearly remembered Mandelson's call. By misleading Blair and Campbell when the problem blew up at the weekend, Mandelson had committed the capital offence of hiding important facts from No. 10.

With Blair due to face a grilling on the issue at Prime Minister's Questions, Mandelson was required on 24 January 2001 to sign a second resignation letter, in which he admitted making misleading statements but once again denied wrongdoing. His departure was as swift as it was brutal. Campbell was blamed for official briefings to journalists questioning Mandelson's state of mind and describing the twice shamed ex-minister as 'slightly detached'. A *Guardian* report remarked that even Jesus came back from the dead only once.

There was no way back for Mandelson. Blair set up an inquiry into the affair under Sir Anthony Hammond QC, a former Treasury solicitor, prompting comparison with Dreyfus by friends of Mandelson's who feared the Government would seek to bury him. They were wrong. On 9 March 2001, five weeks after Mandelson quit the Government, Hammond, an establishment figure, produced a report that effectively cleared him of any wrongdoing, though questions remained about the former Northern Ireland Secretary's dealings with the wealthy Hindujas.

'I do not believe Mr Mandelson has tried to deceive anyone during the course of these events,' said Sir Anthony. Nor, he added, was there 'evidence of an improper relationship' with the Hindujas. The report concluded that he did not 'make representations' on behalf of S P Hinduja – disclosing, however, that he saw classified MI6 material on the brothers before accepting their sponsorship. In the opinion of some commentators, a Scottish 'not proven' verdict, instead of the resounding 'not guilty' claimed by Mandelson, might have been more appropriate. Hammond criticised the lack of proper records, and admitted, 'I have been unable to come to any definite conclusion about the suggestion that Mr Mandelson wanted his contact with Mr O'Brien kept private.'

Mandelson declared, 'I do not desire a return to government,' and insisted he had been vindicated. 'In sum, Sir Anthony's report establishes that I did not lie; that I did not deceive; that I did not set out to mislead. I am grateful to Sir Anthony for clearing my name and restoring my reputation. This was indeed a muddle rather than a misrepresentation and I would like to say how much I regret the part I played in creating this muddle.'

There was no way back into the Cabinet for Mandelson – though a European Commission post may yet be his – but he appears at the time of writing to retain an influence over the Prime Minister. An unbreakable cord seemingly links the two north-east England MPs and keepers of the Third Way flame. Mandelson speaks to Blair most days, acting as an unofficial counsellor. When Cherie Blair was on the rack [see pp.434–43] over Peter Foster's role in buying two Bristol flats, it was Mandelson to whom the Blairs turned.

Mandelson also uses his freedom from red boxes to play a wider political role, organising conferences and touring the world. Two trips have been funded by Asia House, a London-based institute partly financed by the Hindujas. He is also making money. In June 2001, two days before polling day, it emerged that he was to join a new advertising agency, Clemmow Hornby Inge, set up by two executives he helped appoint to run Labour's multi-million-pound advertising campaign. The ex-minister had been invited by one of the founders, Johnny Hornby, to lecture the staff of his old agency shortly after he quit as Trade Secretary. Hornby was a brother-in-law of Robert Harris who made the introductions. Such are the intersecting circles of the New Labour tribe and its friends.

Tony Blair's remark – that he knew he would have fully transformed the Labour Party when it learned to love Peter Mandelson – became famous. For the Prime Minister, Labour's transformation remains incomplete.

GEOFFREY ROBINSON – 1998, 2001

'Money, money, money, it's a rich man's world'

The jibe 'champagne socialist' fell flat when aimed at ministers in Tony Blair's first Labour administration. Not because of a widespread dislike of fizzy white wine, indeed a glass of bubbly was the favoured tipple of many – but because so few would describe themselves as socialists. One of the exceptions was an amiable politician who enjoyed champagne and was rich enough to buy bottles for everybody else.

Geoffrey Robinson, a multi-millionaire industrialist turned MP worth an estimated £80 to £100 million at the peak of his bank balance, was a successful capitalist who liked to think of himself as a socialist put in charge of the nation's chequebook. Appointed Paymaster-General in May 1997 as part of Gordon Brown's Treasury team, wealthy enough not to need to draw a ministerial salary, he seemed to an incoming New Labour government almost too good to be true. He was.

Forced to resign after a secret £373,000 home loan to Blair's lieutenant Peter Mandelson was exposed, Robinson was later suspended from the Commons for three weeks over past undeclared financial links with crooked tycoon Robert Maxwell.

Friends said Robinson was too generous, even naive, and allowed himself to be exploited by senior New Labour figures, particularly in the Blair camp, who later turned on this Brownite. Critics, and they weren't confined to the diehard Blairites, pointed to a tangled web of business dealings which opened up Labour to repeated charges of sleaze. He was to face a police inquiry, a Department of Trade and Industry investigation and four probes by fellow MPs. Robinson was buried under a welter of allegations.

Born in Sheffield, Geoffrey Robinson won a scholarship to a London school. After Cambridge and Yale, Robinson did his

National Service in the intelligence corps before Harold Wilson recruited him as a researcher in Transport House, Labour's headquarters. Very bright, Robinson moved to British Leyland, the troubled state-run motor industry, and by the age of 34, was chief executive of Jaguar. He stood for Labour in Coventry North West, winning a tricky 1976 by-election that preserved Labour's slender Commons majority. A glittering future in politics beckoned. Yet Robinson, with Labour out of power from 1979, preferred the allure of business and concentrated on making his fortune, buying the *New Statesman* political weekly and a seat on the board of Coventry City football club along the way.

When Labour leader John Smith died in 1994, Robinson, now one of the richest members of the House, was persuaded by Brown to play a wider role in Labour's preparations for office. Robinson became Labour's Paymaster-General before he played the role in government. The MP's apartment in the Grosvenor House Hotel, overlooking Hyde Park, became home to the Brownites. When not watching football on TV, they planned how they would run the Treasury.

Robinson commissioned and paid for £300,000 of confidential research from accountants on tax policies, including a £5 billion windfall tax on privatised power and water utilities, and it was in the Grosvenor House that Brown announced he would grant independence over interest rates to the Bank of England. Blair and his family holidayed in Robinson's Tuscan villa and his flat in Cannes on the French Mediterranean, enjoying his hospitality. And, during a dinner in the Grosvenor House apartment on 23 May 1996, Robinson and Peter Mandelson first discussed the loan that was to cost both their ministerial posts in December 1998.

All had looked set fair for Robinson in May 1997. The new Paymaster-General joked that he was the man from the Treasury, there to help. Brown believed he could 'solve the unsolvable' and Blair regarding him as the 'unconventional minister' with a Midas touch. The calm was first disturbed in November 1997 with the public disclosure that he was the beneficiary of a tax-saving offshore trust based in Guernsey. The Orion Trust had been set up by the aptly named Joska Bourgeois, a Belgian national resident in Switzerland. Bourgeois had taken a shine to the MP when he was at Jaguar and she imported cars. She bequeathed her fortune, including a twenty-bedroom Lutyens mansion in Hampshire and the flat in Cannes, to Robinson on her death in 1994.

The minister protested that it was a blind trust beyond his control. He had told Terry Burns, the Treasury's Permanent Secretary, of its existence, he said, and been assured it complied with the ministerial code of conduct. Robinson's version of events was disputed and the damage was done. Labour was committed to plugging tax loopholes, yet here was a well-off Treasury minister benefiting from a tax-saving offshore fund. To make matters worse, Robinson was poised to announce plans to reduce the amount middle-earners could put into tax-free investments by replacing TESSA and PEP share schemes with more limited ISAs.

As Robinson reeled from the offshore trust row, he was hit by a fresh scandal: his links with Maxwell, the former *Daily Mirror* publisher who plundered £400 million from pension funds before he drowned in 1991. Robinson had been a director and chairman of a number of Maxwell companies from the mid-1980s and faced accusations ranging from asset stripping to accepting an undeclared £200,000 as well as failing to list all of his interests in the MPs' register. He denied receiving the £200,000 in 1990 for management services provided to A M Lock, a subsidiary of Maxwell's Hollis Industries conglomerate. A report by the Commons Standards and Privileges Committee published later in November 1998 accepted assurances that he never accepted the payment but Robinson was still required to apologise to the Commons for failing to register four directorships between 1984 and 1992. The 54-second apology he duly made was considered excessively brief.

Robinson was under severe pressure. Blair was only persuaded to reprieve his holiday host and Paymaster-General in the July 1998 reshuffle by the intervention of Gordon Brown who pleaded his case. Robinson failed to attend a No. 10 appointment with Blair at which the PM intended to sack the minister. When Robinson did not turn up, Blair meekly backed down.

No. 10 spin chief Alastair Campbell, turning up the spin cycle, briefed heavily against Robinson. But no one, including Campbell, expected the minister's eventual departure from office to be so spectacular. In December 1998, Robinson was forced to resign along with Peter Mandelson, the Trade and Industry Secretary, when the secret £373,000 home loan was exposed. Mandelson maintained that Robinson had offered him the money.

In *The Unconventional Minister*, his memoirs, Robinson is adamant that Mandelson was 'looking for a loan' when the pair met for dinner in May 1996. 'There is almost the implication that I put him up to it. I find this most objectionable. Intentionally or not, Peter has contributed to the image that certain sections of the press have tried to create of me buying influence, power or even office.'

If Robinson had somehow survived the home loan scandal, he would probably have been knocked down by another blow. The allegations were multiplying. There were more stories about his dealings with Maxwell. TransTec, a car components firm he had set up in 1991, had collapsed and been put into receivership on Christmas Eve 1999, and Robinson was accused of hiding a disastrous £11 million compensation claim from Ford. A DTI inquiry was launched. It concluded in February 2001 that Robinson, who had resigned from TransTec's board in 1997, was never told about the company's crippling debt. West Midlands police looked into claims that TransTec had fraudulently obtained government grants, but decided not to proceed with any action.

Robinson claimed he was vindicated and was the victim of 'dirty tricks'. Then the inquiry into the £200,000 Maxwell cheque was reopened. In an illuminating biography of Robinson, investigative journalist Tom Bower published evidence in the form of an invoice stamped 'Paid' and sent from Robinson's address. In May 2001 the Labour backbencher was criticised by the Standards and Privileges Committee for failing to provide 'full answers' and withholding information on the £200,000 plus failing to register another financial interest.

Robinson declared he was 'determined to prove I did not receive the payment'. MPs granted him three months to do so. He failed. In October 2001 the former Paymaster-General was suspended from the Commons for three weeks. He apologised for 'inadvertently' misleading the Standards and Privileges Committee and giving less than 'full and frank' answers to questions. His Commons colleagues, however, decided not to back the finding of the Parliamentary Standards Commissioner, Elizabeth Filkin. She had concluded that it 'would be stretching coincidence beyond the bounds of credulity' to claim there was no payment. The MPs' failure to back her finding saved Robinson a back tax bill of £80,000 plus interest.

The disputed cheque had been drawn on the Pergamon AGB company owned by Maxwell and transferred to a bank where Robinson and TransTec both had accounts. Robinson said it was his engineering firm TransTec, not he personally, that was owed £200,000 for management services to Lock, one of Maxwell's companies. 'The money was owed and the company was asked to pay it, but I completely deny that either I or any company associated with me either directly or indirectly received it.'

Shortly before Christmas 2002 Robinson was caught up in a bizarre incident. Police searched his home in Godalming, Surrey after a wrap of white powder was found on the floor of a police van when the MP was arrested for driving his Jaguar 'erratically' on the A454 in Walsall. He had been stopped after watching Coventry City (he had given his chauffeur the day off to go to a pantomime, he said). Laboratory tests showed that the powder was cocaine but there was nothing to link it to the former minister. Robinson pleaded guilty in August 2003 to failing to provide a breath test, receiving a £1,000 fine and a twelve-month driving ban.

Robinson is aware that he will always be remembered as the minister who loaned Peter Mandelson £373,000; the house deal overshadowed anything he achieved in the Treasury. He also protests the innocent nature of his dealings with Maxwell, insisting he did not receive the £200,000. Heavily out of pocket after the collapse of TransTec, and with his political reputation in shreds, Robinson once mused that he would be considerably richer if he had stayed out of politics. The days when he had enough in the bank to try to buy the media tycoon Rupert Murdoch's apartment in St James's are long gone.

JEFFREY ARCHER – 2001

Prisoner FF8282

A character so over-the-top, so far-fetched, so outrageous in a political thriller might well have readers throwing down the book and protesting 'Come on! no one will believe this.' Which is what makes the extraordinary story of the irrepressible Jeffrey Archer so much stranger than fiction and without doubt more interesting than the novels he sold in their millions, amassing a huge fortune along the way – though that too is part of his tale.

It is the true story of a life of fantasy and deception culminating in a four-year jail sentence for perjury and perversion of the course of justice. Lord Archer of Weston-super-Mare, a former MP, former Deputy Chairman of the Conservative Party and darling of Conservative activists, ennobled by John Major in 1992, was a rascal who demonstrated the qualities of a human rubber ball. It is difficult at the time of writing to see how even one so irrepressible as he could bounce back from a public humiliation such as his final jail sentence. But no doubt he is trying.

In turn deceitful, charming, mendacious, funny, pushy, resilient, tactless, gullible, bullying, reckless, calculating, naive, self-obsessed, quixotic, shameless, Archer was corrupt and corrupted others. With his Krug champagne and shepherd's pie parties at Tory conferences, or his Thames-side penthouse flat with its grand view of the Houses of Parliament, he played the genial host to the cream of Conservatism, captains of industry, luvvies, Archbishops of Canterbury and a media either fascinated by the knave or fooled into believing he was a jolly good chap. Guests seeking the way to the lavatory in Alembic House were directed by this dapper little man barking instructions to go past the Picasso and turn left at the Matisse.

Archer could also be menacing, threatening writs against those he feared – quite rightly as it turned out – to be delving too deeply into his affairs. As many journalists and others know, he was always ready to deploy the 'I know your boss' line to deter inquisitors. In this case he really was telling the truth: he did know their bosses.

But finally the contradictions in his life were such, the scale of his lies so shocking, that Archer became the author of his own downfall. Sheridan Morley, one of his oldest friends, put it like this: 'The best way to think about Jeffrey is to treat him as if he comes from another planet. He will drive over a cliff and then be amazed that he's falling. He thinks he's Peter Pan, that he'll never die. Everything he does he thinks is going to be all right in the end.'

Truth and Archer ceased meeting more than occasionally long before Mr Justice Potts sentenced the peer to four years' imprisonment at the Old Bailey on 19 July 2001. The blurring of fact and fiction and the genius he showed for embellishment are the story of his own life.

His wife, the Cambridge academic, Mary Archer, understated memorably – yet put her finger on an important truth about him – when she said he had a gift 'for inaccurate precis'. For Archer's stories were not plucked from a vacuum: though not always, there was sometimes a grain, sometimes a fair measure, of truth within his distortion, and in many fields he really did have solid achievements to boast about. At various points in his life he has been an athlete, a councillor, a policeman, a fundraiser, an MP, a peer, an auctioneer, a best-selling novelist, a playwright, an adulterer and a jailbird. Among the few consistent threads running through all this, however, are a hunger for fame, a talent to entertain and a habit of outrageous deception.

Michael Crick called his superb biography of Archer *Stranger Than Fiction* after uncovering a breathtaking number of fibs. Some were small lies and, on their own, of little consequence. Why did Archer bother to claim he was born in Somerset when he was born in central London, near the City Road in 1940? Sometimes it has seemed as though Archer finds the truth insufficiently challenging to a restless spirit in search of risk.

Perhaps, though, it was understandable when the then aspiring politician, anxiously climbing a greasy social as well as political pole, painted his father as a war hero rather than the bigamist he was, a man who fled to New York on his dead employer's passport in 1914 to avoid arrest for fraud. Many people have misled employers about their qualifications but few on the industrial scale practised by Archer. He attended a little-known Somerset private school called Wellington yet led people to believe it was the more famous Wellington College in Berkshire. Applying to train as a teacher, his letter of application claimed he possessed six O levels and three A levels rather than the three O levels and no A levels he gained before leaving (the other) Wellington.

One CV listed a year at Sandhurst military college and an army physical training instruction course, though his apparent attendance is still a surprise to Sandhurst and the Ministry of Defence. The three A levels that never were secured him a place on a one-year diploma at Brasenose College in Oxford. But thereafter he repeatedly gave the impression he had completed a full degree course.

Later, teaching physical education at private Dover College in Kent, Archer turned up for a school photograph wearing a graduate gown though he had never received any degree or attended any graduation for which he might have worn it. Elected to the Greater London Council in the 1960s, Archer offered to fill in the expenses forms of colleagues in return for a 10 per cent cut. He was also accused of fiddling his expenses while fundraising for the United Nations Association. And there was his arrest in Toronto, Canada, in 1975 for allegedly shoplifting three suits. Though Archer was released without charge, his unofficial biographer, Crick, savages his subject's claimed explanation that a mistake was behind the charge.

But Archer did meet the Beatles and enlist the support of the Fab Four for one of his fundraising drives. He did win an Oxford athletics blue (even if his false starts and eligibility were queried). He did briefly make the England team. And, in 1966, he did marry Mary Weedon who went on to become an expert in solar energy and who would be his most trenchant public champion.

Elected Tory MP for Louth in Lincolnshire in December 1969, Archer was then the youngest member of the House of Commons. A glittering political career seemed to lie ahead. He was brash, he was bright and if he stuck to politics he might have been all right; but he ran straight into his first big fall. Gambling on making millions by investing in Aquablast, a Canadian company manufacturing a gadget that supposedly reduced petrol consumption in cars, Archer borrowed heavily. Like so many get-rich-quick schemes it was an illusion and a fraud; the rising political star fell to earth heavily with debts of half a million pounds.

Fighting bankruptcy he resigned his Commons seat in 1974 and lost the family's house when, with one son to feed and another on the way, he and Mary were forced to sell up. Down and apparently out, Archer turned to writing in an effort to clear his debts. The result was *Not a Penny More, Not a Penny Less*, a novel slated by the critics but loved by a public who were to make Archer a multi-millionaire.

It was an unlikely success story. Archer had bounced back. The books flowed out and the money flowed in. Now a successful author, he became a major draw on the constituency rubber-chicken circuit, an entertaining if hammy speaker capable (we have witnessed it) of a truly mean turn with a gavel, raising thousands and thousands of pounds as an auctioneer for the Tory Party and causes he supported.

Margaret Thatcher liked his energy and admired the way he had bounced back. Mindful of his popularity with the grassroots, she made Archer Deputy Chairman of the Conservatives in 1985 against the better judgement of many of her Cabinet. William Whitelaw, for one, regarded him as 'an accident waiting to happen'. Mr Whitelaw did not have to wait long. Archer was accused in October 1986 by the *News of the World* of paying money to a prostitute. 'Tory boss Archer pays off vice girl' made for a sensational story.

The Sunday tabloid had secretly photographed Archer's friend Michael Stacpoole, a PR executive who collaborated on fund-raising deals, on a platform at Victoria station handing £2,000 in £50 notes in a brown paper envelope to Monica Coghlan, a woman who travelled from north-west England to London to ply her trade at weekends. It was a classic tabloid 'sting': the paper paid Coghlan to ring Archer and tell him journalists were asking questions about their session. Archer admitted giving money to Coghlan yet denied ever meeting her, implausibly insisting he had hoped to help her leave the country because of her claim that she was being hounded by journalists. It was, maintained Archer, an 'error of judgement', but no more than that.

A few days later the *Daily Star* went further than the *News of the World*, asserting (on the say-so of Coghlan's nephew) that Archer had slept with the prostitute. Archer, it was said, paid £70 for sex with her in a seedy hotel, making his intentions known to her shortly before 1 a.m. by flashing the lights of his Jaguar just as she was about to climb into a car with another client. He quit his Tory post and sued.

And that is the point. *He sued.* Like Oscar Wilde a century before, or Jonathan Aitken a decade later, Archer might have been left alone if he had been prepared to let matters lie. He was now seeking to enrich himself at the expense of a newspaper which had reported the truth. This self-destructive unwillingness to accept a stand-off when in the wrong is often overlooked by sympathisers of all three men. In Archer's and Aitken's case, too, it has also been overlooked by those surprised either at the severity of the sentences in the criminal cases that followed, or by the fact that the Crown Prosecution Service pressed charges for perjury in the first place. It is perfectly true, of course, that guilty men in the dock regularly lie in order to defend themselves, yet a charge of perjury rarely follows their conviction. But Archer and Aitken were not (at this stage) in the dock. They were not defending themselves. They were the plaintiffs. They were using the law to attack someone else. They were putting other (innocent) men in the dock by lying under oath. That is what so angers the law.

Archer was originally alleged to have met Coghlan on the night of 9 September but the *Star* admitted an error and at the trial said it had been 8 September. Archer produced alibis for both. On the 8th, he said, he had dinner at Le Caprice in St James's Place, one of his favourite restaurants, then met film agent Terence Baker. Baker testified in the 1987 trial that he was driven back to his Camberwell home in South London around the time Archer was accused of being with Coghlan. The second alibi, for the 9th, was supplied by Ted Francis, a TV producer, who signed a statement detailing how on the night in question the pair dined at Sambuca, an Italian restaurant near Sloane Square. Francis said they met to discuss TV and film projects, and he had left for home at 9.45 p.m. to take a business call from the USA. Around 11.20 p.m., Francis added, he spoke to Archer over the phone, thus extending the alibi to near midnight. He had at first thought (he was later to say) that he was covering up an affair.

The libel trial was described as the best free show in London. One of the best known and most popular politicians in Britain, a man whose blockbusters were read by huge numbers of people, was going to court (as Archer would have it) to uphold his honour against accusations that he had slept with a prostitute. The stakes could not be higher. With the date in question now 8 September, Francis's statement relating to the 9th was irrelevant. Archer produced a diary showing he was with Baker on the 8th and his friend testified that the pair had indeed dined at Le Caprice, Archer had been driving him home at the time it was alleged he had been in the Albion, a hotel in Victoria, London, with Coghlan.

Coghlan was not an entirely convincing witness. Admitting that she could not be sure the client in question was Archer, she said the man she was with on the night had a scarred back. Archer's legal team insisted he did not fit that description. Coghlan was angry that the *Star* had relied on the testimony of her nephew whom, it emerged, she had not spoken to at the time. But the star of the libel trial, the absolute diva, turned out not to be Archer or Coghlan or Baker, or the redundant statement from Francis, but Mary Archer, his long-suffering wife. She conjured up an image of a happy family life, a devoted couple shuttling between their Thames apartment and the Old Vicarage (the former home of the poet Rupert Brooke) in Grantchester just outside Cambridge where she taught chemistry. With her husband's reputation on the line, she had now come riding to the rescue.

She captivated the judge, Mr Justice Caulfield, who in a summing up still capable of making the legal establishment wince, all but instructed the jury to find in the Tory's favour. With such a vision of 'elegance, fragrance and radiance' as Mary Archer before them, he asked, how could they believe that Jeffrey Archer was 'in need of cold, unloving, rubber-insulated sex in a seedy hotel'?

The jury obliged, and found in Archer's favour. He was awarded £500,000, emerging triumphant on the steps of the court in July 1987 with the fragrant Mary to declare that justice had been done. A wronged man had been cleared. Emboldened, he stepped up his work for the Conservative Party, increasing his velocity of circulation round the local constituency circuit. Now regularly on television to offer his assessment of the issues of the day, he resumed his writing: television adaptations and serialisations adding to his wealth.

And the ever-generous Archer grandly announced that the £500,000 libel damages would be donated to charity. Only at his 2001 perjury hearing was it disclosed that the sum he actually did give away was £130,000. He held on to the rest.

When Margaret Thatcher was ousted at the end of 1990 and succeeded by the Huntingdon MP, John Major, Archer found himself at the heart of what the media called an 'East Anglian mafia' around the new Prime Minister, with whom he was quick to consolidate his friendship. Mr Major needed friends badly. After he had scraped home in the 1992 General Election he rewarded Archer with a life peerage and even considered making him a minister in David Mellor's Department of National Heritage. Wiser counsels prevailed, but the (now) Lord Archer of Weston-super-Mare had been triumphantly rehabilitated.

He loved his new title and, basking in his status, continued writing, politicking and charity fundraising with gusto. Archer visited several Conservative Associations and made speeches. It is rumoured that horrified Conservative Association chairmen and presidents reported being taken aside by the lord after his performances and asked to write personally to the Prime Minister in praise of all the trouble he had taken to grace them with his oratorical skills.

But Willie Whitelaw had been right once and was about to be proved right again. Archer remained an accident waiting to happen. Another crash was just around the corner.

In January 1994 he bought 50,000 shares in Anglia TV shortly before a takeover bid sent them soaring, netting him a £77,219 profit. A shrewd piece of business or insider dealing? Mary Archer was a non-executive director of Anglia. Archer once more protested his innocence, insisting he had bought the shares on behalf of a friend. But the friend turned out to have no money, nor any record of buying or selling shares, let alone receiving sensationally good stock market tips. He claimed he had received the tip at a dinner party hosted by Nick Lloyd, editor of the *Daily Express*. A puzzled Lloyd said the dinner party had taken place *after* Archer's Anglia purchase. Mary Archer claimed she had no involvement in the deal and an inquiry ordered by Michael Heseltine, President of the Board of Trade, who had been enraged by Archer's behaviour, cleared him of insider dealing.

His lawyers admitted their client had made a mistake but denied any wrong-doing. Archer, tipped in the press as a future chairman of the Tory Party, was once again viewed as a liability. Tony Blair's parliamentary avalanche of May 1997 meant that one door to disaster – government office – was now closed; but with the new government's introduction of elected mayors, another opened. The occupier of an apartment with one of the finest views of the capital decided he wanted to be London's first elected mayor.

With typical enthusiasm and hyperbole Archer threw himself into the task first of securing the Tory nomination and then of winning at the ballot box. He assembled a high-powered campaign team and presented himself as a man of the people, targeting ethnic minority communities in particular as a source of votes untapped by rival candidates. Guests at his penthouse tell of being taken aside by Archer and steered, arm on shoulder, to the plate-glass picture windows, where he would point to buildings he did not like on the skyline. '*That* will go,' he would bark, 'and *that*, when I am mayor.'

But a ghost from the past was waiting. Ted Francis, the TV producer who had supplied the peer with a redundant alibi for the Coghlan libel trial, had fallen out with his old friend and decided to take revenge. Following the libel victory Archer had promised to put £25,000 into Francis's £100,000 TV project on Enid Blyton, but when Francis went to collect the cheque it was for only £12,000. 'I don't expect to see this back, you know,' said Archer, who made it clear the money was a gift rather than a loan or investment.

The reduction, however, soured their relationship. And it comprehensively curdled at one of Archer's parties. As Francis chatted to an actress, Archer breezed by and told her: 'You want to watch this man, you know. I lent him £20,000 once and I'm still waiting to get the money back.' Humiliated, Francis approached the publicist, Max Clifford, and in return for £12,000 from the *News of the World* for his story, which he used to buy a second-hand car to replace his old Audi, Francis organised a sting against his former friend – because, he said, he 'disapproved of the idea' of Archer becoming Mayor of London.

Clifford approached the *News of the World*, the paper that originally linked Archer to Coghlan, with a secret tape-recording of a conversation Francis had contrived with Archer, in which Francis told the novelist he had been approached by journalists about the alibi.

'You said, "tell them we had dinner here, didn't we?" I said "Yes fine, if you say". Do you remember?' Francis asked Archer. Archer replied: 'We've got to be careful, Ted. We don't want to end up in a court of law with this.'

The newspaper's subsequent scoop in November 1999, revealing that Archer had lied in his 1987 libel trial, began his downfall. Archer was forced to pull out of the race to be Mayor of London. The Tory leader William Hague, declaring there was no other course of action open to the man he had only recently applauded as a candidate of 'probity and integrity,' was made to look a complete idiot. Hague was later to remark that he had come close to resigning his leadership of the Conservative Party at this point.

Archer's expulsion from his party followed in February 2000. His arrest the following April came next. A disbelieving press and public smacked its lips at the prospect of yet another Archer spectacular.

So perhaps, and in his strange way, did Lord Archer. It did not seem to occur to him to go quietly to the dock. The self-proclaimed great storyteller pushed chutzpah (and the law of contempt) to its limit by not only writing but starring in a play staged just before the trial, about a prominent man who defends himself in a case revolving around whether the character had lied about a sexual relationship. The play was called *The Accused* and opened in September 2000 at The Theatre Royal, Windsor. In another Archeresque touch, each night's audience was asked at the end to vote on the guilt or innocence of the supposedly fictional figure. Archer, to his satisfaction, was found not guilty on the opening night.

The run-up to the trial was to take a sad twist when in April 2001, two weeks before it opened, Coghlan was killed in a car accident in Yorkshire when her Fiesta was hit by a Jaguar driven by a fleeing armed robber. Only two people will have known for certain whether Archer and Coghlan slept together, and one of them – Coghlan – is dead.

The Old Bailey trial opened in May 2001 with Archer, now 61, facing seven charges: four of perverting the course of justice, two counts of perjury and one of dishonesty. Next to him in the dock was Francis, facing a single charge of perverting the course of justice. In sharp contrast to the scene of marital bliss presented in 1987, the press in 2001 was agog at tales of Archer's philandering with Andrina Colquhoun, a former debutante and personal assistant: an affair which had been going on at the time when Mr Justice Caulfield was inviting the jury's incredulity at the very possibility of extramarital sex.

Francis recalled: 'He said, "What were you doing on September 9 last year?" I said, "God, I don't know," – bearing in mind this was four months later. I said, "I don't know, I could check in my diary," and he said, "could we have been having dinner? I want you to do me a favour and say we were having a dinner. I was having dinner with somebody else on that night but it would embarrass me with Mary. So will you say it was with you and not with Andrina?'

Francis went on: 'I was a bit reluctant to do it at first. I said, "Yes, but if it's going to end in divorce or anything, I'm not going to commit perjury for you." I knew that he and Andrina were close and I connected it automatically with that. I guess there had been strains on his marriage from his relationship with Andrina.'

Every bit as explosive – arguably more so – was the testimony of Angela Peppiatt, Archer's personal assistant and secretary for two years before the 1987 libel trial. Enjoying the trust of her boss, she bought presents for the women in his life; Archer had once given his wife and Colquhoun identical sets of jewellery. Peppiatt said Archer and Colquhoun – he calling her Roonette, she calling him Moon – had started their affair in 1979 and ended it after the libel victory.

Peppiatt's fatal thrust, however, was the disclosure that shortly before the libel trial Archer had asked her to produce a fake diary to account for his movements, filling in a blank 1986 diary with a list of names he provided. He then delivered this to his solicitors. Peppiatt said that the fake diary was used in the libel trial but she had kept the genuine diary when she left his employment in December 1987, copying the new diary pages before and after she wrote the extra entries. 'I was seriously concerned about becoming involved in a deception,' she told the court. But, worried about losing her job, she complied.

Something of a fanatic in the business of keeping documents, fourteen years on she was able to produce the crucial appointments diary – much smaller than the version Archer used in the libel trial. Colquhoun confirmed that there had been an affair, and confirmed too that Archer's excuse to Francis, that he was having dinner with her, was bogus. Colquhoun said she had been in Greece at the time and had a stamp in her passport to prove it.

Enter Lady Archer who told the Old Bailey she knew of his affair with Colquhoun, adding that he 'could hardly have been the first aspiring politician to have had the first fling'. As in the libel trial so in the perjury trial, she stood by her man. But the picture she painted was very different from her work of fourteen years earlier. 'I think we have explored the further reaches of "for better or worse" – far more than some other couples,' said Lady Archer.

Archer was doomed. His alibi for 9 September 1987 had been destroyed. Although not part of the perjury trial, the 8 September 1987 alibi, the one deployed, was also in shreds. In addition to the diary evidence presented by Peppiatt, grave doubts had been raised as to whether Terence Baker had been in Le Caprice that night. Before the case went to court, senior TV executive Nick Elliott had signed an affadivit saying that Baker, who died in 1991, had admitted to him that he did not dine with Archer in Le Caprice; but that he had been pressed by Archer to say he did, to cover up an affair.

The case gripped Courtroom 8 for seven weeks and the proceedings were followed around the world. With an international audience watching, Archer, the great storyteller and perpetual seeker of attention, broke a lifetime habit and decided to remain silent. His legal team was left to fight his corner.

On 19 July 2001 the jury returned: Archer was guilty of six of the seven counts of perjury and perversion of the course of justice; Francis was acquitted of the single charge. Mr Justice Potts told him: 'These charges represent as serious an offence of perjury as I have had experience of and have been able to find in the books.' As Archer sat impassively, Lady Archer unflinching in the public gallery, the judge strained credulity by declaring: 'Sentencing you, Lord Archer, gives me no pleasure at all.' It had been, he added, 'an extremely distasteful case'. He sent Archer down for four years with an expectation of serving two if he behaved well.

A clamour began for Archer to be stripped of his title. 'There is no precedent for a life peerage being removed. I would think treason would be the only exception,' said an exasperated House of Lords spokesman. John Major commented: 'I am deeply, deeply sorry at the outcome. I hope at this difficult time everyone will also remember the many kind and generous things Jeffrey has done.' Peter Bottomley, a Tory MP and a friend of Archer, called him a rubber ball – with 'ways of bouncing back that most of us would envy'.

Other former friends of Lord Archer's – Tories who had never thought it beneath them to be seen at his parties when his parties were fashionable – suffered a curious amnesia about the society they once kept. All at once (it seemed) an amusing chap whom they may have recognised as a bit of an embroiderer, but in whom we had seen such tendencies as more lovable than culpable, was readjusted in a thousand recollections. They had always known he was a rogue; they had had a bad feeling about that man from the start; well, yes, they did accept the occasional invitation to lunch in his penthouse – but only to be polite. Thank heavens, they said *we* had kept our distance.

Michael Crick, Archer's biographer of some years' standing by this time, could be forgiven his exasperation. Much of what was now being greeted with shock and amazement had been carefully set out and fully backed up in his book – yet the world had gone on believing in the man.

Peter Hill, the *Daily Star*'s editor, demanded compensation and relished this unusual opportunity for his newspaper to occupy the moral high ground. 'He is a proven liar, a cheat and a chancer, a man so arrogant that he thought he was above the law,' gloated Hill. 'Now finally he has got what he deserved.'

Prisoner FF8282 was taken to high-security Belmarsh Prison in south-east London, normally used to house terrorist suspects, to start his sentence. Initially classed as Category D, low risk and suitable for an open prison, he was upgraded – or downgraded depending on your view – to Category C after Scotland Yard launched an inquiry into allegations that millions of pounds were missing from a Kurdish fundraising campaign he had masterminded. Archer was transferred to Wayland Prison in Norfolk, a Category C institution, but after his wife protested his innocence over the fund he was transferred two months later to North Sea Camp open prison in Lincolnshire. An audit by accountants KPMG cleared Archer of siphoning off Kurdish funds. A massive discrepancy between the amounts supposedly raised and the amounts actually disbursed was explained (it seems) by the way Archer had inflated his own achievements in collecting for the charity.

On his first day in prison he was said to have been seen shaking the hand of Great Train Robber Ronnie Biggs and within two days of being sentenced Archer was allowed out under guard to attend the funeral of his mother. In yet another (this time sad) example of the twists that had kept occurring all his life, Lola Hayne, his 87-year-old mother, had died during the judge's summing up in the libel trial.

Archer, unusually, spurned the spotlight when his appeal was heard on 22 July 2002 in the Royal Courts of Justice. It turned out to be a good call. The journey from North Sea Camp jail in Lincolnshire to London takes some four hours in the back of a prison van and, if unsuccessful, another four hours back. It took three judges just 110 seconds to dismiss Archer's appeal against his conviction for perjury and perverting the course of justice.

Not that he was to serve his time without attracting attention. It emerged that when behind bars he had signed a lucrative three-book deal with the publishers Macmillan.

Later he used a 'home' visit to attend a drinks party at the home of East Anglian neighbour Gillian Shepherd, a senior Tory MP and former Education Secretary. Archer was allowed out of jail to work in Lincoln's Theatre Royal, helping on community and charity projects before returning to be locked up at night. An inquiry was launched when it was discovered he had enjoyed a restaurant lunch with a female police officer and a senior prison officer during a break from the theatre. The warder resigned, on health grounds, and the chief constable ordered an inquiry into the police officer's behaviour.

An October High Court hearing announced Archer had paid £2.5 million to the *Daily Star*, the original £500,000 damages plus £1.8 million in costs and interest. Archer immediately bounced back by publishing a diary of his three weeks in Belmarsh. Serialised in the *Daily Mail*, it claimed he had contemplated suicide and argued that his writing on drugs and prisoners would spark a national debate.

'I came in very naive about heroin, cocaine and crack. I am now becoming well informed,' said Archer. Complaints were made that he had broken prison rules by identifying fellow inmates with whom he rubbed shoulders. Archer made it clear that he believed any punishment he was likely to receive for speaking out was a price worth paying if it helped improve the drug problem. David Blunkett, the Home Secretary, himself no slouch at attracting press attention, was reported to be 'driven up the wall' by Archer's capacity to thumb his nose at the prison service.

Archer was released on 21 July 2003 after serving two years of his four-year sentence. To the parole service he gave as his address the Thames flat where he had so often entertained prime ministers and prelates. He issued a statement saying: 'I wish to thank my wife Mary and my sons, William and James, for their unwavering and unstinting support during this unhappy period in my life. I should also like to thank the many friends who took the trouble to visit me in prison, as well as countless members of the public who sent letters, cards and gifts.'

On 18 September he agreed to deliver a lecture in Oxford's Randolph Hotel, at a seminar organised by the Howard League for Penal Reform. Critics pointed out that this was the man who at a party conference had urged a Tory Home Secretary to 'stand and deliver' tougher justice.

In his defence, however, it may be worth observing that as a politician his tone had been colourful rather than hateful. He had never been excessively negative or personal in politics. Indeed it might be doubted whether Jeffrey Archer was ever seriously interested in policy at all.

Crick is incredulous at the way a trio of Tory leaders – Thatcher, Major and Hague – were taken in by this man. As he said at the time, 'Any one of those three was surely aware of all the evidence that Archer was a deeply dishonest man, a deeply untrustworthy man, and a man of appalling judgement. And yet they were prepared to go along with him. The answers to all of that are complex. The Tory faithful loved him, he was very good at raising money for the party, and when it came to being Mayor of London he was really the only person who looked like he might have a possibility of winning for the Conservatives.'

Instead of winning, he ended up by reminding voters of the sleaze that had tarnished eighteen years of Tory rule. Two prominent Conservatives, Jonathan Aitken and Archer, had now been imprisoned for perjury. Beyond reasonable doubt he is a scoundrel.

But Archer did brighten up politics, and the remark that he had added to the gaiety of nations, though at his downfall it became a media cliché, struck a chord. 'We all invent ourselves to some degree,' remarked his friend Barry Humphries, the creator of Dame Edna Everage: 'Jeffrey just took it a little further than most.'

JOHN PRESCOTT – 2001

'John is John' – The Rumble in Rhyl

In a General Election campaign distinguished only by its lack of incident, the Deputy Prime Minister's fizzing left hook provided by far the most enduring image of a contest that was over before it even started. John Prescott's political style, always knockabout, proved more pugnacious than even his nervous boss, Tony Blair, had imagined.

The Rumble in Rhyl, matching fiery John Prescott in the red corner with hapless farm worker Craig Evans in the blue, was perhaps the only time Labour connected with the public during four weeks of argument that ended in the lowest turnout at the polls for more than eighty years.

Prescott, an 'old' Labour bruiser in a New Labour government, had come up the rough way. Trade union politics had been his nursery, and his own politics (so far as anyone could guess) were unreconstructed, but he was unswervingly loyal. In turn, Tony Blair needed him partly as an ambassador to, and partly as a hostage from, a great swath of the Party which Mr Blair himself found it hard to reach. Lippy and irritable yet with a folksy appeal, Prescott shot from the hip, famously mangling the English language yet seldom failing to make himself clear.

Sometimes too clear. The Deputy Prime Minister had been dispatched on a national coach tour of marginal constituencies by the party's high command in an effort to keep him out of London, out of trouble and out of the newspapers. But the attempt to suppress him failed spectacularly when he knocked out coverage of Labour's manifesto launch.

Mr Prescott was 62: no spring chicken; but he seemed to have forgotten none of the pugilistic skills acquired in his youth. Sir Anthony Eden, enjoying a cruise on the *Rangitata* through the Panama Canal to New Zealand to recuperate from the illness and political woes that forced him to resign as a Conservative Prime Minister, awarded two bottles of beer and a couple of hours' overtime bonus to a young waiter named John Prescott who had just won a boxing match staged on the liner's deck. According to a biographer, the Deputy Prime Minister's first bout was on holiday at Butlins in Wales. The young puncher from Prestatyn made the mistake of stepping into the ring with someone who could box and found himself on the canvas before he could raise a glove in anger.

When he went to sea in the 1950s and early 1960s, Prescott learned to defend himself to avoid being bullied. Merseyside was a rough port and he was taught by Dom Volante, a Liverpudlian who had been a professional featherweight in the 1930s. Sailors frequently settled arguments with their fists. Brawling, he admitted, was a feature of his younger days. 'When a ship gets in, the lads will go ashore and get bevvied,' said Prescott. 'I have been in some problems, yeah. A Belfast lad pulled a razor on me in New York once. He was drunk. I just moved away. Got him the next day.'

Until 16 May 2001, however, there was no public record of Prescott as MP for Hull East, let alone Prescott the Deputy Prime Minister, actually hitting anyone in anger. Yes, two decades earlier there had been a famous menacing finger-wag at Labour's ex-leader Jim Callaghan in a Commons dining room when the former PM criticised the party's policy on unilateral nuclear disarmament. Once, confronted by a drunk at King's Cross railway station when making a TV film, he had threatened the interloper: 'If you don't get out of this shot, I'll stick one on your chin.' Yet he had kept his hands to himself while drenched by a bucket of iced water thrown by Danbert Nobacon, a singer with the anarchist band Chumbawamba, when Mr Prescott inexplicably attended the 1998 Brit Awards.

And his sparring with French environment minister Dominique Voynet was strictly verbal; the pair blaming each other for the collapse of a Green summit with Voynet dismissing him as an inveterate macho-man. Prescott's reply was memorable 'Macho-man – moi?'

He had come a little closer to violence when he encountered one of the authors of this book at a *Times* Christmas reception at the Reform Club in Pall Mall in London. Prescott had been angered by certain parliamentary sketches describing his lifelong battle with English syntax, a fight which had left his native language slumped and bleeding on the ropes. 'You snob,' said

Prescott, rounding on his victim, 'you with your uppity public-school sneers.' He raised a fist and held it against your author's nose as cameras flashed. Nobody was sure whether this was a joke; perhaps not entirely.

But such matters never came to blows. Until the 2001 General Election. The Prescott Express had pulled up near the Little Theatre in Rhyl on the North Wales coast at 6.40 p.m. on Wednesday 16 May 2001 for what was billed as a political cabaret. About thirty jeering, whistling protesters were on hand, waving placards that defended hunting or accused the Labour Government of failing to help farmers hit by foot-and-mouth disease, an epidemic which had forced polling day to be postponed from May to June. They lined the crash barriers along the route to the venue.

Rhodri Morgan, Labour's First Minister in Wales, had wisely slipped in through the back door. Prescott stepped off the bus. He had a pathological hatred of the pro-hunting lobby, regarding them as toffs and Tories. He had mocked their 'contorted faces' at a Labour Party annual conference. Confronted by more of these faces now, he pointed and scowled at the rather unwelcoming welcoming committee. Sensing his hostility reciprocated, the Deputy Prime Minister asked a police officer: 'Is that the way you want me to go?'

Alas, the constable missed his chance to avert disaster. He failed to divert Mr Prescott. The Deputy Prime Minister appeared to swagger in the direction of the Little Theatre, the enemy within a few feet on his left, a low wall to his right. The tension showed as he passed a 29-year-old with an unfashionable mullet haircut. An egg hit him hard on the left ear.

Prescott moved instinctively and fast. He landed a strong left hook on the chin of the bloke we now know to be farm worker Craig Evans. A clenched right fist looked ready to follow, when Evans lunged over the barrier straight at him. Pandemonium broke out. Prescott was pinned against the wall by Evans. Two of the Deputy PM's aides were knocked to the ground. People fell over. Confused demonstrators pulled at the grappling duo. A hand, someone's hand, was in the Deputy Prime Minister's face. It was like a game of Twister. The North Wales constabulary waded in to rescue Prescott, arrest Evans and restore order. The extraordinary brawl, all captured on camera, had lasted ten long seconds.

As a shaken Prescott, egg splattered across his suit and face, was helped, half walking, half dragged, into the Little Theatre in Rhyl, there were wimps in Westminster – quite senior figures among them – and in Labour's Millbank Tower headquarters, who feared Prescott might just have cost them the election.

Every detail of the unedifying brawl had been filmed flawlessly by a Sky television crew. Those ten seconds were to be replayed endlessly. The jaw-dropping shock of seeing a Deputy Prime Minister smacking and brawling with a voter finally if moment-arily brought to life one of the most boring elections in memory.

Gordon Brown, a powerful Chancellor and chair of Labour's campaign, was hosting a strategy meeting with Douglas Alexander (his chief lieutenant) and Charles Falconer, the younger Tony Blair's first flatmate and unofficial legal adviser. Lord Falconer had been a successful lawyer before accepting a life peerage when he joined the Government. With Prescott's reputation hanging in the balance, he advised that the Deputy Prime Minister was in the wrong and could be charged with assault. Mr Alexander urged caution, arguing that Prescott had clearly been provoked.

Blair had not enjoyed the best of days himself. Since launching Labour's manifesto in Birmingham he had endured an uncomfortable, if less physical, confrontation of his own. On the doorstep of the city's Queen Elizabeth Hospital he had been ambushed by a woman, Sharron Storer, who demanded to know why there was no specialist cancer bed for her ailing partner. This too had been televised.

Driving back to London with spin doctor Alastair Campbell, Blair consulted the Millbank team from the back seat of the chauffeur-driven car. He feared that a giant spanner had been thrown into their previously smooth election machine. As a politician who had made his mark in opposition with the soundbite 'Tough on crime, tough on the causes of crime', he at once saw the problem – a big problem. The Tories, he anticipated, would have a field day. Labour would be the party of law and disorder, a bunch of street-fighting hooligans.

Blair rang his deputy and ordered him to apologise. The call, by all accounts, was as short as it was fraught. 'I'm not going to fucking apologise,' Prescott spat back down the phone, by now, even more enraged. 'He never said sorry to that lad on the *Guardian*.'

The 'he' in question was Campbell; the lad was Michael White, the *Guardian*'s political editor. At that time Campbell held the same position on the *Daily Mirror*. He had taken a swing at White in 1991 when (the *Mirror*'s proprietor Robert 'Bob' Maxwell having just drowned in mysterious circumstances) he took violent exception to White's improvised adaptation of the song 'Bob, bob, bobbing along'. John Prescott was correct to observe that there was no apology on record for this.

The result was a statement from the Deputy Prime Minister referring to a 'frightening and regrettable incident', and pinning the blame on Evans. 'I arrived in Rhyl this evening for the meeting. I got off my bus into a clearly hostile crowd. I walked through all the jostling and I was attacked by an individual. In the mêlée that followed I clearly defended myself.'

Blair believed that the strategy was wrong and Prescott should have said sorry. It was with trepidation that the Prime Minister faced an excited media in London at a pre-arranged press conference the following morning. Braced for tough questioning, the plan was to stonewall as best he could and put fresh pressure on Prescott if things went badly.

Addressing the only issue on the agenda, Blair was preparing the ground for a gentle admonition of his deputy: 'In respect of John, of course it would have been better if the whole thing hadn't happened, but I want to say something to you about John Prescott. You could not wish for a deputy more loyal, more true and more decent. He cares about his country and he cares passionately about his politics. But John is John . . . '

At the phrase 'John is John' a chuckle was heard from the hacks. Soon most of Fleet Street was laughing at an explanation that explained nothing, settled nothing, and yet somehow laid the affair to rest.

Blair quickly realised it was going to be treated as a joke. Already derided as 'two Jags' for a fondness for luxury cars which conflicted with his exhortations to the rest of the country to use public transport, Prescott was fast dubbed 'two Jabs' even if he had only managed one.

Opinion polls showed a groundswell of support for Prescott. Admiration for a man who had taken on someone half his age was particularly evident among working-class voters who rang radio phone-ins to claim they would have reacted, or liked to have reacted, in the same way. Actor Sir Sean Connery, victor in many a battle with screen baddies as James Bond and a prominent bankroller of the Scottish National Party, sent a message: 'The whole of Scotland is behind you.'

Tory leader William Hague, aware of the groundswell in favour of the punchy politician, merely suggested Prescott should 'learn to keep his cool', adding that for his own part he found it best during elections to try to avoid hitting any of the voters. Simon Hughes, a prominent Liberal Democrat, conceded that 'none of us is perfect'.

When Prescott arrived in Edinburgh the morning after the night before, anti-privatisation campaigners held placards declaring: 'Stop Two Punch Prescott's Postal Sell Off'. Soon the Deputy Prime Minister was joking: 'I wish I had ducked a bit quicker at Rhyl. Mind you, I think the other guy thinks that as well.'

Prescott claimed he had been set up by blood-sports activists who tipped off Sky News, ignoring the presence of other camera crews (Sky, admittedly, got the best shots but there was no evidence to back the allegation). Evans, it emerged, was a disgruntled farm worker, scraping a living doing odd jobs, who had found himself left outside the walls of the New Jerusalem promised by New Labour.

Prescott's impromptu ten-second punch-up all but obliterated coverage of the carefully and expensively stage-managed hour-long launch of the Party's manifesto that day. But the cloud had a silver lining. Amid all the excitement and fuss, the Labour leadership was able to duck probing questions about whether a Labour government would raise National Insurance contributions. The Party's General Secretary, Margaret McDonagh, was instructed to send a letter to TV channels accusing them of complicity with the hunters in Rhyl. The epistle was promptly leaked to newspapers and that row, rather than National Insurance, became the story.

And Mr Prescott's ten-second bout, far from becoming a vote loser, proved a triumph. Labour went on to win a second Westminster avalanche in the June 2001 election. Blair moved Prescott from the Department of Environment, Transport and Regions, and created a new post within the Cabinet Office for his Deputy to co-ordinate implementation of a manifesto over-shadowed by his fist-fight.

In September the Crown Prosecution Service quietly announced that no action would be taken against the throwers of either the egg or the left hook. After studying video evidence and witness statements, the CPS ruled that there was no good prospect that prosecution of Prescott would succeed against a defence of self-defence. Nor would prosecution of Evans serve any useful purpose, because of the minor nature of the incident. The Rumble in Rhyl had been officially declared a draw.

We doubt most readers would now dispute the justice of that outcome. Britain decided to treat the incident as a joke, and trivial. But why, and precisely when, it became so is less clear. Mr Blair's deft 'John is John' probably helped, and a fund of public affection for the roughest diamond in New Labour's tiara made a difference too. Many will remember, however, that at the time the mood of both public and media seemed quite delicately balanced between viewing the fight as a very serious misjudgement by the Deputy Prime Minister, and regarding it as just one of those things.

The lesson, if there is one, seems to be that if you're going to do something silly in politics, be sure to have a reputation for that kind of thing already. 'Herod is Herod' would never have done the trick, but 'John is John' just about did.

STEPHEN BYERS – 2002

'Liar Byers . . . pants on fire'

Al-Qaeda fanatics flew two hijacked airliners into New York's World Trade Center twin towers on 11 September 2001, killing some 3,000 innocent people in arguably the most dreadful terrorist outrage ever recorded. Countless millions of people around the world watching the terrible destruction on television saw office workers trapped in the burning buildings jump to certain death to escape the flames. Both blocks collapsed, crushing rescuers and those they were trying to save.

Tony Blair, in Brighton to address the TUC, watched the tragedy unfold on TV like so many others. The shaken Premier made a short speech, talking of the awful threat posed by modern terrorism, before heading back to London under tight security to decide what emergency plans needed to be implemented in order to protect the population. Elsewhere in the Brighton conference complex, groups of ministers, numbed by the destruction, wandered around in a state of shock before heading back to the capital to see what, if anything, they could do.

In London Ms Jo Moore, special adviser to the Transport Secretary, Stephen Byers, tapped the 'send' button on an email to colleagues at 2.55 p.m. When her infamous message – 'It's now a very good day to get out anything we want to bury. Councillors' expenses'? – Jo.' – popped up on the screens of two colleagues, it plumbed new depths of spinicism. Taking advantage of the deaths of thousands of people to release details on a subject as mundane as attendance allowances on the street furniture sub-committee was beyond parody. It pictured New Labour as addicted to fighting over every headline, a government promising a New Britain yet concerned to avoid the possibility of a few lines of criticism on the most mind-numbingly dull of topics.

When Moore's extraordinary instruction – sent to a policy colleague and to Alun Evans, director of communications in the Department for Local Government, Transport and Regions (he left his job within a month) – surfaced on 8 October, it triggered justifiable calls for her resignation. And Stephen Byers, Moore's boss, compounded her cynicism by deciding not to sack his pushy spin doctor. It was to prove the biggest error of his political career and was ultimately to cost Byers his Cabinet post. The decision to hang on to Moore after such a huge error underlined how obsessed the Government remained with spin and cocked a significant snook at decency in public life.

Moore, a hard-nosed former Labour Party chief press officer, owner of an ice-pick brooch designed to taunt Trotskyists and with a stick insect named after her in London Zoo, had been put on the public payroll at £50,000 (for a three-day week) to improve her boss's image. Mr Byers, an engaging MP popular with backbenchers and union leaders, had now unintentionally tied his own fate to that of his stricken adviser.

Her credibility gone, his disappeared too. Yet in no sense can he be blamed for her error of judgement, and his failure to sack her, though arguably arrogant and insensitive, cannot really be called an abuse of office. A couple of years later most people, asked why it was that Stephen Byers had resigned, would be stumped for an answer. The former Cabinet minister only makes it into a book on parliamentary scandal because of the huge wave of public and media anger that engulfed him – in retrospect rather mysteriously. Perhaps he became a lightning conductor for a negative charge building up among the public in its attitude to the Government's techniques of communication. Whatever the cause, for sheer, unrelenting abuse, the attacks on Byers will take some beating.

Newspaper headlines daily branded him a liar, without even the use of qualifying quotation marks. A *Sun* headline in February screamed 'Liar Byers . . . Pants On Fire', while the *Daily Mirror* pictured him with a long nose under the heading: 'Spinocchio: The lie keeps growing and growing . . . until it's as clear as the nose on your face.' The trigger for the attacks was generally not policy initiatives but his trustworthiness.

Moore had attempted to stage-manage an apology on 16 October for her 'terrible error of judgement' but looked shifty rather than shameful. Blair the following day told MPs the email was 'horrible, stupid and wrong,' yet he did not follow the criticism through to its logical conclusion, declaring instead that she would stay. The decision puzzled seasoned watchers of the Whitehall scene. Tony Wright, Labour chairman of the all-party Public Administration Committee, considered her action 'inconsistent with any notion of public service'. Jonathan Baume, general secretary of the First Division Association, the senior civil servants' union, called on her to 'step aside and let the professionals get on with it.'

As Byers read the increasingly desperate headlines, the spinning itself became ever more desperate. On 27 November, the day of Chancellor Gordon Brown's pre-Budget report to Parliament, Moore leaked minutes of a controversial meeting between Byers and the head of Railtrack. In a move popular with Left-wingers the Transport Secretary had pulled the plug on the controversial rail company in October, plunging it into administration and effectively taking public control of the network. When it began to look as if Railtrack shareholders would lose out, Byers counterattacked through Moore. Brown, however, was furious at his stolen thunder, while the notes seemed to contradict Byers' account of a key meeting. Spin once more became the story.

Come new year, a new spin row. In the middle of January 2002 it emerged that Byers and Martin Sixsmith, a veteran former BBC correspondent hired as a communications director, had had a 'blazing row' over moves to hand a senior PR job to a Labour Party friend of Moore's rather than a civil servant. Then on Valentine's Day, 14 February 2002, an email from Sixsmith was leaked. Purportedly sent to Moore, it banned the use of Princess Margaret's funeral to bury bad news – on this occasion, poor train punctuality. 'There is no way I will allow this department to make any substantive announcements next Friday,' wrote Sixsmith. 'Princess Margaret is being buried on that day. I will absolutely not allow anything else to be.' By 9 a.m. Moore was dismissing the email as 'completely fictitious . . . complete and utter lies'. A couple of hours later Godric Smith, one of Blair's official spokesmen, described it as a 'fabrication' and Robin Cook, leader of the Commons, took the same dismissive line.

An email did exist, however. It had been sent by Sixsmith to Byers, Moore's boss. Byers was at the end of his tether, unable to make a speech or unveil a policy initiative without it backfiring in a spin row. He decided Moore must go – along with Sixsmith, whom he suspected of briefing against him. The following day, 15 February, Sixsmith was summoned to a meeting with permanent secretary Sir Richard Mottram, who told him Moore had tendered her resignation and Byers would only accept it if both spin doctors went. Sixsmith agreed to think about it and left for a hospital appointment, only to emerge from the visit to a doctor to hear on the radio that he had quit.

In a farce worthy of *Yes Minister*, Sixsmith tried to arrange a meeting with Byers but he was unavailable. Mottram admitted to Sixsmith there had been a 'complete cock-up', but nevertheless issued a statement saying that both had resigned though details had yet to be finalised. With Sixsmith continuing to insist he had *not* resigned, the Tories called once again for Byers' head. The row rumbled on. Mottram issued a rare public statement on 25 February confirming that Sixsmith had agreed to resign, although details of his departure had not been finalised when his resignation was announced. Sixsmith retaliated 24 hours later on the BBC, blaming Byers for the false announcement of his resignation. Byers in turn told MPs in a statement that Sixsmith had agreed to resign and insisted that there was a 'concerted attempt by a very small number of civil servants in the press office to undermine' the department. Amid the confusion, efforts to improve Britain's creaking transport system were paralysed as Byers fought for his political life.

At the beginning of May 2002, the department finally conceded that Sixsmith had not resigned in February but would now depart at the end of the month. Contrary to what Byers had said in the Commons and on TV on 15 February, the statement admitted: 'The department regrets that, while acting in good faith, they announced that he had resigned on what turned out to be an incorrect understanding of earlier discussions that day.'

Byers was accused of deliberately misleading the Commons. Tory front bencher Tim Collins insisted with perhaps a trace of hyperbole that it was the 'most clear example in human history of a man being caught out lying'. In the Commons on 8 May, Tony Blair claimed Byers had acted in 'good faith'. 'It was clear the Secretary of State had been told Mr Sixsmith had agreed to resign. It was equally clear that Mr Sixsmith disputed that he had resigned,' he said. 'Therefore, the parties were not in agreement. There had to be negotiation . . . terms have now been agreed and he has indeed departed.'

It was a farcical row. On one level an internal Whitehall personnel issue that might have been of interest only to political anoraks, against the backdrop of that infamous email it was a drama made into a crisis. Newspaper reports said that Mottram dispensed with mandarin-speak in a conversation with a Whitehall colleague: 'We're all fucked. I'm fucked, you're fucked, the whole department's fucked. It's been the biggest cock-up and we are all completely fucked.' Mottram was soon to be exiled to the Siberia of Whitehall, the Department of Work and Pensions.

No matter how mundane the twists and turns of the dispute, it had ground Byers down. He was accused by a spokeswoman for survivors of a 1999 Paddington rail crash of deciding to collapse

Railtrack weeks before the official announcement, a claim which if true would have risked compensation claims from aggrieved investors. The weekend before he accepted the inevitable defeat, a report by the Labour-dominated Commons transport committee branded the Government's ten-year transport plan 'incomprehensible'. Deputy Premier John Prescott detected the 'final knife in the back of Stephen Byers'.

While the Commons was in recess and MPs were away from Westminster, Byers quit on 28 May 2002. Unusually he announced his departure in Downing Street as No. 10 threw a protective arm around him while simultaneously pushing him out of the door. Byers said it was 'the right thing to do for the Labour Party and the Government.' He had tried to 'behave honourably', he added, 'the people that know me best know I am not a liar. What is clear to me, however, is that I have become a distraction from what the Government is achieving, that the debate we need to have about key policy issues is being distorted by my involvement, that by remaining in office I damage the Government.'

Sixsmith formally left the civil service three days later and began a comic political novel about a purely fictitious Cabinet scandal involving wholly imaginary techniques of spin, bearing no relation to any real persons, living or dead. When last heard of, Moore was training as a primary school teacher in North London, her days of spin over. Byers is tipped for a return to the Cabinet. Why on earth would he want to?

TONY BLAIR – 2002 ONWARDS

'Sometimes the Balls Get Dropped: the Crook, the Premier, His Wife and Her Guru'

No Prime Minister in contemporary politics did trust like Tony Blair, elected on a wave of revulsion at the perceived degeneracy of the final Tory years.

Or that was how it started. The mantra was 'trust in Tony', as New Labour's leader preached a personal credo of honesty, virtue and good faith at times so motherhood-and-apple-pie that this self-styled 'pretty straight sort of a guy' came to be lampooned in *Private Eye* as the poisonously saccharine Vicar of St Albion. After seven years of John Major (whom at the Commons Dispatch Box Mr Blair had once described as 'knee-deep in dishonour', though he was quick to protest when his own honour was impugned), Blair's ministers would be, he promised, purer than pure. He would clean up politics, restore standards in public life, open up the books to clear the stink hanging over party funding and, by his seemingly endless contracts with the people, just do (in one of his favourite phrases) 'the right thing'.

This is not quite how much of Britain and its news media came to see him. A mixture of cronyism, dodgy donations, bad decisions, over-spun prospectuses and a fickle press meant that Blair's reputation for virtue fast began to fray. Part deserved and part unfair, the change in mood meant that by 2004 Tony Blair led a pockmarked administration – more a case of bad skin than major scarring – as distrusted as any that had gone before it.

But Mr Blair's good fortune was to lead Britain through a sort of prolonged post-Thatcher shudder. Glancing back over our shoulders at an era of almost traumatic change, we were easy to remind that if that was the alternative, then Blair's big-mouthed but often timid programme remained a lesser evil. And whether he pleased or infuriated, the Prime Minister remained a consummate entertainer with a cheesy grin, an engaging line in visionary patter, and a certain star quality: one of life's winners. This (along with a seemingly endless economic summer) guaranteed another easy victory for Labour in the 2001 election.

Public trust, however, was leaching away.

At the time of writing it is too early to say why. When did it start? What crime, if any, should head the charge-sheet? Dip into the sawdust for anything hard enough to justify the term 'corrupt' and your hand returns empty; or clutching worthless incidents, mere rumours, little fibs, slight evasions, much bragging and a great deal of empty and self-regarding nonsense – tales of an unedifying but mostly trivial kind. The suspicion nags that there was something insubstantial about the promises, something untrustworthy about the preacher's pitch; but the big betrayal or downright lie is hard to identify, let alone stand up.

Throughout the period Tony Blair was persistently caricatured as a grinning salesman, or as slippery, or fey. Words like 'charlatan' became tempting because they conveyed the aura of deception without demanding the proof. By early 2004 there was no proof, and perhaps there never will be. One is left with a string of small, troubling but inconclusive stories, and the lingering impression of a playground cheat plus the killing fields of Iraq.

The reader in search of a Great Parliamentary Scandal which history can attach to Tony Blair will therefore search this book in vain. Some believe that his assurances to Parliament before the US-British attack on Iraq – that Saddam Hussein possessed quickly deployable weapons of mass destruction – will be shown to amount to a scandal of this kind. Books are being written on the affair and in time this book may (or may not) include a chapter on it; but it is a chapter as yet unclosed.

Just as likely is that when Mr Blair leaves office he will leave it rather as, more than a quarter of a century before, the late Harold Wilson did. Admired by most for dexterity, dismissed by many for vacuity, and suspected by a few of villainy, but with nothing proved, he will quit the stage in a flash of magnesium and a puff of smoke, leaving the faint impression that we have seen something exotic but insubstantial: a conjurer.

A sense of it is conveyed by the following randomly selected and completely insignificant story from 1999, at a time when Tony Blair's predominance was pretty much unchallenged. At Prime Minister's Questions he was taunting the then Leader of the Opposition, William Hague, about the Conservative Party's hostility to European Union plans. The House was in a rowdy mood. Let the Tories name one EU country, Mr Blair cried, which agreed with the Tory approach.

Having apparently picked up a response from someone on the Tory benches, the PM's gleeful shout pierced the hubbub. 'Norway?' he shouted, 'Norway isn't even *in* the European Union!' A gale of laughter swept the whole House. Mr Hague grinned foolishly. Some as yet unidentified Tory, it seemed, had made an idiot of his whole party.

Blair's victory was almost total, hardly marred by the fact that nobody in the Press Gallery or the Chamber could afterwards be found who could point to – or had even heard – a Member shouting 'Norway'. Within ten minutes a rumour began among journalists that Blair had confected the entire incident by pretending to hear the shout, then hitting back with a prefabricated response. On reflection most of us concluded that this was unlikely: too clever by half, it could so easily have backfired.

What was remarkable, however, was that only two years into Blair's premiership it had occurred simultaneously to so many hearers to ask not whether we might have missed something in the noise, but whether the Prime Minister might have cheated. Already he was being seen (and not unadmiringly in some quarters) as a chancer with a dash of rascality to his nature.

Other incidents were more serious, or alleged by Blair's enemies and some of the press to be so. But none have approached proof sufficiently to be detailed in a book of parliamentary scandals. Depending on commentators' points of view they have been called calumnies against an innocent man, or dark hints of deeper stories that never surfaced. In the paragraphs which follow we shall run through them more by way of a toxic medley of disagreeable gossip than an exhaustive summary of established fact. We repeat: many of the tales listed below have been described in one quarter or another as serious scandals but none has come close to being proved. Some are self-evidently trivial.

Take, for example, Tony Blair's claim (in a TV interview with Des O'Connor) not long after being elected that, aged fourteen, he had tried to stow away on a flight from Newcastle Airport bound for the Bahamas. A quick check with the airport revealed it did not offer, and never had, flights to the Caribbean. When

Blair was a teenager its destination list had been topped by Jersey and the Isle of Man. Nobody at school with him at the time could be found who remembered the incident, or anything like it.

Then there was his attempt to reinvent himself as a sports fanatic, remembering (it seemed) a past as a football-crazy Newcastle United supporter. The recollection occurred at about the time when Nick Hornby's book *Fever Pitch* was re-casting football for the middle classes and it was becoming fashionable at London supper parties to be following a team. The PM told a Tyneside radio station in 1997 how, as a lad, he had sat in the Gallowgate End of St James' Park and watched his hero, Jackie Milburn. Listeners pictured the scene: the young leader-to-be, wrapped in black and white, cheering on the Magpies with thousands of other ordinary people.

Unfortunately Milburn stopped playing for Newcastle when Blair was three – an age, incidentally, when Blair lived in Australia. Nor (regardless of whom he was watching) could the young Blair have *sat* at the Gallowgate End. Seats were only installed there when Blair was in the Shadow Cabinet.

Such stories caused only mirth. The press was less amused, however, by the first serious scandal alleged against him and his administration: the so-called Bernie Ecclestone affair. In November 1997 the new Prime Minister was leader of a Labour Party that had accepted a £1m donation from the top figure in British motor racing. Blair also agreed to postpone a ban on tobacco sponsorship in the sport. The coincidence struck many as suspicious, though Blair has consistently claimed that it was no more than that. The coincidence would have remained secret had initial denials been accepted. In the end, and after a furore in the press, the Party returned the cheque.

Far less serious (but still a perennial big-hitter in each summer's silly-season headlines) have been the Blairs' holiday destinations. Instead of flicking through brochures or consulting serious travel literature, the family developed a taste for staying in the homes of more or less distant (but always rich and famous) friends and acquaintances, including a Tuscan count they barely knew. The British Press made merry with the fact that the Italian authorities closed entire beaches to the Latin hoi-polloi in order to ensure the Blairs' privacy.

Millionaire socialist Geoffrey Robinson was another chosen provider of beds in his holiday homes until his public fall from grace, though even he was heard to grumble that Mr Blair failed to pay for the tennis lessons provided at his Italian villa and Mrs Blair once took home with her most of the books in his South of France apartment – no doubt easy mistakes for tired, busy people to make.

In 2003 the Blairs all went on a summer holiday in the £3 million Barbados mansion of Sir Cliff Richard – not just for a week or two but three. The Tory-leaning Peter Pan of Pop had apparently rung up No. 10 to offer his place (complete with pool) because he thought the PM looked gaunt and tired after the invasion of Iraq in March. Undisclosed donations were made to charity and, required to buy their own air tickets, the Blairs flew economy.

Blair did indeed look grey, and as if he was losing weight and having trouble sleeping. In November of that year he was to require hospital treatment, Downing Street insisting it was a minor complaint and a one-off. The latter comment may have surprised former US President Bill Clinton and the Queen, both admitting they had known of Blair's heart problem for years.

Thrift was accompanied by a passion for alternative or holistic therapies. An unlikely interest for a pair so closely associated with Christianity, it nonetheless led to the couple smearing each other with mud and screaming inside an Aztec rebirthing pyramid when they stayed on in Mexico for a private holiday, after an official trip to Latin America.

Or perhaps it was the media back at home they were screaming at. Pathologically unwilling to distinguish between serious scandal and a good national giggle, the British press seemed more determined with every passing year to find something to cause the Prime Minister embarrassment – or worse. Downing Street's reaction became increasingly contemptuous. This was understandable but not always wise.

The Hindujah brothers affair, and the Mittal affair in 2002, when Blair wrote to the Romanian Premier supporting Lakshmi Mittal's application to purchase a privatised steel plant after the Indian billionaire had donated £125,000 to Labour, were alleged by some to touch the Prime Minister's own judgement. Both, however, appeared to trigger the same response from sources close to the Prime Minister: an almost automatic dismissal of press interest or concern as ridiculous.

Thus there were fewer ready to believe stern Downing Street denials when it was alleged that pressure had been applied to secure Blair a more prominent role during the mourning following the Queen Mother's death in March 2002. A tremendous (some might say disproportionate) media fuss ensued, in which the truth emerged as somewhat more complicated than initial denials had suggested.

What seemed to be emerging was a perhaps unconscious collective wish (on much of the media's part and some of the public's too) to catch the Prime Minister out. Quite trivial incidents, as much as more serious ones, provoked the same response: an energetic scrabbling for possible ammunition against him – and flat official denials. The denials only inflamed the appetite to score a palpable hit against Blair. Curiously this did not at first coincide with any comparable movement against his party in the opinion polls. It was as if people were sure he was somehow tricksy and wanted to see him slip up and be shown to have cheated – yet without any corresponding disposition to remove him as Prime Minister. Perhaps all they really wanted was to see him given a public slap.

The picture, however, turned nasty when in 2002 Iraq began to surface as the impending big national story. The story is not covered here. What is worth noting, though, is that when an inquiry by a retired judge, Lord Hutton, into circumstances surrounding the suicide of the government weapons-expert, Dr David Kelly, began its researches, press and public alike followed it eagerly and seemed to admire the thorough and painstaking way Lord Hutton was proceeding. Yet when he reached his emphatic conclusion – that the Prime Minister and his government had been almost without blame in the affair – public and media opinion immediately turned *against* Tony Blair. Opinion polls found most of the electorate unready to believe him, regardless of what Lord Hutton thought. A majority even said they believed the PM should resign. Yet the conventional wisdom in Britain – almost unchallenged – continued confident that Labour would be easily re-elected in a General Election that was by then probably little more than a year away.

Friends and foes alike of the Blair administration and of Mr Blair personally took some comfort from this apparent paradox. It seemed a political leader may be widely distrusted – regarded by some as scandalously delinquent – without this necessarily translating into a determination to remove him from office.

Perhaps this is because the electorate need to trust an alternative, as well as distrust an incumbent, before they switch. Perhaps it is because many do not mind having someone they consider a cheat as leader, as long as he's *their* cheat and as long as he gets away with it.

At the time of writing, Westminster is awash with rumours that Blair is to be toppled by a putsch, to be replaced by Gordon Brown. Newspapers are full of stories about how he will be pushed unless he jumps. Certainly the photographs of coalition troops abusing Iraqi prisoners undermined what public support there was for the military invasion. No weapons of mass destruction, no links to Osama bin Laden and now human rights abuses.

Whatever the truth, there can be no doubt that as his years in office lengthened, the nation and its newspapers took increasing pleasure in trying to catch not only the PM, but his whole household, red-handed at *something*, however trivial or bizarre.

Which is why one small scandal in late 2002 chimed so well with the mood of the media and the public. Downing Street deployed its spin machine to cover up the use by the Prime Minister's wife of a former conman to help the couple buy a pair of flats in Bristol.

In itself the purchase of the smart city centre flats – partly an investment, partly a potential home for their son Euan at university in the city – was not extraordinary. Nor was Cherie Blair's decision to enlist outside advice to choose the property a surprise – she was, after all, a busy woman. What caused a stir was first her exotic choice of adviser – a curious spiritual and fashion consultant – and second the tendentious efforts by No. 10 to deny the whole thing once it became public.

At the centre of the whole affair was Carole Caplin, one of the oddest people in recent years to reach the heart of British politics. Despite having posed topless for magazine photographs and being an associate of Exegesis (a New Age cult which persuaded people to reveal their sexual secrets and charged them to do it), she became part of the Blairs' inner circle after starting as Cherie's fitness trainer. Going on to become what the press called a lifestyle guru, she was reportedly paid several thousand pounds a month for duties including choosing some of the Prime Minister's clothes.

Caplin introduced Cherie to her mother, Sylvia, a former ballet dancer who claims to make contact with the dead via 'energy-channelling crystals', sitting clients on the floor of a darkened room to consult heavenly spirits. Both mother and daughter holidayed with the Blairs. Mrs Blair's mother Gale, it is said, on one occasion castigated Ms Caplin for wearing a revealing top at dinner in front of the children.

The family's unusual reliance on Caplin remained tittle-tattle, little more than gossip, until shortly before Christmas 2002 when the *Mail on Sunday* newspaper claimed on its front page: 'Blair Used Fraudster To Buy Flats'. The opening paragraph read: 'Tony and Cherie Blair were plunged into a damaging sleaze row last night amid claims that they used a notorious fraudster to buy them two luxury flats at a knockdown price.'

The paper went on to claim that an Australian, Peter Foster, a convicted conman jailed on three continents and fighting deportation from Britain, had helped negotiate the purchase of two £270,000 Bristol apartments in the Panoramic, an exclusive development in the fashionable Clifton quarter with far-reaching views of the city and Mendip Hills.

It transpired that Mr Foster, known in Britain as a former escort of the *Sun* newspaper's page three model, Samantha Fox, and once exposed by Esther Rantzen on her TV show as behind a slimming scam, was Caplin's boyfriend. Caplin, it emerged, had a pass to Downing Street and found it easier to gain entry into No. 10 than most Cabinet ministers.

Downing Street went into overdrive, denouncing the claims as 'ludicrous'. Two official spokesmen, Godric Smith and Tom Kelly, stonewalled, insisting there was no truth whatsoever in the allegations. Foster had never been a financial adviser to Mrs Blair, they said.

For four days the denials from No. 10 were as emphatic as they were frequent. Every question about the affair was shot down as Downing Street ridiculed inquisitors trying to get to the bottom of the affair, seemingly affronted that anyone could be so gullible (or malevolent) as to suspect there could be a shred of truth in these outrageous accusations.

Then publication of email correspondence between Mrs Blair and Foster demonstrated his involvement in the Bristol deal. No. 10 was forced into a humiliating handbrake turn.

The emails showed Mrs Blair and Foster discussing the purchase of the two apartments, one to rent and the other for eldest son Euan to live in while at university. Foster's emails included cheesy phrases such as 'your pleasure is my pleasure'.

It is likely that Foster exaggerated his involvement, creating an electronic record to be used later to his own advantage. But involved he certainly had been, despite the official denials. After he had travelled to Bristol and spoken to people concerned, Mrs Blair had emailed Foster: 'You are a star, I have sent them [the mortgage forms] off'. After further help from him she wrote: 'thank you so much Peter, I appreciate that'. And when Foster said he had 'put a rocket under a letting agent to strike a good deal', Mrs Blair said she could not 'thank you enough Peter for taking these negotiations for me'. She hoped to see him again 'soon'.

The Downing Street U-turn forced No. 10 to admit that Foster had, after all, been involved 'for a couple of weeks'. They insisted that a £20,000 discount on each of the flats was available to all buyers and was not a special arrangement struck by Foster.

Nor, they insisted, had Mrs Blair accepted Foster's offer to use his own accountant. Spinners who had spun that there was nothing in the original claims now spun to save their own reputations. They implied to journalists that Mrs Blair had not told them the whole story.

Downing Street's communications chief, Alastair Campbell, who had assured journalists the allegations were without foundation, apparently complained that he too had been misled. In a statement Mrs Blair tried to spare the blushes of spokesmen in the firing line by saying that if there was 'any misunderstanding between the No. 10 press office and the media that is unfortunate and I regret that'.

The affair developed theatrically, thanks to Peter Mandelson who is said to have drafted the televised *mea culpa* that followed. Ten days after the start of the scandal, Mandelson slipped into No. 10 to write (it is said) what is known as a 'non-apology apology' for the Prime Minister's wife.

TV crews were hastily summoned to an early evening education reception attended by Mrs Blair where, in front of a sympathetic audience, she read from the prepared ten-minute text: 'The reality of my daily life is that I am juggling a lot of balls in the air,' she said in her statement, 'trying to be a good wife and mother, trying to be the Prime Ministerial consort at home and abroad, and being a barrister, a charity worker. And sometimes some of the balls get dropped. There just aren't enough hours in the day.'

Downing Street declared the scandal over and so it was: over, that is, for 36 hours until another disclosure thumped onto doormats with the morning newspapers of 12 December. Mrs Blair was now accused of intervening in Foster's deportation battle with the Government. Court papers, it was alleged, had been faxed to her Downing Street study and she had taken part in a conference call with his lawyers in mid-November.

Again Downing Street denials were issued. Again evidence was produced, this time a three-page document faxed at 5.19 p.m. on 22 November, taking 57 seconds to go through, shortly after Mrs Blair did speak to Foster's solicitor.

Caplin later claimed she had badgered Mrs Blair into having a short conversation with Foster's lawyer. The documents, insisted Caplin, were faxed to her, not Mrs Blair, though she used the No. 10 fax machine. 'I'm appalled that her phone call to the solicitor, which was a simple act of friendship to me, is being interpreted in this way and I have apologised to Cherie for the embarrassment and difficulties that has caused her,' she said.

The entire episode left the Prime Minister depressed, Mr Blair blaming himself for heaping too much responsibility for the family's affairs on his wife.

There will be those who argue, not without cause, that the Blairs were a victim of a sting by Foster who deliberately targeted them through Caplin. And there will be some who argue that if a scandal at all, it was not a parliamentary scandal because it involved the PM's wife rather than the PM. But New Labour had used the government machine to deny what was true, even if the Premier avoided misleading the House of Commons. None of this helped Tony Blair's credibility.

Carole Caplin picked herself up shrewdly from the fiasco. She invited TV cameras into her life to make a documentary and secured a column with the Sunday newspaper that had exposed the scandal.

Mrs Blair found the affair harder to shake off. She was to be embarrassed again by her involvement with Caplin, in the autumn of 2003. *Marie Claire*, a women's magazine, published toe-curling pictures of Caplin applying lipstick to Mrs Blair while the pair sat, in the Prime Ministerial bedroom, on the Prime Ministerial bed; a £3,500 king-size, well-sprung Norwegian model.

BIBLIOGRAPHY

Among the many books and works of reference we have found helpful (often acknowledged in the text) it is worth mentioning here just a handful of those upon which we have particularly relied:

ALLEN, Louis, *et al*: *Political Scandals and Causes Célèbres Since 1945*, Longman: Pearson Professional, 1991

BESSELL, Peter: *Cover-up: The Jeremy Thorpe Affair*, Simons Books, 1980

BOOTHBY, Robert: *Recollections of a Rebel*, Hutchinson, 1978

BOWER, Tom: *The Paymaster: Geoffrey Robinson, Maxwell and New Labour*, Simon & Schuster, 2001

BROWN, Colin: *Fighting Talk: The Biography of John Prescott*, Simon & Schuster, 1997

CLARKE, G. N.: *The Later Stuarts 1660–1714*, Oxford University Press, 1956

COLQUHOUN, Maureen: *A Woman in the House*, Scan, 1980

COOK, Margaret: *A Slight and Delicate Creature*, Weidenfeld, 1999

CRICK, Michael: *Jeffrey Archer: Stranger than Fiction*, HarperCollins, 1995.

CULLEN, Tom: *Maundy Gregory, Purveyor of Honours*, Sidgwick and Jackson, 1974

CURRIE, Edwina: *Diaries 1987–1992*, Time Warner, 2002

DOIG, Alan: *Westminster Babylon*, Allison and Busby, 1990

DOIG, Alan: *Corruption and Misconduct in Contemporary British Politics*, Penguin Books, 1984

DONALDSON, Frances: *The Marconi Scandal*, Rupert Hart-Davis, 1962

Greer, Ian: *One Man's Word*, André Deutsch, 1997

HARVEY, Ian: *To Fall Like Lucifer*, Sidgwick and Jackson, 1971

HYDE, H. *Montgomery: A Tangled Web*, 1986

KEAYS, Sara: *A Question of Judgement*, Quintessential Press, 1985

KEELER, Christine: *Scandal!*, Xanadu, 1989

KNIGHTLEY, Philip, and KENNEDY, Caroline: *An Affair of State: the Profumo case and the Naming of Stephen Ward*, Cape, 1987

LEIGH, David and VULLIAMY, Ed: *Sleaze: The Corruption of Parliament*, Fourth Estate, 1997

LEWIS, Chester: *Jeremy Thorpe, A Secret Life*, Fontana, 1979

LYONS, F. S. L.: *Charles Stewart Parnell*, Collins, 1977

MACINTYRE, Donald: *Mandelson: The Biography*, HarperCollins, 1999

MARLOW, Joyce: *The Uncrowned Queen of Ireland: The Life of Kitty O'Shea*, Weidenfeld and Nicolson, 1975

McKIE, David: *Jabez: The Rise and Fall of a Victorian Scoundrel*, Atlantic Books, 2004

PARKINSON, Cecil: *Right at the Centre, My Autobiography*, Weidenfeld and Nicolson, 1992

RAWNSLEY, Andrew: *Servants of the People: The Inside Story of New Labour*, Hamish Hamilton, 2000

RHODES-JAMES, Robert: *Bob Boothby, A Portrait*, Hodder and Stoughton, 1991

RIDLEY, Jane, and Thomas, Stephen: *The Young Disraeli 1804–1846*, Sinclair Stevenson, 1995

SEARLE, G. R.: *Corruption in British Politics, 1895–1930*, Oxford University Press, 1987

STONEHOUSE, John: *My Trial, Wyndham Publications*, 1976

VASSAL, John: *The Autobiography of a Spy*, Sidgwick and Jackson, 1975

FAMILY-VALUES, Norman: *The McTory Book of Bonks*, McNaughty Books/BS Randle, 1994

WASSERSTEIN, Bernard: *The Secret Lives of Trebitsch Lincoln*, Penguin, 1989

INDEX

MacDonald, Ramsay 102–3
mace incident 285–8, 342
MacInnes, Alaisdair 249
McKie, David 61, 63–5
Macleod, Iain 165
Macmillan, Harold 103–9,
   116, 157, 165, 174, 177
Mad Monks of Medmenham
   12
Major, John 234, 266–72,
   296, 316, 318, 361
male prostitutes 71, 274, 386
male strippers 263
Mandelson, Peter 382, 388,
   394–402, 404, 442
Mangold, Tom 179
Mann, Peter 161
Mann, Sir John 136, 138
Marconi scandal 80–3
Mardy Jones, R.I. 109–11
marijuana 156, 161, 188,
   245, 386
Marlow, Tony 240
Martin, Paul 332
Mates, Colonel Michael 249
Mates, Michael 313–17
Matthew, H.C.G. 39
Maudling, Reginald 181–7,
   233, 360
Mawhinney, Brian 335
Maxse, Leo 81
Maxwell-Fyffe, Sir David
   121
Maxwell, Robert xiii, 32, 35,
   63, 79, 84, 136, 341, 396,
   403, 405–7, 426
Mayhew, Clare 139
Mayor of London 415

Mellor, David 267, 271, 280,
   295–304, 315, 322, 414
members' interests 117, 360
mental illness 26
Merchant, Piers 333–5
MI5 226
Miller, Eric 183, 230
Millhench, Ronald 228, 230
Milligan, Stephen ix, 325
Milroy-Sloane, Nadine 366
Miss Whiplash 193, 305,
   307, 309
mistresses 12, 42, 49, 63–5,
   87, 159, 160, 194, 196,
   198, 240, 251, 253, 255,
   286, 303, 321, 323, 327,
   333, 342, 381, 383
Mittal affair 433
Moncrieff, Chris 312
Moore, Jo 429–31, 433
morality 39, 175, 318
Morgan, Rhodri 424
Morley, Sheridan 409
Morrison, Herbert 123
Mosley, Sir Oswald 102, 103
Mottram, Sir Richard 431–2
muck-raking 58, 175
Mulholland, Brendan 154
murder plots 199, 200, 202,
   207, 209, 212, 214, 222–3
Murray, Alexander 80, 81,
   83

Nadir, Asil 313–17
nationalism 47, 48, 91
national security 178
Newcastle United 437
newspaper barons 99